P9-DNB-756

DATE DUE

DEMCO, INC. 38-2931

Virtual Justice

Virtual Justice

The Flawed Prosecution of Crime in America

H. Richard Uviller

Yale University Press *New Haven and London*

345.05
3945
U94v

\

Published with assistance from the foundation established in memory of Philip Hamilton McMillan of the Class of 1894, Yale College.

Designed by Rebecca Gibb. Set in New Caledonia type by The Composing Room of Michigan, Inc., Grand Rapids, Michigan. Printed by Vail-Ballon Press, Binghamton, New York.

Library of Congress Cataloging-in-Publication Data

Uviller, H. Richard.
    Virtual justice : the flawed prosecution of crime in
America / H. Richard Uviller.
        p.   cm.
    Includes index.
    ISBN 0-300-06483-7 (cloth : alk. paper)
    1. Criminal justice, Administration of—United States.   I. Title.
KF9223.U88   1996
345.73′05—dc20
[347.3055]   95-38687
                                                     CIP

A catalogue record for this book is available from the British Library.

The paper in this book meets the guidelines for permanence and durability of the Committee on Production Guidelines for Book Longevity of the Council on Library Resources.

10 9 8 7 6 5 4 3 2 1

To my students,
from whom I have learned so much
and who have always indulged graciously
my improvisations on the theme of justice
over the past twenty-five years

Contents

Acknowledgments

I thank, first, Marie Winn, who sparked the idea for this book. I am grateful, too, to my imaginative and discerning colleague, Jerry Lynch, for his insightful comments on the design and structure of the book, along with a number of critical details. Joe Ferrer, friend and perceptive commentator, read a draft and offered thoughtful and critical reactions along with general encouragement. I am especially grateful to my new colleague, Debra Livingston, for the thorough, knowledgeable, and helpful criticism she contributed. She gave me full benefit of her experience as a prosecutor, her scholarship, and her editorial skills. I appreciate also the prompt and authoritative research generously provided by Claudia Tuchman, my student and able young research assistant. And I warmly thank my wife of thirty years, Rena, not only for her wise commentary on the draft and her richly flavored accounts of the work of the courtroom where she presides (which help keep me in touch with the scene at the front), but for her fond and unflagging encouragement in the production of *Virtual Justice*. The Walter E. Meyer Foundation provided some financial assistance for the project, which I acknowledge with thanks.

Introduction

Americans, who are avid consumers of criminal justice—in news and entertainment, if not by firsthand experience—sometimes have the uneasy feeling
that it's not working. Do police have the laws they need to do the job? Or are
the laws—and especially the courts' constitutional interpretations—actually
making things needlessly difficult, leading to the release of dangerous felons
for no discernible good reason? Are juries really competent for the critical
task assigned to them? Can they recognize the truth in the tangle of evidence? How well are they served by the rules that filter the data provided to
them? And what of the lawyers—do they contribute anything of value to the
process, like shielding the innocent from unjust conviction or keeping the
government honest? Or do they simply hinder the important and primary
task of law enforcement: removing the predators from among their victims?
And how do the prosecutors fit into the process? Are they choosing targets
wisely, are they focusing law enforcement attention where it is most sorely
needed? Or are they, with the connivance of the court, selling out justice in
the plea bargaining process while inducing the innocent to plead themselves
into prison with can't-refuse deals? Finally, where do trial judges fit into our
peculiar adversary model of criminal justice? Are they effective, empowered
figures who guide the process toward a just outcome, or does the adversary
system induce a sort of judicial passivity that allows lawyers and jurors to take
the process on excursions to DisneyWorld, far from the realms of truth?
Does this amazing, cumbersome, clanking contrivance we call (without

irony) our system of justice actually deliver an acceptable approximation of justice?

The criminal justice system of the United States is, in many ways, our proudest boast, incorporating the best of a post-Enlightenment society and daily demonstrating the free and final authority of the ordinary people, sitting as juries, to rule the state's awful power to punish. Yet the system often seems to defeat the very principles it purports to serve: the fair and efficient separation of guilty from innocent, according to law, in a dignified and rational proceeding, with appropriate respect for the sovereignty of the individual. Too often the burnished ideals are borne on the back of a stumbling creature, lost in a fog of uncertainty. Common sense finds itself groping through a legal maze, common practice has an aura of questionable legality, and many common assumptions—of law enforcement people as well as spectators—turn out to be contrary to the requirements of law. Occasional public exposure of these failures contributes to a general belief that the law is indeed an ass (at best)—inept, pretentious, and misguided.

To perceive that a prized national institution is failing in some important respects is a bitter and demoralizing discovery. For the ends of justice are a vital social interest. I take as a premise that the criminal justice system is more than a contribution to the national entertainment industry called news, that it affects the social peace and confidence of the nation. And our faith in our criminal justice system contributes heavily to the belief that we live in a civilized society.

Of the many ways we strive to make sense of the chaos that surrounds us, the quest for justice is one of the most urgent. The moral imperative—the need to have things come out right—is a major driving force in the way we seek to order our world. I do not quarrel with those who insist that sex or religion is the motive engine of human endeavor, or that the libido is fueled by greed or by the esthetics of style. I believe it all. I merely submit my sense that it is also terribly important to us personally and to our pride in the society we inhabit to believe that rewards and punishments are distributed in accord with what the collective ethic deems just deserts. The anger of the crime victim as she watches her assailant walk free out of the courtroom must count as one of the great rages of a civilized society. The fury of the innocent defendant convicted by a confident though mistaken jury is no less intense. And, with only slight cooling, the bitter disappointment is transmitted from the immediate parties to the disinterested spectator who beholds the grim spectacle of a process off its bearings.

Sadly, most of us are resigned to the injustice of "life." We don't really expect nature to bless the virtuous or plague the evildoer. But we demand more of our government. And government's most visible agency for dispensing justice is, of course, the court system and especially the ever-newsworthy criminal court. In an unjust world, we expect—we demand—recognizable justice from our courts.

Yet we know, from reason or painful experience, courts are hardly a perfect system for the delivery of true, gratifying justice. Error is built into the fact-finding process, for one thing. After all, we are trying to reconstruct a truth that is all but hidden even to the honest witness. And sabotage is prevalent. Cleverly inserted among the bits and pieces from which our assiduous fact finder hopes to build a facsimile of truth are bound to be false fragments. And, like expert forgeries, these pieces may be indistinguishable from the genuine shards. What level of accuracy can we expect of a system so burdened? But while we uncomfortably accommodate the existential uncertainties of our imperfect fact finding, even the resolutely realistic among us are offended by the foolish or unnecessary impediments to actual justice.

This book is about the appearance of justice, virtual justice that often passes for the real thing. It is my purpose to examine a number of aspects of our facsimile of justice, to explore the gaps, the contradictions, the mythology of practice and principle, and to inquire whether the prized process comes as close as possible to the genuine article, the product that merits our confidence.

Let me be clear. My title does not suggest that what passes for criminal justice in America today is *simulated.* No one in our legal establishment is trying to *imitate* justice instead of *doing* justice, trying to fool people into thinking just results are being turned out by a machine secretly geared to corruption and oppression. History has known such systems, and no doubt such oppressive "justice" still thrives in some parts of today's world. Some may think ours is such a system; I do not.

Nor do I address injustice attributable to ordinary incompetence—bad cops, stupid judges, misguided juries. Infuriating, sometimes tragic as such miscarriages can be, I regard them as the unavoidable cost of any system resting on the human faculties of perception, recollection, recital, reception, and judgment. They are *occasional* failures, due sometimes to a visible screwup, more often to a breakdown stemming only from simple human error on a particular occasion.

The virtual justice that engages my attention here is delivered by a process operated in good faith by men and women seriously trying to produce true justice.

And often the congruence is close enough to be called perfect. Of course, neither I nor anyone else can say confidently when virtual justice matches historic reality and the dictates of the collective ethic, or when the process that produced it conforms to our notions of civilized legality. The historical past is only a synthesis to us, as it was to the jury, and we usually have no better way of reconstructing it than that used by the fact finder in court. So too, the process by which the result was reached—some of it invisible, some confused—cannot always be fully and wisely judged. So we must concede at the outset that there's a big chunk of this business that is simply (and probably perpetually) unknown and unknowable. *Ignoramus,* as the old grand jurors might have said.

But I also know that there are elements in the process—systemic flaws— that tend to bend virtual justice without distorting its apparent correspondence to true justice. In places, law fails the needs of the investigators, of the lawyers, of the fact finders; at critical junctures action is improvised and adversary confrontations cast the players in roles that do not enhance the reliability of the synthesis. It is these aspects of the process on which I will focus. Here, perhaps, we may see whether the virtual justice generated by the adversary system has an acceptably close correspondence to the true justice that our collective libido demands.

The shape and design of the House of Justice—to say nothing of the goings-on within it—fascinate all consumers of evening news bites and tabloid expositions. And with good reason. Great and moving stories, morality tales of the clash of good and evil, high drama of escape and vengeance are enacted here every day. Stars and bit players strut and fret their hour (after hour, after tedious hour) on the stage. It is at once a theatre for the enactment of Parables of Our Times and a lecture hall on the Great Values of Our Society. And it's free.

In the pages ahead, I shall conduct a short tour of this bedeviled edifice. We will enter a number of rooms, some well-lit and open to the public, others hidden beyond dim passages. Each will be a small adventure in itself;

sometimes the connection between them will be little more than their common roof. Occasionally, I will point out a flaw of plumbing or wiring for which I can propose a remedy. In other rooms, I will attempt to describe the architectural peculiarities, some structural weakness perhaps, but—sadly—I will have no repair or improvement in mind. And from time to time, like a good guide, I will simply point out a quirk, like the hidden staircases at Monticello. Perhaps an odd, habitual turn of the legal mind will be amusing, perhaps an unsuspected doctrinal wrinkle will raise a casual eyebrow. Harmless sport. Disappointing, perhaps, to some who seek more aggressive commentary. But it is my prime purpose merely to engage, to reveal, and to share some of the wonder I feel as I wander through these familiar premises.

My plan is this: I will spin for you a modest collection of tales in which I take you to the site of common and perplexing events in the collection of evidence and the trial of criminal cases. These accounts will be fictional—made-up characters with made-up names attending to made-up cases—but they will not be altogether fictitious. The little events that make up the scenarios will be familiar to every cop on the beat, every lawyer at the criminal Bar. In short, the stories will not be *artificial*—the sort of hypothetical puzzles that generations of law students have grappled with in classrooms, never to encounter again. My tales will be *virtually* true: true to life, but imaginary. Each is designed to raise a question of some difficulty. Each will illuminate a place where the law has failed to provide good guidance to conduct or judgment, an example of where the legal system has failed.

Actually, in real life, much of what goes on in the squad cars, precincts, and courthouses is routine. Not dull, exactly, but calling merely for the normal procedures of indisputably appropriate response. This book is surely not a manual of conventional procedure. I would not tax my time or your attention with labored description of that unremarkable landscape. (Nor, by the way, is this a collection of anecdotes, culled from a career in court, demonstrating the wit or prowess of the hero.) What I hope to do is sketch for you some common events and situations that present genuine and critical problems. Sometimes we will doubtless shrug, sensing that the failures are inevitable, the anomalies interesting but trivial. Often, however, we will find that these baffling dilemmas result from a discontinuity between the dictates of common sense and the governing principles of American law. And from time to time, we will confront fundamental faults in the structure, all but concealed behind a careful blind of endemic oblivion.

You will soon discover that this tour is enlivened by no footnotes and precious few legal citations. This discovery, I trust, will be unsettling only to resolute scholars. My defense (to them) is that I do not mean the book to be a scholarly work, to reflect upon or to reply to the musings of others on contiguous subjects. I do regret (to some small degree) that my choice to abandon the academic convention prevents me from acknowledging the work of the many scholars (good and bad) who have contributed over the years (in one way and another) to my own thinking on the subject. To any who feel that I have stolen a precious idea without compensating credit (an unlikely accusation), my apologies. Your thought has become so embedded that I mistook it for my own.

Along the way, I promise to evade at least two questions that are bound to recur throughout our tour: One, just what is the relation between crime and the criminal justice system? And two, should we worry more about the conviction of the innocent or the acquittal of the guilty? These, I regret to announce, readers will have to wrestle with on their own. My reticence comes not from lack of interest in those nasty, persistent imponderables. Over nearly forty years of thinking about crime, the Constitution, and the law, I've made more than one attempt to come to terms with them. My diplomatic avoidance comes rather from my reluctance to admit how little progress I have made in squeezing out some decent answers.

The lesson that this tale will teach (if it teaches anything at all) is that "the law" that empowers our response to violent and destructive behavior is not a solid and coherent corpus of principles, the comforting societal analogue of the wise, strong parent's injunctions, edicts, and accommodations that we would like to believe it to be. Rather, we will discover that within a loose collection of principles expressing the uncertain limits of social tolerance, the law is manifest in a process, an ongoing, ever-changing approach to the resolution of the problems—often insoluble—generated by human interactions in a stressed society.

Law is not "applied" to cases like some healing salve to a sore. Nor is it "applied" like a formula—$A = \pi r^2$, let us say—to solve a mathematical puzzle. The good citizens of our beleaguered polity—including many students entering law school—would love to think that the ancient guild of lawyers keeps the rituals and mysteries of the temple, performing like an anointed order the verbal incantations and ceremonial gestures that create corporations, sever marriages, induce harmony between landlords and tenants, and identify criminals while keeping in check the natural inclination of a police force to transform itself into a brutish monster. Would it were so.

In truth, we lawyers make it up as we go along. Courts, no less than cops in the field, hang their practical solutions on the several fixed parameters of the structure. Their ornamentation waving in the breeze is noticed by other travelers coming the same way, who modify it or augment it according to their own notions until eventually these flapping fragments begin to serve as a guide to others on the same path. Often they prove reliable clues, and those who heed them have the satisfaction that they have come out right. Many times, signals are few, confused, and without secure connection to the underlying structure. The traveler is left to improvise as best he can. Thus, we "do justice" by taking a set of inexact legal metrics, consulting our various fragments of moral ethics, appealing reverentially to common sense, and hoping the outcome accords with some shared notion of the appropriate response of a civilized people to a cruel affliction.

I will be not be greatly troubled in these pages with the idea that human law, unlike the law of nature, is a variable in life, driven by circumstances and obedient to peculiar human responses and personal dispositions. Perhaps some will say that our current approximation serves social demands adequately well—at least it would if querulous scholars would refrain from poking at it and undermining public confidence. I wish I thought so too. But even in a relaxed, modern, relativistic frame of mind, I will insist that our courts must sort the guilty from the innocent with the highest possible factual accuracy within a process that accords due deference to basic principles of human dignity. And I may lead this exploration to the conclusion that our brand of virtual justice is a sham, that acceptance of it as true justice lulls people into a false faith, and that the process must be redesigned to justify the boast that our liberal democracy is honored by its criminal justice system.

Overview of the American Criminal Justice System

Before addressing some particular (and peculiar) aspects of the American criminal justice process, it might be helpful to sketch a map of the system as a whole. This description is probably the closest semblance of a *system* of justice to be found in the book—a *virtual* map, at best—and it should be regarded with appropriate caution. To those familiar with the contours of the territory, this sketch may be superfluous; I won't be insulted if you skip it.

Jurisdiction

In the United States, crime comes in two brands: state crime and federal crime. One action may violate both state and federal laws at the same time. Sell a half-kilo of cocaine, rob a bank, run an underworld extortion ring, drive a car you stole in another state, kidnap someone, or set up a mail-order scam in fake jewelry, and you will commit both federal and state crimes simultaneously. Whether you get busted by local cops or federal agents, prosecuted in state or federal court, whether you serve your time in state or federal prison may depend on no principle more weighty than who made the case against you first. This duplication is the result of our marvelous federal structure of overlapping jurisdictions, which, despite its evident inefficiencies, is being emulated in newborn democracies from South Africa to Eastern Europe and the European Community.

The framers of our federal design did not originally contemplate such pushing and shoving. Crime and criminal law enforcement was traditionally a local (that is, *state*) concern. All the ordinary crimes—murder, rape, assault, robbery, burglary, larceny, and so on—were (and remain) violations of state law, and many extraordinary offenses like gambling, insurance fraud, and labor racketeering were written into state statutes.

For the first hundred and fifty years or so of our nationhood, federal crimes were relatively few, and they were distinctly national in character: treason, smuggling, counterfeiting, presidential assassination, and the like. In the first quarter of the twentieth century, kidnapping was added in the wake of the crime against the Lindbergh baby. Criminalizing interstate "white slave" (prostitution) traffic, enforcing the constitutional prohibition against alcoholic drinks, and countering wartime espionage further widened the reach of federal law enforcement agencies. Then, as part of the New Deal in the thirties, a whole new chart was drawn, redefining the scope of federal authority, and federal criminal jurisdiction expanded apace, covering lots of local crimes that made use of interstate communication or commerce. In the sixties, with Robert Kennedy as Attorney General, the federal government got into counterracketeering in a big way. In the eighties and nineties, drug enforcement has become more and more obviously a national imperative. And so the central criminal law enforcement apparatus has finally enlarged to the point that it nearly equals—indeed in some areas, exceeds—traditional state authority.

Still, criminal law enforcement remains primarily the task of local and state governments. By 1995 there were some 10,000 FBI agents distributed across the nation (the FBI being the primary federal criminal law enforcement agency), but there were approximately 30,000 cops in New York City alone. And the overwhelming majority of the overwhelming prison population of the United States is securely housed in state prisons, serving state time for state crimes.

Investigation and Accusation

The government, federal or state (and for purposes of this discussion county, city, or town prosecutors and cops are considered state officers because they are usually enforcing state laws through state courts), gets into action to enforce its criminal laws in one of two ways: either by responding to trouble or looking for it.

The Responsive Mode

Most police work begins with a complaint, usually by a victim or witness. Police respond when they are called. Sometimes, it's easy. The complainant knows the perpetrator, maybe even knows where to find him. Some paperwork, a fast collar, an interrogation, maybe a lineup, some loose items of evidence to collect and send down to the lab: case closed.

More often, police must *investigate*. Even when they start with a specific, known crime and a cooperative victim or witness, getting from complaint to collar may be an arduous undertaking. Let the victim of the holdup sit and look at photos, books full of them, computers stocked with mug shots filed by age, race, sex, and customary mode of operation. Comb through the murdered woman's date books, phone books, files, correspondence; interview everyone who knew her. Shake your stoolies, chase down tips, visit all your suspect's hangouts, bug his family and friends, keep your eyes peeled; maybe he'll turn up one of these days. Homicide clearance rates are surprisingly high, burglary is very low, but across the board, cops are making collars, stuffing the holding pens—and eventually the courts—with cases for adjudication.

In the usual sequence, the case is turned over to a prosecutor after the arrest is made. At this point, the prosecutor (a lawyer, but frequently a young one) goes over the case, perhaps directing some additional investigation, and decides whether it should be further prosecuted or dismissed. Many cases are thrown out at the outset for a variety of reasons: bad police work, weak evidence, reluctant witnesses.

Soon after the arrest (it should be *very* soon after), the defendant is brought before a judge for *arraignment*. That first court appearance is an occasion for a judge to go over the papers to inquire whether there is a legal basis to hold the accused and proceed further, to inform the defendant of the charge on which he is being held, to ascertain whether the defendant has a lawyer or can afford one and to assign counsel if not, and to fix the terms of the defendant's release pending further proceedings. Generally pretrial release is on bail, a monetary bond, which will be forfeit if the defendant skips, but the court may order him released without posting bond—"on his own recognizance" or on the assurances of a friend or relative.

Next, an accusatory instrument may be returned—an *indictment* (for a felony, a crime carrying a possible punishment of at least a year's imprisonment) or an *information* (usually for a misdemeanor)—after a presentation of the skeletal case either to a grand jury or a hearing judge. Unless the defendant waives the right, federal felony accusations are by grand jury only—a requirement of the Fifth Amendment of the U.S. Constitution. Although this is one of the few provisions of the Bill of Rights that is not binding on the states, about half the states still use grand juries, by choice. If the grand jury or examining judge confirms the initial charge—as they usually do, sometimes elaborating the accusation with additional counts—the defendant is arraigned again on the formal charge now embodied in the indictment or information.

The Investigatory Mode

The U.S. Department of Justice, both in Washington and through its many United States Attorneys around the country, several other federal agencies, and the better local prosecutors and police agencies *initiate* investigations. They go out and look for crimes in places where they suspect illegal activity flourishes out of sight. Staking out the site of a possible crime, police may be able to watch it happen. Occasionally, they will participate and help make it happen. Sitting on a roof, peering through binoculars, police monitor drug sales in the street below them, broadcasting descriptions to teammates waiting around the corner to pick up the buyers. Or cops, unshaved, in hooded sweat shirts, buy drugs with marked money as their cohorts wait to swoop in for the bust. Or, wearing designer sneakers and gold chains, agents help smugglers arrange to bring large quantities of drugs into the country, collecting evidence on the conspiracy (but, alas, doing little to stem the flow).

Investigation may be set off by little more than the faint alarms of suspicions. Too many civil servants bought high-priced tickets to a political fundraiser; some illegal arm-twisting, perhaps? Concrete recently poured to build a highway has begun to crumble; could bid rigging, bribery, or other chicanery be the invisible clause in the contract? Is a linen supply company, owned by the brother-in-law of the local Mafia chief, signing up all the restaurants in town without any apparent reason? Hmmm. The investigation moves without complaint, often without suspect, and sometimes without even good reason to think that a crime was committed. Maybe, months and millions later, it will come up dry. But with a good nose and a lot of luck, these drillings may hit a gusher. Difficult and expensive as it is, the investigatory mode is virtually the only way to attack corruption of government officials, extortion, commercial fraud, and underworld domination—a vast variety of quiet, hidden, criminal activities.

Apart from an occasional public eruption, the rackets generally work unseen. Many, like loan sharking, vice, and drug distribution, provide a service to a willing clientele. Others, like commercial bribery and sweetheart unionism, are tolerated because they facilitate legitimate enterprise. But they all threaten to replace fair competition, free choice, and confidence in law with the exploitation of dependence, corruption of authority, and brutal terror. They are the perennial targets of government-initiated investigation.

These prosecutor-initiated investigations are typically longer and more complex than responsive investigations, and they are likely to use more sophisticated detection techniques. Electronic surveillance, tails, infiltration, scams, search warrants, and a great deal of tedious analysis of documentary records are typical elements of these protracted pursuits. Sometimes the hunt is not for the criminal who committed a known crime but for the crime committed by a known criminal. At the end of the day, if the investigation has been fruitful, an indictment is returned, the defendant is arrested, and the case joins the more common fare in the judicial hopper.

Adjudication

Before a defendant reaches trial, a number of *motions* are usually made on his behalf. These may address everything from the bona fides of the accusation to the evidence that may be adduced against him at the upcoming trial. Some of these issues may require hearings at which evidence is heard and the judge makes findings of fact. The outcome of these motions may critically affect the triability of the case; granting a motion to suppress vital incriminating evidence, for example, may effectively terminate the prosecution. The accused has the constitutional right to be present at all of these proceedings, represented by counsel, and to challenge by cross-examination any testimony introduced against him. But these pretrial questions are not tried to a jury—the Sixth Amendment right to jury trial does not extend this far.

Each side is also allowed some preliminary look at its adversary's case—called *discovery*. But it is not a very revealing discovery. The prosecution may be entitled to know whether the defense will be insanity or whether the defendant will claim to have been elsewhere at the time of the crime (an *alibi* defense, in the strict use of that misused term), but not much else. The defendant gets somewhat more. He is entitled to have all the potentially exculpatory evidence that the government's investigation may have turned up and which the government does not expect to introduce at trial. He will get all documents and records that may contain material that might impeach government witnesses. He may also get a preliminary ruling from the court on such matters as which of his prior convictions or misdeeds the prosecution will be allowed to adduce against him should he elect to testify in his own behalf. He may also receive other material bearing on the case: a chemist's report or the coroner's certificate, for example.

But in most jurisdictions the defendant is not entitled to a preview of the evidence supporting the accusation. He will not learn the identity of the prosecution witnesses nor what they are expected to say on the stand. Because discovery is thus limited in criminal cases, defendants frequently use pretrial motions—and the factual hearings that accompany them—to learn as much as they can about the government's case.

In addition to making, answering, and adjudicating pretrial motions, this period is frequently a time of intense negotiation between the prosecutor and defense counsel on the possibility of a disposition by *guilty plea,* a disposition that will sweep seven, eight, even nine out of ten cases off the docket. The adversaries may also discuss cooperation by the defendant in a continuing investigation, consolidation of outstanding charges, or even—once in a great while—dismissal of the charge as false.

Finally all pretrial maneuvers are done and, for those relatively few cases that survive, the *trial* begins. The trial is, in essence, an orderly, controlled way of presenting evidence in its most reliable form to a neutral and diverse body of citizens who were previously ignorant of the crime and open-minded on the issue of guilt. The rules of evidence control the admissibility of evidence, and the judge rules on objections to proffered testimony or physical evidence according to her best understanding of the law. But the *producers* of the trial are the lawyers. Counsel for both sides are in complete control of who testifies, about what, and in which order. They also select the physical evidence that will be submitted to the jury. Of course, they are stuck with the people who can be found who know something about the case. But we American lawyers (unlike our European counterparts) may groom and rehearse our witnesses—and do. However we may espouse the value of spontaneity in the search for truth, we see no deception in coaching. Does coaching, which is to some extent truth-defeating, validate in some small way the worst people say about lawyers? Does this minor, all but unnoticed element in our tradition reveal our process as false and theatrical?

Undeniably, the parade before juries of defendants dressed in suits and ties they never wore before, backed by hitherto neglectful or neglected family members (or their stand-ins) in the gallery, makes one wonder whether the jury system invites subtle deception. The prosecutor, too, must often rely on co-conspirators, stoolies, and assorted felons, spruced up to pass for pillars of society. Is this charade really the best way for the jury to get the true picture?

Yet trial lawyers argue, with some basis, that the raw stories told by happenstance witnesses are apt to be incomplete, inconsistent, and unconvincing, even when entirely true. Most people are simply not natural witnesses, not adept in any one of the three faculties implicit in the term *witness:* perception, recall, or recital. And, for better or worse, the jury's prejudices will interfere with judgment if they see the defendant or the other actors before them in their customary street garb, employing their customary locutions.

To most consumers of the evening news—to say nothing of the evening's entertainment—the general contours of the trial are familiar. It is, in the Anglo-American model, *adversary* in nature. That is, we believe that a true verdict is most likely to emerge from the dialectic collision of opposed versions, each with a full opportunity to discredit the other. The role of the judge in this process is to control the proceedings, rule on questions of law, and see that the jury is well and fully instructed on the principles of law that should govern their consideration of it.

When all the evidence is in, the lawyers' closing arguments have been voiced, and the judge's charge has been solemnly intoned, the jurors retire and, in private, argue themselves into unanimous agreement on a verdict. If this proves impossible after a really serious effort, the court will accept their profession of hopeless deadlock and declare a mistrial. They have become, in that odd but universal phrase, a hung jury. That means that the case may be retried from the beginning before a fresh jury, a prospect that is joyfully greeted only by the defendant who was certain he was done for.

The *verdict* in a criminal case is either *Guilty* or *Not Guilty.* Defense counsel regularly remind the jury that they are not asked to vote whether the defendant is innocent; *Not Guilty* means only that, innocent or not, the defendant has not been proved guilty beyond a reasonable doubt. The jury answers no specific questions (Did the defendant fire the gun at the deceased? Did he do so intending to kill him? If so, was he acting in self-defense?) and gives no explanations. If the verdict is *Not Guilty*, the defendant literally walks out of the courtroom a free person. He may not be held another minute and, regardless of any errors in his trial, he may not be retried in the same jurisdiction for that crime—or any crime based on the same underlying event—ever again. Retrial in the same jurisdiction for the same criminal conduct after acquittal, even erroneous acquittal, is the heart of the prohibition against *double jeopardy*.

If the verdict is *Guilty*, the judge fixes a date for sentence and the defendant is either continued on bail—perhaps the amount is raised somewhat in view of the added motivation to flee provided by the verdict—or remanded to jail. He will receive credit against his sentence for any time spent in jail awaiting trial, during trial, or awaiting sentence. With a probation report in hand and perhaps a sheaf of letters from partisans of the defendant and the victim, the trial judge will hear from the lawyers and others in open court and then pronounce sentence. The term imposed will be more or less controlled by statute, from the tight parameters of the federal sentencing guidelines to the wide perimeters of the typical state statute, which sets out a maximum and, in some states, a minimum term, usually leaving the judge wide scope. It is not unusual for a state judge to find an available range of legal sentences for a given felony from a year or two behind bars to ten or fifteen. But it is in the selection of the appropriate sentence that the judge earns his keep: an exercise of *discretion* with the most serious consequences. By discretion we usually mean that the decision of the trial judge is virtually unreviewable, but in reviewing sentences, appellate courts will sometimes intervene to smooth out gross disparities in the judgments of individual judges.

Review

A jury verdict of acquittal is unreviewable. No matter how many or how damaging to the prosecution the errors of the trial may have been, no appellate court will ever consider them. Recognition of those errors on appeal would require an order for a new trial, and a second trial on the same charge—even after a clearly erroneous verdict or acquittal—would violate the basic prohibition against multiple prosecution.

The verdict of conviction and the sentence are together called the judgment, and that judgment is reviewable as a matter of right by at least one level of appeal and, in most jurisdictions, by leave of court on another. On appeal, the reviewing court is bound by the record as established in the original court proceedings; they will not take evidence or find facts to amplify that record. Nor will they second-guess the trial jury on the credibility of witnesses or the question of the defendant's guilt or innocence; if there is some evidence in the record on which the jury could have found the defendant guilty, that verdict will stand. Actual guilt is never an issue on review.

To some this principle appears anomalous; how can the basic issue of innocence ever be precluded? Isn't there some sort of constitutional right not to be punished for something you didn't do? In 1993 the Supreme Court undertook to explain, in a capital murder case called *Herrera v. Collins,* in which the evidence of guilt presented at trial was very strong. Chief Justice William Rehnquist began by conceding the intuitive response to the basic proposition:

> Petitioner asserts that the Eighth and Fourteenth Amendments to the United States Constitution prohibit the execution of a person who is innocent of the crime for which he was convicted. This proposition has an elemental appeal, as would the similar proposition that the Constitution prohibits the imprisonment of one who is innocent of the crime for which he was convicted. After all, the central purpose of any system of criminal justice is to convict the guilty and free the innocent. But the evidence upon which petitioner's claim of innocence rests was not produced at his trial, but rather eight years later. In any system of criminal justice, "innocence" or "guilt" must be determined in some sort of a judicial proceeding. Petitioner's showing of innocence, and indeed his constitutional claim for relief based upon that showing, must be evaluated in the light of the previous proceedings in this case, which have stretched over a span of 10 years.
>
> A person when first charged with a crime is entitled to a presumption of innocence, and may insist that his guilt be established beyond a reasonable doubt. Other constitutional provisions also have the effect of ensuring against the risk of convicting an innocent person. All of these constitutional safeguards, of course, make it more difficult for the State to rebut and finally overturn the presumption of innocence which attaches to every criminal defendant. But we have also observed that "[d]ue process does not require that every conceivable step be taken, at

whatever cost, to eliminate the possibility of convicting an innocent person." To conclude otherwise would all but paralyze our system for enforcement of the criminal law.

Once a defendant has been afforded a fair trial and convicted of the offense for which he was charged, the presumption of innocence disappears. Here, it is not disputed that the State met its burden of proving at trial that petitioner was guilty of the capital murder of Officer Carrisalez beyond a reasonable doubt. Thus, in the eyes of the law, petitioner does not come before the Court as one who is "innocent," but on the contrary as one who has been convicted by due process of law of two brutal murders.

Based on affidavits here filed, petitioner claims that evidence never presented to the trial court proves him innocent notwithstanding the verdict reached at his trial. Such a claim is not cognizable in the state courts of Texas. For to obtain a new trial based on newly discovered evidence, a defendant must file a motion within 30 days after imposition or suspension of sentence.

Claims of actual innocence based on newly discovered evidence have never been held to state a ground for federal habeas relief absent an independent constitutional violation occurring in the underlying state criminal proceeding. . . .

[W]e cannot say that Texas' refusal to entertain petitioner's newly discovered evidence eight years after his conviction transgresses a principle of fundamental fairness "rooted in the traditions and conscience of our people" [the standard for a violation of due process]. This is not to say, however, that petitioner is left without a forum to raise his actual innocence claim. For under Texas law, petitioner may file a request for executive clemency. Clemency is deeply rooted in our Anglo-American tradition of law, and is the historic remedy for preventing miscarriages of justice where judicial process has been exhausted.

So much for the law's concern, postverdict, with "claims of actual innocence," *facts* that might have led a jury to acquit. Errors of *law* that might have affected the verdict, however—usually mistakes made by the trial judge, but occasionally serious errors by the prosecutor—will cause a reversal of the judgment with either a direction to dismiss or, more likely, a remand for a new trial. No trial is perfect, however, and appellate courts will not reverse a judgment for what they deem to be *harmless error.*

Sometimes the judgment is vulnerable for reasons that do not appear on the record: defense counsel was drunk, or never admitted to the Bar, or failed to interview the witnesses supplied by her client; or the prosecutor knowingly adduced perjured testimony from a critical witness; or the defendant was incompetent by reason of temporary, drug-induced disorientation. Such infirmities, which cannot be reached by direct appeal, call for *collateral attack.* The ancient remedy by the writ of error *coram nobis* or its modern statutory descendant allows the defendant to raise such claims after judgment by a motion addressed to the trial court. The court holds a hearing and if the claim is sustained, the conviction will be set aside. In either case, the trial court's ruling on the motion is itself reviewable on appeal.

All in all, it sometimes takes years to get a judgment of conviction finally affirmed. And since some postconviction remedies may be pursued whenever the underlying facts come to light, collateral attack is theoretically never exhausted.

Once the regular appeals are over and collateral attacks have been tried to no avail, as the *Herrera* Court noted, the convicted person's only recourse is a petition for *executive clemency.* The chief executive officer of the jurisdiction—the President of the United States in federal cases, the governor in state cases—enjoys a residue of the absolute prerogative of monarchs: the power of pardon. As the *Herrera* Court indicated, these officers, responsible only to their own consciences, entertain petitions to pardon, commute, or reprieve all of their citizens—even, as Richard Nixon's successor Gerald Ford demonstrated not so long ago, those who have not yet been convicted of any crime. Obviously, though, it is prisoners who are the regular petitioners, and most chief executives grant only a very small number of their petitions each year.

One further practical point should probably be made about appeals. The United States Supreme Court is a constitutional organ of government, one of the famous three branches of the American model. But it is also a *court,* a judicial body charged with the primary responsibility of deciding *cases.* Its decisions, often interpreting basic provisions of our Supreme Charter, have important impact on policy. And the Justices are surely aware of the implications of their opinions, which define and redefine institutions of government, the authority of its agents, and the entitlements of its citizens. But our Court does not answer questions submitted to it in the abstract. It will address only those questions that are necessary to resolve actual disputes and decide actual cases.

We have a strong tradition of requiring our high courts to explain their decisions—to convince us, in effect, that those decisions are correct. And in these expositions, we find a wealth of material on the broader issues of the day. But when it comes to the *holdings* of the court (in contrast to the *dicta*), the general rule of decision is: the narrower the better. And in our common-law tradition, we do not proceed from general principles, encoded in statutes, to particular cases. Rather, courts decide individual cases, each on its peculiar circumstances and the instinct for justice, and then accumulate the results until we can detect enough common elements to distill a principle that we can call law. This is not code making, the work of the democratic branch—the legislature—where a great deal of American law is created. But it is an equally important component of our legal system: court-made law. We might term this common-law process of cumulative, case-driven, judicial lawmaking *improvisation*.

1 Virtual Legality in the Field

Fact Gathering at the Scene of the Crime

Lawyers talk a lot about *the facts*. Good lawyers can be found who will tell you that facts are the whole story. All the rest is rationalization, window dressing to make the fact-driven outcome seem like the product of reasoned, principled choice. But what are "facts"? To courtroom lawyers, facts are the relics of past events, things that actually happened out there in the real world. Today the events are gone, vanished into the elusive, misty realms of memory and cause. Now, in court, we must produce some *evidence* of those vanished events. Only a moment's reflection brings any thoughtful observer up against the Great Evidentiary Riddle—a basic, inescapable, and deeply perplexing uncertainty in the relation between present fragmentary and subjective data and the objective past. To what extent is the knowable, transmissible *fact* the *reality* that it purports to represent? How well do the fragments of the past that come to us by the selective process of memory or the happenstance of preservation represent the complex reality of the former present?

Fortunately, the law ignores these troubling philosophical issues and operates on a far simpler set of premises. The law postulates that most events, so far as our senses inform us, have some impact on the physical world or on the perceptions of human witnesses. These traces—often blurred, light, or ambiguous—are the evidence we seek. Organized, interpreted, well presented, this is the stuff of litigation. Preparation, in the American tradition, is extensive and, at its best, meticulous. Facts must be located, dug up, and assembled to tell a coherent story. Shards must be analyzed by experts.

Human witnesses must be found, examined, and cajoled to divulge their recollections.

In criminal cases, the burden of persuasion is always on the prosecution. And to a high degree of certainty: "beyond a reasonable doubt." That allocation of burden—and only that—is what we mean by the presumption of innocence. It is the codification of the basic tenet that we will willingly suffer the acquittal of many guilty defendants to avert the horror of the wrongful conviction of a single innocent person.

Whether the presumption actually fulfills its vital mission is another question for another day. For now, I invoke this basic principle only to emphasize that primary responsibility for assembling the facts is on the prosecution. Not that the defense is oblivious to facts; a good defense will bend every effort to collect data and present an alternative, exculpatory story. But the defense is under no obligation to do so. A good and often successful defense consists of nothing more than poking holes in the prosecutor's case. The prosecutor, however, *must* go out there and get the evidence. Otherwise it's over: case dismissed.

Sometimes the prosecutor actually directs the investigation of a case. In complex cases or those built on financial records, local prosecutors or U.S. Attorneys, perhaps working with grand juries, may be directly involved in the collection and selection of evidence. But in the vast majority of cases the investigation belongs entirely to the police. Or to whichever initialed federal law enforcement agency happens to be performing the police function on the case: ATF, FBI, DEA, INS, IRS, or what have you. The cops pick up the pieces and deliver them to the government lawyers. The lawyers inspect, weigh, augment, perhaps improve the data they receive from their field officers, and if, in their judgment, it adds up to a case, they take it to court. Trundling the case to the minds of the jurors, like a shopping cart filled with bits and pieces of assorted ingredients, the lawyers try to keep it steady and clear, to hold its integrity intact despite the agitation of the trial process and the depredations of witness forgetfulness (to say nothing of treachery).

So as we enter the process here, we are at the early, fact-gathering stage: police work. Of the many and various repositories of evidence, one of the best is the scene of the crime. If the crime is homicide, the investigation starts with the place where the body was found. And if it looks as though the body was found at the site of the murder—especially if that place is someone's residence—police want to make an immediate and meticulous search of the general vicinity for clues to how the crime was committed and by whom. The crime is not only a puzzle to be solved—though it is that, too. Police are aware that they are taking the first steps toward the creation of a case, a legal construct that will be presented in court. It will have to survive rigorous scrutiny and vigorous challenge. They know that the case will be only as strong as the evidence that supports it. And they know that if they can't read the scene when it's fresh, collect the large and small traces of the event, somewhere down the line their perpetrator is going to walk away smiling.

The four-to-midnight tour is not yet half over when the radio dispatcher breaks into the slow conversation between officers Casey and Triani, driving aimlessly around their quiet sector. Leaving a bit more space between their sentences, the cops half listen without appearing to pay the slightest attention. The dispatcher's voice is their constant companion, eight hours every day on the job, and they've learned to hear and sort the messages without missing a beat of their customary discussion of sports, vacation time, and the renovations of basements. This time, though, something catches their interest, and in an instant the pace shifts. The unfinished donut and coffee go out the window, the car picks up speed, and the crownlights can be seen reflected in the windows they speed past.

Someone identifying herself as "just a citizen" has phoned 911 and told the operator that she is worried. She has not seen her neighbor for days, the mailbox is stuffed, and now there seems to be a strange odor coming from the apartment. The case goes out on the radio as a suspicious disappearance, possible homicide, at a given address.

Another patrol car is already there when Casey and Triani arrive at the address. Officer Maria Lopez is talking to a gray-haired woman on the street as Sgt. Lucas Kincaid stands by listening. Casey and Triani get out and approach the others. The sergeant tells them to go to apartment 6 on the second floor and check it out. They mount the stairs by twos. Drawing their guns as they approach, they pound on the door and try the knob. It's locked. They look at each other. They recognize the odor in the air around the door: the putrid smell of death.

They stand, momentarily undecided. The presence of a sergeant on the scene inhibits their initiative. If they'd been alone, one of them probably would have immediately applied the sole of a boot to the latch, but the boss might have different ideas—and hey, there's no percentage in making him mad. They head downstairs to report back to Kincaid.

"Sarge," Triani tells him, "it's locked. But there's a stiff in there, no doubt of that."

"Maybe the dog died," Lopez offers.

"This woman says the super might be down in the basement," the sergeant tells Triani. "See if you can get a key."

A man approaches and identifies himself as the super. "What's the problem, officer?"

"Do you have the key to apartment 6?" the sergeant asks.

"Sure," the super says. "I have keys to all the apartments. You want to go in?"

All four officers follow the super to the second floor. "Who lives here?" the sergeant asks.

"I know who pays me the rent," the super says. "Name of Powell, Paul Powell."

"Open it up," the sergeant says.

The super steps forward, keys the lock. Casey brushes past him, swings the door open, and quickly crosses the threshold.

The scene is a familiar one to any cop with some mileage on the job. The room is in disorder. Furniture has been overturned, broken glassware is on the floor, uneaten remains of a meal are rotting on a table—the place is a mess. In the middle of the room, a corpse is sprawled on the floor in a stain of dried blood.

The smell is overpowering, sickening. "Jesus!" says Casey, crossing the room. "Let's get some air in this stinkin' pigsty." Before he reaches the window, the sergeant calls him back. "Hey, Tommy," he says, "you want to fuck it up for the crime scene guys?" Casey stops midway to the window and withdraws. A few neighbors have gathered outside the door, where Triani and Lopez are standing. Kincaid enters and looks briefly around the small apartment, opening a few closet doors. Satisfied that no one else, living or dead, is in the place, he too steps back into the hall. "You sick?" he asks Casey, a rookie, who looks a bit green. "Go down and get some air. And make sure crime scene is on the way."

Sergeant Kincaid notices the super in the group buzzing in the hallway. "Hey you," he says. "Come here. I want to ask you something." He leads the reluctant super a few feet into the apartment and points to the corpse. "Take a look at this guy; is this what's-his-name, Powell?"

"Oh, no," the super says. Then after a few moments, "I've never seen this guy before."

"Didn't live here?" the sergeant asks. "You sure?"

The super shakes his head. "Never seen him before," he repeats solemnly.

When the super rejoins the growing crowd at the door, Kincaid asks, "Anyone know where we can find the people who live in this apartment?" No one answers. "Okay, Triani," he says, "let's move everybody out of the hallway." Then, "All right, folks, down on the street, please, clear the area." Lopez appears with some yellow plastic tape and they seal off the apartment, waiting for crime scene to arrive.

So far, everything is kosher. Most police departments have a specially trained and equipped unit like the one I am calling "crime scene." They are called to the scene of every serious crime. As soon as the first officers arrive to discover what the case is about—a homicide, let us say—they are supposed to leave everything untouched and keep the curious from entering the space. When the special investigatory group arrives, they diagram, photograph, and measure the scene. Then, as the medical team takes the body away to the coroner's shop for a careful examination, they begin poking around for whatever might suggest how the killing happened and—most important—who did it.

Here's where the problem arises. In a desk drawer, suppose there is an undeveloped roll of film on which several frames show the deceased with his arms around Powell and a third person. In an address book next to the bed is the name and address of a person who turns out to look very much like the third person in the photo. And on a dish bearing the moldy meal, a single clear fingerprint will match the prints on file for a person bearing the name found in the address book. Not enough to solve the case, perhaps, but very important evidence. It seems perfectly sensible for the police to go through the apartment with care, looking into all the potential repositories of tidbits like these—indeed, not to do so would seem nothing short of incompetent. If asked their authority, they are likely to greet the challenge with surprise and reply with something like: "You don't seem to get it, friend, we're talking murder here!" Or, "Who's around to object, the stiff?" Or, "We're cops. What are we supposed to do? Tip our hats and walk away?"

Yes, *but.* Who was it—it must have been a lawyer—who said that if he had only one word in the English language to take with him to a desert island, that word would be "but." Commonsensible as the search may be—and common as the sensible practice may be—we have a major grade *but* here.

The Fourth Amendment to the United States Constitution provides that people shall be secure in their persons, places, and possessions against unreasonable intrusions by the government. There can be little doubt that what the crime scene police intended to do in that apartment would have amounted to a search and seizure within the constitutional definition. Intrusions under the terms of court-issued warrants, as described in the language of the Amendment itself, are reasonable. So are searches without warrant in a variety of fairly well-delineated situations—usually defined by some exigency that would make the trip to the courthouse highly impractical, like the search of the clothing of a person immediately following his arrest.

The cops have only two lawful ways to search a crime scene. One is to proceed by warrant, the other is to satisfy the court after the fact that the search was reasonable without a warrant. The institutional inclination, for local police, at least, favors the latter option. Crime scene search warrants were long unheard of. And for years, crime scene people like our fictional ones have been vacuuming for fibers, opening drawers and closets, and thumbing through photo albums and address books largely untroubled by constitutional scruples. The product of their scene scans apparently has met little more trouble in court than in the field. Either the eventual defendant turned out to be a person with no standing to complain of the intrusion or else dulled or lulled lawyers neglected to raise the point. For one reason or another, the crime scene search passed for years without challenge. But eventually a prosecutor was forced to defend a crime scene search against a constitutional attack, and defend it all the way to the Supreme Court. Two others cases landed before the High Court shortly thereafter.

The first was a murder case. And a bad one—a cop killing. Justice Potter Stewart, writing for the Court in 1978, described the facts of *Mincey v. Arizona*:

> On the afternoon of October 28, 1974, undercover police officer Barry Headricks of the Metropolitan Area Narcotics Squad knocked on the door of an apartment in Tucson, Arizona, occupied by the petitioner, Rufus Mincey. Earlier in the day, Officer Headricks had allegedly arranged to purchase a quantity of heroin from Mincey and had left, ostensibly to obtain money. On his return he was accompanied by nine

other plainclothes policemen and a deputy county attorney. The door was opened by John Hodgman, one of three acquaintances of Mincey who were in the living room of the apartment. Officer Headricks slipped inside and moved quickly into the bedroom. Hodgman attempted to slam the door in order to keep the other officers from entering but was pushed back against the wall. As the police entered the apartment, a rapid volley of shots was heard from the bedroom. Officer Headricks emerged and collapsed on the floor. When other officers entered the bedroom they found Mincey lying on the floor, wounded and semi-conscious. Officer Headricks died a few hours later in the hospital. . . .

After the shooting, the narcotics agents, thinking that other persons in the apartment might have been injured, looked about quickly for other victims. They found a young woman wounded in the bedroom closet . . . as well as Mincey's three acquaintances (one of whom had been wounded in the head) in the living room. Emergency assistance was requested, and some medical aid was administered to Officer Headricks. But the agents refrained from further investigation, pursuant to a Tucson Police Department directive that police officers should not investigate incidents in which they are involved. They neither searched further nor seized any evidence; they merely guarded the suspects and the premises.

Within 10 minutes, however, homicide detectives who had heard a radio report of the shooting arrived and took charge of the investigation. They supervised the removal of Officer Headricks and the suspects, trying to make sure that the scene was disturbed as little as possible, and then proceeded to gather evidence. Their search lasted four days, during which period the entire apartment was searched, photographed, and diagrammed. The officers opened drawers, closets, and cupboards, and inspected their contents; they emptied clothing pockets; they dug bullet fragments out of the walls and floors; they pulled up sections of the carpet and removed them for examination. Every item in the apartment was closely examined and inventoried, and 200 to 300 objects were seized. In short, Mincey's apartment was subjected to an exhaustive and intrusive search. No warrant was ever obtained.

The State of Arizona had its murder scene theory upheld in the state court and won again in the United States Court of Appeals. The latter wrote:

We hold a reasonable, warrantless search of the scene of a homicide— or of a serious personal injury with likelihood of death where there is reason to suspect foul play—does not violate the Fourth Amendment to the United States Constitution where the law enforcement officers were legally on the premises in the first instance. . . . For the search to be reasonable, the purpose must be limited to determining the circumstances of death and the scope must not exceed that purpose. The search must also begin within a reasonable period following the time when the officials first learn of the murder (or potential murder).

Gamely, when Mincey appealed, Arizona pressed its novel Fourth Amendment theory in Washington. Attorneys for the state, in their brief to the United States Supreme Court, argued:

The Arizona "Murder Scene Exception" meets both the tests of reasonableness and public need. Homicide is the ultimate of all crimes in a civilized society. Society is entitled to know at the earliest possible moment if, in fact, a homicide has taken place. Similarly, society has the right to see the responsible party held to answer for his act at the earliest possible moment. Arizona's "Murder Scene Exception" was created with the public interest in mind. In addition, the exception is founded on the principle of common sense. It seems only logical that when police officers happen on a murder scene or location where a serious injury has occurred and foul play is suspected, they would be expected to take immediate steps to find out who was responsible for the deaths or serious injury. This necessarily includes an immediate and thorough investigation of the scene.

Alas, the Supreme Court disagreed. The state's desperate, rhetorical effort to cast "society" as an "entitled" party—entitled not only to know but to know at once what happened—was unavailing. So, too, was its brave citation of those venerable friends of the prosecution, logic and common sense, as authority for immediate as well as thorough investigation. No, the Court patiently explained, the fact that Mincey shot someone in his home did not amount to a waiver of his constitutionally guaranteed right to security in the premises. The Court had long insisted that no intrusion may ever be justified by its success and that the criminal, surrounded by evidence of his misdeeds, has the same protection against invasion as any innocent homeowner.

Sure, Stewart agreed, police have authority to respond immediately to a dangerous situation, and the scene of a homicide may be an emergency that justifies entrance and a quick look for other victims or a possible killer still lurking about. And they may later use in court whatever incriminating evidence they happen to see during that incursion. But that's it. Quoting itself, the Court reiterated that a "warrantless search must be 'strictly circumscribed by the exigencies which justify its initiation.'" And there were no such exigencies operative at the time the police ripped apart Mincey's domain. As far as public entitlement goes, the Court noted simply that murder was not the only serious crime, and efficiency or simplicity of investigation has never been a value to override the Fourth Amendment's protection of security.

So the "Murder Scene Exception" was dead. And lest anyone be tempted to read the *Mincey* rule as applying only to the sort of four-day, vindictive search that the furious Arizona cops conducted in the wake of the murder of one of their own, the Court reaffirmed its position in 1984 in a Louisiana murder case that involved a routine two-hour search. The Louisiana court had tried to distinguish the case from *Mincey;* the Supremes set them straight.

The crime scene theory was next advanced in a couple of arson cases, fortified by the argument that the Constitution hardly protects privacy in a pile of charred embers. But again the theory was rejected. Once the firefighters leave the smoking building, Fourth Amendment curtains again descend to protect whatever may remain on the premises in which the owner may still have an interest.

Few things are ever completely safe to say. And when we are talking about law, judge-made law, we must maintain a certain respect for the changing tides of sensibility. But it is probably safe enough to say at this point that our cops hovering on the doorstep of the murder scene, Sergeant Kincaid and his crew, may not step back across the threshold to do what seems to them reasonable, indeed obligatory. Especially without a warrant from a judge authorizing the search and seizure, the careful inspection of the scene of the crime is unreasonable, and any product of the enterprise will be suppressed by any trial court on the motion of a defendant who had any interest in the place or its contents.

Maybe that's not so bad. Disappointing, perhaps, even surprising to police trained and expected to search crime scenes. The point of the Fourth Amendment, after all, is not to prohibit necessary searches of "persons, papers, houses, and effects," but to put these searches under the control of judges, not cops. It's a simple enough idea, though surprisingly easy to forget. As the proposition comes down to us through coats of interpretive gloss, the Fourth Amendment may be understood to say that, in the absence of some overriding consideration of necessity, what people reasonably and legitimately expect will be secure against casual exposure cannot be inspected or taken for use as evidence by law enforcement people without specific permission from a court. Further, permission will be granted only on the submission of sworn papers demonstrating some good reason to think that particularly described things to be seized are located in a particularly described place to be searched. This central precept, reposing authority to institute intrusion with a judge—a provision originally intended to curtail colonial abuses by curious and intrusive redcoats—is subject to a number of exceptions. But, as we have learned, the supposition that a murder was committed on the premises is not one of them. So that leaves us with the warrant option.

Let Kincaid post Triani and Casey outside the door to ensure that no one enters to disturb the scene. Let him drive down to the courthouse with Lopez, put his observations and suspicions on a piece of paper, find a judge, swear to it, and return with the necessary warrant on which he or the crime scene unit can go in and make their customary thorough search. What's so hard about that? Nothing in that scene is going anywhere in the meantime; nothing will evaporate or turn stale.

I suppose we must acknowledge the factor of logistical fatigue. In many cities, a trip to the courthouse is far from a brief and pleasant excursion. From outlying precincts, at the wrong time of day, the trip alone can take the better part of an hour. Protocol requires that the application be taken to an assistant prosecutor, who then edits it and submits it to the judge. So Kincaid and Lopez will have to scare up an assistant district attorney who is not besieged by more pressing duties and persuade her or him to listen to their discoveries and read the affidavit they have prepared. Maybe a revised draft will have to be typed. That done, the group must find a judge who will interrupt whatever is in progress to read and sign the warrant. This can be a problem, especially between 5 P.M. and 9:30 A.M. All in all, procuring a search warrant as the Fourth Amendment advises may take several hours— with plenty of standing around and some frayed tempers thrown in. There is a release for the logistical fatigue factor and it is as close at hand as the radio transmitter in the police patrol car, but as yet it is largely an undiscovered resource, and a fuller description of it will have to await a later chapter.

Meanwhile, we should note that the logistical fatigue factor is not everywhere operative. (In some blessed, efficient systems, I am sure, the warrant can be obtained with ease within an hour.) And even where it is a factor, it cannot be allowed to figure in the intrusion equation. If the tenant of the flat in which the stiff turned up becomes a defendant in the case, no court will balance his loss of constitutional security against the hassle the cops would have had to go through in order to comply with the Fourth Amendment. So, with sympathies to the hapless warrant seekers, we will ignore the factor of logistical fatigue altogether.

Putting aside the matter of inconvenience, then, the problem for Triani and Casey is the warrant clause of the Fourth Amendment itself. The heart of the provision, at least at the time it was formulated, are the words that carefully and precisely describe the elements of a lawful search warrant. It was not (as it has since become) the definition of a reasonable search and seizure *without* a warrant that concerned constitutionalists. It was the indispensable requisites of a warrant that would protect the citizen against the arbitrary intrusions of the government. So this is important stuff. And what the Amendment says is that a court should not issue the warrant unless the officer can describe with particularity, in advance, not only where he wants to look but what he is looking for.

This provision contains all the protection offered by the Constitution against a primary abuse by the colonial police—one of the precipitating causes of the Revolution, some say. Searches against suspected troublemakers were often made by authority of what was known as a "general warrant," which ostensibly allowed the King's officers to enter suspect premises, look around, and seize whatever they considered evidence. The Constitution's response to this perceived abuse was to require precise, presearch description and specific authority in the warrant to take the items thus described and nothing else. Reading the provision of the Fourth Amendment, the Court explained that nothing in the execution of the warrant must be left to the judgment of the executing officer; the description of the thing to be seized must be so exact that any fool would recognize it instantly if he saw it.

So the real problem with the crime scene search is that the police cannot obtain a search warrant because they do not know what they are looking for and have no way of predicting what particular item of evidence might be found on the scene. Without such advance and particular knowledge, Kincaid and Lopez may as well save the gas. They won't get the warrant.

Now this is a genuine legal hole. Here is good, honest, even vital police investigation—activity that even dedicated cop critics will endorse as an appropriate response. A procedure that all good police do all the time. But it is indisputably illegal, violating basic constitutional constraints. And there is no way to do it lawfully by warrant.

Not that every crime scene search is illegal or that every piece of evidence taken from the scene of a murder should be suppressed in court. Many homicides go down out of doors. Searches of public places offend nobody's secured interests. Murders may take place on premises in which only the deceased was entitled to expect privacy. Or a person may be killed in the home of a person who either consents to the police inspection or who is never accused of the crime. Only those whose security was invaded and against whom the evidence is offered have standing to exclude it. But in the many cases like our hypothetical scenario, in which the corpse is discovered on an absent suspect's turf, there appears to be no way out of the legal hole.

Absurd!

I once had the temerity to try to work out a solution. I had a jerry-built device and—I thought—a halfway decent theory to prop it up. I could interest neither judges nor politicians in pursuing my idea. Still, I have not altogether abandoned hope that the climate may change, that some incident may occur to awaken politicians, that some interest group may someday think it's worth a push.

The idea is, briefly, this: we should pass a statute that authorizes a judge to issue a warrant to search the scene of a recent crime of a certain level of gravity—perhaps named crimes like homicide, rape, arson, kidnapping. The warrant would issue on a sworn assertion that there is good reason—"probable cause," as the Constitution calls it—to believe, first, that the specified crime had been committed on certain specified premises and, second, that evidence of the crime and the identity of its perpetrator may be recovered from the immediate vicinity. If satisfied from the described circumstances that there is probable cause for these claims, the judge should issue the warrant authorizing a search for and seizure of such evidence—notwithstanding the inability of the police to particularly describe in advance the evidence they are looking for or to give any specific reason to think they will find it.

I would not seriously advance such a bold departure from the text of the Fourth Amendment were I not encouraged by a series of decisions in the Supreme Court on what appears to be a tenuously related topic.

Government officers—federal, state, and local—frequently make inspections of all sorts of private premises, especially commercial properties, that are protected by the Fourth Amendment from unreasonable intrusion. Fire inspectors look for faulty wiring or other fire hazards. Health inspectors go into the kitchens and cellars of restaurants to look for roaches and rodent feces. Immigration officers visit small shops to check the immigration status of the workers. Environmental protection officers may inspect incineration or other waste disposal equipment. All of these routine or random inspection searches are carried out under the terms of laws that set the conditions of health or safety.

For a long time, the courts (in obedience to an old case in the Supreme Court) simply deemed these inspections beyond the concern of the Fourth Amendment. Then, in 1967, in what I have always considered an ill-advised revision, the Supreme Court decided *Camara v. Municipal Court of San Francisco.* The Court, in an opinion written by Justice White, not only brought health and safety inspections within the notice of the Fourth Amendment, but refused to find satisfaction of the reasonableness requirement in the simple fact of obedience to a lawful statute. The curious feature of *Camara* is that the Court required inspectors to obtain a search warrant to enter a reluctant occupant's quarters. What I found peculiar about this requirement—and what I now propose to turn to my benefit—is that the warrant the Court had in mind need not be based on any particular reason to believe that the premises contained evidence of the violations for which the officers were looking. Probable cause for the "inspection warrant," the Court held, could be found in the reasonableness of the statute and the conformity of the search to the statutory purpose.

So if an inspection warrant is constitutional under *Camara* without a stated reason to think that any particular evidence of a violation will be discovered, why can't my crime scene warrant—for a search that will likewise conform to a reasonable statutory purpose—pass muster without an advance description of what the cops are looking for or sworn good reasons to believe that it will be found where they propose to look?

My argument, I must confess, is not quite as neat as it appears. These inspection searches—along with their warrantless siblings, the "inventory searches" in which police go through the contents of impounded cars and the like for the safekeeping of valuables they may contain—are frequently justified by their *administrative* aspect, a benign purpose compared with *law enforcement* objectives. The search of the impounded mis-parked car may turn up vials of crack, of course, and the fire marshall's inspection of the warehouse may disclose cartons of stolen TV sets. In short, these administrative intrusions may have criminal consequences, and the evidence discovered by the administrative search may be used in the criminal prosecution. But the initial purpose of these common and routine procedures has nothing to do with the search for evidence of crime.

My crime scene search, by contrast, is entirely dedicated to the discovery of such evidence. Still, it does seem reasonable, doesn't it? And reasonability, remember, is at the heart of the Fourth Amendment, which provides (in its entirety) that "The right of the people to be secure in their persons, houses, papers, and effects shall not be violated, and no Warrants shall issue, but upon probable cause, supported by Oath or affirmation, and particularly describing the place to be searched, and the person or things to be seized."

We cannot know how the courts would regard a crime scene warrant procedure such as mine. That's the fun of it. We live in a legal system that is—by design—perpetually experimental. We have theories and arguments to back our proposals, never assurances and rarely binding precedents. So if you find an insoluble problem and can think up a relatively cost-free solution, try it. Improvise!

This tune needs a few more bars. Virtually all the professionals to whom I sing it respond the same way: very interesting; you're surely right, but is this a *real* problem? The question itself says something about the legal profession. An issue that is theoretical might be interesting, but it need not vex us if it has no pragmatic consequence. And the constitutional barriers to the search for vital evidence at the scene hardly merit a passing glance until the issue plays out in court. Being an academic lawyer, I am somewhat friendlier to the merely theoretical questions but, as an old trial dog, I share the pragmatic viewpoint of the trade. Is this crime scene search problem *real?*

It is difficult to say how often defendants who are in a position to raise the issue actually assert that evidence acquired in a search of the crime scene was illegally seized. It is also difficult to say how often warrants are sought for crime scene searches and with what results. Appellate courts have ruled on some such claims but surprisingly few. Perhaps the issue was raised at trial in many more cases that never made it to the appellate decisions and are therefore virtually immune to research. Still, I think it is fair to say that the issues are not unknown to the courts. So my puzzle is real to some extent.

But I suspect that the challenge to the crime scene search is rarely heard and, when voiced, is rarely successful. So the harder question remains: why is this issue ignored? Why is the inescapable infirmity of these forays glossed over? Why isn't the constitutional issue really real?

It may be that a crime scene search, particularly in a murder case, is so eminently reasonable, so broadly and deeply ingrained as proper police response to the discovery of a homicide, that it does not occur even to the most resourceful and contentious defense lawyer to challenge the product. It may be that judges, despite the instruction of their library, simply will not reject the evidence acquired in the course of what appears to be standard—indeed, obligatory—police work. It may be that all sides have tacitly agreed in these cases to accept, even to prefer, virtual justice.

2 The Magical Moment of Arrest

Capture and Custody

The first contact between a law enforcement agent and a suspect is a moment alive with possibilities. Experienced cops know. Their customary cool and casual manner masks quivering antennae. Unexpected things happen and they happen fast. Why do cops draw their guns as they walk up to a strange doorway, why do they approach a stopped car from both sides, the cop on the right hanging back just behind the occupant's line of sight? Because the lore of the station house, in the cities, at least, is that most folks do not think of a conversation with a police officer as a pleasant social encounter. Bane or blessing, police carry with them an aura of menace. Without even trying to activate their threat glands, they instill an uncomfortable feeling that one's life is about to take an unpleasant turn. And people who have recently committed a crime may feel the pang of panic. Those emotional ingredients can make a lethal adrenaline cocktail. Plus, the good cop knows that the first contact might shake loose an incriminating item—a surprised, unguarded acknowledgment or sudden guilt-inspired flight, perhaps a surreptitiously discarded object or a demonstrably false alibi. All good evidence of culpability. It pays to be alert.

The first contact is loaded also with legal consequence. From the standpoint of law, the adversarial intersection of government and citizen is a defining moment of democracy. The confrontation rings all the tonic chords of social utility and fundamental rights. The basic freedom of the individual to move about at will confronts the civic necessity to stand still and submit to authority. Values of personal sovereignty and the reign of domestic tranquility are instantly and deeply engaged. The overlay of value grids, the reverberation of dissonant analytic systems is almost enough to frighten off the curious tourist.

Yet the moment is so ordinary that it is somewhat embarrassing to make a scholarly fuss about it. That is the peculiar thing about this corner of the system of justice—the most commonplace events are often mined with constitutional ambiguities. As we now invade the precious moment, we will discover surprising anomalies, some of constitutional grade.

Trooper Kevin McCarthy is on highway patrol on Route I-95 a few miles north of Hartbridge one afternoon when he hears a radio call to be on the lookout for a late model red Lumina, plate number ABC 123, which may be headed either north or south on I-95. According to the dispatcher's report, the vehicle was stolen at knifepoint from its owner in the Hartbridge shopping mall near the highway. A handbag containing about one hundred dollars in cash was left in the car, plus the identification of the owner, Elizabeth Adler. Approach with caution, the dispatcher warns, the driver is believed to be armed and dangerous.

Shortly after getting the call, McCarthy—who is in the southbound lane—sees a red Lumina approaching. He does a U-turn across the divider, switches on his crownlights, and steps on the gas. He radios his position and, as he closes the gap, notices that the plate number of the Lumina is ABC 132—pretty close. Now the driver of the Lumina sees the police lights behind him and suddenly accelerates. McCarthy, whose car is prepared for high-speed chases, is soon catching up again, this time with siren wailing to clear other traffic out of the way.

Both cars are doing over 90 when McCarthy finally locks in close behind the Lumina and, over the loudspeaker, orders the driver to pull over. The Lumina slows down and pulls onto the shoulder, the police car close behind. As McCarthy is broadcasting his report to the dispatcher, the car door of the Lumina suddenly swings open, and a man clutching a handbag jumps out and heads for the nearby woods.

"Hey! There he goes!" McCarthy tells his microphone. Switching to the P.A., he says, "Hold it right there or I'll shoot!" His fleeing target does not even look back. McCarthy gets out of his car, draws his service pistol, aims, and fires three times at the back of the suspect, evidently missing him completely. The trooper starts to run now as the suspect reaches the underbrush of the woods bordering the highway. He sees the suspect throw the handbag under a bush as he enters the woods. When McCarthy arrives there a few moments later, he takes careful note of the spot where the bag was thrown. In the woods, the terrain slows the suspect, and McCarthy, an experienced deer hunter, has the advantage. Finally, McCarthy gets close enough to shout again, and the suspect, turning to see the muzzle end of McCarthy's pistol now within range, raises his hands and surrenders.

McCarthy turns the suspect around and snaps a pair of handcuffs on his wrists. Running his hand over the front of the suspect's clothing, the trooper discovers a hunting knife in a sheath inside the suspect's pants. He takes it, sheath and all, and pockets it. As he prods the man back through the woods to the highway, another patrol car pulls up and a second trooper leaps out to lend a hand. Putting his prisoner in the hands of his buddy, McCarthy returns to the underbrush, and from the bush that he had previously marked, he retrieves a woman's handbag. Inside, he finds $110 in cash in a wallet carrying cards in the name of Elizabeth Adler. He takes the property with him.

In this story we have no fewer than four Fourth Amendment events, some quite controversial and one, at least, only recently resolved.

I suppose it should have occurred to me years ago, but somehow I never thought that a cop firing a gun to stop a fleeing suspect was effecting a *seizure* in the sense of the Fourth Amendment prohibition against "unreasonable search and seizure." I knew, of course, that we had accumulated a substantial body of law regarding the use of deadly force by police—and civilians—to avert the commission of violence upon them and to effect the capture of felons. These are troublesome issues. They have generated spirited public debate when a suspected robber in a Halloween costume was killed by a frightened homeowner, when a white subway rider fired at a group of young blacks he thought were about to rob him, when a police officer shot and killed a young man he thought was drawing a weapon after being chased onto a darkened suburban parking lot. But these are policy questions. When is a putative victim's security worth the risk of killing a person when he believes himself to be in imminent danger? How much force may our agents use to prevent the escape of a felon who should face a criminal charge? Tough questions. But matters of social policy are not issues of constitutional dimension; they are questions for legislatures, not courts. Or so I thought.

It was a thoroughly unremarkable case that brought the issue to the Supreme Court—tragic, perhaps, but ordinary. Standard police work. Justice Byron White related the story of *Garner v. Tennessee:*

> At about 10:45 P.M. on October 3, 1974, Memphis Police Officers Elton Hymon and Leslie Wright were dispatched to answer a "prowler inside call." Upon arriving at the scene they saw a woman standing on her porch and gesturing toward the adjacent house. [Hymon said he saw lights on in the house.] She told them she had heard glass breaking and that "they" or "someone" was breaking in next door. While Wright radioed the dispatcher to say that they were on the scene, Hymon went behind the house. He heard a door slam and saw someone run across the backyard. The fleeing suspect, . . . Edward Garner, stopped at a 6-feet-high chain link fence at the edge of the yard. With the aid of a flashlight, Hymon was able to see Garner's face and hands. He saw no sign of a weapon, and, though not certain, was "reasonably sure" and "figured" that Garner was unarmed. He thought Garner was 17 or 18 years old and about 5'5" or 5'7" tall. [In fact, Garner, an eighth-grader, was fifteen. He was five feet, four inches tall and weighed somewhere around 100 to 110 pounds.] While Garner was crouched at the base of the fence, Hymon called out "police, halt" and took a few steps toward him. Garner then began to climb over the fence. Convinced that if Garner made it over the fence he would elude capture, Hymon shot him. The bullet hit Garner in the back of the head. Garner was taken by ambulance to a hospital, where he died on the operating table. Ten dollars and a purse taken from the house were found on his body.

The Court, despite two dissents, had little trouble deciding that Hymon's bullet effected a seizure of Garner's person in the constitutional sense. Because there is obviously no such thing as a shooting warrant (though an arrest warrant might conceivably be endorsed to allow execution by deadly force if necessary where the conditions met *Garner's* criteria for reasonableness), the question for the Court to decide was when seizure by gunshot is "reasonable." Their conclusion? Here again are White's words: "We conclude that such [deadly] force may not be used unless it is necessary to prevent the escape and the officer has probable cause to believe that the suspect poses a significant threat of death or serious physical injury to the officer or others."

As a result, the Court held that young Garner's father might recover damages from the state's violation of the constitutional rights of his son by shooting him as he tried to escape from the burglary he had committed.

We are required to apply this humane interpretation of the Fourth Amendment to McCarthy's pegging a shot at a fleeing suspect who was entering the protection of the woods well ahead of his only pursuer. Unhappily, it is not always easy to follow rules from the Court, even when they appear to be clear and simple.

Even if we assume that McCarthy had probable cause to believe that the man riding in the stolen car had obtained it in the manner described by the dispatcher—and there are a couple of levels of hearsay embedded in that recital, hearsay that might explain the garbled license number or conceal other misreported facts—even on that assumption, we have problems. For one, what would the Court consider a "significant threat"? Elsewhere in his opinion, Justice White writes: "Where the suspect poses no immediate threat to the officer and no threat to others, the harm resulting from failing to apprehend him does not justify the use of deadly force to do so." Unless he thought the suspect an expert knife-thrower, McCarthy could not have considered himself in *immediate* danger. But surely the defense of himself and others against imminent harm is not the only ground on which a police officer is allowed to use his gun. An ordinary private citizen may use deadly force in self-defense (which includes the defense of others). We give our cops *public* responsibilities that require them to go beyond self-defense. In some instances, we expect them to use aggressive force to protect us all against present *and future* harm. Don't we?

It may be significant—and we should always indulge the assumption that judicial authors choose their words with care—that the word "immediate" is omitted when the threat to a third person is considered. White's concern for future harm to third persons appears in several references to the violent character of the fleeing felon and the violent conduct of his crime. At one point, White notes that law enforcement does not benefit from "the killing of nonviolent suspects." At another, he acknowledges that danger might be inferred from the belief that the suspect is fleeing from a crime that "involved the infliction or threatened infliction of serious physical harm." Thus, on a careful reading, the Court appears to hold that a cop may fire to halt a person posing an imminent danger to the cop or someone else, or whose escape portends future harm to some person unknown because of his violent character.

Evidently, White did not consider Garner's burglary a crime of violence, though some—including Justice O'Connor and two codissenters—would argue with good reason that a nighttime residential burglary always carries an implicit threat of physical harm. But our carjacker had committed his crime at knifepoint. So the Supreme Court might find McCarthy's shot constitutional on the theory that a "violent suspect" who would use a knife to steal a car might, if allowed to escape, strike again with physically harmful effect. Obviously, though, the distinction is woefully strained. The actual danger to future victims unknown to the housebreaker and the carjacker is speculative to a point that can hardly support a constitutional principle.

And that speculation ignores the fact that, as the cop raises his weapon, he often knows nothing of the character of the person in his sights or of the crime from which the suspect is fleeing. Maybe young Garner had committed a series of rapes for which he was being sought at the time of the burglary—not the sort of person law enforcement should allow to escape. But can we allow this fact to validate the lethal shot though Hymon was ignorant of it at the moment he pulled the trigger? That would leave the constitutional construction of his conduct virtually to chance. Can't have that. And what if, unknown to Hymon, the resident of the house from which Garner fled was at that very moment lying bludgeoned and unconscious on the bedroom floor—would the police bullet then have been acceptable to the Court?

If not, then the Constitution does require police to allow the escape of dangerous people. Perhaps the old rule, with its implicit assumption that all felons are potentially dangerous, was best. I used to call it the *fleeing felon rule:* police may use force to a degree reasonable in the circumstances for the apprehension of a person reasonably believed to have committed a felony. Under the old rule, at least, when the cop shouted at the retreating burglar, drug dealer, or car thief, "Stop or I'll shoot!" the suspect could not shout back, "You do, and I'll sue!"

Another twist. Unlike the unfortunate Memphis cop, Elton Hymon, our Kevin McCarthy missed. He and the state are, therefore, gratefully relieved of any civil liability for damages. But did his inaccurate aim also dispel the concern over the Fourth Amendment? This is not an empty question. As we will see, important consequences—notably the use of the knife and the handbag as evidence against the suspect—may hang on the answer. Does a gunshot effect a seizure only when the bullet stops the target? Or is the use of deadly force itself an exercise of state power that may infringe on a citizen's right to move about freely? And firing a gun at someone is certainly using "deadly force" whether or not death results. It would be silly to say that a cop who has no reason to believe that the fleeing felon poses any danger may fire his gun at the retreating form—but only if his aim is poor. The response of the Fourth Amendment should not depend upon the notorious vagaries of police aim.

Still, a shot that misses or wings the fleeing felon does not stop him. How then can it effect a seizure of his person? Perhaps because a shot—even a harmless warning shot fired in the air—amounts to a show of authority, an assertion of power that impinges on one's sense of personal sovereignty. That could be a Fourth Amendment event. Even McCarthy's cry of "Halt!" might amount to the sort of gesture that interferes with freedom of movement and thus effects a seizure of the person—though its immediately visible effect is only to quicken the stride of the escaping felon.

By this logic, perhaps we might say that the seizure occurred when McCarthy switched on his crownlights and stepped on the gas. Someone out there might even argue that initiating a high-speed auto chase is the use of *deadly* force; it is probably more dangerous to life and limb than the uncertain accuracy of the police pistol fired on the run. But even if no civil action could be maintained by a chased car thief who has wrapped his car around a telephone pole, a police cruiser, lights flashing, siren wailing, bearing down on a suspect surely amounts to a show of authority. Could it not be maintained that this chase—or the later footrace in the woods, for that matter— impaired freedom of action by pursuit that made the suspect run away, the legal twin of capture that would make him stand still?

Actually, several states, including California and New York, have held that a footrace between cops and suspect amounts to a seizure and that, absent preexisting probable cause, any object discarded along the course of pursuit must be regarded not as abandoned property but as evidence acquired by illegal search and seizure. As such, the evidence could be suppressed.

California's rule reached the United States Supreme Court in 1991 in a case called *Matter of Hodari D.* In that case, as Justice Antonin Scalia told the story, cops became suspicious when a small cluster of boys split and ran in several directions at the approach of the officers' unmarked car. Perhaps it was the word "POLICE" embossed on their jackets that tipped off the group of young drug dealers. Anyway, Officer Pertoso—evidently a pretty talented street runner himself—left the car and pursued the juvenile, "Hodari D.," who threw away a "small rock" just before the officer tackled him. The rock turned out to be crack cocaine. In his possession, Hodari had a pager and $130 in cash. The California Court of Appeal reversed the lower court's denial of Hodari's motion to suppress the cocaine, agreeing with Hodari that he had been seized when he saw the officer running toward him, that this seizure was unreasonable under the Fourth Amendment, and that the evidence must be suppressed as the fruit of that illegal seizure.

The Supreme Court disagreed. A "show of authority" as might be manifest in a chase does not accomplish a seizure, Scalia explained. Only the "laying on of hands"—that is, the application of restraining physical force or the submission of the suspect—amounts to an arrest. The response of New York to this enlightenment from Washington was, in effect: thanks for the lesson in the meaning of the *United States* Constitution; but we'll apply the identical provision in our *state* Constitution to state chases, and, in our unrepentant judgment our New York Constitution still regards a police chase as a seizure.

States may do this. In a rather odd twist on federalism, states are bound by provisions of the federal Constitution only as it sets outer boundaries on the power of government; it is perfectly acceptable to set narrower limits on police authority under state constitutions than the U.S. Supreme Court has set under identical provisions of the U.S. Constitution. And as the Supremes have become less sympathetic to the claims of criminal defendants for extensions of constitutional protection, many states have responded by imposing stricter curtailments on local investigation and prosecution than the federal Charter requires.

The holding in *Hodari D.* must mean that McCarthy's missed shot—along with a wounding hit, a warning shot, and a shouted command—is not a Fourth Amendment event. No seizure of the suspect's person occurred by show of authority alone. And, silly as it seems, *Garner v. Tennessee* applies only to the fatal or disabling shot. If the bullet is viewed as the hand of the cop on the suspect's shoulder, then only the bullet that disables (the hand that restrains)—not the shot that loudly proclaims official authority—constitutes a constitutional event. Of course, we have not yet heard the Court say that. We're just putting two and two together.

But let's remember that McCarthy did actually bring the Lumina to a stop. A driver at that juncture would presumably think that he was no longer free to move as he wished and was thenceforward subject to the custodial authority of the police. That's a pretty good definition of an arrest or a seizure of the person in the terms of the Fourth Amendment. The puzzling question is whether that seizure continues through an escape and renewed flight, or whether it terminates for legal purposes as soon as the person seized breaks free of the control being exercised over him.

Directly relevant to our case, Scalia wrote: "To say that an arrest is effected by the slightest application of physical force, despite the arrestee's escape, is not to say that for Fourth Amendment purposes there is a continuing arrest during the period of fugitivity. If, for example, Pertoso had laid his hands upon Hodari to arrest him, but Hodari had broken away and had then cast away the cocaine, it would hardly be realistic to say that that disclosure [*sic*] had been made during the course of an arrest."

So now we know. If McCarthy seized his fugitive by stopping his car, the seizure vanished with his renewed flight. The gunshot—though indisputably a "show of authority"—did not amount to a seizure because it did not accomplish a physical restraint (as a leg wound might have) or induce a surrender. The foot chase into the woods, though accompanied by shouted commands to stop, was nothing but a sylvan romp until the suspect stopped with his hands in the air. So the handbag thrown under the bush during the pursuit will be admitted as evidence at trial as abandoned property, regardless of whether McCarthy had probable cause to pursue the suspect.

At least, we are authoritatively informed of these interpretations so far as the commands of the U.S. Constitution govern. Where a state officer is doing the chasing (as in our case), we will have to determine whether the local jurisdiction has chosen to divorce itself from federal jurisprudence—as it may—and follow a policy more restrictive in the license granted the police. As we have already noted, a state may construe more generously than the Supreme Court the rights of the pursued, but never the authority of the pursuer.

That leaves us with the final encounter, the physical seizure of the suspect and the removal of the knife from his belt. Here at last we have a clear and simple proposition on which state and federal constitutions are read alike. Incidental to a lawful arrest, it is always reasonable under the Fourth Amendment for police to conduct a full search of the person of the arrested individual and the immediately surrounding area into which he might reach to secure the means of resistance or escape—whether or not the arresting officer has reason to believe that such an object lies ready at hand or that the arrested person is inclined to resist or escape if possible. In the eyes of the law, every arrested person may have both the means and the inclination to fight and run.

The incident search rule, in concept, must be spatially and temporally restricted to its purpose. In fact, both limits have been stretched somewhat. In one case, the Supreme Court indicated that an incident search might be delayed, at least until the morning after the person was arrested, when his clothes might be taken for microscopic examination.

The spatial limit likewise has a subtle and built-in extender. Our carjacker, remember, had the knife taken from the front of his jeans when his hands were shackled behind him. Let's make it harder. Imagine a woman arrested carrying a large handbag. The bag is taken from her and her wrists are cuffed. May police look in the bag? A man is arrested behind a desk. He is told to stand up and directed to the side of the room, where he is manacled. May police go back and look in the desk drawers? All of these places were within "grabbable space" (in the jargon of the trade) at the time of arrest but not at the time of the search. The moment that should be critical for the search to conform to the theory behind it is the moment of *the search*. Once the arrested person is physically constrained or removed from the source of the potential instrument of flight or resistance, the reason for allowing the prophylactic search evaporates. Nothing wrong with that line of argument. But here, despite its avowed and laborious effort to get the scope of the incident search lined up with its rationale, the Supreme Court simply ignored its own logic. It held that the moment of arrest is critical and police may search shortly after the arrest any place from which the arrested person might have grabbed a weapon *at the time of his arrest* (but didn't).

Is it not strange how those who expound the law seek to convince the rest of us that it is a coherent body of doctrine, a logically interlocking web of proposition, inference, and policy? Perhaps they convince themselves. Surely some of them do. How else could they write as they do through an entire career? For the last fifty years or so, a significant number of legal scholars— some judges among them—have argued that the law is not founded on theory nor held together by logic. The Legal Realists, as they call themselves, say that law is only a way of enacting social policy and that its lifeblood is the changeable, vital, personal component of experience and common values among the lawmakers. I have been educated and nourished in the school of Legal Realism, and I acknowledge its influence. Still, I am not altogether persuaded that the law is nothing but the disposition of judges to promulgate their personal or social ethic, to create or perpetuate a society that conforms to their psychological, economic, or political interests.

I have watched and suffered with too many judges, scholars, and students as they wrestled with the intellectual constraints of coherence and consistency to think that the law is nothing but social preference. I cannot believe all that sweat was spilled only in the service of rationalization or the preservation of an empty facade of reason. I have seen people use the law to reach results directly contrary to their interests and inclinations. The federal judges of southern courts during the civil rights era, the many judges who have overcome personal repugnance to rule for disfavored—even dangerous—parties before them wrote a proud chapter in legal history. Contraception and even abortion have been allowed by many judges whose personal credo is deeply offended; disgusting, bigoted speech has been protected by judges who are themselves the object of the bigotry. These and many other instances testify to the proposition that law is a principled discipline, notwithstanding its many self-serving ministers. Doctrine counts.

Perhaps I am saying only that I rank high among our basic drives a need to make sense of things. The human brain is wired, I am convinced, to abstract principles from perceptions, to form theoretical constructs around experience. It is important, then, to keep the faith in these constructs once they have been articulated. And the discontinuities in legal doctrine are disturbing for that reason. They suggest either weakness in the construct or lack of rigor in its application. This may be too harsh a judgment on the flawed human endeavor to keep the governing principles of the law clear and straight. But it suggests that interpretation of law is a sincere and useful enterprise of articulation and clarification.

And I suppose it is not altogether a bad thing—though it is confusing at times—for the central authority, the U.S. Supreme Court reading the U.S. Constitution, to come up with one idea while local authorities, the state high courts reading their state constitutions, choose a different interpretation of the same principle. Some very thoughtful people have regarded such diversity as one of the prime benefits of our federal system. To others it is disconcerting to learn that such basic questions as the right of a cop to fire a gun at a citizen can be answered differently from state to state and according to whether the cop in question draws a salary from the federal or the local treasury. But until our courts are all agreed on the *correct* allocation of rights and consequences in this chase paradigm, that is the legal world we live in.

3 The Marvelous Faculty of Recognition

Eyewitness Identification of a Suspect

Mona Parker, 57, was on her way to the grocery store one evening, fifty dollars in her handbag from a recent stop at the local bank cash machine. Two men who had been standing on the corner as she passed followed her as she walked down the darkening street between the bank and the market. In the middle of the block, one of the men grabs Parker from behind in a choke hold. The other circles in front of her and pulls her handbag from her. As she wriggles and tries to hold onto the bag, the man in front of her slaps her face hard and says, "Don't be a fool, old lady, or you'll be a dead old lady." Seeing that the man is holding a knife in front of her face, Parker stops struggling. The men throw her to the ground and run off into the shadows with her purse.

When they have gone, Mona Parker painfully picks herself up off the ground and walks to the corner, where she telephones the police. A police car pulls up several minutes later and finds the victim, bruised and faint, being tended by some passing strangers. As soon as they hear the story, the officers ask about Parker's injuries and whether she feels strong enough to come into the patrol car for a short tour of the neighborhood to see whether the robbers are still around. But she is bleeding from a cut on the mouth where she was slapped and from some scrapes and bruises she sustained when she was thrown to the ground. On second thought, the police radio for an ambulance and Mona Parker is taken to the emergency room, where she is treated for her minor injuries and released several hours later. The following morning, at the request of the police, she arrives at the local station house to view some photos.

Meanwhile, police have learned that a clerk at the corner market, Nico Gonzalez, was outside the store having a smoke when he saw two men run by. One of them, he noticed, was carrying what looked like a woman's purse. The light from the store window provided good illumination, but the incident happened so quickly and unexpectedly that the clerk was unable to get a good look at the running men. He gave a general description of their clothing and told police he might be able to recognize one of them if he saw him again.

At the robbery unit of the local detective squad, Detective Mary Bailey has caught the case from the uniformed police who responded on the street. As Ms. Parker walks in, Detective Bailey moves toward a row of thick black ring binders on the shelf. They are filled with photos of people arrested for, or suspected of committing, street robberies in the precinct. The photos—copies of official mug shots mixed in with Polaroid snapshots taken when a suspect was in the squad room for questioning—are arranged by sex and race. A couple of preliminary questions inform Bailey which books to pull for her complainant. "Just look through these books," she tells Ms. Parker, seating her at a relatively uncluttered table. "Take your time. Look at each face. If you see anyone you think might be one of the men who robbed you yesterday, just holler, OK?"

A half-hour later, Bailey comes up and looks over Parker's shoulder. Parker is solemnly studying a color mug shot, clear and crisp, front and profile. "Any luck?" Bailey asks.

"Well," Parker says slowly, "I don't know. This looks a lot like the one who held the knife. But I can't be sure. The guy who robbed me looked meaner, angrier, you know what I mean? But it could be him."

Detective Bailey reaches over, slips the photo out of the book, and reads the information on the back. So far so good, she thinks. At least it doesn't rule him out. Not like the victim we had in here last week who described a perp as six-four, maybe five, then ID'd a shot of a mope five-eight. Or the vic last month who made a positive on a heavy hitter who was doing four-to-eight at the time the crime went down.

Mona Parker's choice is a photo, some eighteen months old, of a young man named Henderson, aka Junior, arrested for a stickup of an all-night convenience store. Bailey remembers the case. The evidence against Henderson was not strong and it was his first rap. He pleaded to a misdemeanor and got eight months. To Ms. Parker, she says soothingly, "OK, good enough. This one's the closest so far, right?" Mona Parker nods. "Keep it up. Get through all the books, OK? And don't forget to call me if anything else looks close."

Bailey keeps the photo chosen and retreats, but the session ends with no other suspects, and Parker is given a ride home by one of the other detectives.

Bailey, meanwhile, is painstakingly preparing a "photo array." Picking five other mug shots of men of roughly the same age and pigmentation, she inserts the six three-by-five photos in the numbered slots of a specially prepared mat. "May as well give our eyewitness a chance to confirm the ID," she comments to Marty Marx, her usual partner. Bailey and Marx sign out a vehicle and head for the store where Gonzalez works, the photo array carefully enclosed in a manilla folder. They find their man at work and, with some ceremony, they exhibit the montage. He responds with a long and serious look. "Sorry," he says, "but I really did not get that good a look at these guys. It could be one of these, but I really can't say for sure. This one might be him, and this one, number four, looks something like him, I think. But I really can't say." Officer Bailey thanks the clerk, tells him to "stay loose," and the officers climb back into their car. "At least we got 50 percent," Bailey comments as they drive back to the house. "Our man said Junior was a possibility." "He must have gotten a better look at him than he thinks," Marx says, "or he wouldn't have even given Henderson the half-nod, right?"

Typing up the report of their interview with Gonzalez, Bailey casually opens a conversation with the sergeant, her commanding officer. Cops don't ask advice. That would violate the canon of competence. Never show indecision. Hesitation is weakness in confrontational work. To seek help is to admit confusion. You know your job, you know what to do in all situations. And cops always play from a position of strength. So she doesn't ask the sergeant for help. Still, it's prudent to get the boss's approval before making a move. So she opens, "Got another half ID on that cash machine mugging of the old lady, Sarge."

"You going to try to make one certain ID out of two uncertains?" the sergeant asks. Professional communication in the station house often runs in the mode of jokes, teases, and taunts. It saves everyone's honor. No one on The Job should take crime too seriously. You'd go nuts in two weeks.

"I think I got to try and find this mope, Henderson, and bring him in for a lineup." Telling, not asking.

"Clear it or close it," the sergeant replies. "I keep telling you people, I don't want these nickel-and-dime cases lying around open forever." He's approving Bailey's move, couched in an old complaint to the troops.

For the next two weeks, Bailey and Marx look for Henderson. Not exclusively. They both have other cases they are working on. But looking all the time. They drive by his last known address, ask questions, show the photo. Nothing, no one remembers him. Maybe when he got out of the slammer, he moved in with a girlfriend in another part of town. Maybe. But the officers have the photo with them, and, as they slowly cruise the precinct, they look at the faces silently looking at them, checking their memory from time to time against the photo, now somewhat dog-eared. Occasionally spotting an informant, they'll show him the photo. "Know this guy? Junior Henderson, ever hear of him?" Sometimes they get a tip from one of their contacts, trying to be helpful. "Oh, yeah, Junior. He hangs at the Stag Club." An after-hours drinking joint. Bailey and Marx add the location joint to their late-night patrols, occasionally stopping drunken patrons as they emerge. "Junior? Henderson? Never heard of him." The photo? "Nah, never seen him." They have no reason to want to be helpful to cops.

Then one bright afternoon, there he is, big as life, sitting on a stoop, drinking beer from a paper bag. Marty Marx spots him first: "Hey, isn't that your man?" Bailey stops the car. "Sure looks like him," she says. Both cops are out of the car and strolling up to the stoop. They don't have to display badges or announce their identity. All stoop sitters and street loungers know them instantly as cops. "You Henderson?" Bailey asks.

"What if I am?" is the laconic response.

"Hey, we just want to talk to you, OK?" Marx says.

"So talk," says Henderson, real cool.

"Somebody says you did a mugging a few weeks back." No Miranda. Henderson is not in custody, no warnings are called for.

"Not me," Henderson says. "You got the wrong dude."

"We'd like you to come into the station house and clear this up. It won't take long. If you're right, so long, good luck, no hard feelings. What do you say? You're not doing anything right now anyway."

"I'm waiting for my friend," says Henderson, stalling.

"So? He'll wait for you. You'll be back here in an hour." More like three to six years if we get lucky, Bailey silently amends her prediction.

"Otherwise," says Marx, "you know. It'll be hanging over you." Just what this vague threat means to Henderson is hard to say, but he hesitates only a moment longer before rising slowly to his feet.

"OK. Let's get it over with." He leaves the beer on the stoop as a gesture of confidence in his imminent vindication and return.

"You don't have anything on you now, right?" asks Marx, walking Henderson to the car. Henderson stops and raises his elbows, inviting the frisk. Marx touches him at the waist and pockets, a cursory frisk. Nothing on him. They continue to the car, no cuffs.

Let's interrupt the narrative here for a look at these events through the prism of law. The story has progressed to that portentous moment: the first adversarial contact between an individual, minding his business on a neighborhood stoop, and a couple of purposeful agents of the polity, looking for a collar. But would we call this an "arrest"? I did slip in that little parenthetical hint: Henderson was not yet "in custody" for purposes of the Miranda warnings. I did that, in part, to put off to another chapter the whole Miranda business. But have I dismissed the issue too lightly? A nineteen-year-old man approached by two cops might well think that he was not entirely free to walk away. And if he felt so constrained, that's custody, isn't it?

To peg "custody"—with all its constitutional implications—on the subjective sense of constraint experienced by the suspect is odd in several ways. First, it suggests that more sensitive, more frightened people will have greater constitutional rights than more callous or confident people. Second, it locates the critical factor where it is virtually inaccessible to the prosecution (which is likely to have the burden of proving that the suspect was not in custody): the mind of the defendant. Finally, although the very object of the definition is restriction of the exercise of police power, the subjective reading makes it very difficult to instruct the police on the limits of their authority. It is one thing to tell them: do not seize a suspect with the intent of depriving him of his freedom to move about at will unless you have damn good reason to think he committed a crime. It is quite another to say: do nothing that might give this particular individual the sense that he is restricted in his actions.

The question before the house, then, is: when a cruising cop rolls down the window and beckons to a lounger on the street to come over to the car to exchange a few words, is the gesture sufficient to amount to "custody" such that it must be preceded by probable cause and followed by a set of Miranda warnings? It probably seems false to cops to call this a "seizure." After all, the guy could have just smiled and waved back—or walked away. He had no cuffs on him, no one had a gun under his chin. Still, few would deny that taking a person peremptorily off the street and into police-controlled space is a significant exercise of dominion. As to the consent theory, dear to the hearts of law enforcement people—and much abused by them—the Supreme

Court years ago declared the last word: mere acquiescence to apparently lawful authority is not consent in the sense of a free waiver of constitutional entitlements. In other words, when a cop asks "May I?" the answer, "Sure, go ahead," does not necessarily strip the citizen of any security to which she might be otherwise entitled by the Constitution.

Then, in 1991, the Supreme Court decided an odd little case called *Florida v. Bostick. Bostick* demonstrated that even a perfectly reasonable and realistic belief that one is not free to leave an encounter with police may not indicate that a seizure of the person has taken place. Local sheriffs in Fort Lauderdale, looking for drugs, were routinely getting on buses at scheduled stops and asking passengers for permission to search their bags. On the occasion in question, without any particular grounds for suspicion, they picked out Terrance Bostick, who was reclining on the rear seat of a Greyhound bus. Effectively blocking the narrow aisle, they asked for and received permission to search a piece of his luggage; in it they found cocaine.

Justice Sandra Day O'Connor, writing for the majority of the Court, identified the issue in the case as follows: "The sole issue presented for our review is whether a police encounter on a bus of the type described above necessarily constitutes a 'seizure' within the meaning of the Fourth Amendment. The State concedes, and we accept for purposes of this decision, that the officers lacked the reasonable suspicion required to justify a seizure and that, if a seizure took place, the drugs found in Bostick's suitcase must be suppressed as tainted fruit."

The high court of Florida had answered the question affirmatively, reasoning that no passenger approached by armed officers in the cramped confines of a bus, only partway to his destination, could have reasonably felt free to get up and walk away. Justice O'Connor did not like this ruling, which automatically killed effective drug interdiction programs on public vehicles. Besides, she said, the conditions precluding free departure were not the makings of the police but were inherent in the physical setting. A seizure occurs, she held, only where the police take some action that conveys a reasonable sense of restraint to the object of their interest. In an encounter like the one initiated by the Fort Lauderdale sheriffs, the free-to-walk-away standard is inappropriate; though he might not have felt free to get up and exit, Bostick could have refused to talk to the sheriffs or allow them to search his bag. As the Court put it:

When police attempt to question a person who is walking down the street or through an airport lobby, it makes sense to inquire whether a reasonable person would feel free to continue walking. But when the person is seated on a bus and has no desire to leave, the degree to which a reasonable person would feel that he or she could leave is not an accurate measure of the coercive effect of the encounter.

Here, for example, the mere fact that Bostick did not feel free to leave the bus does not mean that the police seized him. Bostick was a passenger on a bus that was scheduled to depart. He would not have felt free to leave the bus even if the police had not been present. Bostick's movements were "confined" in a sense, but this was the natural result of his decision to take the bus; it says nothing about whether or not the police conduct at issue was coercive.

Because the courts below had not considered the case in that light, Justice O'Connor sent it back for another look by state courts aided by the enlightenment she and the majority had supplied. Concluding, the Court declared:

> Here, the facts recited by the Florida Supreme Court indicate that the officers did not point guns at Bostick or otherwise threaten him and that they specifically advised Bostick that he could refuse consent.
>
> Nevertheless, we refrain from deciding whether or not a seizure occurred in this case. The trial court made no express findings of fact, and the Florida Supreme Court rested its decision on a single fact—that the encounter took place on a bus—rather than on the totality of the circumstances. We remand so that the Florida courts may evaluate the seizure question under the correct legal standard. We do reject, however, Bostick's argument that he must have been seized because no reasonable person would freely consent to a search of luggage that he or she knows contains drugs. This argument cannot prevail because the "reasonable person" test presupposes an innocent person. . . .
>
> Clearly, a bus passenger's decision to cooperate with law enforcement officers authorizes the police to conduct a search without first obtaining a warrant only if the cooperation is voluntary. "Consent" that is the product of official intimidation or harassment is not consent at all. Citizens do not forfeit their constitutional rights when they are coerced to comply with a request that they would prefer to refuse. The question

to be decided by the Florida courts on remand is whether Bostick chose to permit the search of his luggage.

On remand, the Florida Supreme Court simply swung around and affirmed the trial court's order, which denied Bostick's motion to suppress the evidence and the conviction based upon it. A dissent, however, protested this simple response and insisted that, though the Supremes had rejected the blanket finding that a busboard approach is a coercive seizure *in se,* the particular facts in Bostick's case made refusal to cooperate an unreasonable option.

Justice O'Connor and friends were not entirely clear on the question of whether an arrest—a seizure of the person in Fourth Amendment terms—is governed by an objective or subjective standard. Most judges, including at least a few Justices of the Supreme Court, would probably say that an arrest is measured by the understanding of the citizen—provided that understanding is not unreasonable. "Reasonable" means that others in the same position might well feel the same way. This is an objective standard in that the conduct is measured by what some hypothetical normal (innocent) person would think, rather than by what the particular person actually thought.

The preferred solution to the puzzle thus has both subjective and objective components: did this particular person actually feel constrained, and would others feel the same way? If both criteria apply, then regardless of the cops' characterization of the interaction as purely voluntary compliance, the individual is under arrest. Although the standard has a subjective element, it does not require cops to be mind readers: if they figure anyone they put this move on might well feel his freedom had been impaired at least temporarily, they should know that their actions constitute custody. If this particular mope is so cool as to feel unconstrained, so much the better.

So the solution courts have usually elected (confirmed, in a sense, by *Bostick*) is heavily weighted toward the objective criterion: would the conduct of the police have instilled in a reasonable person similarly situated the belief that his freedom of movement had been to some extent curtailed? Police, it is thought, being reasonable persons themselves, should be able to assess their own conduct by this standard and guide themselves accordingly.

There are problems with this solution as well. It is the actual, subjective sense of loss of autonomy, after all, that imperils protected rights. The Constitution is, in this view, a codification of the personal rights of citizens, not a manual of police conduct.

Another problem was illustrated by a celebrated case in New York, where a subway rider named Bernard Goetz fired on a group of four young men who he believed were about to rob him. His plea of self-defense depended on his assertion that he truly believed that these young men were bent on robbery, a surmise that they, of course, denied. After the highest court straightened out its errant lower courts, instructing them that the standard for reasonable belief in New York was objective, the issue remained whether the "reasonable person similarly situated" meant a reasonable person who, like Goetz, had been previously accosted and robbed on the subway. Facing the issue squarely, the Court of Appeals in New York specifically held that personal history may be considered in determining the objective reasonability of belief. As you can readily see, along this path lies a curious merger of objective and subjective standards.

So was Henderson under arrest when Marx and Bailey first approached him as he sat drinking beer on a stoop or was he not? The truth is, we have graded the concept of custody for constitutional purposes. There are brief preliminary interruptions that are constitutional on "mere suspicion," less cause than the "probable cause" required for a "full-blown" arrest. What we call a "stop and frisk" is usually a brief, on-the-spot detention for a few perfunctory questions and, in some circumstances, a superficial pat-down for weapons. The frisk is self-protective and may be done, without arrest, on the barest grounds to believe something illegal may be afoot. Marx's tentative ground for belief that Henderson committed an armed robbery would allow him to take precautions before sitting next to him in the car. That prudent frisk, although a Fourth Amendment event, would be reasonable. Only if Marx felt what he believed was a weapon could he reach into Henderson's clothes to pull out the object. Such was the teaching of a famous 1968 case in the United States Supreme Court called *Terry v. Ohio*. If Marx had felt something that might have been a weapon, the object he extracted would be lawful evidence even if it turned out to be harmless. In a recent modification of *Terry*, the Court allowed that if the officer can plainly tell just by feel, through a layer of fabric, that an object is contraband—even if not a dangerous weapon—the officer can lawfully retrieve it. But I note the lawfulness of Marx's frisk only in passing since he felt and recovered nothing.

We froze our story at a somewhat later frame. Our cops are now taking their suspect into a car, to hold him at the police station so the victim and witness can look at him for a recognition test. The officers have control of the suspect's body, having sharply curtailed his choice of conduct. Surely at this point the police must be said to have him in custody and under arrest. Incidentally, if you asked them, Marx and Bailey would have a fast and confident reply: "Arrest? Are you kidding? This was no arrest. We just asked him did he want to come down to the house, and he said OK. If the old lady had failed to identify him, we would have let him go. He was our guest, not our prisoner." But their appraisal has no bearing on the legal question.

Another question: why are we allowing ourselves to become twisted in this semantic skein? Well, it may sound like legalistic hair-splitting, but we do not engage in it for the exercise. Rather, I am following a trail to another legal anomaly, an apparently insoluble riddle that puts the police in the position of having no legal way to do what they do, what they must do every day. But again, this enigma seems to be a sleeping dog. Except for those who worry about the capacity of the Constitution to govern daily police work, no one seems greatly troubled by the problem. We, too, should probably let these dozing paradoxes lie, but having come this far, I must play with them a bit.

An arrest, we have already noted, is a constitutional event. It encroaches upon the security in one's person that the Fourth Amendment guards. An arrest is thus unconstitutional unless it has been authorized by warrant or is otherwise "reasonable" in the circumstances. In either case, the lawful arrest must be supported by probable cause. *Probable cause* is not a very apt term; it has little to do with probability and nothing whatever with causality. But it is the term chosen by the Framers to describe the degree of suspicion requisite for the government to move into the citizen's private spaces. It means "damn good reason to believe," that's all. Not certainty beyond a reasonable doubt, not even more likely than not. But more than a hunch or suspicion. That's the best we can do to define it. We shouldn't ask for too much precision here; the term is a crude working tool, and its ill-defined contours, oddly, improve its utility.

What's the consequence of an unlawful arrest? We can't suppress the body of the person arrested as we suppress physical evidence seized in violation of the Fourth Amendment. The jurisdiction of a court to try a criminal case is not defeated by the illegal production of the defendant before the court. But there are serious consequences. Evidence obtained by exploitation of the initial illegality—the colorful and inescapable metaphor is "fruit of the poisonous tree"—is barred. And that might well include the reactions of those who see Henderson's illegally detained face and figure in a lineup.

Here, then, is our brain teaser. On the equivocal photo ID by Mona Parker, the police have some grounds for suspicion. The 50 percent hit by Gonzalez didn't add much. We're far short of the level of certainty that would add up to a damn good reason to believe Henderson is the robber. Without that, Bailey can't make a lawful arrest. But we all know that photo IDs are tough, especially when the photo is eighteen months old. Weight, haircut, or facial hair may have changed. A flat, posed, glossy print is just not the same as a life-size exposure in the round. So the logical next step in the investigation is to give the witnesses a look at a live body.

Sometimes that is possible by taking the witness out into the world to see whether she can pick the criminal from the population at large. A woman employee, raped by a fellow worker, may be taken to the plant entrance when the shift changes to give her a chance to pick her rapist from the emerging workers. Or the store owner, held up at gunpoint moments before, may be taken through the neighborhood to see if he can spot the robber on the street. Usually, though, the suspect must be brought to the police station, stood in a line behind a pane of one-way glass with five people of roughly similar age, color, and stature, and exposed to the uncoached witness. If the witness is reasonably certain of the identity of the suspect in a fair lineup, police have probable cause to arrest.

The problem: probable cause is not retroactive. To paraphrase the eminent Justice Cardozo, no intrusion may ever be justified by its success. If probable cause does not flower until the positive corporeal ID, how are Bailey and Marx supposed to produce Henderson to be viewed? If Henderson had been a bit braver or better informed and told Bailey to get lost when she proposed "clearing things up," or if some scrupulous judge refuses to buy the free-consent argument in these circumstances, Bailey and Marx are helpless. Catch-22: without the corp ID, no grounds for arrest; without the antecedent arrest, no corp ID.

It is hard to believe that the law leaves police trapped in this inescapable conundrum, especially with regard to such a regular and ordinary part of their business. They must either abuse the concept of consent (often with the connivance of courts that cannot bring themselves to outlaw fair and necessary lineups) or they must forgo the opportunity to obtain this essential evidence. There must be a way out of this bind.

Actually, we almost had a way out. Some unsung hero, a creative spirit in the anonymous ranks of government drones, came up with a proposal more than twenty years ago that would have solved the conundrum neatly, fairly, and for all time. Congress was too busy debating nonsense and distributing pork to notice a gem in the intake basket, and the measure disappeared into the vortex. Incorrigible optimists reintroduced the measure in successive sessions with, alas, the same result. It was probably too subtle for the wise heads of the legislative branch. Its only beneficiaries were all of us, and we don't lobby effectively.

The ill-fated measure was a modest amendment to the dry old Federal Rules of Criminal Procedure and would have created a rule titled "Nontestimonial Identification." It would have provided that a federal magistrate, on request of a law enforcement officer or government attorney, might issue an order at any stage of the investigation, including before arrest, directing a person to appear and furnish "nontestimonial identification," a term defined to include evidence obtained by "fingerprints, palm prints, footprints, measurements, blood specimens, urine specimens, saliva samples, hair samples, or other reasonable physical or medical examination, handwriting exemplars, voice samples, photographs, and lineups." The order could issue only on sworn affidavits establishing the following grounds: (1) probable cause to believe an offense was committed, (2) reasonable grounds amounting to less than probable cause to believe that the suspect committed the offense, and (3) some basis to believe that the results of a nontestimonial examination will be of "material aid" in determining whether the suspect committed the offense.

Neat, simple, and—as far as I can see—perfectly constitutional. The reason, incidentally, that the measure expressly excludes *testimonial* identification is that as soon as the cops ask the suspect to tell them something that might connect him to the crime, a whole new set of severe strictures is activated. No court can order a person to divulge the contents of his or her mind, supplying data that might be used in some way to help convict that person of a crime. But when it comes to *external* evidence, physical traits, all the government needs is some lawful basis for holding the citizen immobile long enough to take the print, measurement, or whatever, and a relatively safe and painless means of acquiring it. Surgery to dig a slug out of a suspect's body has been held to be too intrusive, but extracting a bit of blood to prove the driver was drunk is OK.

I peg my constitutional call on the fact that the Supreme Court virtually invited such a procedure more than twenty-five years ago in a case called *Davis v. Mississippi.* The Court overturned a conviction based on fingerprints taken from the defendant along with a number of young men who, without probable cause, had been brought to the station house, questioned, printed, and released. Justice William Brennan, writing for the majority, threw this language into his opinion: "We have no occasion in this case, however, to determine whether the requirements of the Fourth Amendment could be met by narrowly circumscribed procedures for obtaining, during the course of a criminal investigation, the fingerprints of individuals for whom there is no probable cause to arrest." In the trade, that's what is called a broad hint. But Congress, for some reason, did not take it.

So what do investigating police do in the absence of the nontestimonial identification order? There is some judicial language expressing tolerance for brief, on-the-spot detentions to take a fingerprint using a mobile print kit. The same principle might work also for a photo, voice or handwriting exemplar, or for a small lock of head hair (though I have not heard of these ID procedures being used on the street). But a urine or blood specimen, pubic hair sample, lineup, and other forms of inspection require some transportation. Federal jurisdictions and two others (Illinois and the District of Columbia) use the subpoena to compel a suspect's attendance before a grand jury and there order him to participate in a lineup and otherwise furnish evidence of the trait that might identify him. As of the end of 1990, nine states (Alaska, Arizona, Colorado, Idaho, Iowa, Nebraska, North Carolina, Utah, and Vermont) had enacted some form of the nontestimonial identification procedure that Congress abandoned. Whether it works and how often it is used in these states I cannot say. Although New York has an ID statute, it would be no help to Bailey and Marx because it cannot be invoked until after the suspect has been indicted for the crime.

Again we ask: in the other forty states, what do our police do in these circumstances? There has to be a way to get the suspect, tentatively identified from a photo, into a carefully structured lineup for a live exposure, doesn't there? Oddly enough, we spectators do not really know what the police do. I suppose they improvise and hope the court will not look too closely. Cops I have watched do pretty much what Bailey and Marx did and, remarkably, the resulting corp ID is rarely challenged as the product of an illegal seizure (as it surely appears to be). It may not be strictly legal, but the virtual justice here is particularly hard to dispute.

Let's return to our story. When we left him, Henderson had agreed to accompany Bailey and Marx, confidently telling his fellow stoop hangers he'd be back in an hour.

In the car, the police talk to each other, ignoring their guest. When he asks, "What's this shit all about?" Marx smiles and says, "C'mon, Junior, you know what it's all about." The subject is dropped. At the squad room, Henderson is left smoking a cigarette and drinking a cup of home-brewed coffee in front of a television set that is never turned off. At that hour, Bailey can find only two civilian clerks at their desks who resemble Henderson closely enough to stand in a lineup with him, so she and Marx go back to the streets to enlist three more citizens of the right race, age, and general physical configuration who are willing to spend an easy hour or so for the five bucks the cops can offer from petty cash. Unless the suspect is really peculiar looking, the street always seems to yield a supply of fitting "fillers." Once the group is assembled, Bailey phones Mona Parker.

"Mrs. Parker," she says with elaborate courtesy, "we'd like you to come down to the station house to view a lineup if it's not too much trouble."

"Well . . ." Ms. Parker says, hesitating.

"Is that knee still bothering you? I know this is a nuisance, but we have to do it."

"Well . . ." Parker repeats.

"Look, I tell you what. If it's too hard for you to get here, I'll come out and get you. Give you a ride. What do you say, can you leave in five minutes?"

Bailey knows that even the best complainants sometimes lose interest. Failure of courage, reluctance to "get involved," or just the various distractions of life—these are powerful deterrents to the cooperation cops depend upon. And they hate to have a good one evaporate. So they treat their witnesses gently. Ms. Parker agrees, and Bailey heads out to escort her in. Marx, meanwhile, tries to call the other witness but Gonzalez is not at the store. He then sets up the lineup room, clearing a space and standing the suspect and fillers facing the mirrored glass. They are told to hold cards with large numbers, 1 to 6. "Just be cool, guys," he tells them, "the witness is on her way." He walks out and closes the door.

The routine is fairly standard. Cops today take precautions. The witness must not inadvertently see either the suspect or the fillers except in the line. Nothing is said to suggest that police believe they have captured the felon. Witnesses are not allowed to view the lineup in each other's presence lest a positive ID by one influence another to point out the same person.

When Ms. Parker arrives, she is led up to the glass as Mary Bailey explains, "This is one-way glass, Mrs. Parker; they can't see you. Now take your time. I want you to look at each one carefully and tell me whether you recognize anyone." A moment after she arrives at the glass, Parker says, "Oh, yes. That's him. Absolutely, that's him." She starts to tremble slightly—the autonomic confirmation cops look for.

"Which number, Mrs. Parker?"

"Number four, no doubt about it."

"And who is number four, Mrs. Parker? You have to say it."

"He's the man who robbed me and knocked me down," she says.

Bailey leads her away from the window, flashing a triumphant smile to Marx, who waits in the background. Marx picks up the battered squad Polaroid and snaps a couple of shots of the group before paying and releasing the fillers.

Detective Bailey takes Mona Parker home, saying only, "Good job," and telling her they will get in touch when they need her next. Meanwhile, Marty Marx informs Henderson that he is now under arrest, "We got a hundred percent hit on you, fella," he tells him. Without waiting for an answer, he snaps a pair of cuffs over his wrists and reads him his Miranda warnings aloud from a large, hand-printed manilla folder taped to the wall: "You have the right to remain silent. Anything you say may be used against you. You have a right to a lawyer present with you during interrogation. If you have no funds to retain counsel, a lawyer will be provided for you free of charge. Do you understand?"

Henderson shrugs. "Yeah, I understand," he says.

"You want to talk to me?"

"Nah, nothing to say."

"Good," says Marx, "I don't want to hear your bullshit anyway." He leads the prisoner to a holding cell and locks him in.

That's it. A thoroughly unremarkable event. Standard procedure. A good solid identification in a fair lineup provides the probable cause for a valid arrest, ornamented with a full and accurate recitation of the famous Miranda quatrain. What's the problem?

Big problems.

The major problem is that people are not very good at recognizing other people. Especially strangers. Especially strangers of a different race. Especially strangers of a different race seen briefly under stress.

I used to think it was just me. My wife is one of those people who can walk up to a person waiting at a bus stop and say, "Isn't your name Eleanor? Didn't we meet about a year ago at a dinner party at Betty's?" And be right. I can look at a student's face in class, four hours a week for fourteen weeks, see him a year later, and he won't even look familiar. Not long ago I was walking up Madison Avenue when a street person twenty-five yards away picked up a trash can and slammed it into the plate glass window of a bank that had not yet opened. After three or four tries, he managed to break a hole in the window and disappeared inside. Police arrived, climbed through the hole after him, and as I waited to see the outcome, I asked myself: could I give a good description of the man? Only in the most general way. Fifteen or twenty minutes later, the police led the man out in handcuffs. I remembered him from his clothes, but if I had seen him groomed for court, I would hesitate to testify that it was the same man who had broken in only minutes before.

It turns out it's not just me. I'm not suffering from some genetic defect in my recognition faculty. The truth is that, within categories, the differences of facial construction upon which recognition is based are minuscule. Of course, a heavy, dark, black-haired man with a mustache would not be mistaken for a fair, slim, clean-shaven person. But in a room full of people of the same general description, what are the differences that would distinguish any one of them from the others in the room? Two millimeters more space between the eyes? A lower lip slightly fatter than the upper? A millimeter's difference in the width of the flare of the nostrils? There's about as much difference between similar people as there is between squirrels. It's no wonder that to me strangers all look alike, or at least like many others who look something like them. And there are plenty of data to prove that most people are like me, not like my wife.

Dr. Elizabeth Loftus is probably the leading and senior expert—and expert witness—on the erratic human faculty of facial recognition, though today we have no shortage of both experimental and testifying social psychologists. Any of them will discourse, with the aid of statistics, charts, and slides, on the several constituent processes of perception, recall, and recognition, as well as the factors that distort them. You might hear of one study in which white clerks correctly identified from photos only two out of three whites who had been in the store earlier that day and misidentified about half the blacks. The expert might also cite an experiment in which an incident was enacted in the presence of bystanders and the subject was shown an array of photos from which to pick the prime actor. Of those subjects who thought they recognized him, 79 percent picked an innocent bystander. From the data, Dr. Loftus or her cronies will also note that the forgetting curve is very steep: in one test, in which some 90 percent of the subjects accurately assessed a critical fact immediately after perceiving it, the rate fell off to about 50 percent (the guess rate) after two days. Perhaps the most troubling—and counterintuitive—of the teachings of social science is the finding that certainty has no correlation whatever with accuracy. People who are mistaken are just as likely to be 100 percent sure as those who are right, and very hesitant picks are as likely to be right as the most confident selections.

It's not hard to see what these baleful data mean for the prosecution of crime. There are cases—lots of cases—where the criminal's identity is not in doubt and others where strong evidence of identity does not depend on the recognition factor: fingerprints or DNA geneprints matching the defendant's are discovered at the scene; the suspect is found with the victim's property in his possession; ballistics can trace the lethal slug to the defendant's weapon. But there are many, many other cases in which the testimony of an identification witness provides the crucial evidence linking the defendant with the crime. And these cases are often serious crimes like rape, armed robbery, or aggravated assault—the kind of one-on-one encounter that may leave no evidence save the victim's recollection of the features of her assailant's face. Inescapably, the fate of the accused hangs by the ability of the victim to make an accurate identification. It is impossible to guess how often eyewitnesses, though certain, are wrong. But the conclusion is inescapable that some of these witnesses are mistaken, leading to the conviction of innocent people who are then locked up for long stretches.

One could greet this conclusion philosophically—as I am inclined to. It is regrettable, but no worse than one would expect from a system of proof that relies upon the ordinary human skills of perception and recollection. The eye is not a camera, the mind is no computer. The price of prosecution by testimony (and what system would be preferable?) is a certain level of error—which is, therefore, tolerable. It is, as I say, one possible response to this disconcerting conclusion. But to espouse it takes a strong stomach.

The Supreme Court of the Warren era had no stomach for such resignation. Show the activist an injustice and a remedy must be found. Show an activist Court a miscarriage of justice and a constitutional remedy must be found.

In the case of the danger of eyewitness misidentification, the task was formidable. The Constitution has no language speaking, even obliquely, to the problem. And the Constitution is the Court's only available text when proclaiming law that binds state as well as federal law enforcement agencies. Undismayed, taking its lead from an earlier, disastrous effort to limit inter-rogation of prisoners, the Court found the answer in the Sixth Amendment's guarantee of the assistance of counsel for the defense. How, you may won-der, can the defendant's right to have expert legal advice and counsel avert the danger that the eyewitness may be mistaken when she identifies the defendant as the criminal? Good question.

In 1967, in two cases (one federal and one state: *United States v. Wade* and *Gilbert v. California*), the Court reasoned that the moment at which a wit-ness comes face to face with a suspect is a "critical stage" of the proceedings, a moment at which the defendant's fate may be sealed without hope of remedy at trial. Surely true. And, the Court went on, the express guarantee in the Sixth Amendment of *assistance* from counsel goes beyond mere trial performance and includes help at any harmful preliminary event that might ineradicably affect the outcome. An exposure to a suspect might convey, overtly or covertly, a suggestion to the witness that the police believe a particular person is the culprit. That suggestion might cause the witness to make an identification, or make it with greater confidence than he would otherwise do. And that identification, once made, will be repeated with assurance at the trial. To prevent that possibility, the lawyer's presence is helpful.

As the states were swallowing their amazement and getting lawyers to attend lineups—even, on the strength of *Wade* and *Gilbert,* throwing out evidence of identification obtained at lineups like the one in which Mona Parker recognized Junior Henderson—the Court dropped the other shoe. In 1972, it held in *Kirby v. Illinois* that, because the Sixth Amendment grants protection only to those who have been formally accused, the right to counsel at a lineup does not apply when the exposure occurs before indictment.

To see how this plays out, let's return briefly to our drama.

Having arrested Henderson on a good ID in the round, Marx and Bailey go out to the store where Gonzalez works to see if they can double their good fortune.

There they learn that Gonzalez has had an emergency call from his family in Puerto Rico and left in haste. He's not expected back for a week or two. A week or so after Henderson's case reaches the court dockets, the grand jury hands down an indictment. The next day, Bailey gets a call from Gonzalez, back from Puerto Rico. "Let's do it," she says to her partner. "It can only make the case better." So she puts in the necessary papers, and the following day the prisoner is produced and delivered to the temporary custody of the detective.

"Hey, Junior," Bailey greets him, "how're ya doin'?"

"OK," wary, surprised by her friendly tone.

"They treating you all right in there?"

"Yeah." What's she getting at?

"See some of your old friends?"

"Yeah, some. What's this about? What are you taking me out for?"

"Listen, Junior, We're going to do another lineup on you. We have another witness. We want him to have a look at you." Doesn't hurt to have your perp think that the case against him is really strong.

"Sure. No sweat."

"Who's your lawyer?" Marx asks.

"Don't have no lawyer."

"Hey, c'mon. You must have a lawyer. Didn't the judge assign a lawyer when you were in court?"

"Well, some kid from the public defender stood up for me and got the bail set, if that's what you mean."

"That's what I mean."

Preparation for this lineup goes much as before, with the addition of a telephone call to the public defender's office. Marx makes the call. After identifying himself, he says to the administrator at the other end of the line: "We've got a client of yours here, Junior Henderson. We want to do a lineup on him. We need his lawyer down here." A moment's pause and some clicking of the computer keys and the administrator verifies that the public defender indeed represents Henderson.

"So how about sending a lawyer down here to represent him like the Supreme Court says?" Marx asks again. Another pause.

"I'm sorry," the administrator says. "All our lawyers are busy at the moment."

"Do you want your client to waive?"

"I cannot tell you that. Only his lawyer can tell you that."

"So what are we supposed to do?" Marx asks, slightly exasperated.

"That's your problem, officer. All I can tell you is this is really a very bad time. All our lawyers are either in court or in conference with clients. I really can't spare anyone at this time."

"Are things any easier around two A.M.?" Sarcastically.

"Look, officer, I said I was sorry. I'll do the best I can."

As Bailey comes in with the last of the fillers, Marx tells her. "We're going to have a bit of trouble in the counsel department." They decide to call Gonzalez. It might take a while for him to get there. Maybe a lawyer will show up in the meantime. Gonzalez arrives and sits patiently waiting. An hour later, a second phone call is made to the public defender with the same result. The process has come to a halt. A simple procedure—likely in this case to produce nothing—is frustrated because of Gonzalez's untimely trip home and the busy schedule of the lawyer's office. The detectives have three choices: give it up and go with the case they already have; return Henderson, let everyone else go, and make an appointment with the lawyer for some future time; or proceed without the lawyer present. None is an attractive option. Cops should not leave possible sources of evidence untapped. The likelihood of getting an overbooked lawyer to travel to the station house at an appointed time is not the best, and to violate the defendant's constitutional rights, even by the most meticulously fair lineup, might have unfortunate ramifications at the trial. The presence of counsel can be waived, but only by the defendant. It cannot be waived by his lawyer, and surely not merely by nonappearance.

So it would appear that a postindictment lineup may be derailed entirely by a lawyer's simply declining the invitation to be present. I doubt that this result was intended—or foreseen—by Justice Brennan and his colleagues. And indeed, it is probably rare. In a well-disciplined jurisdiction (and many federal districts meet this standard), the prosecutor makes the arrangements for the post accusation lineup, accommodating counsel's schedule, and the defense attorney generally shows up. Even in more chaotic places, my experience has been that lawyers usually attend lineups when they are advised in timely fashion. So nonappearance by counsel has not been a major problem. But I have often wondered why it is so easy.

If I were a defense lawyer, I think I would see that service to my client's interest did not require my presence for a lineup at which I could do precious little to prevent the identification—even an erroneous one. If the witness is going to pick him out, she'll very likely pick him out whether I'm there or not. But my *absence* might really help by preventing the prosecution from obtaining this damaging evidence altogether. Perhaps the prosecutor could get a court order directing me to attend. But it would not be easy. The prosecutor might say that my client's right to my assistance implies a duty on my part to assist. I would argue, though—not only vigorously but with considerable merit—that my presence at the lineup only facilitates the prosecution's acquisition of evidence against my client, constituting assistance not to him but to his enemies. I would probably lose, or they would relieve me and substitute more compliant counsel. But I would certainly kick up a lot of dust—and maybe even satisfy my professional conscience.

In any event, this quirk is not among the main faults with the *Wade-Gilbert-Kirby* doctrine. The main faults are true faith shakers. They call into question not only the prescribed ID routine, but the capacity of the Oracle on the Potomac to deal with problems in the precincts. I count four of these major faults.

The first flaw appeared with the Court's perfectly just observation that since the Sixth Amendment right to counsel belongs only to those who have been formally accused of crime, lineup IDs of unindicted suspects may be conducted in the station houses without benefit of counsel. But *Kirby* so grievously undermined the none-too-solid rationale of *Wade-Gilbert* that the doctrine lost its reason for being. If one goes along with the Court's notion that the assistance of counsel at a lineup does in fact prevent the conveyance of a suggestion that might seal the fate of an innocent person, surely that service should be rendered at the first exposure, whether or not a grand jury has formalized the accusation by indictment. But once the Court grants, as it did in *Kirby,* that there is no constitutional right to counsel at a preindictment lineup (when most lineups occur), it is hardly convincing to insist that counsel attend the postindictment exposure. From any rational perspective, there was no difference in Henderson's interest between exposure to Mona Parker (before accusation) and to Nico Gonzalez (after accusation).

Strangely, the Court might have avoided this illogical conclusion with no damage to the Constitution and little practical inconvenience. It might have held that for these purposes, arrest amounts to accusation—as it surely does in some sense—and custody for the conduct of the lineup amounts to an arrest. That, at least, would produce a lawyer at all lineups. Perhaps the

Justices were worried that if an arrest is treated as a Sixth Amendment accusation, it would be very difficult to explain why an interrogation may take place in the absence of counsel. But still, if the Miranda warning suffices to obtain a waiver of counsel's presence and assistance for Fifth Amendment purposes, it could serve the same function under the Sixth Amendment with no great violence to the structure of rights. The Court did not choose this doctrinally neat solution.

The second major fault is this: requiring the assistance of counsel at a lineup puts the lawyer in an extremely uncomfortable bind, perhaps even a compromising position. True, a lawyer may actually do something—or at least suggest something—that makes it harder for the witness to identify her client: request that a filler and the suspect exchange clothing, that the lineup be seated to minimize differences in height, even that a filler more closely resembling the suspect be substituted. Such improvements just might reduce the chance of a mistake. Perhaps, just by her attentive presence, the lawyer might discourage helpful hints from the police. But if the witness recognizes the lawyer's client despite the lawyer's best efforts—a possibility not to be ignored if the client is in fact the criminal—making the lineup fairer makes the identification stronger against her client. One defense counsel once told me, in effect, "The last thing I want to do is make the prosecution's case better. If the *unfairness* of the lineup may be my client's strongest line of defense at trial, why should I—my client's only champion—foreclose it?"

The Court imposed an additional source of discomfort on the defense attorney: it suggested that the lawyer, by observing the lineup procedure, becomes a witness whose credible word may support the defendant's suspect claim of suggestiveness. But lawyers know that, should they actually become testifying witnesses in their client's case, they must resign as counsel. And I have heard lawyers say, "If my client has chosen me as her counsel, my service as witness will deprive my client of my service as her counsel of choice." These are impressive contentions. The wonder is that they are not more generally appreciated by the Bar.

The third fault is more basic. The remedy provided does not address the real and substantial evil to which it is addressed. Insofar as the problem that concerned the Court was the purposeful rigging of the lineup, the presence of counsel to witness the exposure itself cannot possibly deter the dishonest cop from fixing the result. There are always plenty of opportunities to plant the pernicious suggestion out of defense counsel's wary presence. But this is probably not the Court's primary concern. The concern is that, given the vagaries of recognition, the uncoached witness may, in all good faith, pick an innocent person in the line who looks most like the culprit, influenced perhaps by the resemblance he bears to the photo selected from the mug book. It can easily happen. And when it does, that person will be confidently identified by the eyewitness at the trial, because the witness remembers his face and features not from the time of the crime but from the more recent and better studied lineup exposure.

Misidentification is a looming threat of grave proportions. But what, in the name of all reason and reflection, can the physical presence of a person with a J.D. degree at the window at the time the eyewitness makes her critical mistake contribute toward its avoidance? The lawyer is not there to cross-examine the witness and would not be permitted to do so if he tried. And a mistaken identification can as easily be made in the watchful presence of a lawyer as of anyone else.

The final flaw is the most disturbing of all. If the Sixth Amendment has done nothing to solve this awful possibility, has the Court dulled our vigilance—and its own—by invoking it? The awful possibility of misidentification, insoluble by legal improvisation, should remain vivid in the mind. The illusion of prophylaxis, the pretense of remedy, not only does nothing to help, it may aggravate the problem by reducing concern; it supplants existential distress with baseless self-congratulation.

4 The Exclusionary Rule

*The Fabled Doctrine, Its Baleful Side Effects, and a
Generally Ignored Technological Remedy*

The proposition that the criminal is to go free because the constable blundered is by no means self-evident. Yet in peculiarly American jurisprudence, it is now immutably established—established as firmly as though the words had been written by the hand of James Madison himself—that evidence, no matter how convincing, will be excluded from the view of the jury if that evidence was acquired by law enforcement officers in violation of the constitutional rights of the defendant. *The Exclusionary Rule.* Is there anything anywhere in the law of crimes and criminal law enforcement, even today, that stirs the passions, sets judicial conservative against new-age liberal, doctrinalist against social visionary, like the exclusionary rule? Here, as in no other field, do the forces of law engage the legions of policy in full battle array. Like no other, the issue calls into question the basic tenets of the American judicial process, the ideals of constitutional democracy, and the capacity of the legal process to deal with the plague of crime.

Does the judicial rejection of inculpatory evidence acquired by Officer A in the investigation of crime X actually deter Officer B from making an illegal search and seizure in the investigation of crime Y? Surely the question is one of the most inscrutable in the social science of law enforcement. The crudest effort to answer requires a whole set of assumptions, none of which commends itself instantly to full confidence. Was the judicial exclusion of Officer A's evidence based on a legal proposition sufficiently clear and generally accepted that any judge would be likely to do the same thing in similar circumstances? Is Officer B likely to know of the disposition of Officer A's evidence and understand the reason for it? Are the particular facts and circumstances of crime Y close enough to crime X so that B can expect a result like A's if he acts in similar fashion?

Even if (by a stretch of faith) affirmative assumptions are justified on all of the above, a few tough questions remain. What is Officer B's motivation and state of mind as she considers reaching under the front seat to look for a gun in the automobile she and her partner have just stopped? Is she thinking of whether the gun will be admitted into evidence at a possible future trial of the motorist? How much does she care whether or not the gun (assuming she comes up with one) sustains a criminal charge for its possession since in any event she will have confiscated an illegal weapon from a person she thinks is dangerous? She has also improved the likelihood that her child's mother will return home after today's tour. And she will not lose an hour's pay or a day of vacation time if the evidence she recovers is eventually suppressed.

We have not honestly confronted the confiscation wrinkle in the doctrine of deterrence. Although the Fourth Amendment might make a search and seizure unlawful and the exclusionary rule might bar the use of the evidence or any other evidence derived from it in a criminal prosecution of the person from whom it was illegally taken, the law does not require that contraband or loot be politely returned to its former possessor. That would be too foolish even for the most expansive vindicator of rights. The message to cops clangs with dissonance against the stern injunction of the exclusionary rule: if you have a chance to take a gun away from a bad guy, destroy a stash of illicit drugs, return stolen property to its owner, scare a knot of gang members off a rooftop, go right ahead. As long as you don't take the case to court, you needn't even cast a glance over your shoulder at the Fourth Amendment. I suspect that, for many cops, the confiscation alternative goes a fair way to undermine the instructional value of the exclusionary rule—at least when it come to weapons and drugs.

Yet, difficult as the basic question of deterrence may be, its ostensible answer contains the major premise of the exclusionary rule. The primary justification for depriving a fact-starved jury of relevant evidence is that its exclusion will influence police officers, in their future official conduct, to show greater respect for the constitutional rights of suspects. Perhaps it has. Certainly, a case may be made that today, thirty-three years after the exclusionary rule burst upon state law enforcement agencies, police conduct more often (though by no means always) conforms to constitutional strictures. The exclusionary consequence fashioned by the Court underscored the importance of the Constitution's limitation on police authority, but the effect has gone far beyond the Court's suasive powers. The rule has been mediated by departmental training, regulations, and customary usage; and almost two generations of cops have assimilated their department's interpretations of the limits of zeal. These things modify behavior. To this extent, then, the exclusionary rule—a judicially fashioned, courtroom rule of trial—might be credited with enhancing police legality, indisputably an important value of social policy.

The penchant for putting the law to tasks of social engineering developed gradually on these shores, took hold more slowly in Great Britain, and is still in its earliest stages in European systems. Under the common law, as we call the British progenitive law and its early American descendant, evidence that was probative of the issues on trial was admitted without regard to the means of its acquisition. More than fourscore years ago, in the year 1914, the United States Supreme Court, with neither drumroll nor repercussion, elected to abandon the common-law rule and exclude the product of unlawful search and seizure from evidence in the federal courts.

In his opinion for the Supreme Court in *Weeks v. United States,* Justice William Rufus Day was less than clear about whether he had taken the step under constitutional aegis or by exercise of the Supreme Court's supervisory power over the federal court system. It was a matter of little consequence at the time because the Fourth Amendment applied only in the federal courts and state prosecutions would not have been affected even if the exclusionary rule had a solid constitutional predicate.

Thirty-five years later, when the Fourth Amendment was applied to the states, the Court considered whether the exclusionary rule went along with it. In *Wolf v. Ohio,* the Supremes decided that Justice Day never intended to attach the exclusionary consequence to the right of security expressed in the Constitution. For the next dozen years, the Fourth Amendment languished in most state courts; without the stern rule of exclusion, state judges were not called upon to adjudicate the legality of searches and seizures by state officers, and while the Fourth Amendment theoretically governed their conduct, few state officers even troubled to learn the contours of the federal rule.

Then, in 1961, the Supreme Court detonated the case whose name, along with *Miranda,* came to symbolize the "revolution" in criminal justice of the

Warren era: *Mapp v. Ohio.* Actually, the decision simply expressed a second thought on the *Wolf* compromise and held that those states that had not already elected to follow the *Weeks* rule were henceforth obliged to do so by the Fourth Amendment itself. Justice Day, the Court now thought, intended no less. The outcry that greeted the decision drowned the facts that the case did not invent the exclusionary rule (it had been around for almost fifty years), that the feds had lived comfortably with it (even though their criminal jurisdiction was still rather narrow), and most significantly that, by the time *Mapp* came down, more than half of the states had voluntarily fallen into line with *Weeks* and found that they could still enforce their criminal laws.

With the application of the exclusionary rule to the active criminal dockets of the full array of states, the Supreme Court was propelled into a ferociously busy decade of interpretation. Every term brought a blizzard of new opinions on search and seizure. The pages of legal journals sprouted analysis of the latest entries, law school casebooks underwent major annual revisions, and verbal brawls among the Justices of the Supreme Court enlivened academic debate but dismayed the troops in the field who were trying to get a firm grip on unfamiliar doctrines. The excitement has subsided somewhat, but the dogma is still in considerable disarray.

From our present vantage, with full appreciation of the beneficial effects of the rule on the legality of daily police work in the field, and conscious, too, of the aggravated threat of crime today, many people are asking themselves again: can we afford to let the criminal go free because the constable blundered? Has the standard of police intervention advanced, with the help of more than thirty years of instruction-cum-deterrence, to the level of professionalism at which the rule is no longer necessary to maintain an acceptably high level of respect for constitutional constraints?

We have always known that a criminal trial serves social values apart from the separation of the guilty from the innocent. But we had believed that the adjudicative function was primary. Many of us would question whether the criminal trial of X or Y is the most appropriate occasion to instruct officers A and B on the limits of their authority. Couldn't they be more effectively schooled by an administrative procedure that punished the cop for invading a citizen's rights? Losing a promotion or a paycheck probably focuses the cop's attention more sharply than losing a conviction. And without the gratuitous social cost.

Several responses to this sensible administrative alternative may—or may not—convince doubters of the overarching importance of excluding illegally obtained evidence. These arguments augment the rationale of deterrence and, to some, provide reason enough for exclusion even if it could be demonstrated that deterrence is nothing but a judicial fantasy. Some are highly pragmatic, the others sound a more theoretical note.

Law, we are reminded, is not primarily an exercise in social engineering, a means of inclining future police behavior toward desirable restraint. Rather (this theory insists), law seeks to right wrongs while vindicating principle. Thus, in addition to incidental deterrence, the exclusionary rule serves two equally noble functions: it provides a remedy for the wronged victim of illegal intrusion and it vindicates what are sometimes called the interests of judicial integrity.

The theory of remedy is simple. If the proceeds of the invasion of privacy are banished, the wrong is righted to the extent that the case proceeds in court as though the search and seizure had never taken place. The exclusionary rule, it is said, serves the same function as its ancient antecedent, the action in replevin for the return of things wrongfully taken by the government. Their return effectively prevented their use in evidence, hence exclusion was accomplished under a different name. The modern exclusionary rule is but a more sophisticated version of the old physical remedy.

The remedial rationale, however, is not quite as simple as it seems. For one thing, it sometimes seems at odds with the other two rationales: deterrence and judicial integrity. A remedial theory would suppress only evidence taken in violation of the rights of the defendant on trial (only he would have "standing," lawyers would say, to protest the violation). Even if the most egregious police conduct violated only the rights of a person who turned out to be a mere witness at most, the evidence would not be suppressed. And the Supreme Court so held in *United States v. Payner,* a 1980 case of blatant illegality in which the police had intruded knowing that because the injured party was not likely to be a defendant, their illegality would not affect the prosecution. Offended, the Court nevertheless declined to exclude the evidence; neither the interests of integrity nor of deterrence prevailed.

And here's a famous conundrum challenging the remedial rationale as the governing principle in the exclusionary rule's design: on a theory of remedy, if police break into what they believe to be a suspect's motel room (knowing full well that he has constitutionally secured rights of privacy in those premises) and, in a thorough search, discover incriminating evidence, that discovery will not be excluded if it turns out, fortuitously, that the defendant had quietly checked out the day before. Having departed, the suspect has no rights left in the place for the cops to breach; hence no remedial suppression is necessary. There must be something wrong with a pure remedial rationale, some would say, if it precludes application of the rule to such a conscious and intentional breach. It galls the jurisprudential palate. A basic tenet of culpability holds that a person firing a gun at a shape she truly believes to be the sleeping form of her lover, intending to kill him, is guilty of attempted murder even if, unknown to her, the form is nothing but a mound of bedclothes. Factual impossibility is no excuse if one acts with intent to do harm and would have done so had matters been as one erroneously supposed them to be. That's the law. The deterrence-based, moral-toned law of culpability. In *Payner,* however, the Supreme Court shunned this line in favor of the remedial construction of the exclusionary rule: absent actual injury, no remedial exclusion.

Notwithstanding *Payner,* however, the remedy rationale has had an uncertain career on the pages of Supreme Court opinions. In one of its more mystifying pronouncements on the subject, the Court said that by remedy it meant only that illegal searches and seizures would be deterred in the future. But if deterrence were the goal, the cops breaking into the motel room in ignorance of the occupant's departure should be penalized to teach them not to do that in the future. As the motel model illustrates, the deterrence rational should produce a different result from the remedial rationale, and it is difficult to grasp the Court's effort to bale them together. In fact, this definition of remedy as deterrence leads some to think that the Court has virtually abandoned the remedial justification for the exclusionary rule.

Courts use the lofty phrase "judicial integrity" to characterize their obligation, apart from all else, to maintain their dignity. The term expresses the recognition of the importance of myth—in this case, the myth of institutional virtue. Judicially administered justice is effective only to the extent that the courts' processes are deemed worthy of public respect. And to accept in evidence the proceeds of illegal police work is, in effect, to connive at lawlessness—contrary to the interests of judicial integrity.

Another answer to those who argue that there are better ways to teach cops to behave is perhaps the most pragmatic: administrative remedies just don't work. What police commander will discipline an officer who has broken into a suspect's premises and come up with an arsenal? Can you envision any real consequence when the invasion has been productive? To cops—even on an administrative level—solving a crime, coming up with convincing evidence in a case that started on a hunch, is good police work.

And the civil alternative—if your rights were ignored, sue—is not much better. Aside from the problem that damages might not exceed the price of a new lock for the front door, it is difficult to imagine a drug dealer convincing a jury to award damages for the illegal entry that discovered his drug factory. So, it is said, exclusion is the only way to demonstrate that the Fourth Amendment has teeth.

My favorite, unspoken apology for the exclusionary rule is that even if you could devise a working system that visited a painful penalty directly on the officer responsible—a system, say, under which a judge would make the finding of invasion but an administrative rather than an evidentiary consequence would follow—the result might well be overdeterrence. We want a lawful police force but we also want an active police force. We don't want to risk discouraging aggressive police work to the point of lethargy. Cops are, among other things, civil servants. Threaten their benefits and you will sap their initiative. A leaden force, with a prevalent code of "Why should I stick my neck out?" is at least as painful to contemplate as a responsive force that sometimes gives too little consideration to the constitutional constraints on its activity. So, one might be persuaded, for all its crudeness, the impact of the exclusionary rule on police conduct strikes just the right balance between too broad license and too narrow initiative.

I must frankly admit that I have not yet come down securely on one side or the other of the continuing controversy over the exclusionary rule. I regard with the utmost dismay the dubious premises and the disheveled doctrine that so frequently engulf the substantive issues of important cases. I dearly wish for trials of the guilt of a defendant, not the transgressions of the pursuing officers. At the same time, I find it repugnant that courts should tolerate the use of illegal methods by police in the pursuit of those whom they believe to be criminals, even if it should turn out that they were right. And I am not confident that the lessons learned by the police during the years when legality really counted are so ingrained that new generations of officers, cynical about lawyers in any event, would demonstrate the sort of counterproductive self-restraint that proper respect for constitutional values requires.

Perhaps some sort of compromise is possible. In England and many foreign courts, exclusion of illegally acquired evidence is discretionary with the judge, who takes into consideration a variety of factors, only a few of which are hardwired into our rule. The judge may weigh, for example, the seriousness of the intrusion against the necessity of intruding; he may take account of the nature of the crime under investigation, along with the likelihood that the officer knew that he was exceeding constitutional prerogative.

True, such a flexible standard suffers a loss of predictability and, to that extent, of deterrent effect. It also injects an element of whim into the legal process, hanging (in some cases) the prosecutability of a case on the inclination of the particular judge drawn. For many, this introduces the roulette factor, the dread prospect of turning the courthouse into a casino of justice. I am sensitive to this concern, believe me. But. But on balance, I trust judges. I do not believe that the exercise of judicial discretion is a roll of the dice. And I think that the solution to the perplexing dilemma is probably in resort to good sense and an educated decision on whether exclusion is appropriate in all the complex circumstances of the particular case.

I find that I cannot construct a parable reflecting even a small fraction of the problems arising in the application of the Fourth Amendment to the streets. So the story will be but a suggestion of the sorts of questions regularly confronting police and courts in the harsh light of the exclusionary rule.

The FBI has been investigating a terrorist conspiracy planning bombings of public buildings in Washington. The plan is coming close to the operations stage. Then one day, unexpectedly, agents on the case get a call from their inside informant alerting them that one of the prime conspirators, code name Fireworks, has obtained a vital component in the construction of the bomb and is transporting it in his car, a black Chevrolet Corsica. The car is parked at a designated lot for an unknown duration. From prior tails, Special Agents Mulaney and Ricci know the Corsica and set out at once for the lot. At the lot they identify themselves to the attendant and tell him that they want to "have a look at" the Corsica, furnishing the plate number. "Sure, go ahead," the attendant replies, indicating the corner of the lot where the car is parked. "Here are the keys."

When Mulaney and Ricci locate the car, they circle it, peering into the windows. On the floor of the back seat, Ricci sees a small open box containing what appear to be electrician's tools: wire clippers, screwdrivers, pliers and such. Using the key supplied by the helpful attendant, Mulaney then opens the car. As Ricci removes the box of tools [later offered as evidence], Mulaney opens the glove compartment and finds a key stamped with the name of a large public storage locker in town. Mulaney then goes around to the back and unlocks the trunk. As the lid swings up, the agents see a smallish brown paper carton. It is closed but not sealed. The agents look at each other and shrug. Is this what they are looking for? Mulaney reaches into the trunk, removes the box, and opens it. Inside, the agents find a timing mechanism that they recognize as capable of triggering a timed explosive device. [It is later discovered to bear the fingerprints of Fireworks and is, of course, offered in evidence against him.]

Ricci and Mulaney write up the results of their investigation, swear to it, and obtain a search warrant for the storage locker and an arrest warrant for Fireworks. They take the search warrant, authorizing the seizure of "any and all items contained therein which may pertain to the manufacture or installation of illegal explosive devices," and go to the locker. Opening it with the seized key, they find chemical ingredients for the manufacture of explosives. They remove them, take them back to the FBI lab for analysis, and hold them for use as evidence.

Meanwhile, the agents have put out the word that they are looking for Fireworks. Within twenty-four hours, a trustworthy snitch phones with the intelligence that Fireworks has holed up at a safe house with a person called Mother. The snitch provides the address and the additional information that Fireworks is preparing to leave the country and may be gone within a day. The agents waste no time. Armed with the arrest warrant, they head for Mother's place. They are met at the door by a woman who disclaims any knowledge of Fireworks or his whereabouts. "Think we'll just check that out for ourselves," they say, brushing Mother aside. The agents go through the house, looking only in places where Fireworks may be hiding, to no avail.

That is, they don't find Fireworks, who continues to elude them for several weeks. But the venture is not altogether fruitless. In a closet, they come upon some wires and batteries that might be used in the manufacture of timed explosives. This discovery links Mother to the plot and the items are eventually offered against her and the other conspirators.

The Constitution protects our security (or privacy, as it is often called) only up to a point. The protection of the Fourth Amendment is only against *unreasonable* searches and seizures. And even an intrusion without prior court sanction may be reasonable in some circumstances. The Supreme Court has had no trouble extending the reach of the Fourth Amendment well beyond its literal scope: automobiles, business premises, and the spoken word (all entitled to Fourth Amendment protections) are not, strictly speaking, the "homes, papers, persons, and effects" designated as secure by the language of the Constitution. But defining the circumstances of the reasonable search and seizure has occasioned no end of debate among the Justices and uncertainty among the rest of us.

As Mulaney and Ricci approached the stationary automobile, the Fourth Amendment was on alert. It was, after all, an automobile, which, while subject to the protection of the Fourth Amendment, is (the Supreme Court has held) the repository of somewhat reduced expectations of privacy. Still, as it sat on that lot, the car was hardly the "vagrant and fleeting target" that gave rise to the "automobile exception" to the warrant rule back in Prohibition times. It remains a daunting challenge to today's monks and mystics to describe precisely the level of constitutionally insured security to which we are entitled when we place personal items in closed compartments within functional vehicles that are then left locked, unattended, and immobile in public places.

Circling the car, looking in its windows, the agents were still on solid ground. Thanks to the permission of the attendant (who clearly had authority to allow them to enter the lot), they were where they were entitled to be, doing what they were entitled to do. Though what they saw was located in secure space, it was readily visible from outside. Thus it was not constitutionally protected against visual perception. What a person knowingly exposes to casual public view, the Court has said, is not entitled to protection though kept physically in a secure place.

Having seen the tools in plain view, were the agents entitled to open the car and take them? Well, the Court has said, having lawfully perceived contraband in plain view, a police officer is not required to ignore the evidence. That would be plain foolish. But does the lawful search make the seizure lawful? Before officers may seize what they lawfully see, the Court has warned, the object perceived must be immediately recognizable as contraband. Even to pick up a Bang & Olufsen turntable, turn it over, and read its serial number to confirm that it had been stolen (the Court held) is to go beyond the limit of a legal "plain view" seizure. So here, though they saw the tool box lawfully, the agents probably cannot justify the seizure of the tools—

hardly contraband, and not immediately recognizable as connected with the bomb conspiracy.

But can't the government justify all the seizures from the vehicle by the consent of the attendant, a person who had lawful custody and control of the car and gave his permission freely? The theory of consent has been troublesome. For one thing, it was overused by law enforcement people who were forever telling courts that their intrusions were invited. "I asked him if I could come in and look around and he said, 'Sure; be my guest'" was heard in nearly every case in which a search and seizure was challenged. That led to the Court's first stricture: mere acquiescence to apparently lawful authority is not "consent." So when the lot attendant gave Mulaney and Ricci the keys and allowed the search, we must ask: did he really want them to search or was his cooperation the product of fear, some implicit threat that he would suffer some disadvantage if he refused the FBI's "request"? Not an easy question to answer. The Court has made it somewhat easier by holding that a person's acquiescence to even the most polite official request is presumptively coerced simply by the popular apprehension that refusing cops is likely to bring unpleasant consequences—a charge of "obstructing justice" or worse. The government might well persuade a court, based on the attendant's apparent disinterest, that the consent was free and voluntary, but this decision cannot be confidently predicted.

Even if the government succeeds thus far (as I think it should), the most touchy element of the consent doctrine still bedevils its case. Though the personal right to security may be vicariously surrendered (if A stashes his drugs in B's handbag, he can hardly claim that B has no authority to allow police to look inside if she wishes to), what sort of authority did the attendant have to waive the rights of the owner? They were hardly like roommates or spouses who both have dominion over jointly used spaces. Each of joint users, the Court has held, may consent to a search of common property (though the other—the one against whom the discoveries were eventually used—would surely have objected). And to what extent were the FBI agents entitled to rely upon the lot attendant's apparent authority? The Supreme Court had a case once in which police officers, looking for robbers, came to a hotel where their suspects stayed and obtained the key to their room and the desk clerk's cheerful permission to go in and look around. The evidence they found was suppressed because an innkeeper, though he keeps a key and has authority to enter for housekeeping purposes, has no more authority than a landlord to consent to a search of a guest/tenant's premises. The clerk had no "right at stake." And the police had no right to rely—though in good faith—on the clerk's ostensible authority.

To discover the attendant's agency, we should ask what the owner contemplated when he surrendered the car key to the attendant. If he expected that the attendant in the normal course would enter the car, see what was in plain view inside, and use the trunk key under certain circumstances—perhaps to change a flat tire—then a good argument might be made that the owner had ceded to the attendant the right to consent to a police officer's invasion to the same extent as the attendant's own license. Under this theory, Mulaney and Ricci's discoveries in the car would be available to the government as evidence. On the other hand, it might be argued that the attendant had no rights of privacy in the vehicle himself (as a joint user would)—no right at stake—and hence no greater authority to consent than the hotel clerk. In this view, the same argument that might be used to prove that the attendant's consent was free and voluntary might demonstrate that he had no authority to consent. Which of these is the more persuasive argument is a matter on which courts might differ.

Even if Mulaney lawfully opened the trunk and saw the carton, did he make a second—and unlawful—intrusion when he opened the carton and looked inside? The Court has had a notable struggle with the problem of closed containers aboard mobile vehicles. The containers are, like the cars that carry them, "vagrant and fleeting targets," likely to be gone by the time the cops get a warrant. And if the Fourth Amendment recognizes cars themselves as containers with reduced immunity to police penetration, how is the closed carton any different from the closed trunk that holds it? If the agents have a right to look inside one, why should they not have the right to look a bit deeper into the other?

On the other hand, small boxes, luggage, packages, and such are all mobile, but the Supreme Court will not allow diluted protection of them on that account. How is the right of security in the contents reduced by the mere happenstance that they happen to be aboard a vehicle at the moment the police come upon them? After all, the searching agents could have removed the carton (nullifying its inherent mobility) and then applied for a search warrant to open it.

Finally, in 1991 after several short-lived experimental models, the Court crafted its current doctrine in *Acevedo v. California:* authority to search a car—either with a warrant or pursuant to the "automobile exception" or some other—includes the authority to search closed containers aboard the vehicle. So it looks like Mulaney and Ricci are on solid ground in their discovery of the timing device. Prior to *Acevedo,* the Court would not have allowed the search and seizure of the interior of the closed carton unless Mulaney and Ricci could demonstrate that they not only had good reason to believe the timing device was in the car (from the informant's tip), but that they had reason to believe it was within a closed container within in the car. At least things have gotten a little simpler.

However the challenge to the evidence seized from the car is handled, the trial judge would have to consider separately the admissibility of the explosive chemicals seized by search warrant from the locker. The Fourth Amendment, only one sentence long, specifies the ingredients of a lawful warrant: "no Warrants shall issue, but upon probable cause, supported by Oath or affirmation, and particularly describing the place to be searched, and the persons or things to be seized."

The requirement of a particular description is an important element; as I noted earlier, the framers put it in to protect against the infamous "general warrants" of colonial times, which allowed crown soldiers to enter anywhere, almost at will, to look for anything they thought might be seditious. Our "place to be searched" is pretty clearly described, but the "things to be seized" are ill-defined. Items "pertaining" to the manufacture and installation of a bomb leaves a great deal to the judgment of the executing officer. Still, courts have allowed description by reference. Does our warrant contain a clear, narrow, and specific description, one that would allow any reasonably intelligent officer to recognize at once the thing described? Or does it require knowledge and judgment; is it broad and inclusive enough to fetch material that the judge never intended it to cover? The particularity clause is a problem.

Even more problematic is the core component of the constitutional search: probable cause. What it means, simply, is that no warrant should issue without a good reason, given under oath, to believe that the invasion entailed by the search will produce an item of evidence: that the precisely described item exists, that it is evidence in some case, and that it is located in the designated place. What is "good reason to believe"? Much has been written on the subject, but it remains a pragmatic and flexible standard: reliable information that would lead a reasonable person to conclude that the fact was reasonably likely to be true. Could very well be true. Something like that. Our problem: from the fact that a suspected conspirator in a terrorist plot has a key to a public locker, would a reasonable person infer that the locker contained the fixings for a bomb? It might be a good guess, or a sound hunch, but those standards of belief are below the level of probable cause, generous as that criterion may be. Admittedly, when the subject is terrorist bombs, many judges will be inclined to relax even further the uncertain bounds of probable cause. But there are still many doctrinal conservatives who (especially when the danger has passed) will insist that our warrant is worthless for lack of a stronger inferential link than mere possibility.

Before giving up on the vital evidence acquired by that defective warrant, we must take a strange detour. For years, many people argued that the deterrent policy of the exclusionary rule cannot work when a field officer believes in good faith that the search he is about to make comports fully with the Constitution. Only by "punishing" cops for conduct they know or should know is wrong may we hope to educate them. The argument made a lot of sense to many critics of the exclusionary rule and, with a change in the High Court's composition in the early 1980s, observers expected a *good-faith exception* to be engrafted onto the exclusionary rule. Such an exception would allow unlawfully seized evidence to be introduced at a trial, provided that the officer honestly thought his search was legal. Most cops could convincingly— and even truthfully—testify that they believed they were acting lawfully, in part because most cops try to do the job according to the rules and in part because the rules themselves are so uncertain that courts split on their application. If appellate courts had even numbers of judges on them instead of odd, many of the search and seizure cases would never be resolved at all. Thus, in effect, the good-faith exception would be a reasoned and principled way to kill the exclusionary rule. Which is exactly what most of us thought the new majority would like to do.

But, to everyone's surprise, it didn't happen. Instead, the Court in 1984 handed down a strange little case called *United States v. Leon.* In the decision, the majority, speaking through Justice Byron White, began by reminding us that the exclusionary rule is not itself a constitutional right:

> The Fourth Amendment contains no provision expressly precluding the use of evidence obtained in violation of its commands, and an examination of its origin and purposes makes clear that the use of fruits of a

past unlawful search and seizure "work[s] no new Fourth Amendment wrong." . . . The wrong condemned by the Amendment is "fully accomplished" by the unlawful search and seizure itself and the exclusionary rule is neither intended nor able to "cure the invasion of the defendant's rights which he has already suffered."

Having thus set the stage for the good-faith exception, the Court offered this further tease: "We have frequently questioned whether the exclusionary rule can have any deterrent effect when the offending officers acted in the objectively reasonable belief that their conduct did not violate the Fourth Amendment." Almost casually, the majority appends: "This is particularly true, we believe, when an officer acting with objective good faith has obtained a search warrant from a judge or magistrate and acted within its scope." The Court then goes on to hold that normally police officers act in objective good faith when they rely upon a warrant signed by a judge, supported by an officer's affidavit, and in such a case, exclusion of evidence on a later determination of invalidity of the warrant is not justified. Thus, except in the most egregious cases (when the officer must have known that the warrant was defective on its face), *Leon* held that even an invalid warrant insulates a search and seizure from the exclusionary rule. Judges are supposed to know what amounts to probable cause and particular description, officers are entitled to rely on their judgment, and the exclusionary rule is an inappropriate instrument for the instruction-by-deterrence of judges.

The net result is that, although the probable cause supporting our warrant is highly dubious, the evidence acquired under it will not be suppressed on that account. For all practical purposes, the warrant, once issued, is invulnerable.

Even as this book gets its final editorial polish, the scene it describes is changing. Congress is writing some law. Bills have been drawn that, when reconciled and compromised, will doubtless make it to the books. Aside from codifying *Leon*—a meaningless gesture, but unobjectionable—the new law will enact a true good-faith exception. As the House version currently stands, it provides that evidence obtained, by warrant or otherwise, in violation of the Fourth Amendment shall not be excluded in federal courts if the search and seizure was made in the reasonable belief that it was lawful. Although constitutional approval from the Supreme Court is no sure thing, my best guess is that the Court will defer to congressional wisdom on this one and allow that exclusion is not required to deter intrusions that law enforcement officers have some objectively reasonable basis for believing are perfectly lawful. They haven't said so yet, but they haven't clearly said no, either.

Congress cannot force a good-faith exception on the states, but if the Supreme Court tolerates the idea, federal courts—and those states that choose to follow the federal lead—could well find the eighty-year-old exclusionary rule, like the witch in *The Wizard of Oz,* shriveling before their eyes. Except in the most outrageous cases, law enforcement agents could believably claim honest confusion, justified by uncertain case law or badly written rules. Lawyers and trial judges will readily confess to uncertainty on the legality of many searches and seizures. Even appellate courts frequently split, and if the minority have a reasonable basis for their opinion (as they always do), why not a field officer? After all, the next case is always a little different from the last. The understandable mistakes of law enforcement personnel will insulate their discoveries from the ravages of the old-fashioned exclusionary rule. And what about the remedial virtues of the exclusionary rule? The Court has already said that the remedy lies in the deterrence of future violations. So allowing the evidence where no deterrence is possible does not conflict with the remedial rationale—at least as that idea was strangely reconfigured by the Court.

A different sort of warrant underlies the excursion in our scenario to Mother's place, a trip that ultimately produced important evidence against both Fireworks and Mother, namely the electrical components of a bomb. That warrant was not a search warrant but an arrest warrant, and the execution of the arrest warrant presents problems of its own.

The arrest warrant lives in the twilight zone of the Fourth Amendment. In its normal form, it is not a full-blown warrant to search for and seize the person of a designated human object. Yet it is in other respects like a Fourth Amendment document. It is a judge's order based on probable cause as set out in a cop's sworn affidavit, and it directs the seizure of a particularly described person. It is, in short a "seizure warrant" for a human being. It enforces constitutional guarantees of security in one's person; it does nothing whatever to enforce security in places or inanimate objects.

For most of our history, in most places, arrest warrants were more a courtesy than a constitutional necessity. Arrests, though constitutional events, were "reasonable" (as well as lawful under prevailing statutes) on probable cause alone. At least in public places, the inherent mobility of the human target invariably supplied the element of exigency that removes the necessity of a side trip to the magistrate's chambers. So comfortable were we with this notion that some states—notably New York—did not even have a provision in the state law under which a cop could obtain an arrest warrant for an unindicted suspect if she wanted one.

Then in 1980, in a case called *Payton v. New York*, the United States Supreme Court resoundingly reaffirmed the ancient legal proposition that one's home is one's castle. The longstanding license of the constable to arrest without warrant, they decided, extends only as far as the castle gate. Within his home, the Court held, the suspect is secure against arrest without express authorization from a judge. The arrest warrant is, to be sure, a bit thinner than the conventional search warrant; it doesn't require police to tell the judge where they think they'll find their suspect, and the warrant itself, unlike the search warrant, need not authorize the search for the subject in particularly described places. Writing for the Court, Justice John Paul Stevens put it this way: "If there is sufficient evidence of a citizen's participation in a felony to persuade a judicial officer that his arrest is justified, it is constitutionally reasonable to require him to open his doors to officers of the law. Thus, for Fourth Amendment purposes, an arrest warrant founded on probable cause implicitly carries with it the limited authority to enter a dwelling in which the suspect lives when there is reason to believe that the suspect is within."

So with their arrest warrant, based on probable cause, the agents had authority to arrest Fireworks wherever they happened to find him. And with their reliable tip that he was holed up in Mother's safe house, they had good reason to go there and look for him. When they brushed by Mother and forcibly entered and searched the house, they were doing no more than the Supreme Court had approved. If they had found him there, his arrest would have been in full accordance with the Constitution.

But they didn't. Instead, they came up with implements that might be involved in the alleged conspiracy. If they could lawfully seize a person, were they prohibited from taking these inanimate objects discovered in the course of a lawful intrusion and search for the person?

On its face, it would seem anomalous to deny them that seizure. Exclusion is meant to deter excessive zeal or to remedy unlawful damage. Here the zeal was appropriate and the damage was nil. As we have already noted, an axiom of Fourth Amendment jurisprudence, repeatedly reaffirmed by the Court, is that when law enforcement officers are where they are entitled to be, doing what they are entitled to do, they are not required to overlook evidence of crime that comes within their plain view.

Yet one year after they handed down *Payton,* the Supreme Court rejected just such an acquisition. In *Steagald v. United States,* the Court held that the *arrest* warrant does nothing to assure the homeowner that his security in his *home* has been respected; it serves only to override the suspect's security in his *person.* In that case, Drug Enforcement Administration officers were armed with an arrest warrant for a fellow named Lyons, who, they had been informed, was holed up in Steagald's pad. The DEA agents were slow in acting on their tip, and missed Lyons. While looking for him, however, they came across evidence in Steagald's home on which they arrested and prosecuted Steagald. The Supreme Court held that the arrest warrant, though it would have legalized the seizure of Lyons, did not authorize the search of Steagald's home in defeat of Steagald's reasonable expectation of privacy in his place and its contents.

It's a bit odd. Inept as they were, the DEA people were where they were entitled to be, doing what they were entitled to do—hunting for Lyons, for whom they had a lawful warrant. What they discovered was in plain view. Still, the Court found that Steagald—now the defendant, after all—was entitled in his own right to the intervention of the magistrate's judgment, expressed in a warrant, before having his privacy in his home invaded to search for evidence *against him.* The arrest warrant for Lyons, the Court held, did nothing to vindicate that interest.

So at this point, we can witness the baroque minuet that the Fourth Amendment exclusionary rule has become. It goes something like this:

1. If Fireworks had been found standing in one of Mother's closets, the incriminating wiring at his feet, the entry and his indoor arrest would have been lawful under the warrant. And the incriminating items could have been seized as incident to that lawful arrest, and used in evidence against anyone to whom they were relevant—including Mother.

2. If Fireworks had been arrested in Mother's place hiding under a bed and the wiring had been found *thereafter* in a closet, it could not be used against Mother. Most probably, it could not be used against Fireworks either because, as Mother's guest, he was lawfully on the premises and could assert a security interest in the place that was not overcome by the warrant for his arrest.

3. If Fireworks had been arrested hiding under a bed in Mother's place and the wiring had been found in the closet in the course of searching for him but *before* he was discovered, it could probably be used against him since it was found in plain view while police were doing what they were authorized to do under the warrant—look for him. (But they were not authorized to make a general search of the premises after finding him.) In light of *Steagald,* however, it is extremely doubtful that the evidence could be used against Mother.

4. As it happened (in the absence of the elusive Fireworks), the evidence, though unlawfully seized, could be used against Fireworks, assuming that some connection could be established between him and the wiring, unless he could come up with some convincing evidence of his standing to protest the invasion of Mother's home in his absence. Such evidence might include proof that he resided there with some regularity or kept clothing there. Mother, however, would have no trouble excluding the evidence against herself, though the police were acting completely lawfully when they acquired it.

Can anything be done to fix this, to neutralize the anomalies and allow these rather commonplace events to be sorted out and the puzzle resolved by ordinary human intelligence? Well, simplicity is not always a virtue. It just might be that, despite our yearning, the contending principles are too complex for a neat formula. Removing the exclusionary rule would provide some relief. If the pending good-faith exception goes through Congress and is signed into law, perhaps the exclusionary rules will fade into virtual obsolescence. And without the evidentiary consequence, the dance of rights would be relegated to the academic forum, where dispute could continue to rage without disturbing anyone engaged in the real business of law enforcement. Some diehards, no doubt, would mourn the loss of impact, the essential urgency that underscores the proposition that principle counts. And we can be quite certain that, regardless of what Congress does, many state jurisdictions will continue to adhere to the old-fashioned exclusionary rule as a matter of local choice.

Perhaps the doctrinal mess is attributable to the haphazard way in which doctrine develops in our common-law tradition. It's put together piecemeal, case by case, as seems best in a succession of particular circumstances—not a method designed to produce coherence. If we sat down to write a comprehensive code of criminal procedure (as the Europeans did), we might come up with a somewhat simpler, more harmonious set of injunctions.

If I were writing on a clean slate on the subject of arrests, I don't think I would elevate the aphorism about homes and castles to constitutional stature, as the *Payton* Court did. The idea of one's home as a sanctum sanctorum, entitled to a special, enhanced level of constitutional protection, has a certain romantic appeal. But it is too crude in too many ways to be apt. Think of automobiles, offices, motel rooms, and other people's houses. In all we enjoy Fourth Amendment security, but hardly on the basis of a drawbridge metaphor. I would probably try to write an arrest warrant procedure closer to the search warrant procedure. Generally, where police have advance reason to believe that the person sought is in a particular place—indoors or out, residential or not—a search for him there should be specifically authorized by a judge. The ordinary probable cause and specificity requirements of the warrant would, of course, apply.

Where police have probable cause to believe a suspect committed a crime and ample time to take their suspicions before a magistrate, but they have no reason to think he will be found at any particular place, I would also require an arrest warrant, because the suspect deserves protection for the security of his person, wherever he may be. But, of course, such a warrant could be (as they are at present) free-ranging. That is, the suspect could be hunted and seized anywhere, indoors and out, on the basis of any hunch or late-breaking reason to think he might be found—except, of course, if such reason affords ample opportunity to acquire advance judicial authorization for the search of designated private spaces for him. This would be a change in the law since, today, all outdoor arrests are presumptively made in exigent circumstances dispensing with the need for any advance warrantlike authority.

In cases of true exigency, my clean slate would reflect the Supreme Court's approval of arrests without warrant of any sort. This leaves only the problem of defining "true exigency."

This imp, *exigency*, bedevils much of Fourth Amendment jurisprudence. It covers two quite different grades of necessity. Urgency—a situation's imperative demand for prompt action—characterizes most law enforcement fieldwork. If we allowed urgency to substitute for the warrant, there would be little work for the magistrates. Emergency, by contrast, suggests a compelling demand for immediate action, often a matter of life or death in a literal sense. Police must search at once through the pockets of a pedestrian lying unconscious on the street, must rush into a house in response to a cry for help, must immediately disarm a violent person in a shopping mall. Many of these actions are not primarily law enforcement activities. If the Fourth Amendment applies at all, its provisions are easily satisfied by the obvious reasonableness of intrusion in a true emergency.

Where in the broad range between common necessity and vital emergency should I locate the arrest of a suspect at large upon whom the police have only recent information and the risk of escape? Here is the situation I would like to call true exigency—true, but moderate exigency. In these cases, I would allow police to take the suspect without warrant, even if it meant barging in on some person's protected space to do so. And, on my clean slate, the plain-view doctrine would allow in evidence, against anyone incriminated thereby, anything the police might happen upon during the lawful pursuit of a suspect under circumstances of true, moderate, exigency. So I think I would have come out the same way as the Court did in *Steagald* but for different reasons. I would exclude that evidence not because the warrant failed to take account of Steagald's rights but because the police had not moved rapidly enough to justify a claim of exigency in their pursuit.

The exigency question is inextricably bound up in the practical matter of logistics. Though the Supreme Court has never deemed it worth consideration, the question of when police may dispense with a trip to the courthouse depends largely on how long it actually takes in a particular town to get the warrant—the time of day or night that it is sought, the distance to and from the courthouse, and the local arrangements to facilitate its issuance. To some, these may seem oddly pedestrian factors on which to peg a constitutional right as important as the mediation of the neutral and detached magistrate between the citizen's right of security and the zeal of the pursuing posse.

And if I were given the magic powers not only to write the laws but to establish the tradition of their enforcement, there is one simple fix I would love to make. A nice technological solution to an ancient problem. Part of its beauty is that it would relieve me of the miserable job of wrestling with that imp exigency.

Behind the *Leon* rule is the Court's historic reading of the Fourth Amendment to encourage police to take their suspicions to a court for approval before breaching a citizen's security. At one point in his opinion, Justice White (using a nested quotation from prior decisions of the Court) puts it this way: Because a search warrant "provides the detached scrutiny of a neutral magistrate, which is a more reliable safeguard against improper searches than the hurried judgment of a law enforcement officer 'engaged in the often competitive enterprise of ferreting out crime,'" we have expressed a strong preference for warrants and declared that "in a doubtful or marginal case a search under a warrant may be sustainable where without one it would fail." The thrust of this warrant preference rule, taken together with the *Leon* good faith exception, is unmistakable, though not always understood by law enforcement authorities: the exclusionary rule is not intended to deprive juries of probative evidence but merely to encourage law enforcement officers to use the warrant route to get it.

The prime reason police do not go to court before they enter secure spaces is logistical. It's a hassle. And next to insolence, what cops hate most is a hassle. In most places—certainly the large cities—it can take hours to go down to the courthouse, type up an affidavit, find a young prosecutor who will take the time to read it, correct it, approve it, and take it to a judge who will interrupt other business to read it, question the officer, and sign it. And late at night or on weekends, forget it. The word is out: in a fast-breaking situation, improvise and clean up the act later. Mulaney and Ricci know the ropes. If they were making a planned and considered strike, they would have run the whole operation by an Assistant United States Attorney, who would have gone over the plan and provided all the necessary paper to make it legal. Let us hope that most state police officers have a similar routine for those deliberate searches carefully planned well in advance. But that does not describe the usual case where cops make a search—the kinds of cases that end up in suppression disputes and may result in rejection of vital evidence. It seems obvious that if a search warrant could be gotten without hassle for the ordinary sort of search, like Mulaney and Ricci's hit on Fireworks' car, the painful operation of the exclusionary rule would be practically obviated.

Remarkably, a technological solution is at hand—but virtually ignored.

The Fourth Amendment, some wise soul noticed recently, speaks of a supporting statement "on oath or affirmation" but not of a *written* affidavit. The affidavit, laboriously composed, submitted, edited, revised, and taken physically to a judge by the officer—this is the source of the hassle. Let's try to dispense with it and see what is left.

What if we had a permanent, round-the-clock, three-way radio hook-up connecting the police radio in the field to a prosecutor on call and a judge on regular, rotating duty. Let's put a scrambler and an automatic recording device on the line and a pad of blank search warrant forms in every patrol car. When an officer like Mulaney gets his hot tip, jumps on the case, and locates the Corsica, he gets on the radio and in minutes is connected to the prosecutor and the judge. The judge puts him under oath and the agent describes over the air where he is, what he knows (or has been told), and what he wants. He is questioned by both the prosecutor and the judge. If the judge feels the probable cause is weak, she may decline the application and the prosecutor may advise the cop how to beef it up. If the judge is satisfied, she will direct the agent how to fill out the warrant form and will authorize the agent to affix the judge's name. Mulaney will then proceed just as he and his partner did until the next move, requiring new authorization, must be made—the recovery of the key or the search of the briefcase—at which time a new radio call will provide a new warrant if appropriate.

Thanks to *Leon*, courts will not be concerned with motions to suppress any of the evidence seized under these oral search warrants—unless, of course, one is preposterous on its face. But even in those state jurisdictions that still allow challenges to seizures by warrant, the recorded avowals, under oath, will furnish dispositive data indistinguishable from the written affidavits of old.

It's flawless. It accomplishes all that the Court has been urging for so long: warrants become the ordinary and customary way to accomplish searches and seizures. And we do not have to suffer the anomaly of lost prosecutions of guilty criminals in order to protect people against unreasonable invasions of security.

Yet, so far as I know, only San Diego, California, uses this godsend on a regular basis. Other states have provided themselves with a statutory framework—to the extent that that may be necessary—and in the few cases in which the issue has come up, courts have approved the legality of the method. It is even employed sporadically, on an "emergency" basis, in a few places. But it has certainly not swept the country as the beautiful deliverance it is. Why not?

Surely, bureaucratic inertia deserves some of the credit. Then there is the modest outlay required to install the equipment. And special duty rosters of judges and prosecutors would have to be drawn up—though I suspect most jurisdictions keep a judge and prosecutor on nominal twenty-four-hour alert even without the oral-warrant hook-up. Perhaps judges are reluctant to agree to receive far more calls, frequently at inconvenient hours—though that is precisely the intended result of the exclusionary rule.

But I suspect that the major impediment to the rapid and grateful deployment of the system comes from the prosecutors' offices. Though direct evidence is scant, I am convinced that if a prosecutor's office enthusiastically promoted the idea, it would happen. I have tried repeatedly to get my local District Attorney to install it, or at least to give a good excuse for dragging his feet. I get neither, but I do get a sense of the source of his stubborn inaction. The oral–search warrant system puts the field officer in direct and immediate communication with a judge—as the Fourth Amendment design contemplated. It virtually bypasses the prosecutor, who is on the line more as a matter of courtesy than anything else. With conventional warrant procedures, the prosecutor is in charge. The prosecutor hears of the proposed venture before anyone else. He exercises some control over the investigation, has the opportunity to participate at an early stage in what are normally police decisions. He may deny this venture, he may direct further investigation before submitting the warrant. Then, when the prosecutor has approved the affidavit for submission, he may expect a certain deference from the court. A busy judge trusts the prosecutor to submit only the applications that he is confident he can sustain under later challenge. Thus the prosecutor enjoys power both upward and downward while maintaining the image of detachment in the exercise of professional judgment. It is a role not easily surrendered.

The sad thing is that their fears may be ill-founded. Some jurisdictions that use a telephone warrant system have kept the prosecutor's role prominent—though the office may have lost the control of a gatekeeper. But beyond this consideration, there is something profoundly ironic in the prosecutor's resistance. Prosecutors are uniquely concerned with the suppression of good evidence. They, of all the players, want verdicts based on all the relevant evidence that can be obtained on the case. Yet they decline the proffered means of clearing away a major obstacle to that end. It is sad, still somewhat mysterious, and ultimately infuriating.

If I were a prosecutor, I would be out in San Diego watching how the system works; if it works as they say, I would be back pushing the idea with the Department of Justice, the Congress, the state legislature, the local law enforcement agencies, with all the energy I could command. Bless the electronic age and make the oral search warrant an ordinary mode, I would proclaim, and the exclusionary rule, that ugly old monster, the prime distortion factor in criminal verdicts, the gunk that clogs the court dockets, would be largely purged. Virtually banished to the rare and unusual case, the motion to suppress would attract curious young lawyers and send judges back to the old cases to learn the Byzantine doctrines that once dominated the criminal trial. And only an occasional tear would be shed by some sentimental old timer as he remembered his youth, misspent on Fourth Amendment litigation.

5 Stops of People and Vehicles

Some Radical Proposals to Get the Guns Off the Streets

As the millennium draws to a close, murder has become one of the most grievous afflictions of the great American city culture. Freud was right: the chief impediment to civilization is the human instinct for aggression. Aided, in no small measure, by the pervasive handgun.

The statistics are grim. According to the FBI, the murder rate in the United States increased 62 percent between 1987 and 1992, when 13,220 Americans were murdered with handguns. That number compares with a total of 367 in Great Britain, Sweden, Switzerland, Japan, Australia, and Canada combined, countries whose aggregate population of 239 million is comparable to the 249 million in the United States. Handguns were also used in 917,000 nonfatal crimes—assaults, rapes, and robberies—in the United States in 1992, an increase of 21 percent over 1991 and 50 percent over the average of the preceding five years, according to the United States Department of Justice. In 1992 in the United States, 3,336 children under age twenty were murdered with firearms, 1,429 committed suicide with guns, and 501 were killed in accidental shootings—a total of 5,266, or an average of more than 14 young people killed by gunfire every day. A certain (unrecorded) number of these tragedies were doubtless slaughter by weapons legally possessed. But a substantial proportion were surely the result of illegal access to lethal firepower.

If there is any fact of urban life that shames the boast of law enforcement, it is the helpless failure to get the guns out of the pockets, the waistbands, the duffel bags, and the cars of the predators who prowl the city streets. Why is it so difficult? Does the Fourth Amendment stand so firmly in the way of effective police work that it constitutes a fortress for the felons against the rest of us, their victims? Is it hopeless, a fact of urban life that will have to await the arrival of a Messiah to reform the aggressive instinct with which God or Nature negligently endowed us all?

There have been a few ideas, even a move or two aimed at disarming the gunslingers. I am not optimistic.

Point-of-delivery interdiction seems promising to some. To disarm the populace, these starry-eyed reformers argue, you control distribution. How can we complain of the number of handguns in circulation when some states allow anyone to walk into a local gun shop and simply buy an implement good for nothing but killing? Of course, some states have stringent gun laws, virtually prohibiting pistols in private hands, others make more or less perfunctory checks on buyers (at least screening for a criminal record), but many just sell guns like fishing poles. And if a person can easily buy a handgun just across the border, stringent state controls on sales are a joke.

Federal legislation aimed at distribution points was proposed to bring the free-purchase states up to some minimum standards of limitation. Dubbed the Brady bill, for the man wounded in the 1981 assassination attempt on President Reagan, the proposal called for a waiting period and a background check of the purchaser. The electorate shouted approval as loud as it could, the President of the United States got down on his knees and begged—and Congress barely had the courage to disappoint the National Rifle Association. This free-spending, wide-bore gang seems committed to assuring every American the firepower to emulate the heroes of movies and TV and blast away at anyone who seems to deserve it. It might seem odd that these lofty ideals could have kept the majority of freely elected guardians of the people's welfare in thrall for all these years. But that's politics, folks. Anyway, *mirabile dictu*, the Brady bill squeaked through.

Before we get into this and other strategies to reduce illegal gunplay, we should dispose of a notion that has some currency: that all such efforts are unconstitutional interference with everyone's right to "keep and bear arms." Supported by a few real scholars, legions of NRA propagandists have filled the pages of tracts and journals with this argument. It's just noise. In spite of its seemingly plain language, the Second Amendment to the United States Constitution does not guarantee to every individual citizen the right to have a gun.

The Second Amendment, in its entirety, provides:

> A well regulated Militia, being necessary to the security of a free State, the right of the people to keep and bear Arms, shall not be infringed.

The Textualist contingent of the Individual Rights gang make a close reading of the language, pointing out that the militia clause is really nothing but an introductory piece of explanatory chat. As written, they aver, the heart of the provision is the solemn recognition of a right, lodged not in the states but in "the people," not only to bear arms (as soldiers do) but to keep them as well (as citizens do). How can this provision be read, as their adversaries read it, merely as recognition of the right of states to maintain militias? Moreover, they remind us, this individual right to have a gun is absolutely and resolutely protected against government infringement of any sort. The Historical Intentionalists chime in to say that the clear purpose of the Framers should control construction of the provision forever.

They have a point. But, like everyone else who sets finger to keyboard in this field, I am confident that I have the true explanation of the meaning of the text and its contemporary significance. It's not exactly original. In its only discussion of the issue, the United States Supreme Court took the same line. It goes like this:

In the late eighteenth century, citizens of the new American nation were extremely wary of concentrated power in the central government and extremely proud of their local militia—rag-tag, civilian bands of young men who had brought their smooth-bore muskets to drive the great and brightly clad British Army from their shores. After King George's surrender, those local heroes, banded together under their regional colors, were widely regarded as the citizens' protection against the threat of tyranny in the guise of the newly hatched democracy. In the meantime, the Framers in Philadelphia had written into Article 1, Section 8 of the new Constitution various powers enjoyed by Congress regarding military forces, including arming the militia.

Because citizens still considered their military units a last-ditch defense *against* the federal government, these provisions were worrisome. The local troops were still expected to bring their own weapons when they were called to fight in their regional armies. If Congress could use their powers to deprive the men of their guns, local control of the militia would evaporate.

The principal impetus for the whole Bill of Rights was to protect individuals and states from what they feared was too much power in the central government. The First Amendment, relating to religion, speech, press, assembly, and protest, might have begun, "Freedom of conscience and expression, being necessary to a free society, Congress shall make no law . . ." In the same tenor, the Second Amendment might be paraphrased thus: "Our local militia being very important to our sense of well-being, Congress shall make no law to weaken these units by depriving our brave young men of the weapons they require to arm themselves for our defense." In this sense, the Second Amendment did establish a personal right to have a gun—but only insofar as personal arms were the general and exclusive source of armament for the communal armies. Certainly, the Individual Rights contingent is on firm ground when they argue that the Second Amendment did not assure the states a right to maintain a militia. If there was any such assurance, it would have to be read into the vague language of the Tenth Amendment, which reserves to the states all powers not delegated to the central government by the Constitution. In view of the substantial express delegation of Article 1, Section 8 regarding the militia, however, this argument would be difficult to mount.

State militias developed armories of standard-issue military hardware during the middle of the nineteenth century, and, by the end of the Civil War, personal arms could no longer be brought to service even by those rustics who might prefer them. With that transformation, the Second Amendment lost its entire reason for being. It became, as even important provisions sometimes do, a fossil. It's not the only one in the constitutional garden. The Third Amendment provides: "No Soldier shall, in time of peace be quartered in any house, without the consent of the Owner, nor in time of war, but in a manner prescribed by law." Once an issue throbbing with urgency to the oppressed recent colonists; today nothing but an empty outline left in the stone.

However passionately scholars (and quasi-scholars) may construct and deconstruct the constitutional text in the legal journals and reviews, the law of the Second Amendment comes from the courts. And from that quarter, not the slightest breeze propels the proposition that the Second Amendment precludes state and federal regulation and restriction of individual access to guns.

In the year 1939, the Supreme Court decided a case called *United States v. Miller,* a decision conveniently overlooked by the gun-lovers but still alive and well in the courts. Miller was prosecuted for the interstate transportation of a sawed-off shotgun in violation of the National Firearms Act. The case came to the Supreme Court on direct appeal from the trial court, which had bought the argument that the Act violated the Second Amendment. The Supreme Court made short work of the idea. Justice James C. McReynolds keeping a judicially straight face, wrote: "In the absence of any evidence tending to show that possession or use of a 'shotgun having a barrel of less than eighteen inches in length' [the language of the indictment] at this time has some reasonable relationship to the preservation or efficiency of a well regulated militia, we cannot say that the Second Amendment guarantees the right to keep and bear such an instrument." Taking us through a detailed history lesson on colonial militias, emphasizing that citizens were required in those days to furnish their own arms, the Court said: "With obvious purpose to assure the continuation and render possible the effectiveness of such forces[,] the declaration and guarantee of the Second Amendment were made. It must be interpreted and applied with that end in view." Some have argued that this, the Supreme Court's one holding on the Second Amendment, means only that citizens have no right to possess weapons like sawed-off shotguns, which are not standard ordnance of a militia. By that reasoning, of course, the decision could be cited to assure private possession of grenades, rocket launchers, and machine guns. Absurd. The Court's meaning is plain: now that the states themselves maintain the arsenals for their militia units, the Second Amendment confers on the people no independent right to bear arms.

All courts have read *Miller* thus. No piece of federal gun legislation—and there have been several—has ever been struck down on Second Amendment grounds, and several lower federal courts have reaffirmed the proposition that the Second Amendment refers to the states' right to maintain a militia, not independent individual rights to have guns. And in 1972 the great outdoorsman Justice William O. Douglas, writing a dissent in a stop-and-frisk case called *Adams v. Williams,* noted in passing: "A powerful lobby dins into the ears of our citizenry that these gun purchases are constitutional rights protected by the Second Amendment. . . . [Citing the *Miller* decision, the Justice continues:] There is under our decisions no reason why stiff state laws governing the purchase and possession of pistols may not be enacted. There is no reason why pistols may not be barred from anyone with a police record. There is no reason why a State may not require a purchaser of a pistol to pass a psychiatric test. There is no reason why all pistols should not be barred to everyone except the police." Apart from the good Justice's casual reference to *state* laws in his discussion of *Miller* and the Second Amendment, his view accords with that of all courts that have thought about the meaning of the Second Amendment.

Most laws restricting sale or possession of firearms—or simply making possession of an unlicensed gun a crime—do come from state legislatures, not the U.S. Congress. There's an even simpler reason than the *Miller* rule why they have never stumbled on any provision of the Constitution: the Second Amendment does not apply to the states. Like the others in the Bill of Rights, this Amendment was written as a restraint on the power of Congress. But unlike most of the others, this one remains a restraint *only* on the power of the federal government. Along with the right to indictment by grand jury of the Fifth and the right to a jury trial in a civil case of the Seventh, the right of the Second Amendment (such as it was) was never incorporated in the Reconstruction Amendment, the Fourteenth, to become equally binding on state courts and governments. Admittedly, the case in the United States Supreme Court so holding, *United States v. Cruikshank,* is 120 years old (1875), but it has never been overruled. And as recently as 1992, the Court of Appeals for the 9th Circuit, reviewing and rejecting all arguments to the contrary, affirmed that the Second Amendment still does not bind the states and hence has no impact whatever on state gun control measures.

The problem with these legislative responses that focus on the point of distribution is, therefore, not constitutional. The problem is that a five-day waiting period (as the Brady bill provided) might be a minor inconvenience to the law-abiding gun buyer, but it will do virtually nothing to take the guns away from criminals.

True, a number of handguns, legitimately purchased, find their way into the jeans of felons. Found in a stolen car, taken in a burglary, a pistol may be transferred from even the most stringently licensed owner to the felonious gunslinger. Little can be done about that. There are probably also some enterprising black marketeers who travel to easy-purchase states and smuggle the hardware back to sell to the predators in the back alleys of their hometowns. Tightening up on legal sales might inhibit this trickle of guns into unlicensed hands. But there are so many loose guns already out there circulating illegally on the streets of our cities that, even assuming that obstacles like those the Brady bill imposes could significantly inhibit lawful sales, it is naive to hope that control of the point of distribution will significantly reduce the firepower of criminals.

And regardless of how restrictive we make point-of-distribution laws, they still do not assure that legality of purchase means legality of use. Only days afterthe much publicized Brady bill finally became law, a man named Colin Ferguson traveled from New York to California and, patiently waiting out the two-week delay period there, bought a weapon. After returning to New York, he walked through a commuter train with that lawfully purchased gun, killing six people and wounding nineteen others who happened to be in his line of fire.

As this book goes to press, I note the emergence of another idea that won't work. Reacting to rising public anger concerning crime and citizens' growing sense that the paid police forces can't handle it, several states have relaxed (or are in the process of relaxing) handgun licensing restrictions. Make it easier for the good guys to carry concealed weapons, the champions say, and the bad guys will back down. Reverse strategy: more guns out there, less gun crime.

The big numbers are not yet in, and the little experience we have yields somewhat equivocal data. The most recent study published, by the Violence Research Group of the University of Maryland, tracked homicide rates in four cities that had recently relaxed their concealed-weapons laws. In three (all in Florida), homicides by gunshot increased by between 22 and 74 percent. The other city, Portland, Oregon, registered a 12 percent decline—a number, researchers said, that might be explained by a tightening of gun purchase laws at about the same time as carrying laws were eased.

Apart from statistics, allowing more citizens to walk around packing legal handguns is a foolish strategy.

In those states where a gun license is somewhat easier to come by than a driver's license, something like two or three in a hundred adults get the licenses. Of that number let's suppose that one or even two actually go out and buy a gun. My guess is that most of those soon discover that a gun carried in a holster under your clothes or in your handbag is heavy, bulky, and uncomfortable, and it doesn't do much for the way your clothes hang. I doubt whether, after the novelty has worn off, more than one in five hundred will regularly carry a weapon at all times in public. Believe it or not, when a bad guy draws in a city like New York, he is a lot more likely to be in the presence of an off-duty cop than of an armed civilian good guy, who might return fire (or whatever it is that they expect to do). That does not seem like much of a deterrent.

And all we can do is hope that the hero who does keep his ordnance at hand does not drink too much, take offense easily, or get into a dispute at the end of a bad day when a guy cuts him off in traffic or takes a parking spot he had his eye on. Let us pray that none of these civilian guardians of the peace is ever in a bitter domestic quarrel, that none ever comes home sleepy or shortsighted to see a shadowy figure in the darkened alley, a figure who turned out—when the gunsmoke had cleared—to have been a spouse putting out the garbage.

Meanwhile, the guns of those other discouraged Wyatt Earps will be lying forgotten in the trunks and glove compartments of automobiles, in desk drawers, and under the socks in the bedroom dresser—where they can easily be found by youngsters to use in their games or stolen by the casual car thief or burglar.

Maybe I'll be proved wrong and the NRA right; maybe the vigilante troops will rescue our violent nation from its own firepower. But it seems contrary to all experience and common sense. More handguns lawfully in civilian hands will not reduce deaths from bullets and cannot stop the predators from enforcing their criminal demands and expressing their lethal purposes with the most effective tool they can get their hands on.

Another civil disarmament program seems little short of whimsical. Guns turned in to the local police station pursuant to this initiative would be exchanged for a $100 gift certificate at Toys-R-Us. Get rid of your unwanted armaments and get the kids a nice Christmas gift with the same stroke. Started in New York before Christmas 1993 as a modest, seasonally correct gesture of goodwill, the idea caught the fancy of the press. Before long, all sorts of firearms were pouring in—to the well-publicized amazement of the cops. The program soon outran the generosity of its first sponsor, but other merchants contributed and similar programs were set up in other cities with like results. Where did all those guns come from? we marveled. Who would have guessed there was that much unused weaponry out there?

But for all the wonder, for all the guns stripped from the backs of closets, the bottoms of dresser drawers, can we really say that the firepower of the dangerous people was significantly reduced? I doubt very much that these hundreds or even thousands of guns came from the arsenals of the neighborhood thugs. People who carry guns for no good reason do not turn them in to the cops to buy a bicycle for the kid. When the Christmas season receded and the cops recovered from their amazement, no decline in armed crime could be detected.

Still another idea surfaced in the spring of 1994 in the wake of a spate of intolerable carnage in Chicago's Taylor Homes, where residents complained that they felt unsafe going out of doors at any hour and some three hundred gunshots were counted during a single weekend. Police and housing security guards, cheered on by the vast majority of tenants, had tried a variety of measures to get the drug dealers and gun toters out of the project: searches of empty apartments, metal detectors in the lobbies, surveillance cameras. At the misguided urging of the American Civil Liberties Union, a federal district court judge struck down these initiatives as invasive of the privacy of nonconsenting tenants. President Clinton then proposed that public housing authorities include a clause in leases by which tenants would "voluntarily consent" in advance to searches of their apartments without warrant.

It is a dubious solution. Without offense to the Constitution's Fourth Amendment—to say nothing of serious damage to basic tenets of equal protection—residents of low-income public housing may not be required by the government, as the price for shelter, to relinquish the ordinary constitutional barriers against arbitrary intrusion.

Only a few weeks before the administration's idea hit the press, the eminent authority on law enforcement, Professor James Q. Wilson, proposed an ingenious technological solution in an op-ed piece. I am always attracted to technological solutions for constitutional problems, so I pricked up my ears.

Professor Wilson suggested that it might be productive to put some of our brilliant, underemployed military technicians to work to devise a metal detector that works at a distance of ten to fifteen feet. His thinking must have been that using today's hand-held metal detectors out on the street—effective as they may be in providing the beep that would entitle law enforcement officers to look into bags, pockets, and waistbands—requires that the subject be briefly halted. As we have already seen, that halt, absent at least some reasonable suspicion that the subject is armed and dangerous, amounts to an unconstitutional interference with liberty. But if cruising cops could simply aim an improved detector, like a radar gun, at a moving subject, they could provide themselves with the requisite grounds for a search without the problematic antecedent stop.

The trouble with Wilson's idea is that courts and commentators seem to agree that the use of metal detectors constitutes a "search" in the Fourth Amendment sense apart from any incidental stop. To be sure, some twenty years ago, when several lower federal courts last thought about the issue (mostly in the context of airport passenger screening), they noted that the intrusion was minimal and easily "outweighed" by the evident benefits of airport and aircraft security. So, too, courthouse magnetometers, though making "searches," were considered "reasonable" and therefore tolerable under the Fourth Amendment without demonstrable grounds for suspicion.

Although we've had no direct test of the idea in the courts, Wilson's mobile surveillance teams, turning their implement on any passing person who attracted their notice, occupy shaky legal ground. The Supreme Court has sent out several signals that it does not like random groundless searches by roving patrols. These have been mostly in the context of illegal immigration interdiction, but the message is clear: police discretion—the polite way to say hunch searches—may be easily exercised in a racially discriminatory manner. Such execution aggravates the feature of unreasonability. Unfortunately, no unemployed electronics engineer can cure this hitch in the Wilson plan.

Perhaps Professor Wilson was thinking of the narcotics cases where trained dogs have been the chosen instrument for searching suspicious packages or luggage. These canine sniff cases have been generally approved, the courts holding either that fine-tuned olfactories make no intrusion on privacy, hence no search in the Fourth Amendment sense, or else that the minimal intrusion of a whiff requires only slight suspicion to be reasonable under the Fourth. This clever canine sniff seems not too different from the sensitive electronic perception of magnetic emanations. But analogy only gets you so far in legal reasoning. And there has been some talk that the metal detector does not really measure emanations but makes an electronic penetration to where the metal object lies hidden. That bit of medieval reasoning erodes the analogy for constitutional purposes. So, lacking a fixed search point, a high security risk, or solid suspicion, I wouldn't bet on the courts' nod for James Q. Wilson's idea.

But one idea sometimes generates another, and an idea that attracts the attention of a good funding authority can generate some neat hardware as well. According to the newspaper, I was not the only one who read the Wilson op-ed piece with interest. President Clinton was intrigued by the idea and took it to his Attorney General, and we may be on the edge of a new technology. Inspired by high-tech military gear, the Justice Department is developing a camera that can read from twelve feet away silhouettes against the "millimeter waves" emitted by the human body—genuine emanations, it seems. Plastic as well as metal weapons show up clearly on the camera's screen. Production models are two or three years off, the paper says, but Wilson likes the technology: "Long overdue," he called it. Constitutional scholars, of course, are scratching their heads. Can this electronic sniff be deployed at random because, making no intrusion into the body's protected privacy, it is beneath the notice of the Fourth Amendment? Or is the enhanced vision that reveals objects concealed beneath clothing a *virtual* penetration of the personal aura, the sort of police activity that requires both demonstration of "reasonable" necessity and "reasonable" deployment? Unlike Professor Wilson, who thinks it will pass muster, I'm not yet ready with my prediction.

Clinton and Wilson are both on the right track, however. To disarm the bad guys, the good guys must go out there and take the guns from them. It's the only way. Minor limits on lawful sales will not work; encouraging voluntary surrender will not produce the guns we want. And the traditional method, punishment for those caught using or carrying guns unlawfully—even severe and mandatory prison terms—has now fully proved its own ineffectiveness as a deterrent to armed crime. And the new hi-tech search implements will be a while coming; I don't know whether our beleaguered cities can wait.

In the meantime, here's another idea, mine this time. A low-tech fantasy:

Crime was not just the number one political issue to the good citizens of the city of Megapolis; it was a daily fact of urban life. In some quarters of town, the streets were Sarajevo, USA. Petty disputes on the street were settled by gunfire. Holdups of local merchants ended with a shot from the door, just for good measure. And stray bullets often found unintended targets. Everyone in the neighborhood knew someone who had been shot. Sometimes it was a friend or relative who had taken a bullet while on the way to the corner for some lo mein. Or a neighbor's child who was hit as she sat at the window doing her homework. In these sections, people were literally afraid to step out of their front doors, to sit near windows in their own homes. Youngsters had to walk through metal detectors to get into their schools. The prevalent spirit in these communities was equal parts anger and desperation, seasoned with a sense of utter despair.

Nor were the depredations of armed criminals confined to these neighborhoods. Everywhere, people eyed with suspicion the young men who seemed to have nowhere to go, nothing to do, who moved slowly, menacingly through the busy parts of town. Did those loose-fitting jeans conceal a gun? Could a look in the eye, a failure to give way as you approached be interpreted as an insult? Would an unconcealed glint of gold jewelry, an involuntary tightening of one's grip on a handbag be considered an invitation to aggressive crime? Just enough incidents of violence were reported by the press to make everyone nervous and suspicious of strangers. Do I dare ride my bike in the park early in the morning? Jog along the river? How do I get home safely from my night shift job?

The politicians and police brass did their usual act. In even-numbered months, they assured the people that the city was safe, cops were on relentless community patrol, "quality-of-life" arrests were up, the media were only stirring up hysteria. In odd-numbered months, they decried the rising tide of crime, blamed one another, and promised the people that new initiatives would soon be undertaken to combat lawlessness. Meanwhile, the sober statistics: rape, robbery, murder, and mayhem—mostly with illegal handguns—continued to rise from their intolerably high levels the previous year.

Finally, the good citizens of Megapolis rebelled. They threw the politicians out of City Hall and elected as mayor a former police sergeant, Martin Browning, who had had a career in law enforcement in the precincts, not at headquarters, and who promised some radical measures. Browning was a big man, handsome, with the inflection of the streets still in his speech. If he'd learned one thing from his twenty-two years in the Department, it was to recognize bullshit when he heard it—both the official and the unofficial varieties. Soon after Mayor Browning was installed, he got down to the business for which he was elected. He appointed an old buddy, a former partner, Leroy Hendricks, as police commissioner and sat down with him and a couple of bold lawyers to draw up a plan of action.

"Number one," Browning opened, "guns. We know they're out there. And we know the courts can't do a damn thing about it. It's up to us to collect them."

"Yeah, Marty, right, right," Hendricks said. "But the Constitution's in their pocket, not ours. There's not much we can do to get out from under. Legally, that is."

"Not so fast, Leroy, I've heard that complaint too often. We've got a couple of smart young lawyers here. It's our move." Browning turned to the lawyers.

"What's the question, Chief?" one asked.

"It's not a question. I want you to forget what they taught you in law school about what we can't do. I want to know what we can do—and haven't tried yet."

The lawyers looked at one another. It was an interesting commission. High risk, but hey, that's what they signed on for—make a difference. "Give us a couple of days, Chief. We'll get back to you on that one."

As soon as they were alone together, the mayor's young legal staff went to work. "The way I see it," Mike Andreotti ventured, "we have three targets: persons, cars, and premises."

"All different for constitutional purposes," Lauren Gold said, picking up on it. "Let's think about them one at a time."

"Looking for guns on people is tough," Mike said. "Fourth Amendment security in one's person means we can't touch. The Supremes have been pretty clear about that. As I recall, the cops must have some good reason to think this particular person is armed and dangerous or has committed some crime. Not much we can do about that, is there?"

"Hold on, Mike," Lauren laughed. "That's just the kind of negative thinking the boss wants us to forget about."

"Sure, it's easy for him to say," said Andreotti. "But it's our job to keep him legal, isn't it?"

Lauren thought for a moment. Mike poured himself a cup of coffee from the stale brew perpetually warming on the hot plate. "How about this?" Lauren said at last. "The Court has said OK to roadblocks to catch drunk drivers, right?"

"Yeah, but what does that have to do with . . ."

"Hear me out. Why couldn't we have a streetblock to catch illegal gunslingers?"

"You mean, no more roving patrols stopping every black or Latino kid in the wrong haberdashery? Well, that's a plus, at least."

"Right," Lauren said. "Fixed checkpoints, the way the Court likes them. Everyone has to pass through. No discretion, no discrimination—isn't that the formula?"

"So, Lauren, you think that gunslingers are as dangerous as drunks behind the wheel? I think you'd have to sell that to the Court right at the top."

"I'm willing to try that one—in this town, at least. I think I'd have more trouble convincing them that my hit rate will be in the same range as the drunks picked up by roadblocking. What was that, about 1.5 hits in a hundred stops, something like that?"

Mike shrugged. "We can't know until we try it, I guess. And what rate is high enough to make the intrusion worthwhile? Who knows?"

"Myself, I'd settle for disarming one in five hundred, but I don't know if that's good enough for the Court. Depends on what neighborhood we set up in, I suppose. I'll bet I can find you a couple of corners where I can score one in ten!"

"Careful," Mike said. "There goes your 'indiscriminate' feature, the linchpin of your legality."

"Why? Can't the troopers can set up their roadblock along tavern row on a Saturday night? Same thing: we triage to the highest gun crime areas first. Then we stop everyone who passes by—indiscriminately."

"It's an idea," Andreotti conceded. "Your hand-held magnetometer doesn't make much more of an intrusion than a Breathalyzer, I guess. But even granting legality, how are you going to do it? Just put a walk-through magnetometer up in the middle of some block and have everyone walk through it—like in an airport? What makes you think the guys packing sidearms are just going to line up and wait for the beep that puts them in jail?"

"That is a problem," Lauren grimaced. "It's a little harder when you're driving to do a U-turn without calling attention to yourself. But pedestrians can probably dodge any sidewalk metal detector without being noticed. Damn! I can handle the law, it's the practicalities that shoot me down."

"You and everybody else."

Lauren hijacked Mike's cup, took a sip of bad coffee, cold now. "There must be some places you could set up temporary fixed detectors. How about the turnstiles where people come off a train? They have to get off that platform, and there's only one way out. Or how about making everybody leaving a rock concert walk past my magnetometers?"

"Not bad, not bad," Mike nodded in admiration. Then he smiled: "How's your imagination when it comes to indoor searching? Want to take a crack at that?"

"I have a lot more trouble with that," Lauren said. "My professor kept saying the Court still thinks a home is a castle, or at least some kind of a sanctum. Even with probable cause, cops can't go in there to make an arrest without a warrant—though they could arrest the same guy on the same grounds on the street. I don't know how we can go in there to look for guns without . . ."

Suddenly animated, Mike cut her off. "Now it's you who's remembering what you learned in law school," Mike said. "Let me take a swing at this one."

"Good luck," Lauren said cheerfully.

"Well, if you'd gotten into a better law school, you might have heard of the administrative search."

"Hey, even at Yale we heard of the administrative search. What does that have to do with the price of beans? That's where inspectors are out looking for oily rags in the closets and rat shit in supermarket basements, right? Health and safety violations, fire hazards, that sort of thing. Not the criminal possession of firearms."

"You think looking for the VIN numbers of stolen cars in a body shop is a health and safety code violation?"

Lauren looked interested. "Right. The Court held that was OK, didn't they?"

"Without a warrant, without probable cause."

"I think I hear what you're saying, Mike. You're a genius."

"If a law enforcement officer can go into someone's residence or place of business to look around with nothing but a rubber-stamped piece of paper that says 'search warrant' in big letters across the top, with a judge's signature— signed by the cop—on the bottom, and no reason whatever to suspect a violation, if that's constitutional, why can't our gun patrol do the same thing?"

"What makes an administrative search legal," Lauren added, getting into the spirit of it, "is a good statute. It's coming back to me. The administrative search has to be a regular or random visit, reasonably necessary to enforce a reasonable statute or regulation. Right?"

"That sounds like the sentence I wrote on my final for Uviller. Or what I should have written. So—why can't we write a reasonable gun control statute that requires periodic site inspections? Wouldn't that be as reasonable as the chop shop inspection?"

"And naturally, if your inspectors just happen to discover evidence of crime, there's no reason for them to turn away, is there?"

"They're law enforcement officers. Every reason for them to make the collar."

Lauren made a face. "I'm still not sure, Mike. It's someone's home. And guns are small. Are you going to let them put their fat hands all over the residents' personal stuff? It could take hours to go through a flat to find all the guns that might be hidden there. It's not like checking the fenders and motor blocks in some greasy body shop. Come on, Mike, get serious. We're talking privacy here."

"I know, Lauren, I know. But you're forgetting the technology," Mike argued. "I'm talking about inspectors with the latest metal detection gear. You can go over walls, floors, upholstery in minutes. You can go through closets and dressers without touching a thing—until your wand beeps. I'm not saying it's no search, but I think we can minimize the intrusion. We'll write the regulation with that in mind. Plus, I'm talking about specially trained troops. Polite. Efficient. In and out with a minimum of fuss and disturbance." He paused and examined Lauren's expression. "You don't think it's possible?"

"I don't know, Mike, I just don't know. Maybe it's worth a try."

The young lawyers are tired now. It's late and the office has a kind of hollow, nighttime sound to it. But they push on. Just a bit further, then let it simmer till tomorrow.

"How about automobiles?" Lauren asks wearily. "Any bright ideas?"

"I don't know. When I was in the D.A.'s office, it always seemed to me we were doing OK in the interdiction department. Guns in cars was the one thing the cops used to bring in pretty regularly."

"Maybe we already have pretty much everything we need for car searches. For one thing, we have the roadblock. While we're looking for drunks there's no law says we can't keep our eyes open for guns."

"Right," Mike said, "and apart from roadblocks, police already have a host of reasons—let's not call them pretexts—for stopping cars on the road: a taillight dark, no turn signal, erratic driving, etc., etc. Once we have them lawfully pulled over, the alert officer is shining that flashlight around the interior, looking for a suspicious glint of metal."

"I suppose experienced cops are also pretty good at spotting the vehicles that are just cruising, looking for some crime of opportunity."

"They always say they had a hunch, a feeling, something looked funny, smelled funny. I once pressed a cop whose nose was remarkably good, 'What do you mean, it smelled funny? You pulled alongside at a red light and looked at these guys. What was funny?' I got a really good answer."

"Yeah?" Lauren asked, curiosity battling fatigue.

"'Of course,' my guy says, 'they took one look at us and knew we were cops. You might not make us,' he tells me, 'but these people know. So suddenly, the guy in the back seat ducks out of sight. Or the guy on the passenger side reaches down like he's doing something on the floor—maybe sliding the gun out of sight under the seat. Or the driver starts jerking at his jacket trying to get it closed around his waist, just to make sure the butt of his gun isn't sticking out. It's really comical sometimes.'"

Lauren smiled. "A lot of departments, I read, are beginning to see traffic patrol as an important move in the war on guns. I guess we need to teach the cops to articulate the bases for their hunches. If we can convert that 'something funny' into a reasonable and particular basis for suspicion . . .'"

"Our problem is, of course," Mike said, "we have no grounds for going deeper into the vehicle on these roadblock and traffic stops. If everything that flashlight can reach looks kosher, we have to tip our hats and say, 'Have a nice evening.'"

"Right," Lauren said. "Now even you, even at this hour, can't come up with a way of looking in the trunk of that car without real probable cause to think there's a gun or some other contraband in there. You can't even look under the dashboard without probable cause to arrest one of the occupants. Admit it."

"Can you?"

"Not at the moment. But I'm working on it, I'm working on it."

"You won't let go till you sweep up that last bit of gunpowder, will you, Lauren?"

"Damn right. I'd like to see men go back to carrying canes as the symbol of their precious masculinity."

Pure fantasy, of course. But our young lawyers seem pretty well educated. The law (such as it is) is as they describe it. The Constitution—as generations of judges of all political stripes have read it—takes a distinctly dim view of police officers following their hunches and sticking their keen noses into other people's business. And searches of people and residences for no better reason than that they happen to be in the wrong neighborhood are even more onerous. Closed packages and compartments cannot be opened by cops at will merely because they happen to be surrounded by an automobile. In our constitutional ordering of priorities, we allow government invasion of private domains only for reasons a lot better than that. And it helps not a bit to get a judge to issue a blank check for any swoop and scoop that might seem appropriate to the officer in the field. "General warrants" and *"lettres de cache"* are among the gentler pejoratives applied to such open-ended authorizations. And they are often cited among the causes of the American Revolution and as just the sort of colonial police work that the Fourth Amendment was written to prohibit. Furthermore, the urgency of social concern has never erased a single penstroke of the Fourth Amendment injunction (though airport searches come close).

And yet. And yet there is such an animal as an administrative search. Health and safety inspections, as Andreotti said, are recognized as reasonable under the Fourth Amendment when they are carried out pursuant to a well-drawn statute and according to a rational plan. In Chapter 1 I cited a little case (that I never liked much) called *Camara* to justify my proposed crime scene search warrant. It was helpful because it said that probable cause for a warrant might be found in the general reasonableness of the inspection program even though the inspectors had no particular reason to think that a violation would be found in the particular premises they wanted to enter. And the chop shop case in the Supreme Court that Mike and Lauren remembered, a 1987 case called *New York v. Burger,* did indeed apply the concept to validate periodic, unannounced inspection raids on automobile body shops suspected of dismantling stolen cars.

Is there any reason, then, that Mayor Browning can't call his gun hunt an administrative action, aimed primarily at securing the general community safety and well-being and only incidentally carrying criminal consequences for the gun keepers? It's an accurate description. If Gold and Andreotti know what they are doing, they should be able to draw a statute to keep the Fourth Amendment happy. It would have to be meticulously fair and even-handed, and it should have a clear and obvious connection with a public policy of public safety as compelling as any community interest in faulty wiring or rodent droppings. When they come to argue for the statute before the Supreme Court (as they doubtless will), they will emphasize that the key concept in the Fourth Amendment is *reasonableness*—the people, the Constitution provides, shall be secure against unreasonable searches and seizures. Reasonableness is a flexible idea. It should take account of the urgency of social necessity as well as the unavailability of lesser intrusions to accomplish the purpose. Browning and Hendricks might well be told by their lawyers that there is at least a chance that today's Court would buy such a plea.

There was a brief moment when I considered cars inherently dangerous instrumentalities, not unlike dynamite sticks. The state, I imagined, had the right to license operation of these useful but deadly items for the safety of all.

A perfectly reasonable condition for the license, I thought, would be a general waiver of the security of the Fourth Amendment to allow random stops just to make sure there is no obvious impediment in either driver or vehicle to reasonably safe operation.

The Supremes set me right in 1972 in a case called *Delaware v. Prouse.* Justice White for the Court put the issue clearly: "The question is whether it is an unreasonable seizure under the Fourth and Fourteenth Amendments to stop an automobile, being driven on a public highway, for the purpose of checking the driving license of the operator and the registration of the car, where there is neither probable cause to believe nor reasonable suspicion that the car is being driven contrary to the laws governing the operation of motor vehicles or that either the car or any of its occupants is subject to seizure or detention in connection with the violation of any other applicable law." The answer the Court gave was: yes, it is an unreasonable seizure. The case arose when a highway patrolman stopped a car for no apparent reason, smelled marijuana smoke as he approached, and spotted some of the drug in plain view on the car floor. First, the Court made it plain that "[t]he Fourth and Fourteenth Amendments are implicated in this case because stopping an automobile and detaining its occupants constitute a 'seizure' within the meaning of those Amendments, even though the purpose of the stop is limited and the resulting detention quite brief." Justice White (no pushover when it comes to law enforcement) went on to find that

> [a]n individual operating or traveling in an automobile does not lose all reasonable expectation of privacy simply because the automobile and its use are subject to government regulation. Automobile travel is a basic, pervasive, and often necessary mode of transportation to and from one's home, workplace, and leisure activities. Many people spend more hours each day traveling in cars than walking on the streets. Undoubtedly, many find a greater sense of security and privacy in traveling in an automobile than they do in exposing themselves by pedestrian or other modes of travel. Were the individual subject to unfettered governmental intrusion every time he entered an automobile, the security guaranteed by the Fourth Amendment would be seriously circumscribed.

The result: random stops and spot checks, even in the interests of highway safety, are unconstitutional.

In 1990, however, the Supreme Court approved roadblocks for automobiles, without abandoning the idea that the stop of a car, however brief, is a Fourth Amendment event. In *Michigan Department of State Police v. Sitz,* the Court decided that the grave danger of drunken driving justified the minimal intrusion of stopping a driver for a field breath test without any particular grounds for suspicion. The Court distinguished *Delaware v. Prouse* as follows:

> In Delaware v. Prouse, we disapproved random stops made by Delaware Highway Patrol officers in an effort to apprehend unlicensed drivers and unsafe vehicles. We observed that no empirical evidence indicated that such stops would be an effective means of promoting roadway safety and said that "[i]t seems common sense that the percentage of all drivers on the road who are driving without a license is very small and that the number of licensed drivers who will be stopped in order to find one unlicensed operator will be large indeed." We observed that the random stops involved the "kind of standardless and unconstrained discretion [which] is the evil the Court has discerned when in previous cases it has insisted that the discretion of the official in the field be circumscribed, at least to some extent."
>
> Unlike *Prouse,* this case involves neither a complete absence of empirical data nor a challenge to random highway stops. During the operation of the Saginaw County checkpoint, the detention of the 126 vehicles that entered the checkpoint resulted in the arrest of two drunken drivers. Stated as a percentage, approximately 1.6 percent of the drivers passing through the checkpoint were arrested for alcohol impairment. In addition, an expert witness testified at the trial that experience in other States demonstrated that, on the whole, sobriety checkpoints resulted in drunken driving arrests of around 1 percent of all motorists stopped. . . .
>
> In sum, the balance of the State's interest in preventing drunken driving, the extent to which this system can reasonably be said to advance that interest, and the degree of intrusion upon individual motorists who are briefly stopped, weighs in favor of the state program. We therefore hold that it is consistent with the Fourth Amendment.

So we must put aside our confusion over the substantive significance of the distinction between the random stops by roving patrols and the equally random stops of everyone who happens to pass through the temporary fixed checkpoint. We accept the distinction and, like Mike Andreotti and Lauren Gold, try to fit ourselves comfortably on the legal side of the line.

But is the dream that the Browning administration is preparing to sell really a nightmare in disguise? Maybe, as a walk in the Alps teaches, it's all a matter of perspective. If you are the one being put up against the wall, the person whose home is suddenly invaded by cops sticking their tools into your closets and drawers, the raids may seem more like the intrusions of a fascist state than a benevolent social program. And if you know that your neighborhood, relatively poor and populated mainly by "minorities," was selected for the hit, you may be tempted to apply the word racist to the operation. These are serious concerns.

On the other hand (as we lawyers like to say), we know that the terrified victims of the scourge also live in these neighborhoods. And they vastly outnumber the bad guys. Can't we count on them to support the program even if their homes are searched, their teenage sons frisked on the street?

We have had considerable experience with similar programs, and new ones are being hatched all over. A recent report of the Crime Control Institute of Washington, D.C., describes the efforts of police in various American cities to improve their capabilities in getting the guns off the streets. Some places have better records than others, and aggressive patrol tactics, specifically directed against handguns, are a prime order of business around the country. None appears to be as daring as Mayor Browning's plan, but it is clear that these aggressive initiatives, in one shape and other, will soon become common creatures in the law enforcement stables.

On this question, I am frankly torn. Aggressive police patrol carries an unmistakable whiff of fascism. We can't let civic fear put basic liberties at risk. At the same time, I deeply believe that before we can call ourselves civilized, the government must do what it can to secure the physical safety of its citizens; in today's urban world, that means first and foremost: get the guns off the streets. I also believe that there is no other way to make meaningful progress toward this objective than to go out into the communities where the illegal guns are prevalent and take them by unexpected, forceful police action. No other way. Believing as I do, it's hard to deny that the program is compatible with basic values of our society.

As a parting shot, Mayor Browning may be tempted to remind his old partner, Hendricks, that the Fourth Amendment does not require the return of weapons seized illegally; it prohibits only their use in evidence in a criminal prosecution. So forget the Fourth Amendment, he may say, only half joking; go on out and confiscate the guns. We won't try to introduce them in court—we'll dump them in the lake. You'll be doing us all useful service even if you don't make a single prosecutable collar. We can only trust that Andreotti and Gold will remind their chief that it's not good politics to counsel illegal conduct by law enforcement agencies even in pursuit of a worthy goal.

I mention again the dirty little secret ploy of confiscation only because it seems to fit into my discussion of this stubborn affront to the boast of law enforcement, the seemingly ineradicable, pervasive urban handgun hazard. That discussion sounds one of the repeated themes I mean to play: the continuous struggle between effective illegality and the blunter but prouder tactics of lawful law enforcement. Where police work must be done and where the law seems helpless to provide an effective way to do it, imagination takes over. So far, improvisation has not helped much. Maybe the new and determined administration of Megapolis will push us a step further toward an accommodation between strict legality and social necessity. Stumbling toward a fair balance, the Court may someday find that in virtual compliance with constitutional precepts, true justice may emerge. And the American people may be able, through lawful action, to reclaim their towns from the murderous hands of the predators. If serious initiatives like the ones that Lauren and Mike are thinking about are deemed tolerable, maybe we can get our numbers down from thousands to hundreds, and the criminal justice system will again have some legitimate claim to doing justice in a civilized society.

6 Privacy and Privilege

Defeating Truth in the Name of Justice

There are lots of things we know that we would rather not tell the government, especially the government's prosecution corps. When the FBI, the local cops, or the prosecuting attorney (perhaps with a grim-faced grand jury arrayed behind him) starts asking questions, our wariness level rises rapidly. Unless we are in a singularly vindictive mode, heedless, or supremely confident, we are gripped by reluctance. Even those whose consciences are clear—if any such can be found—feel a certain foretaste of trouble. Trouble is what the criminal law enforcement branch is all about. The cerebral neurons are firing in volleys. Can these words I am speaking, or the information they convey, possibly be used to destroy me, or if not me, someone who trusted me? Am I, wittingly or unwittingly, supplying the tilt evidence to bring about my own downfall or some friend's grief?

The answer is: yes, quite possibly I am. That's why I am being questioned, most likely—to obtain incriminating evidence to be used in a criminal prosecution against me or others. Of course, if the only "other" against whom my evidence could be used is my attacker, I am happy to cooperate. Or if the other is some stranger about whom I just happen to have some information, I will neutrally—maybe somewhat fearfully—tell what I know and let the chips fall as they may. But if I sense that the likely target of my evidence is me or someone important to me, I find myself asking, must I do this? Is there any escape?

And for most of us, the sense—at least to some extent—is that we are being compelled to "cooperate," that we have lost the precious option to clam up. Of course, we may still ask: how important is the perfect right to refuse to assist the government? How worried should we be that the government demands that the person who has helpful information surrender it? These are harder questions.

It is not only that I am uncomfortable in the role of involuntary accuser. I also have this terrible feeling that my government is ransacking my most personal preserve, my mind, and robbing me of the essential human dignity of control over its contents. My thinking self, I say (mangling Descartes), is the essence of *me*. And what it means to live in a liberal democracy is that my sovereignty over myself is respected by my government. So get your subpoenas off my cerebrum!

But personal disinclination is only one side of the story. The social imperative that has been with us at least since people began to write about social imperatives is that, along with their taxes, citizens owe the government a duty of disclosure. "The state is entitled to every man's evidence," is the way one ancient annotator put it. And that includes cognitive evidence along with documents and such. And it means the state may compel its production from the disinclined—by jail time if necessary. Cognitive privacy has only one refuge and that is the precept, writ large in our Constitution's Fifth Amendment, that the state may not compel a person "in any criminal case to be a witness against himself."

The language chosen by the Framers sounds like it means only that the prosecutor may not call a criminal defendant to testify on the witness stand in his own case. It certainly does mean that, and not only directly but indirectly: the prosecutor may not prod the defendant to testify by commenting to the jury on his failure to do so, asking the jury to infer from his silence that he has something inculpatory to hide. But in addition, the constitutional right of silence has long been understood to mean that no one may be compelled to furnish evidence at any time that may eventually be used against him—or may lead to other evidence that may be used against him—in a criminal prosecution. Being a witness, in other words, equals furnishing evidence.

The prohibition is not absolute, however. The government may compel you to turn over documents in which you have recorded information inculpating yourself. That always comes as a bit of a surprise to my students. "What?" they marvel. "The government may take my diary in which I confessed to myself that I did the dastardly deed and may read my words aloud to the jury? That's not compelling me to be a witness against myself?" Right. The Supreme Court has clearly informed us that you are compelled to be a witness only where "testimonial or communicative evidence" is forced from you. Meaning, evidence pried from your *mind*—cognitive evidence, I have been calling it. Evidence previously expressed freely—though privately— and then wrested from you in its recorded form is fair game.

In ancient times, there was an attempt to endow citizens with the fundamental right to withhold evidence incriminating to others. In religious inquisitions, some of the persecuted contended that no one should be forced to accuse others of heresy. But the idea never took root in English soil and has never been sown again. Other than the self-inculpatory variety, the only cognitive evidence an American may withhold today is evidence protected by some subconstitutional privilege, like the doctor-patient, priest-penitent, lawyer-client, or spouse-spouse privileges. About which, more later.

For now, let's conjure up a case:

For some months, the federal government has been investigating fraudulent promotions by investment agents. One day a story in the financial press, citing a confidential source, reports that the investigation has turned to the real estate investment market. Sam Franklin, an investment broker, visits Maud Shepherd, Esq., the following day. Shepherd, having made something of a reputation as chief of the Frauds Division of a large United States Attorney's Office, has been in private practice for eight years, specializing in white-collar crime. Franklin brings a thick briefcase with him.

After the introductions, they get right down to business. "I need some good advice," Franklin opens.

"I'll do my best," Shepherd says.

"Did you happen to see yesterday's *Financial World*?"

"I glanced at it."

"Well, I'm in the investment business, and right now I'm promoting a major shopping mall deal."

"I see."

"Does that give you some idea of why I'm here?"

"Not a very clear idea, I'm afraid. Could you spell it out for me?"

"Well, I don't know how much to say right now," Franklin hesitates. "We haven't signed a retainer agreement yet. I haven't paid you a dime."

"Don't worry about that, Mr. Franklin," Shepherd says. "We'll sign that piece of paper and agree on our fee arrangement after I hear a bit more about the case and decide whether I can take it."

"Well," Franklin says, "I don't know if I can tell you any more until I know that you represent me."

"Oh, I see," says Shepherd. "You are concerned about the privilege. Well, let me assure you that what you tell me now—even if I decide I can't take the case and you never pay me a fee—everything that you tell me is completely protected by the privilege. And everything that I tell you. So long as you speak with me in confidence on a legal matter, I assure you I will not and cannot be compelled to disclose a word of what you tell me. The privilege also covers any conferences I may have with members of my firm—or yours, for that matter— or experts I may need to help me render the legal service you seek. OK?" Shepherd's more or less standard allocution is completely correct.

Reassured, Franklin confides to Shepherd his fears that representations he made in mailings to potential investors might be construed by government in- vestigators as fraudulent. Shepherd takes careful notes, asking questions from time to time to clarify the story. Finally, Franklin opens his briefcase. "These are the documents I'm most concerned about," he says.

"What are they?"

"They are land surveys and local zoning rules for several of the proposed malls," Franklin says, handing Shepherd the papers.

"And?" she says.

"And they do not support the sales pitch. That's the long and short of it." Shepherd looks them over.

"Please," Franklin says. "Keep them. You can study them at your leisure. Along with any other documents you need."

"Yes," she says. "I think I should."

By the conclusion of the conference some hours later, Shepherd has agreed to represent Franklin and they have executed a retainer agreement.

Within a few days, Franklin receives a subpoena from the federal grand jury calling for him to appear and bring with him copies of surveyors' reports relat- ing to several named proposed development sites for shopping malls promoted by the Franklin firm. He goes at once to Shepherd, who immediately files a mo- tion to quash the subpoena. In her motion she asserts that Franklin is not in possession of the documents called for, and that, in any case, the subpoena violates his privilege under the Fifth Amendment.

During oral argument of her motion in court, Shepherd is asked by the judge

whether she has the documents in question in her possession, whether she received them from her client, and if so, whether she will turn them over to the
court. Shepherd declines to answer the questions or comply with the request
on grounds of privilege.

Shall we interrupt our story at this point to inquire how the court should rule
on these motions and deal with Shepherd's refusal?

Lawyers have always really loved the attorney-client privilege. They say it
enhances candor. And without a full and honest disclosure in the office, they
insist, they cannot render the professional service the client is paying for.
Maybe so. But skeptics like me persist in doubting both propositions. I'm not
entirely sure that a client's trust is much affected by the privilege. At least in
criminal cases, I have good reason to believe that few clients actually tell their
lawyers the whole truth—I once heard a room full of criminal defense
lawyers admit as much. Most criminal defendants come to the lawyer with a
story, and if that story is shot down, the client looks to the lawyer to suggest a
sturdier one. In some cases, the truth may be the best story. So much the
better, but the truth is rarely the best story for a guilty defendant—and most
defendants are guilty. I assume that most of these guilty people who do not
want to fold and settle for a negotiated term want to arm their counsel with
the most persuasive exculpatory story they can come up with. And I seriously
doubt whether the standard advisory about the rock-bound privilege alters
their assessment of their best interests.

I also have considerable doubt whether criminal defense lawyers really
want—or need—to hear the truth from their clients. Yes, they need to have
the adverse evidence plausibly accounted for, so they need to know from the
client what they are up against. That may require some truth telling. But I
suspect that a lawyer can perform as well—and perhaps with a good deal
more inner conviction shining through—if his client falsely insists that he
was mistakenly identified and produces a credible, albeit perjurious, alibi. No
lawyer, of course, can suggest such a tactic to a client, but few would look too
closely at the teeth of the steed should the client arrive riding it.

I have an irreverent suspicion that the privilege betokens just that: privilege. Judging from the number of trades that line up at the state houses every
season petitioning for the enactment of a law bestowing a privilege on them,
I think the privilege must confer a sort of professional caste on the privileged
practitioners. Could it really be sought as a device to induce their clients to

be more forthcoming in their disclosures? Will the candor quotient of the patrons of accountants, dental hygienists, architects, or Alcoholics Anonymous support groups actually rise if they are assured legal confidentiality? It was not too long ago, remember, that the status of Ph.D. shrinks was elevated by according them the privilege that theretofore was the entitlement of M.D.s only. Do you suppose the candor of their patients was enhanced? Or is the professional privilege just a mark that society considers their relationships as important as those between lawyer and client, doctor and patient, priest and penitent,

I am mindful, too, that even the strongest privileges can occasionally be made to yield to overriding public necessity. California and nineteen other states require psychotherapists to warn "foreseeable and identifiable" future victims that their patients have threatened to harm them, notwithstanding that these threats were communicated within an indisputably privileged relationship. Three other states follow in modified form this Tarasoff rule (named for the California case in which it was first articulated), several others lean toward adoption, and only two have rejected it (Michigan and Florida). I can imagine situations that would give rise to an overriding necessity to abrogate other privileges, including the sacrosanct attorney-client privilege.

But notwithstanding these small dents, the privilege protecting the confidentiality of communications between attorneys and their clients is deeply embedded in our jurisprudence, enjoying nearly constitutional status in criminal cases, where, it is asserted, the privilege is an element of the Sixth Amendment right to competent professional assistance. The privilege protects the client against all efforts to obtain from her lawyer the communications between them that were intended to be private and were made in the course of legal counseling. And handwritten notes, like those Shepherd was making, are generally within the privilege as "work product."

But the privilege does not protect everything that passes between a lawyer and a client. The name of the lawyer's client, for example, the fact that he sought the lawyer's services, the fee, and the name of the person who paid it—though learned by the lawyer from communications of the client in the course of their professional relationship—are usually not covered by the privilege. Unless there is some special, extraordinary reason to think otherwise, these facts are not considered confidential. That means that the judge may ask whether Mr. Franklin had sought the services of Ms. Shepherd, a well-known criminal lawyer, the day after it was announced that the government was opening a criminal investigation of business concerns like his. Though the courts refuse to acknowledge that there could be anything suspicious about consulting a criminal lawyer, you and I—and surely, Sam Franklin—know better.

The privilege also accords no protection to objects, including documents, turned over to the lawyer by the client even if they are necessary to the rendition of legal service and intended by the client to be confidential. The logic is that anything that could be obtained by compulsory process from the client cannot be put beyond reach simply by delivery to a lawyer. Lawyers do not want to become safe repositories of damaging physical evidence, though its examination is helpful to preparing a defense. Oral evidence, yes; physical evidence, no.

So this means that the propriety of the judge's request that Shepherd turn over the documents she had received depends upon whether Franklin could have successfully resisted a subpoena calling for the production of the survey reports had the documents still been in his hands. But how could he refuse to surrender the documents? Didn't I already say that there is no constitutional privilege to withhold self-incriminatory documents? Brace yourself—here comes a really cute twist, the kind of thing that makes the whole subject of privilege dear to the hearts of legal scholars with a medieval sense of humor. It comes, as usual, from the Highest Authority: a 1976 case in the Supreme Court called *Fisher v. United States.*

Franklin cannot resist the subpoena on the grounds that the *contents* of the documents are inculpatory, but he can if the *production* of the documents in response to the subpoena is itself somehow inculpatory. And just how can the production of a document be incriminating? By bringing the surveyor's reports to the grand jury, Franklin is implicitly testifying that such documents exist, that the documents produced are those described, and—most importantly for us, assuming the documents contradict assertions he made in his sales pitch—that he had those documents in his possession and knew their contents. The question then becomes: was the prosecution making use of this implicit testimony in its case against Franklin? That question is not always easy to answer.

Some may disagree, but I do not regard these odd discontinuities as true holes in the concept of privilege; wrinkles in the fabric, perhaps, but not holes. Perhaps it is because I do not love the privileges. I see them as scattered barriers to accurate verdicts, creatures of social policy designed to obstruct truth in the interest of some other social value (such as the candor of a therapist's patient). I'm not sure that the guilty should go free or the innocent be shipped off to jail in the service of the values supposedly advanced by the privilege. To be honest, I deem it an outrage that to protect a murderer's trust in his therapist, lawyer, or priest (however valuable their services may be), we allow an innocent person to be convicted by a jury who will be kept ignorant of the true murderer's privileged confession. Nor am I completely reconciled to acquitting a rapist who has made a full, voluntary, and verifiable confession to a psychotherapist while seeking relief from his pangs of guilt. For that matter, I'm not really happy about acquitting the arsonist who confessed to a police officer before being given his Miranda warnings. So perhaps my contentment with the limitations on the privileges should be discounted by my view that privileges, as impediments to justice, should be suspiciously viewed and narrowly construed.

My skepticism toward privileges is not a reaction to their odd shapes and exotic distinctions. That might be the expected result of strong and conflicting pressures brought to bear, under some heat, on an essentially malleable principle. Rather, I am acutely aware that privileges are truth-defeating; they operate to withhold some relevant fact from the fact finder. That is their acknowledged purpose. Close to despair over the extraordinary difficulty of twelve strangers arriving at a confident—and correct—conclusion on the issue of guilt, I am loath to keep from them any data that might assist in reaching the right result.

On the other hand, the constitutional right to withhold evidence is rightly deemed one of the defining elements of the form of government we prize. Not because a liberal democracy wants those with self-inculpatory information to escape their just deserts in a court of law. But because in our design of limited government power, we want even criminals to retain sovereignty over their own cognition, to be licensed to thumb their noses at one of society's most important objectives when it threatens to invade the core element of their individual dignity: their minds. That's a pretty impressive tenet.

The subconstitutional privileges rest on somewhat more dubious values. I would not only limit them (as indeed they are) to very few, very special relationships, but I would try to build in many releases that would allow disclosure of confidential, privileged, communications in the interests of what I deem to be values more urgent than their supposed enhancement of candor for a supposedly superior purpose.

Let's start (as California already has) with a rule requiring a psychotherapist to warn an intended victim when a patient makes a credible threat within the therapeutic relationship. It would also be easy for me to penetrate even the sacred attorney-client privilege when disclosure is necessary to prevent the conviction of a falsely accused person. I would even extend that exception to any evidence *tending* to prove innocence. In addition to exceptions for warning future victims and exculpating the innocent, there are times when withholding privileged information just offends plain decency. Not long ago, for example, a community in upstate New York was up in arms when a lawyer refused to disclose his client's account of where he had hidden the bodies of two women he had murdered, for whom a frantic search was under way in the vain hope that they might still be alive.

And I suppose I must admit that, like members of my clan, I would more readily puncture the privilege of shrinks, priests, and even spouses than that of lawyers. It is difficult to imagine a legal system capable of providing criminal defendants with a meaningful defense if every inculpatory word they spoke to counsel could be disclosed to the jury simply by serving a subpoena on the lawyer. One could shrug, I suppose, and say, "Only the guilty would suffer, and to hell with them." But to make defense counsel into listening posts for the prosecution cuts too much ground from under the right to effective representation guaranteed by the Sixth Amendment to the Constitution. And we're not about to repeal the Sixth Amendment.

I must curb my rhetorical zest. There's no profit in indulging in a polemic on the fair configuration of subconstitutional privileges. It's a matter of bitter dispute between irreconcilable positions, neither of which can be fully supported or wholly refuted. Instead, let me return to our narrative and pursue the tale a bit further.

About a week later, Sam Franklin is returning a few phone calls when his secretary comes in looking worried. Two people who say they are FBI agents are waiting outside. They ask whether it would be convenient for Mr. Franklin to talk with them for a few minutes. No fool, Sam immediately phones Maud Shepherd. But Maud is out, and Sam, rather than appear to have something to hide, decides to see the agents. After all, he can always end the interview and throw them out of the office if it gets uncomfortable.

A middle-aged man and a young woman come in, and Franklin shuts the door behind them. They smile and show him what appear to be official identification papers in black vinyl wallets. Franklin, too nervous to read them, nods and accepts their credentials. The older man does most of the talking.

"Nice office you've got here, Mr. Franklin," he says.

"Thank you."

"Good of you to see us," he says. "Barging in on you like this."

"Not at all," says Franklin. "What can I do for you?"

"Well," says the agent, looking a bit embarrassed, "The name of your company came up in an investigation we're on, and we just thought you might be able to clear up a few small points."

"I'll try," says Franklin.

"Let me see," the agent says smiling with momentary confusion. "Last year, around this time, you had a piece of a deal involving a shopping mall called the Madison Market Place, about three miles out of Madison, right?"

Franklin hesitates.

"So far, this is all public record," the agent says reassuringly.

"Yes," says Franklin. "I was involved in a small way in that proposal."

"And you knew, I suppose, that a major share of the financing was coming from Madison Equity. Am I right?"

"Yes, I'd heard that," Franklin says. "Anything illegal about that?"

"Just asking, Mr. Franklin. We're not trying to suggest anything. Do you know an individual named Harry Bellman?"

"I know him. He's not a friend of mine, but I know him."

"Could you tell us a bit about his involvement in the Madison deal?"

Sam obliges and so it goes. Franklin finds himself confirming, denying, explaining more than he thought he would. His caution gradually evaporates and he supplies the agents with information that ultimately proves damaging to his claim of innocence. After they leave, friendly handshakes all around, he feels like a fool. How could a smart operator like him get suckered into a conversation like that—with the FBI!

Three weeks later, the same two agents are back. This time their manner is quite different. "Mr. Franklin," the older one announces, "You have been indicted by the grand jury. I have a warrant for your arrest." He hands Franklin a sheet of paper. Franklin can't read it, his hands are shaking too much. He hands it back. "You may consider yourself under arrest."

"May I make a phone call?" Franklin asks, his mouth suddenly dry.

"You will have an opportunity to make three phone calls from headquarters. For now, I think it is best if you took your coat and came with us. We do not want to take you out in handcuffs."

Franklin takes the hint and accompanies the agents without protest. There is no conversation during the ride to FBI headquarters. Once inside and seated in the interrogation room, Franklin is addressed by one of the agents. "Now please listen carefully, Mr. Franklin." Then, pulling out a small card, the agent reads as follows:

"You have the right to remain silent. Anything you say may be used in evidence against you. You have the right to counsel present with you during any interrogation, and if you have no funds to retain counsel, a lawyer will be provided for you free of charge. Do you understand what I have said?"

"I understand."

"What do you want to do? Will you answer questions now without a lawyer present or not?"

"I have nothing to say," Franklin says.

"Does that mean you refuse to answer questions?" the agent presses.

"That's right," Franklin says.

"OK. There's the phone. No more than three calls, and no long distance please."

Franklin calls his wife, his lawyer, and his office. Because there is an agent within earshot, the conversations are brief and cautious. "Be calm," someone at his attorney's office tells him. "Keep your head, answer no questions till Shepherd gets down there. She'll be there as soon as possible." The hours pass. Late in the afternoon, an agent whom Franklin has never seen before comes in and sits across the table.

"I just thought you'd like to know," the agent begins, "we've been talking to Harry Bellman down the hall. He says you are involved in a whole different deal, a shopping mall in Independence. In fact he says you were the center of this scam. That you brought in the others, it was your baby."

"What?" Sam exclaims.

"Wait a minute," the agent interrupts, before you say anything, I want to read you your rights again." He produces the card and reads. Sam listens impatiently.

"Yeah, I know, I know. I was just told all that."

"So what do you want to do now?"

"I'd like to tell you my side of the story. Bellman doesn't know what he's talking about. He's just trying to get himself out from under."

"OK, you'll get your chance," the agent says, showing Franklin his palm, fingers up. "But first you'll have to sign this waiver form." He pushes a printed page across the table. "It says you agree to talk to us without your lawyer." Franklin glances at it, signs, and says to the agent, "All right, suppose you begin by telling me what that miserable bastard has told you about me." The conversation proceeds from there.

In fact, the agent is lying to Franklin. Bellman has never said the things the agent now relates to Franklin. But the ploy works. In the course of heatedly denying Bellman's putative accusations, Franklin furnishes the agent with enough acknowledgments and false denials to strengthen considerably the prosecutor's case against him. In the course of his earnest efforts to convince the agents of his honesty, Franklin several times says, "I told my lawyer the same thing. You can check with her."

Now, how will these clever probes into the suspect's cognition survive challenge in court? Can the government get away with all this? Can they use the words of Sam Franklin against him without trashing the Constitution? And may they add insult to injury and call Maud Shepherd to the witness stand at trial to testify to the damaging things her client told her on the grounds that Franklin waived his attorney-client privilege in his final conversation with the duplicitous agent?

This is my cue to tell of the long and colorful history of the famous, or infamous, decision in *Miranda v. Arizona*. It is an oft-told tale, and quite possibly—unlike Hamlet's—these issues are not immortal. Still, it has a vast progeny and has become an integral part of the jurisprudence of privilege. And, if you haven't heard it before, it's not a bad story. Like all good cultural legends, it has as many versions as there are tellers. This is mine.

It all begins with the proud boast that ours is an adversary, not an inquisitorial, system of justice. The very word *inquisition* is surrounded with taboo. It connotes horrors like the Spanish Inquisition of the late fifteenth century, or the British period of brutal religious persecution symbolized for us by the Star Chamber. Inquisition is inextricably linked in our cultural mythology with physical torture. Can you say the word "inquisition" without immediately associating to the words "the rack and the screw"? In fact, modern western European criminal justice is, for the most part, inquisitorial. It has not aroused the interest of the Human Rights Watch. But the evolved version that prevails today does not still our deeply ingrained hostility to the idea.

Basically, what we mean by an adversary system is one in which a suspect is never regarded as a primary source of evidence, where the state gathers its evidence elsewhere and presents it against a well-defended, fully informed defendant who has an opportunity to challenge it vigorously in an open forum before neutral fact finders—the lay jury—who decide whether it amounts to sufficient proof to convict.

The stage is set for *Miranda*'s entrance by the realization that ours is not a purely adversary system. It has a highly visible adversary component when the case reaches the courthouse, what one commentator has called the Mansion of Justice. But in the Gatehouses of Justice—the police precinct houses, or, for that matter, in the field—the state has inquisitorial access to the mind of the defendant. Forget about lawyers, formal accusation, confrontation by accusers—just the cops asking questions, seeking evidence from the suspect herself. Barring physical abuse or the threat of it, no one thought that even intense police interrogation of a suspect under arrest compelled his responses. For most of our life as a nation, the Supreme Court, too, ignored this inquisitorial window. When the Court eventually focused on the word "compelled" in the Fifth Amendment, they took it beyond physical force or intimidation to encompass psychological compulsion as well.

Supreme Court Justice Arthur Goldberg was the first to express concern about the inquisition in the station house. In his ill-fated opinion for the Court in *Escobedo v. Illinois,* he spoke of the "focus of suspicion" that could convert a station house interrogation into an accusatorial proceeding at which a suspect is entitled by the Sixth Amendment to the assistance of counsel. What Goldberg sold the Court was a half-baked idea that would have transformed some station house interrogations—though not all—into adversary proceedings. Meaning, of course, that they would be precluded because no lawyer would permit his client to submit to questioning in that setting (as the Supreme Court itself, in a burst of candor, once acknowledged). At the same time, Goldberg tried to preserve some opening of the inquisitorial window. The result: as the police conversation with suspect approached confession—and suspicion began to "focus"—the window would be slammed shut. The short-lived holding of *Escobedo* led to some bizarre lower-court decisions, as judges tried to determine just when suspicion had "focused" sufficiently to require that a lawyer be provided for the suspect.

This foolishness could have been avoided easily had Justice Goldberg and the Court taken the idea of the Sixth Amendment seriously. Doctrine will readily support the view—which accords with common sense as well, for what that's worth—that a person under arrest becomes officially "accused" as that term is used in the Sixth Amendment. In that status, a person is entitled to the assistance of counsel at all critical stages—of which police interrogation is doubtless one. The virtue of doctrinal coherence is, perhaps, offset by the consequence of a virtual end to confession evidence. Understandably, the Court would not go the distance.

Then, in 1966, when Ernesto Miranda's case reached the Supreme Court in a group of four unrelated cases, Chief Justice Earl Warren had another idea. Somewhere (I imagine) he had run across the British "Judge's Rules," a set of administrative directives to the Metropolitan Police that, upon arrest, they should inform prisoners according to a certain script set forth in the Rules. This was neither a judicial nor parliamentary edict, and no exclusionary consequence was specified. In *Miranda v. Arizona,* the Chief Justice painted the British Judge's Rules—only slightly modified—into the center of his masterpiece of creative constitutionalism.

In a long, elaborate opinion, Warren, writing for the Court, set forth his reasoning. Custody, the majority held, was inherently coercive. A person held against his will in a police-dominated atmosphere would feel a certain apprehension—even in the absence of explicit threats—that he had better render what is demanded of him or suffer unknown ill consequences. Even if what was demanded was self-inculpation. Thus, arrest itself amounts to coercion, and any statement taken by police interrogation from a person in custody is "compelled" in violation of the Fifth Amendment.

So far, so good. Those who still think of coercion as heavier intimidation might quarrel with this liberal construction of the concept, but there is a certain undeniable logic in the idea that police custody implies some loss of the option to resist. But the Court's theory, rigorously applied, threatened once again to obliterate all confessions obtained from suspects in custody. To be sure, the Court would have to refine the terms *interrogation* and *custody* (which they have since done), but once those elements are established, the confession would be out.

Virtually all confessions are obtained by police interrogation of suspects under arrest. Again, the Court was looking down a long dark road of criminal prosecutions without access to confession evidence. And again, at the last moment, they could not accept the product of their own logic. They swerved at the brink and found a miraculous release for the consequence of their own theory: the British Judge's Rules!

This litany (in the American version, the one that Franklin heard in our story), solemnly intoned at the appropriate moment by the police themselves, would purge the atmosphere of its inherent coercion and allow the suspect to make a free and voluntary election whether to cooperate with his interrogators or not. And after an express waiver of the rights read to him, the suspect in custody could make a free inculpatory statement in response to interrogation. The Chief had rescued American society from a confession-free, totally adversary system of prosecution while at the same time creating the illusion of the truly voluntary confession.

No one really knows the results of this ingenious piece of judicial sleight of hand. There are some who say that it has made no difference whatever in the rate at which foolish suspects contribute to their own convictions. Which, of course, would suit many of us just fine. Others say a certain number of confessions are lost—and with them, convictions of the guilty—by the arousal of caution induced by the warnings. Most people I have spoken to say the warnings have become largely an empty ritual, embarrassing to cops and superfluous to suspects.

From my limited experience, I suspect that, except for the rare cases of outright brutality or the threat of it, most confessions are not produced by custodial pressure to confess—and few ever were. Most confessions either result from overwhelming remorse (as in family or lover killings) or boasting, or else they begin not as confessions at all but as misguided attempts to talk oneself out of trouble. These adventures in outwitting the dumb cops sometimes run into unexpected contravention, necessitating changes in course that occasionally end up with an unavoidable surrender.

The Supreme Court, while adhering to the general principles of *Miranda* through the years—and (surprisingly) through the changes in its membership—has performed a piece of surgery on the Fifth Amendment that manifests disdain for constitutional principle as much as disillusion with the doctrine it created. In 1974, in *Michigan v. Tucker*, the Court announced that its *Miranda* rule was not founded in the Constitution but was a mere "procedural safeguard" to protect the constitutional right against compulsory self-incrimination. Violations of the Fifth Amendment itself (distinct from violations of the *Miranda* rule) were still the old-fashioned type of overwhelming physical or psychological pressure. This detachment of *Miranda* from its Fifth Amendment underpinnings is fine as a matter of principle if the Court decrees observation in federal courts only. They can do that without authority in the Constitution. But the Court is without jurisdiction to impose the dogma of *Miranda* on state and local police (as it continues to do) without a clear constitutional predicate. It's enough to shake your faith.

How, then, shall we apply the *Miranda* doctrine to our story?

In his first conversation with the FBI agents, Franklin was not advised of his right to remain silent or to have his lawyer present. He evidently understood that he had those rights, however. Does his sophistication in the matter of constitutional entitlements excuse the agents' failure to deliver *Miranda* warnings? Not at all. The Court has made it clear that even an arrested detective who has read the warnings dozens of times to suspects, even a professor of constitutional law is entitled to hear the advisory from his or her interrogator.

The obvious reason for the blanket rule is to save the trial courts the nuisance of inquiring in each case what the particular suspect's level of understanding happened to be. There is a deeper reason. In most cases today, suspects about to undergo questioning are well aware of the substance of the ritual warning. They have heard it on TV, in movies, and in many cases on their own prior arrests. The purpose, then, is not to educate but to assure the suspect that the police officer knows the limits of his own authority and is prepared to honor them. From that assurance the suspect may derive a bit of courage to refuse cooperation.

But the blanket rule does not cover all conversations—even when conducted, like this one, in an interrogatory mode—between police and suspects. "Compelled" is still the operative word in the constitutional prohibition, and "custody" is the *Miranda* Court's translation of that term. Was Sam Franklin in custody when he gave his first harmful replies? Courts have wrestled mightily with this one. Under arrest, in handcuffs, behind bars in a holding pen, that's easy. But not long after *Miranda* was decided, in a case called *Orozco v. Texas*, the Court made it clear that they meant more than that. A suspect alone in his own bedroom, asked three questions by two cops, was deemed by the Court to have been in custody for purposes of *Miranda*. The setting, they felt, gave rise to a sense that the suspect was, however briefly, under police control.

Was our hero, Franklin, in his own office, under the impression that he was not in control of the interview? Perhaps we should ask him. But, of course, trying to exclude his improvident statements, he will now say that he felt severely constrained by the agents' presence. If we ask the agents—as courts frequently, irrationally, do—whether they considered the suspect in custody, whether they would have stopped him if he had attempted to leave, we can guess their answer. But it is irrelevant. As I have already explained, custody is in the mind of the prisoner (the *reasonable* prisoner, that is), not the custodian.

My guess is that in our scenario, most courts would conclude that there was nothing in the interview to suggest constraint, that Sam Franklin understood that he could terminate the interview at any time, and all things taken together, this was not a police-dominated situation calling for *Miranda* warnings. And since there was obviously none of the old-fashioned sort of coercion, the statements would be admitted in evidence.

In the next encounter, the FBI agents (as they invariably do) delivered the warnings letter perfect. Lying as they did so, of course, as they—and all law enforcement officers—always do. The fourth part of this familiar quatrain, remember, promises that if the suspect elects to have a lawyer with him during questioning and lacks the funds to hire his own, some J.D. "will be provided." To the extent that this promise conveys the impression that the interrogating officer will go out and, by appropriate incantation, cause a competent, dedicated attorney to materialize to assist the suspect, free of charge, during the interrogation, it is wholly false. None of the hundreds of thousands (millions, maybe) of agents and cops who have faithfully read warnings to suspects in the decades since *Miranda* has had the slightest intention of doing such a thing—or the remotest idea of how it might be done—and none of their prisoners believed for a moment that it would be done. Any prisoner who elected to have the free assistance of appointed counsel during interrogation would simply find that the interview was terminated.

In our case, Franklin elected not a conference with his counsel but silence. As we will see, this choice—which has the identical effect of terminating the interview—was significant. When Franklin declined to waive his right to silence, agents asked no more questions. At this point, only the suspect himself may revive the conversation. By an unsolicited expression of willingness to talk, the suspect may, in effect, cancel his own prior assertion of his constitutional right. The only question—not yet definitively decided—is: if the prisoner does initiate a further exchange, are follow-up questions by police allowed without repeated warnings and an express waiver?

The next conversation in our case was elicited by a new agent on a new matter after repeated warnings and a waiver. Now here comes one of the nastiest twists in the doctrine, which demonstrates how far the Court has strayed from the precincts of reality. If Franklin had responded to the first advisory by saying, "No, thanks. I choose not to talk to you until I talk to my lawyer," or words to that effect, he could not be reapproached until he had had the conference he requested. And the rewarning and waiver would be meaningless. "[I]t is inconsistent with *Miranda* and its progeny," the Supreme Court intoned in 1981 in a case called *Edwards v. Arizona,* "for the authorities, at their instance, to reinterrogate an accused in custody if he has clearly asserted his right to counsel."

But having said instead, "No, thanks. I choose not to talk to you, period," the prisoner may revoke his decision upon a rewarning. At least with regard to a new matter. Here are the words of the Court in 1975 in *Michigan v. Mosely:* "[A] blanket prohibition against the taking of voluntary statements or a permanent immunity from further interrogation, regardless of the circumstances, would transform the *Miranda* safeguards into wholly irrational obstacles to legitimate police investigative activity, and deprive suspects of an opportunity to make informed and intelligent assessments of their interests. Clearly, therefore, [no passage] in the *Miranda* opinion can sensibly be read to create a *per se* proscription of indefinite duration upon any further questioning by any police officer on any subject, once the person in custody has indicated a desire to remain silent."

The weight given to the *form* of refusal to be interviewed is vastly out of proportion to its significance to the prisoner. The button pushed of the several offered, the precise form of words used by the suspect to signify his wish to be left alone with his thoughts, is surely a matter of small consequence and less purpose to him. Moreover, as demonstrated in a 1993 dissent by three Justices to the Court's refusal to hear an appeal on this subject (one vote shy of the number required to grant certiorari), the differential rule is causing considerable confusion in the lower courts when the choice of counsel is less than clearly explicit. These are the exasperating, stupid smudges that make one doubt the integrity of the line: can police renew a conversation with a prisoner, for example, after he has said, more to his muse than his interrogators: "I wonder if I should run this by a lawyer"?

So, having obtained a good waiver on the new matter, the agent obtains incriminating statements from Franklin. But he does so by deception. The oldest ploy in the books, and still one of the best: your buddy ratted on you. Here, too, the Court has sliced the doctrine much finer than most practical people find sensible.

The legitimacy of deception appears to depend upon when it was employed. If the waiver was obtained by trick, it is probably null; if the confession was obtained by trick, it is probably good. Does this sound like a distinction crafted by cloistered medieval monks debating scholastic dogma? I once had trouble convincing a seasoned police detective that our own Supreme Court really came up with this one. But there it is. The opinion in *Miranda* itself says the waiver is meaningless if the prisoner was "threatened, tricked, or cajoled." But if the waiver is properly obtained, nothing in the doctrine precludes interrogation by deception short of such as might induce an innocent person to confess (a feigned threat to involve a family member, for example, or a promise to tear up the complaint on receiving a confession). The old trick employed in our case would hardly procure a confession from an innocent suspect; you might call your allegedly faithless buddy a liar, but you wouldn't confess to a crime you never committed.

Finally, the government might try to get Maud Shepherd to tell the jury what her client had disclosed to her on the grounds that Sam Franklin had waived his privilege by telling the agent what he had told his lawyer. This is a small but annoying glitch in the attorney-client privilege.

Like all privileges, this one may be waived. And the waiver need not be formal and express. One good index of implied waiver is some indication that the holder does not wish the communication to be confidential. So when the client fully and truthfully reveals the words spoken between him and his lawyer, it may be fair to say that he has voluntarily lifted the curtains of privilege and made the lawyer an ordinary witness.

The hard cases are mainly of two sorts, and on these neither courts nor commentators have spoken clearly. The first is the case where the client speaks publicly about the same *matter* as he conferred about with counsel without recounting the *conversation*. Some think that by discussing the subject, the client implies that he has no secrets in the matter. Unfriendly as I am to privileges in general, this seems wrong to me. Even assuming (a large assumption) that my unprivileged statement is true, I am not relinquishing my wish for secrecy regarding those details that I revealed to my lawyer and have carefully omitted from my public statement.

The other hard case is where the client, referring to conversations with counsel, purports to reveal at least some of the words that passed between them. First, there is the question of whether the client is actually recounting his conversation with his lawyer truthfully. If he is just dropping in false and gratuitous allusions to bolster his present assertions—as Franklin appeared to be doing—he has hardly signaled abandonment of confidentiality. How is the trial court, offered Shepherd's testimony, to know whether Franklin's earlier comments to the agent were a true relinquishment of privilege or a mere rhetorical gambit? (I see no way.)

Second (and more to the point), even if truthful, should some selected disclosures operate to cancel the privilege on all related topics? Hard, hard, I mean *hard* question. We do have some parallel authority. Addressing waiver of the privilege against self-incrimination, courts have said that any voluntary disclosure of any part of the inculpatory matter deprives the witness of the privilege with regard to any other part. Even if the answer was not in itself inculpatory. I call it *anticipatory waiver*. An answer to the question, "Did you ever have dinner with a man named Frank Felon in March of last year?" may preclude the assertion of privilege to the next question, "Wasn't the purpose of that dinner to arrange for a bribe to the commissioner of markets?" So if Sam Franklin told the agent that he had told his lawyer that he never had any dealings with Harry Bellman, Maud Shepherd might be released to testify not only that Franklin told her he had dealt with Bellman but also what those dealings were.

On the other hand, those who love the attorney-client privilege (and that includes most lawyers and judges) would be loath to give the waiver such broad scope. Intent of the holder, they would say, is the key. And the inference from partial disclosure to total abandonment is unreasonable. Maybe so. Parallel authority never was the most persuasive kind.

Before closing the chapter, perhaps I should say a few more words on the subject of confession. The basic outlines of the doctrine that we can derive from the Constitution have already been related. But for most of us, the law has left the subject in an awkward posture. When it comes to confessions, we—like Chief Justice Warren—are deeply ambivalent. Prosecutions strengthened by confession would seem to figure mostly in cases against the weak, ignorant, and friendless. Why would anyone else confess to a police agent? Those defendants wise or fortunate enough to have lawyers on call, or even to know of the enormous benefit they would receive just for asking for counsel, enjoy an advantage that appears wholly inconsistent with basic paradigms of equal justice. Plus, even without explicit threats or false promises, there is something about the inquisitorial probe of the isolated and helpless individual that rankles our liberal conscience.

The remedy for this inequality and the offensive spectacle of the inquisitorial interrogation of the solitary suspect is not hard to find. All but spontaneous confessions could be banned from evidence as irretrievably coerced under the Fifth Amendment (a conclusion toward which the Supreme Court seemed headed). Or, as I have suggested, the moment of official accusation could be advanced to the point of arrest and the attached right of counsel decreed unwaivable except in the presence of counsel (as some local jurisdictions have elected to do). The effects of both options are virtually identical. No lawyer will permit a client to waive his right to counsel during police interrogation, and no lawyer will allow the client to say anything inculpatory in such an interview. So providing an unwaivable right to counsel is tantamount to prohibiting interrogation.

Looking boldly at the prospect of a law enforcement landscape stripped utterly of confession evidence, we cannot suppress a shudder. How many horrible, vicious crimes we remember that could not have been prosecuted without the confession of the felon—unsolved serial murders, brutal rapes. Imagine a particularly vicious culprit under arrest, who gives a full and voluntary confession, which is verified by checking out its details. But the culprit is released by the court when the confession is thrown out as having been implicitly coerced or delivered without the guiding hand of counsel. Public anger would be so intense, I can see the return of the lynch mob. Or, if police simply adapt to the new dogma and abandon all attempts to get an acknowledgment of guilt, we will see a sharp downturn of clearance rates, especially in homicides. It is all very well for liberal courts and commentators to demand that the cops get up off their duffs and go out and find some witnesses or some forensic evidence: let's make these cases the hard way, the adversary way. First, it must be said that the inquisition that produces a confession does not obviate the need for objective evidence. In fact, as I noted, a great many confessions are obtained only by confronting the suspect with the product of arduous fieldwork that convinces him that his position is desperate or by digging up the extrinsic material that refutes the false exculpation the suspect has been trying to sell to his interrogators. Beyond that, where eyewitness or forensic evidence is lacking, the gap in the proof is not, in the main, attributable to sloth; often, evidence of this sort is just not out there.

True, both solutions suffer from the same virus as most constitutional limits on police conduct: they may be defeated by perjury. Cops may testify falsely that the statement they actually obtained by impermissible questioning was tendered as a spontaneous and unsolicited gift. Police perjury is the wild card in all efforts to adjudicate constitutional rights at the trial. Police seeking to convict the guilty, learn—and may not scruple—to testify to a version of events designed to preserve the evidence that they laboriously acquired. The principal remedy for police perjury is courtroom cross-examination and contradiction. And this device—whatever it might otherwise be worth—has been blunted by overuse: today virtually every cop is accused of perjury by the defense (a charge many jurors are predisposed to consider sympathetically). Yet unhappily, the possibility of perjury remains a pervasive factor, and the best we can make of it is to keep it in mind and ignore it simultaneously.

What all this means is that if the law tries to compensate for the inequalities of targets in the inquisitorial phase, attempts to put the poor, dim-witted, arrogant, or frightened captive in the same position as the smart, confident, or counseled suspect, the only course is pretty much to shut this window of opportunity altogether. And that is a very costly move. Some, from a disposition to protect the hapless suspect at hazard or from a strong sense of enforced equal protection, are doubtless ready to pay the price. Like the Court, I am not.

7 The Right to Counsel

Dramatic, Deceitful, and Dilatory Assistance

Popular contempt for lawyers is nothing new. In the seventeenth century the practice of law was prohibited in several colonies, Massachusetts Bay, Virginia, and Connecticut among them. "A base and vile thing to plead for money or reward," proclaimed the Fundamental Constitutions of the Carolinas. Nonetheless, in the late eighteenth century, a criminal defendant's entitlement to "the assistance of counsel for his defense" was included in the basic catalogue of trial rights that is the Sixth Amendment to the Constitution. The meaning of this provision has been the subject of heated debate since.

Let's take a case:

As expected, Senator Stephen P. Hardy has been indicted after a long investigation, charged with a complex scheme of corruption in violation of the racketeering law known as RICO (the Racketeer-Influenced Corrupt Organization Act of 1970). Hardy immediately retains Sylvia N. Meade, a trial lawyer who has made a reputation successfully defending abused women accused of assault or homicide against their companions. She is a flamboyant courtroom performer, a widely read author, and a regular guest on TV talk shows, where she has impressed viewers with her earnest commitment to her clients' cause. Hardy is affected by her sincerity and verve. An energetic and convincing trial performer with an impressive track record—what more could he ask? A lawyer like Sylvia Meade, he thinks, could lend credibility to his case, especially with women (one of his important constituencies).

For her part, Sylvia Meade is very pleased to have Senator Hardy as a client. He is a high-visibility figure in a position to pay a full fee. Although she knows nothing of the devious ways of political corruption and has never even read the statute, much less represented anyone in a RICO prosecution, she is confident that she can handle it. Anyway, she had been feeling lately that she was in a rut, and the opportunity to branch out into white-collar crime—and in a case that would advertise her services in that field—is just the ticket. A thought occurs to her, and she decides to voice it up front.

"Senator, I'm happy to represent you in this matter. But let me put a proposition to you. If you don't like it, just say so. As you may know, I have published articles in the popular press and a book based on some cases I handled. Now it occurs to me that your story might be the subject of a book. I don't say I will write that book, but if you will give me a right of first refusal on your story, I would be willing to adjust my fee accordingly. Of course, you have my assurance that I will not betray any confidences and that anything I say in print—my book or someone else's—will be specifically released by you. How does this idea strike you?"

"Well," Hardy says slowly, "I trust you. So why not? It sounds OK to me."

After a mutually acceptable fee arrangement has been drawn up and signed, Hardy says, "Look here, Ms. Meade, there's something I have to say right at the get-go. Let's face it: I'm up against a vicious media campaign here. The government has been leaking every bit of slander they can find. If this keeps up, I'm convicted without a trial."

"Do I understand you to be saying, Senator, that these stories are untrue?"

"Well, no," Hardy says. "I'm not saying that exactly. Listen, do we have to get into all that at this point? I mean, I'm entitled to a fair trial whether all this garbage is true or not, right? I'm no lawyer, but that seems pretty basic to me."

"Right," Meade says, "but you're not asking me to defend you in the courtroom just now, I take it. You are asking for a defense against the media, right?"

"You're darned right I am!" Hardy says. "If this smear keeps up, I'm finished. It's not enough for me to keep saying I'm innocent. Every two-bit crook says he's innocent. I need someone credible to stand up in front of those cameras and say she believes me. That's where you come in."

"I thought I understood your drift. But before I put my own credibility on the line, I just thought you might want to tell me what the truth is."

"The truth? The truth is that I need a vigorous defense—outside the court-room as well as in it. I'm entitled to no less, right? And you have agreed to give it to me. I want you to be my lawyer partly for your courtroom skill but—I'll be honest with you—partly because you have a high public credibility profile, if you know what I mean. People believe you. When you get up and say 'Believe me, Senator Hardy is innocent, the victim of a political vendetta, and we will prove it in court,' public confidence in me will be restored. At least we'll be playing on a level field when we get to court."

"Well, let me give that some thought," Meade says.

"Another thing," Hardy continues, "I'm not in any big hurry to get this thing tried. I've got my seat in the Senate and I'd rather live under a cloud than a conviction, you understand?"

"I understand," Meade says.

"Well, I just want to confirm this. The word around the courthouse is that you are backed up for about two years. To put it crudely, word is that a notice of appearance filed by you is as good as a two-year adjournment. Is that true?"

"I am very busy," Meade says. "I can't promise you two years, but the case I'm starting next week is about that old. But you should know that I am fighting with judges every day about my commitments. Some of them can get pretty nasty about accepting my affidavits of actual engagement."

"Well, I just wanted to check on that because, as I say, I can use the delay. And I don't suppose the government's case is going to get any stronger with the passage of time."

"That is generally true," Meade says.

What Sylvia Meade does not tell her new client is that some five or six years before, she had a client named Mary Dumont, a woman of about 26, who worked for Senator Hardy for a time. She had come to complain that the sena-tor had made unwelcome sexual overtures on several occasions, touching her in ways she found offensive. Meade and Dumont had discussed the whole situ-ation, and Ms. Meade had learned a good deal about the way in which the senator ran his office, treated his female staff, and kept his financial accounts. Ultimately, after carefully considering her options, Mary Dumont had decided not to press the matter. A short time thereafter, she was able to secure a good position elsewhere. Meade dismisses the thought of disclosing the mat-ter to Hardy; it really has no bearing on her dedication to the case at hand—and bringing it up might impair Hardy's confidence in her and sour the deal.

On the date when the case against Hardy appears on the court calendar, Sylvia Meade files a notice of appearance. She is now on record as counsel to Senator Hardy. On on her way down the courthouse steps, Meade finds a bank of microphones set up and a mob of reporters and photographers waiting for her and her client. It is a familiar scene, and she plays it like the pro she is. With an aside to Hardy, "Just look confident," she takes center stage. "I cannot tell you how it saddens me to see a devoted public servant like Senator Hardy fall victim to political blood lust. A good and innocent man if I ever met one. But you all know what pols are: they must have their ritual slaughter and they think they have found their lamb. Well, we have confidence in the American system, and I tell you now: justice will triumph, the innocent will be set free!" To a barrage of shouted questions, Meade works variations on her theme, earnest sincerity (her trademark) shining in her eyes.

Going over the case with her client, Meade decides that the best defense—indeed, the only defense—is to cast the blame for the irrefutable numbers in the government's case upon Senator Hardy's former campaign chairman, Edwin M. Kurtz. Unbeknownst to Meade, her former law partner had represented Kurtz during the time in question on matters involving financial affairs between Kurtz and the bank of which he was then president.

During the following months, at a succession of court dates, Sylvia Meade rarely appeared in person. Motions were filed in due order, accompanied by lengthy memoranda of law, all prepared by a young associate in Meade's office and filed with hardly a glance from Meade herself. (The associate was becoming quite knowledgeable in RICO law.) Eventually, all the motions were decided, all the pretrial negotiations concluded, and the process of setting a trial date commenced. Meade is an expert on adjournment, and she used all her skill to resist the increasing pressure of the court to begin the trial. Finally, even the elusive Sylvia Meade ran out of escapes and trial began, some eighteen months after the indictment had been returned.

To Meade, a trial is theatre, and before the jury she played all the roles in a drama of her own direction. To the jury she was the ingenue, simple, sweet, innocent. To the judge she was all confidence and righteous indignation. To the prosecutor she was scornful, and to adverse witnesses she flashed aggression and pity, manifest disbelief and moral outrage. Besides blaming Kurtz, Meade's basic strategy was to confuse the government's witnesses, make them appear inept, inconsistent, or forgetful; to give the jury the impression that all the documentary evidence was too complex to be understood; and to suggest whenever she could—though with no support whatever—that the government had fabricated vital evidence.

This strategy was, as near as the presiding judge or the watching press could tell, highly effective. It became apparent to the judge from the outset, however—and shockingly evident to the prosecutors—that Sylvia Meade lacked rudimentary understanding of the law in a RICO prosecution. As the trial progressed, this impression was confirmed over and over. At several points, the judge thought that, for all her posturing, Meade was eliciting evidence that fortified the government case and overlooking opportunities to make points favorable to her defense.

During one long night strategy session with her associate, Meade proposes calling a witness she has kept hidden. "It will be a great moment," she tells her associate. "Really dramatic."

"But," the young associate offers deferentially, "what this witness has to say can only hurt the case."

"I think the witness has something important to add," Meade says. "And don't underestimate the dramatic effect of a surprise witness." In addition, she cannot help thinking, the appearance of the witness will make a great moment in the book.

The witness testifies. Senator Hardy is convicted.

As an indicted person—an "accused" in the language of the Sixth Amendment—Hardy was entitled to the assistance of counsel, which means, essentially, a professional performance characterized by competence, fidelity, and zeal. Reciprocally, these are the basic ethical obligations of the lawyer to the client. Until 1963, not every criminal defendant was entitled to counsel. I find it remarkable that in my professional lifetime, at least one state took the position, "If he's going to plead guilty, what does he need a lawyer for?" And at least one other state would put an indigent defendant on trial for a felony without counsel, maintaining, "We can't afford to pay for counsel for every poor person who gets accused of a felony."

Gideon v. Wainwright (1963) fixed that. Today, we understand that every criminal defendant enjoys the constitutional right to counsel at every critical stage of the prosecution following formal accusation. As we have seen, critical stages may occur outside the courtroom—at lineup identifications, for example, and interviews with police or their covert agents at which some incriminating admission may be elicited. But the core of the counsel clause (the true meaning of the provision, some—like me—would argue) is the promise of professional assistance at the most critical stage: courtroom proceedings. A trained guide to help the lay person through the baffling maze of trial and pretrial procedure, to produce and respond to paper advocacy, to advise on the plea negotiations, to pursue the postconviction reviews, and (most important) to speak for the defendant in court when a trained voice might help his cause.

The hard question is how to recognize a lawyer's performance that falls below the level of meaningful assistance. And the harder question is what a presiding judge should do to assure the defendant on trial the benefits of adequate professional representation. But the hardest question is whether an advocate's full commitment to the tenets of competence, fidelity, and zeal inevitably translate into the worst sort of advocacy: obstruction, aggression, and false sincerity.

Although I assess the competence of attorneys all the time, often bemoaning the ignorance and ineptitude of the run-of-the-mine trial lawyer, I am hard-pressed to define the quality of professional performance that will satisfy the client's entitlement. Sylvia Meade illustrates the major sticking point. She turned in a performance that satisfied the client's expectations, including dramatically "effective" courtroom work, but, to a sophisticated observer like the judge, she was ignorant of the law, examined witnesses ineffectively, and displayed questionable tactical judgment. Plus, she lost. (But let's be fair: the case was a loser.)

On his appeal, one of the points that Hardy (now represented by a new lawyer) will probably raise is the incompetence of Meade, his trial counsel. There was a time when lawyers were reluctant to challenge their colleagues' competence; the next time around, they might be on the receiving end. But the loosening inhibitions of guild solidarity and the goad of competition have changed the picture: such claims are commonplace today.

How will the appellate court look at the issue? The dominant consideration, I can confidently predict, will be expressed in one of two overworked metaphors: "20-20 hindsight" or, more likely, "Monday morning quarterbacking." Behind these weary aphorisms lies the simple disinclination of a reviewing court to label the quality of assistance "inadequate." It's not just image control—though judges do not like to let the public in on their private grievances against the incompetence of the trial Bar. Nor is it entirely the sympathy of fellow warriors—though most judges were once in the trenches themselves. It is not just the reluctance to rate performance by its result— though only the losers appear on the appellate docket, where the issue of incompetence of trial counsel is ultimately adjudicated. Nor is it explained completely by judicial humility in the application of a standard that tends to become no more than: "could I have done better with this case if I'd been the trial lawyer myself?" Courts' well-known aversion concealed behind the customary aphorisms is probably attributable in some small measure to all of the above in combination.

But the overwhelming reason courts are reluctant to tag a lawyer incompetent is uncertainty in the measure of professional skill and the usual ambiguity of the evidence of ineptitude. Meade's theatrical skills, her rapport with a jury, her instinct for the best way to embarrass a witness—these may outweigh her weak grasp of the governing law. Judges are often appalled by the ignorance of lawyers who regularly win tough cases with juries. There is a certain mystery in rhetorical prowess. The magic of a confident bearing and an attractive manner is often more persuasive than firm control of the evidence and mastery of the formalities of procedure.

The truth is that the trial lawyer's job is so amorphous that skill is almost impossible to calibrate. The same lawyer may be brilliant and insightful in putting in his defense in one case and clumsy and woefully mistaken in another; can a trait like "competence" fluctuate so widely? The best and most skillful lawyer can get into disputes with the defendant that effectively destroy client confidence. Can a lawyer's performance, however pleasing to the judge, be deemed competent if the client has lost all trust in the lawyer's judgment? Then, too, the most learned in the law may be unable to persuade an ordinary jury of the most obvious proposition.

As recently as 1984, in *Strickland v. Washington,* the Supreme Court took its first swing at the question of "actual ineffectiveness" of counsel at trial. The result is disappointing. Justice Sandra Day O'Connor purports to shun specific guidelines and to content herself with the vacuous assertion that counsel's performance must not fall below "an objective standard of reasonableness." The measure of competence remains "[r]easonableness under prevailing professional norms," she writes. She does, however, list specific duties of counsel, including "a duty to bring to bear such skill and knowledge as will render the trial a reliable adversarial testing process."

If that seems an impossibly broad standard, not to worry. The opinion goes on to emphasize that a court should be loath to find a lawyer's representation deficient. "Judicial scrutiny of counsel's performance," Justice O'Connor says in a remarkable sentence applying a constitutional entitlement, "must be highly deferential." Meaning, as she explains, that "a court must indulge a strong presumption" of competence. By this decision, the Supreme Court has ratified the general disinclination to reverse convictions on the appellate assertion of incompetent lawyering at trial. In the four years following *Strickland*, claims of ineffective assistance were sustained by federal courts of appeal in only 4.27 percent of the cases.

Lawyers have also adopted Canon Six of the Code of Professional Responsibility. "A Lawyer," it reads (in solemn initial caps), "Should Represent a Client Competently." And in the more modern version, The Model Rules of Professional Conduct, Rule 1.1 specifies that competence includes "legal knowledge," along with "skill, thoroughness, and preparation." If these codes express a "prevailing professional norm" (as one would certainly think), Meade's first foray into a strange field, in which she knows virtually no law, might qualify as substandard and perhaps even overcome O'Connor's strong presumption of competence. Certainly the explanatory language of the Model Rules seems to advance that theory: "In determining whether a lawyer employs the requisite knowledge and skill in a particular matter," the text reads, "relevant factors include the relative complexity and specialized nature of the matter, the lawyer's general experience, the lawyer's training and experience in the field in question, the preparation and study the lawyer is able to give the matter."

But don't bet on it. The Model Rules go on to take Meade off the hook: "A lawyer need not necessarily have special training or prior experience to handle legal problems of a type with which the lawyer is unfamiliar. A newly admitted lawyer can be as competent as a practitioner with long experience. . . . A lawyer can provide adequate representation in a wholly novel field through . . . the association of a lawyer of established competence in the field in question." The self-schooled familiarity of Meade's associate probably qualifies as "established competence" and rubs off on Meade to qualify her to handle Hardy's case—at least as the codes see it.

Although they call for "punctuality" and condemn useless "delay," there is nothing in the codes or in the Court's definition of competence that specifically recognizes an obligation of counsel to appear for trial when summoned. The criminal defendant has a right enshrined in the Sixth Amendment to a "speedy trial" (by which the Constitution means a prompt, not a short, trial) but no obligation to stand trial at an early date. The relatively few criminal trial lawyers—and especially the handful of sought-after champions—are heavily booked and stretched thin. Like Ms. Meade, they are constantly jockeying court dates and fighting prosecutors and judges for adjournments. And it is generally true that time erodes the prosecution's case considerably more than the defendant's. So, at least for the defendant who is out on bail, a high-priced lawyer whose competing obligations guarantee a long pretrial interval earns part of his fee simply by being otherwise engaged.

Prosecutors are pretty helpless in the battle to start the battle. But judges have some weapons available. For starters, they can order counsel to be present and ready to go on a selected date. And that order—with the threat of a contempt citation to back it up—should preclude voluntary avoidance. Yet judges, boiling with anger over the difficulty of simply getting some notorious lawyer into court on an appointed day ready to start the trial, are somehow reluctant to use the contempt power they have. If I were a judge and I had exhausted efforts to cajole and implore counsel to try the moldering case on my calendar, I think I would devise a draconian contempt penalty that would impose geometrically increasing fines until even the client would beg for the trial to commence. It's easy for me to say; I've never had to do it.

The offending lawyers are full of excuses, of course. If the excuse is that the lawyer is actually engaged before some other judge who also has ordered the lawyer to go forward despite her protests, a contempt citation probably will not stick. It can get pretty frustrating, and I have seen some angry and unseemly battles between judges for the body of some hapless lawyer who committed himself to two courtrooms on the same date. I remember a case in which a state-court trial judge had finally assembled nearly the full cast on the appointed date—prosecutor, witnesses, defendants, and two of the three defense lawyers—only to be informed that the third lawyer was actually engaged before a federal court. When an urgent message to the lawyer to attend at once produced the reply: Sorry, my federal judge won't release me, the state judge blew his top. He got on the phone with his federal colleague; entreaty failed.

"If you don't send that lawyer to my courtroom at once," his honor stormed, "I am sending over two armed court officers to arrest him and bring him here by force!"

"They will be met at the courtroom door," the federal judge replied coolly, "by four armed federal marshals." The Constitution says federal law is supreme; the shootout was averted, and once again the state trial was adjourned.

Apart from the contempt option, a judge might believe that counsel who is too occupied with other matters to give prompt attention to a client's cause is, for that reason, incompetent to represent that person. That brings the vexing question of lawyer availability into the realm of professional ethics and raises the harder question of the presiding judge's ongoing obligation to take immediate action necessary to accord the defendant on trial the competent representation to which he is entitled.

The trial judge has prime responsibility to assure the defendant a fair trial, and, inasmuch as competent representation is part of that right, the judge should respond to indications of incompetence. She might find the manifestation of incompetence in prolonged unavailability. She might also be alerted to it by the lawyer's displayed ignorance of the exceptions to the rule against hearsay or the statutory definition of racketeering. But just what should a conscientious judge do when the alarms of professional incompetence become too loud and insistent to ignore?

The simple answer: relieve the lawyer. While this is not written out in so many words, judges, in their general role as masters of the courtroom, probably have the power to remove lawyers from a case simply by voiding their previously filed "notices of appearance." In practice, this almost never happens—even for the best of reasons—without the application of either the lawyer or the client.

In the case of a lawyer who has been assigned to an indigent defendant, the main consideration is the inconvenience of introducing a new lawyer into the case and getting him up to speed. Only if a new start or other substantial delay is required for new counsel to take over effectively would a judge be inclined to deny the client's plea. When the lawyer requests relief, it is only slightly more sticky. Judges are not heedless of a trusting relationship that may have developed between a defendant and assigned counsel, but the person without funds to retain a lawyer acquires no vested interest in any particular attorney. Just as the court is not bound to assign a particularly requested lawyer in the first place, the trial judge has broad discretion to grant the urgent request of an uncomfortable assigned lawyer.

But it is a rare case in which the court (*sua sponte*, as lawyers say) will relieve counsel over the protests of both lawyer and client. It would take a compelling reason. Does what appears to the court—midtrial, let us say—to be incompetence amount to such a reason? Perhaps the judge gets the impression in the argument of some legal point that the lawyer is not familiar with the law on the subject, perhaps the lawyer makes a tactical call that the judge feels bodes ill for the defense, perhaps the court is exasperated with the lawyer's habitual tardiness and requests for adjournment—do these amount to a failure of fundamental professional responsibility such that Justice O'Connor's presumption falls and the lawyer should be discharged despite his and his clients professed satisfaction with their relationship? It's a tough call.

I have been talking of cases where the lawyer-client relationship has been made by the court by the assignment of counsel to the indigent defendant. Where the defendant has chosen and retained the lawyer, things get even murkier. As recently as 1989 the Supreme Court, with a little jolt to the Equal Protection Clause, recognized a somewhat stronger right to the services of a particular lawyer on the part of those defendants of financial means. I had frequently heard it said that a defendant has a constitutional right to counsel of choice. This baffled me. The only source for the right is the Sixth Amendment and that promises the assistance of a loyal, diligent, and faithful lawyer—but not counsel of one's own choosing. The right to choose counsel implies a duty on the part of lawyers to represent any client who seeks their services, and no lawyer would concede any such ethical obligation.

Then in a group of cases decided in the late eighties, the Supreme Court appeared to concede some right to counsel of choice—at least if you could pay the fee. In *Drysdale v. United States* and its companion, *United States v. Monsanto* (1989), Justice Byron White articulated a presumption in favor of the lawyer selected by the defendant. But in both cases, the Court went on to find that the entitlement—such as it was—did not preclude the government seizure of the defendant's funds that would otherwise go to pay counsel fees. One year before, the Court had overridden a similar claim of denial of counsel of choice when it found that a potential conflict of interest was sufficient to disqualify the chosen lawyer, notwithstanding the defendant's willingness to waive the impediment.

So I conclude that, because Sylvia Meade was the choice of a defendant who was paying her fees, the judge would need some really good reason to force her off the case, but the O'Connor-White presumption of entitlement would probably yield either to the exigencies of calendar control or the judge's perception of professional ignorance. Which suits me just fine. I am more inclined to the rigorous enforcement of professional standards in this beleaguered profession than I am to honoring the wishes of a defendant to be represented by a maladroit lawyer. And I am even less sympathetic to the marginal lawyer's claim to the opulent fees that defendants of this sort can pay from their illegally acquired war chests. But if the judge in our case is anything like the rest, Meade is unlikely to be removed.

There must be many judges who share my impatience with the blathering argument and vacuous showmanship of incompetent trial lawyers. Their motivation and obligation to intercede are high. Why do so few exert their powers to remove a lawyer like this from a case?

As near as I can tell, their reasons are several but their policy is ill-formed, for few have thought through the problem—vexing and common as it is. There is, first, the ordinary disinclination of a judge to interfere in the relationship between a defendant and his or her lawyer. It's hard enough to get them all paired up without predictable personality clashes, conflicts of interest, and hopelessly overlapping engagements. Once matched, the judge hates to see them split over tactics, fees, or a host of other disputes that can sever this delicate relationship. Judges, wisely, do not really want to know what goes on between lawyers and their clients. And to start asking questions relating to the professional performance of counsel may be to sow the seed of distrust that will eventually pollute the relationship.

Prompt response to indications of incompetence during trial has other hazards. If a judge relieves counsel early in the trial, the new lawyer may be able to continue with only a brief postponement to get into the case. But with some trial time under the bridge and a few prosecution witnesses already excused, there's no way a new lawyer can simply pick up the oars and row on. That means a mistrial and a new start. Further delay, additional scheduling conflicts, and all that precious trial time down the drain. Can that reluctant prosecution witness be persuaded to come and face another bout of bruising cross-examination from another, more skillful lawyer? A judge finds many reasons for not intervening at the first—or even the third or fourth—sign of the incompetence of defense counsel. Maybe, the judge hopes, the lawyer will shape up, maybe he has something up his sleeve, maybe the jury loves him in his bumbling, ignorant way. Let's just watch and wait.

Then, too, many judges respect the outcome as a measure of competence.

They are loath to relieve a lawyer who may win an acquittal for the defendant. Waiting to see the outcome and dismissing the incompetent only after a verdict of guilty—ordering a new trial with new counsel—is to put the jury through the agony of deliberation knowing that the verdict of conviction will become an instant nullity. That's hardly fair to the jury. And the burden on the prosecution and the prosecution witnesses is that much greater than they would suffer from a prompt mistrial. The deferred mistrial on grounds of lawyer incompetence has little to recommend it.

But the major problem is of a different order. If neither the defendant nor the lawyer requests it, the court must act on its own initiative. To leap in and relieve this fool before he does any more damage is to vouchsafe the right of the defendant to the assistance of a competent trial lawyer—an obligation the conscientious judge must take seriously. But the judge knows the risk of stopping the trial without the motion or consent of the defendant. If no substitution of counsel is possible without a fresh start, then when the prosecutor tries to move the indictment to trial a second time, the defendant will hustle up to the appellate court and claim that the first trial judge had wrongly perceived counsel's work as below par. And if the trial judge's judgment of "manifest necessity" is not shared by a majority of the reviewing court, the principle of double jeopardy will preclude a retrial. The defendant will walk away. And, taking full account of the uncertain boundaries of competence—and the vagaries of appellate judgment—many judges appreciate the serious risk of aborting the trial even on what appears to them to be evident incompetence.

The net result of the trial judge's reluctance to look over the quarterback's shoulder is a choice to let the matter go and put the issue before the reviewing court on appeal. Let them fix it. At least if the defendant convinces the appellate court that he got a substandard defense, he won't be able to block a retrial by an assertion of double jeopardy. Of course, the appeal option means that the convicted defendant—possibly suffering consequences of an inadequate defense—waits behind bars for months, maybe a year or more, for appellate relief. And the defense, when it finally gets the issue before the appellate court, is up against that old judicial disinclination to replay the tactical moves of the trial. Appellate judges, working from the cold record at some remove from the trial, are really being asked to do some Thursday afternoon quarterbacking. That status only enhances their reluctance. The claim doesn't fly. Judicial tolerance of lawyer incompetence sits stubbornly impervious, like parental indulgence of the unruly child.

The best response a trial judge can make in this fix, I suspect, is also one of the trickiest to pull off. At the earliest clear indication of an inferior defense performance (assuming, of course, that incompetence is recognizable), the judge should halt the proceedings and explain to the defendant his rights and the concern of the court that he is not receiving his due. Telling him his options fairly, the court should encourage a motion by the defendant *pro se* (on his own behalf) to relieve counsel and substitute a new attorney (with appropriate time for preparation). Skillfully tendered, this advice might produce the request that will allow a midstream substitution or a mistrial without risk of double jeopardy.

Of the ingredients of a full Sixth Amendment guarantee of professional assistance, fidelity lends itself to more ample definition than competence. Lawyers pride themselves in taking the role of "last true friend" to the outcast, the desperate, and the beset. All others may desert you, the whole world may be intent on your destruction (we tell the client) but you can trust me; I alone will stick by you, acting only in your interest, never doing anything to harm you. In addition to the privilege, which reinforces the lawyer's claim of loyalty, lawyers are enjoined to take no interest, financial or other, that might conflict with the interests of the client. Thus, for example, a lawyer may not represent a landlord on one matter and a tenant against that same landlord on another.

Sylvia Meade had two possible conflicts. By taking rights to a book as part of her fee, she might have put her interest in a salesworthy story in conflict with the client's interest in a favorable disposition. The conflict became apparent (to our omniscience, anyway) with her decision to call a witness more for dramatic than for evidentiary advantage. Meade's interest in the book might also have influenced her advice to Hardy about whether to accept a plea bargain. The government might have offered a disposition that would save the senator's honor but kill the publication potential of his story. In fact, the Code of Professional Responsibility directly addresses the question. Disciplinary Rule 5-104(B) is a flat-out prohibition: "Prior to conclusion of all aspects of the matter giving rise to his employment, a lawyer shall not enter into any arrangement or understanding with a client or a prospective client by which he acquires an interest in publication rights with respect to the subject matter of his employment or proposed employment."

Meade's second problem is somewhat dicier. Simultaneous representation of two or more clients with conflicting interests is a fairly simple matter: it's forbidden. Conflict of interest gets only slightly more difficult when clients' interests appear harmonious but may conflict in the future: both spouses in a friendly divorce, two people going into partnership, the buyer and seller of real estate, and so on. The multiple clients must be advised of the potential for conflict, they must consent, and if conflict materializes, the lawyer must withdraw from the representation of both or all.

Our Meade problem is in the category of successive representation. A successful lawyer will represent a great many clients in the course of a career; add in those represented by partners and the number and diversity rises dramatically. One way or another, a new client's life, plans, and business interests are likely to intersect with those of another client, or a former client. The new client may be suing a company whose executive officer is the present wife of a man whom the lawyer's partner previously represented in an ugly matrimonial. A defendant may come to a criminal lawyer who, in an earlier role as an Assistant U.S. Attorney, had prosecuted his new client's business partner. Are such former commitments an ethical bar to present representation? If conflicts between present and former clients are counted as disqualifying, a lawyer must be wary indeed.

The Code of Professional Responsibility, oddly enough, makes no direct pronouncement on the subject of successive representations. But the more recently promulgated Model Rules of Professional Conduct, in effect in many jurisdictions, do address the issue. These Rules provide (and other authorities in other places pretty much agree) that "a lawyer who has formerly represented a client in a matter shall not thereafter represent another person in the same or a substantially related matter in which that person's interests are materially adverse to the interests of the former client unless the former client consents after consultation." Construction of this standard requires some nice judgment on when matters are "substantially related" and what are "materially adverse interests." But I suspect there is little opportunity for judicial musing on these questions. The Rule constitutes merely an advisory to a lawyer that whenever there is a possibility of such a conflict, she should phone her former client, explain the prospective client's position, and obtain the old client's consent to representation. It's a good reason for leaving old clients on good terms.

One small but troublesome issue on which the Model Rules offer no help is how the lawyer is to explain the area of possible conflict to the old client without breaching the new client's privilege of confidentiality. The point of the prohibition on successive representation is that the lawyer owes a contin-uing duty to all clients, past along with present, to keep secrets and hold all communications in strict confidence. The new representation may require the lawyer to reveal or otherwise make use of privileged matters to the detriment of the former client. So one would think that to give true, informed consent to the possibly harmful successive engagement, the first client would have to know a good deal about the new client's case. To supply that informa-tion the lawyer would, it seems, inevitably compromise the privilege owed to the new client. It's tricky.

For obvious reasons, Meade chose to avoid the problem altogether by keeping quiet. Had she called Mary Dumont, her former client, and sought Dumont's permission to represent her former employer and tormenter, her attractive new engagement might well have been torpedoed.

Unlike multiple contemporaneous clients, all do not have to consent to a single lawyer's taking on the possibly conflicting interest. So Meade was under no ethical obligation to inform Hardy of her prior representation of Dumont. This may seem odd. Identifying with a client might well influence a lawyer's attitude toward a subsequent client toward whom the former client bears ill will. Having represented a wife in a bitter divorce, wouldn't a lawyer feel conflicted about taking on the husband as a client in a new matter in which the good faith of the man was critical? And wouldn't Hardy feel uncomfortable if he knew that Meade was privy to all the office dirt—to say nothing of the personal denigration—that his angry former employee had told her? Nonetheless, strictly speaking, Meade was not obliged to disclose her former business with Dumont to her new client. And the quality of her representation of Hardy should not be affected by a breach of ethical obliga-tion to Dumont, if any.

On the separate question of whether Meade committed an ethical offense against Mary Dumont, we would have to wrestle with those nice questions of whether the two matters were substantially related and whether the interests were materially adverse. Although on the face of it, there seems little relation between a sexual harassment complaint and a RICO crime, we would proba-bly have to look behind the face, and there we would find that information learned in the course of one case (the financial operation of the senator's office) might well illuminate the financial aspects of the alleged racketeering. But were Dumont's and Hardy's interests adverse in this respect? Hard to say, but probably not—at least not "materially." So Meade is off the hook.

But it is strange. Meade would be required to make use of privileged information in her representation of Hardy even though his financial interests were not materially adverse to Dumont's. Why should successive representation be precluded in the interests of preserving the lawyer-client privilege only in cases of conflict between present and former clients' interests? Violations of the privilege of confidentiality occur even where there is no demonstrable harm to the client from the breach. The answer is probably that, despite their avowed commitment to the privilege, lawyers want to keep themselves as free as possible to take on new business where there is no actual damage to former clients that can be anticipated from the new engagement.

There is another problem. Meade's partner had represented Kurtz, her selected fall guy. Here is a clearly adverse position on a clearly overlapping matter with no informed release from Kurtz. Is Meade in the same conflicted position as her partner would have been, with all his ethical responsibilities attributed to her by virtue of their former association? On this one, the Model Rules of Professional Conduct also speak. Absent consent of the prior client, a lawyer is to take no new client in a substantially related matter and whose interests are materially adverse to the former client of another lawyer with whom the new lawyer was associated *if* (and only if, the Rule provides) the new lawyer knows of this potentially conflicting situation and the new lawyer herself has acquired from her former partner privileged information delivered by his former client.

That rule seems to put Meade safely in the clear. She did not know of her former partner's connection with Kurtz. Even if Meade had been in a law firm where the names of prospective clients are routinely circulated to discover any conflicts members of the firm may have (or other objections to taking them on), and even if this formal notice overcomes her present protestation that she had forgotten all about it when she took on Hardy, her attack on Kurtz would be ethical because she did not learn of, use, or disclose any protected material acquired by her former partner during his professional relationship with Kurtz. Once again, despite the usual rule of attributed intelligence when dealing with an interlocking organization like a law firm, the rulemakers have construed the privilege to allow ex-partners pretty free rein in developing new clientele from among the clients or adversaries of their former associates.

The duties of fidelity to multiple clients in simultaneous and successive representation gets a nice twist when they are combined. Imagine a lawyer who represents two defendants charged as accomplices in the same crime. Such joint representation, though frowned upon, is allowed on the express wish of the clients after full advice concerning the pitfalls. One client suddenly turns and offers to testify as a prosecution witness against the other. The lawyer should immediately withdraw as counsel for both, but suppose the remaining defendant insists that he wants to keep the same lawyer. Suppose further that the case is very complex and long in preparation, and that a substitution on the eve of trial would derail the schedule and waste a great deal of time. So the judge is prepared to allow the lawyer to remain. May that lawyer now cross-examine her former client on behalf of her remaining client without offense to the lawyer-client privilege?

It is generally said that there is no residual attorney-client privilege once joint clients are estranged. Should they fall out, get new lawyers, and sue each other, either may call their former lawyer-in-common and ask him to disclose otherwise privileged communications made in the course of their joint representation. Another way of putting it is that either may waive the privilege. That would seem to indicate that the lawyer remaining in the case may cross-examine her former client without fear of betraying the privilege, which her present client (formerly one of joint holders of the privilege) has waived.

So it would seem. But the few courts that have passed on this question have appended a cute exception: except, they hold, where the joint representation is on a case in litigation. In such a case (for reasons not immediately apparent), the privilege may not be waived except on the agreement of *all* of the former joint clients. I assume "in litigation" includes cases the lawyer expects will go to trial as well as those actually being tried. Thus, a lawyer who represents two or more defendants in a criminal case (and I would call them all "in litigation" regardless of the current stage of the proceedings) would never find herself in the position of cross-examining a former client on behalf of a surviving client. The former client–cum–adverse witness would not consent to the lawyer's continuing representation of the other, and without the consent of both, she could represent neither.

So our hypothetical lawyer may not remain in the case, despite the urgent wishes of the client (and his fervid waving of the banner of the Sixth Amendment entitlement), because she cannot provide effective assistance when her cross of the hostile former client is hobbled by the privilege. And though the right to representation under the Sixth Amendment may be waived altogether, the right to be represented by an unconflicted attorney may not be waived; it is an element of a fair trial in which the court itself has a vital interest—an interest that supersedes that of the defendant affected. Over the client's objection, therefore, the court will order a substitution of counsel. Strange, is it not?

In addition to the lawyerly duties of proficiency and loyalty, there is the energy factor. Diligence. "A Lawyer Should Represent a Client Zealously Within the Bounds of Law," Canon 7 proclaims. Today, the criminal client seems to expect zeal more on the courthouse steps than in the library, more in the trial than in the preparation for it. A vigorous defense has come to connote the spurious obligations of aggression, public relations, and the earnest espousal of falsehood. True, there *are* some politically motivated prosecutions, overblown indictments, and genuinely innocent defendants, but counsel's predictable declarations of outrage, the confident boasts of vindication, and the on-camera professions of wounded innocence make one wonder whether the criminal defense Bar still clings to any pretense of personal honor.

Several scholars who have written on the question have developed various frameworks of analysis and theories of justification. Some are quite elegant. For instance: individual lawyers should not take it upon themselves to ration access to the exclusive service they provide according to some personal calculus of deserts or theory of social merit. This implies, I suppose, that every client is entitled to the same profession of wounded innocence as the occasional wounded innocent. Another theory: putting the client in control of the conduct of his defense enhances "autonomy" and curtails the elitist tendency to professional arrogance. Thus, I infer, the lawyer shouldn't tell the client the limits of the lawyer's conscientious commitment. It is the client who must always be in charge of the defense, I surmise, with the lawyer offering advice and assisting in the execution of the client's will. Like a good carpenter.

I am skeptical. I think that when a criminal defendant puts his case in the hands of a lawyer, professional control of the defense is more important than egalitarian pretenses of autonomy. I know a criminal defense lawyer of the old school who lays it out plainly to clients at the outset. You get to make three decisions: whether you want me to be your lawyer, whether you will plead guilty, and (if you go to trial) whether you will testify; I decide everything else. That sounds about right to me.

On a more pragmatic level, I have actually dared to take the question to several acquaintances in the defense Bar. "How can you do it?" I asked. "Case after case, year after year. Putting your own integrity on the line for a clientele that is, in the overwhelming proportion, guilty and ungrateful?" Most lawyers do not quarrel with the premise—at least those who know me well enough to be candid. The answers I get almost invariably fall into one of three sorts:

1. It's fun. I've heard a number of variants on this theme. One lawyer was honest enough to confide, "All my life, I've wanted to sass a cop and get away with it. Now I do that almost every day—and get paid for it!" Some are a bit more oblique; they are contrary by nature. They seek to establish their individuality by opposition—often opposition for its own sake. To them, government—and, in particular, its repressive forces—has always been anathema. Representation of an accused felon is not so much working for him as it is fighting against the government. Others have a less political motivation. For these lawyers, the trial itself is a high and representing an accused is a special challenge. The strength of the prosecution case puts the odds where the occasional victory will taste the sweetest. Frequently, lawyers like this make no secret of their contempt for most of the people they represent. They do it not for love of the client, not for hatred of the establishment, but for love of the adversary forum.

2. I do it not for the client, but for society at large: to keep the government honest. While this seems a bit pretentious, the claim of social utility has a certain amount of truth. The right of security protected by the Fourth Amendment, for example, becomes living law because it is invoked on behalf of drug dealers, gun toters, and worse. Police who honor that right stay off the backs—and out of the houses—of law-abiding citizens as well. And that's the way we want it. In the past, and in too many governments today, police notoriously abused their authority and the society as a whole suffered. It is almost entirely owing to the vigorous defense of criminals that we have a constitutionally restrained police force.

3. Do you know any better way to protect the occasional innocent defendant? "Look," one lawyer told me, "at the start, I don't know any more than you do which ones are innocent and which are guilty. My guilty clients generally tell me they're innocent, and for all I know, the innocent say they're guilty. But some—few, perhaps—are truly innocent. And I believe in the American jury system. In the hot light of cross-examination, the liars are usually separated from the truth tellers. So I figure if I try my best to get everyone acquitted, the jury will sort it out somehow." Defense lawyers, despite the common tales of juries gone awry, are great believers in the hot light of cross-examination. It is their stock in trade.

I hesitate to reply, but yes, I think I do know a better way. As I shall expound at greater length in another chapter, I am becoming increasingly dubious of the capacities of the lay jury to sort it out. Even under the hot lights. But I am far from sure. Perhaps the hostile confrontation is the best way to expose flaws in the case, errors and lies in the testimony. It may be that the honest and accurate account stands up best under the pummeling of adversarial examination. No social scientist has yet made a serious study of the question.

But even accepting the premise that truth frequently emerges from the controlled combat that is the American model of a trial, one might question the contribution of lawyers like Sylvia Meade to the process. Unfortunately, most of the lawyers drawn to trial work seem to be enamored with the *production*—the rhetorical game that is the presentation of a case. Few are willing to let the *text* of the case—the facts—speak for itself. The random blows of casual aggression, the tedious and pointless pursuit of minor matters, the posturing and pouting, the hints of evidence never adduced—surely these contributions cannot enhance the accuracy of the jury's judgment. The adversary model works best when the lawyers respect the text above the production.

But there is something in the adversary role that attracts or makes personalities of a distinctive hue. Until women entered the ranks of criminal trial lawyers in significant numbers, I was inclined to attribute the personality associated with the job to an excess of testosterone. Two bucks, locking antlers, pushing and shoving, stamping and growling, until one is declared the winner—that seemed to me the primal paradigm of the advocates' courtroom dance. Reluctantly, I must abandon the image—too simple.

Although there are some similarities between prosecutors and defense counsel, and there is some crossover—a few defense lawyers become prosecutors and some prosecutors follow a short career on low wages working for the state or federal government with a long career defending well-heeled clients—they are basically different types. Both feel truly alive only in the adversary forum, both love to win. The main difference—how to tell them apart in kindergarten—is that the prosecutor has to feel he or she is one of the good guys. A staff of well-chosen assistants, generally younger than their counterparts in the defense Bar, is likely to develop an esprit founded on the shared belief that they are the final—and most trustworthy—repositories of justice in the system. By their lights, judges are often old, inclined to be lazy, and sometimes of doubtful integrity. And defense lawyers, for the most part, are nothing but a pack of hired guns. The eager, idealistic young prosecutors consider themselves the true champions of the hurt, the abused, and the helpless—the victims of crime—and, with their shining "quasi-judicial dis-cretion," they take seriously their obligations to a just result. I glimpse my youthful self in this picture, of course, and for several years as a prosecutor I took my sword and cape to court to meet the challenge of duel-by-jury, trying—not very successfully—to cultivate the role traits of combat courage, fact skepticism, and moral conviction. To the defense Bar, naturally, this attitude translates as arrogance, overlaid on righteous rigidity, and clad in robes of inexperience bordering on hopeless ignorance.

I know these generalizations are overdrawn. But I would go further and describe the prototypical defense lawyer thus: he is an individualist who needs to put his personal mark on every aspect of the case. Where he is not masterminding a complex production of an alternative defense scenario, he is busy spoiling the prosecution—and always in his own style. The defense lawyer, born to the role, is a person who is more concerned with appearances and perceptions than with underlying facts; who puts greater reliance in "personality" (including his or her own) than in knowledge; who has little concern for general public disapprobation despite a high ego investment. Above all, the natural-born defense lawyer is a person for whom challenge is always enticing and an occasional victory obliterates many defeats and vali-dates inordinate labor.

My friends in the defense Bar will protest: "Caricature! Stereotype! Lawyer-bashing!" I'm sorry, but I believe that in a calmer frame of mind even they will recognize the traits in themselves and colleagues. Some few defense lawyers have, from time to time, protested publicly that they represent only the "oppressed," the culturally deprived defendants, the victims of social injustice. Maybe so, but even among this self-styled rescue squad, I have heard little disagreement with the proposition that nearly all their clients are guilty. And I have observed little difference in the personality traits and professional tactics of the defense bar dedicated to the deserving and the undeserving clientele.

I do have a paradigm in mind for the virtuous criminal defense lawyer. In a sense, it is the antithesis of the type I have described, but many lawyers combine traits from both categories. And I think—and I try to teach students about to enter the profession—that the practice of trial law can be an honorable craft if the lawyer can manage to develop this alternative list of characteristics. Some trial lawyers do and, in my opinion, constitute the best of the Bar. Unfortunately, they are not the predominant caste.

Before I propose my model of virtue at the Bar, I hasten to note that I would find it difficult to argue that this virtuous defense lawyer provides more effective counsel to clients or even serves the system better. As I have conceded more than once, it may well be that the most effective defense is provided by a theatrical champion, master of dissimulation and sleight-of-tongue. But I do believe that the virtuous model has certain advantages in the adversarial game. He or she can more easily gain the confidence of judges, for example. A good working relationship of mutual respect with colleagues and adversaries also brings rewards. But the main thing must be a sense of honor, of professional competence, the sort of thing that makes it all worthwhile.

The virtuous defense lawyers I have in mind resist coming to early conclusions. Most of us arrive at an ultimate opinion as soon as respectably possible. We hate unresolved issues—of fact or morality—and we use the faculty of judgment to put the world in order as quickly and firmly as we can. The good lawyer has heard too many persuasive "other sides" and is wary of even the most attractive version without exploring the contrary hypothesis. The best lawyers are also great story tellers. They have a natural (and nurtured) facility to find in discursive accounts or jumbled fragments the inferential links that make them into a coherent story, a narrative that makes sense to people of dissimilar experience and appeals to most people's inherent vein of sympathy.

Gifted trial lawyers are people with an insatiable appetite for detail. However energetically they may try to sell the big picture, they are not broad-brush types at heart. Long after most of us would be nodding over the sixth repetition of peripheral detail, impatient to get to the heart of the matter, the good lawyer wants more. The lawyer knows that trivial detail is the grout of a convincing story. And sifting through the ignored or discarded details may reveal the telltale of truth or falsehood.

Finally, a good defense lawyer must be comfortable with the role assigned by courtroom protocol. There is something artificial about the structure of a trial, and role playing is essential to keeping the structure viable. Lawyers who insist on stepping out of role—to be judge, or witness, or prosecutor—will only succeed in annoying everyone.

In a sense, the criminal defense lawyer is a breed apart. His or her work is among the most taxing at the Bar, and the rewards are few. Occasionally, a lucky defender might acquire a client she would be pleased to have as a friend. Once in a great while, a lawyer may have a case he knows is a grave and false misaccusation. Now and then, a really appreciative client might even materialize. But for the most part, in the quotidian slog, the client claiming the lawyer's devotion is not the sort of person to whom it would otherwise be given.

And the grim practice of giving your all to the vicious, guilty, and ungrateful is rarely lightened by the respect of your peers. Judges seem perpetually on the point of exasperation while your most earnest efforts are met with only polite scorn from the self-righteous prosecutors. Even one's friends and family, I suspect, are faintly embarrassed by the work, their celebration of your rare victories muffled by the thought of the predator you freed prowling his old hunting grounds again.

And I'm sure the feeling of professional isolation is not improved by the appearance of a law professor asking, How can you do what you do?

Perhaps for this law professor, at least, the work of the defense Bar in the adversary system would seem less reprehensible if so many did not feel called upon, as a matter of diligence, to lie for their clients. Or at least to speak without personal conviction. From the pretrial declarations on the courthouse steps to the final arguments before the jury, defense counsel offers unblinking support, earnest or outraged as the occasion may warrant. Is this a market phenomenon? As soon as one lawyer steps up to the microphone to vouch for his client, must all lawyers sell the same service? I do not think this segment of the Bar will persuade the rest of us of their integrity as long as vouching remains commonplace.

Surprising as it may be to courthouse buffs and casual observers alike, the codified ethical imperatives of the Bar—the Code of Professional Responsibility and the Model Rules of Professional Conduct—both provide that a lawyer shall not knowingly make a false statement of law or fact to a tribunal. While that does little to inhibit endorsements like Meade's on the courthouse steps, it should deter the fiction weaving that customarily passes for argument to a jury. If the word "knowingly" is too easily flung around the wholly conjectural, amply refuted assertion, my solution is: let's change the word and enjoin lawyers from making statements they have no good reason to believe are true. I would go further and extend the lawyers' obligation of truth telling to public and professional situations beyond the courtroom walls—but the world is probably not yet ready for so radical a proposal.

It may well be that the ugly side of criminal defense work is ineradicable, generated by the supposed virtues of the adversary mode itself. The role of the advocate demands, supports, or instills the very traits of competitive zeal that generate the sort of lawyering that impugns the detachment of a professional approach.

It's too bad. We need good and committed counsel for defendants: And it would be good to be able to encourage a new generation to enter the field without having to warn them of the demands on personality, the peculiar sources of gratification, and the ethical hazards of the job.

8 Executive Discretion
Hard Choices and the Role of the Prosecutor

Prosecutors have no clients. This is a liberating, even exhilarating, position for a lawyer to be in. Professional decisions are not dictated by the personal, parochial preferences of the client. And prosecutors are rarely shackled by fidelity to objectives they find morally repugnant. Unlike defense attorneys, who are ethically bound to seek the earliest release of even the most dangerous and reprehensible criminals they represent, the prosecutor is enjoined never to prosecute those he believes to be innocent. Here and there, a prosecutor may find herself constrained to prosecute capital cases despite her personal opposition to capital punishment, another to prosecute anti-abortion protesters despite his own "pro-life" philosophy, a third to prosecute a doctor who assists suicide though the prosecutor personally believes in a "right to die." But these are rare and exceptional situations; for the most part, those who seek the post of public prosecutor believe in the penal laws of the jurisdictions they will serve. And the occasional embarrassing case can usually be dealt with in a way to minimize bruises to personal moral compunctions. Generally, the prosecutor is free to cultivate his own conscience and to move in accordance with social principle as he sees it. It's a heady professional prerogative.

At the same time, the judgment of the prosecutor is played out in a very public arena. The prosecutor's choices are the fair game of the community— and its most hostile and widely published critics. Her decisions often have loud political repercussions and she must strive to maintain the boundary between professional and political judgment—a line that too easily becomes indistinct in the smoke of public controversy and the haze of private ambition. The prosecutor will discover that public responsibility—which, in the inflamed imagination of the diligent media extends to everything that goes wrong in the administration of criminal justice—is considerably broader than control. The prosecutor can do little, for example, about police brutality or perjury. But let an instance of one or the other surface in the jurisdiction and the next two questions shouted by the news people will be, "Did the prosecutor know about it? And if not, why not?" Or let a grand jury fail to indict or a petit jury fail to convict some prominent citizen, and the media will soon be sniffing around in the country club records to learn whether the D.A. ever played a round of golf with the suspect.

In exchange for their vulnerable high profile, prosecutors are granted some real power in the system. And except for those few who have been grievously wounded by the slings and arrows of the outrageous media, it's a favorable exchange.

We have abolished the ancient prerogatives of private prosecution in the United States and lodged exclusive authority to commence and conduct criminal actions with the public prosecutor. The prosecutor combines the responsibilities of a lawyer with the authority of a public official. This mix gives him far greater clout than the defense lawyer acting on behalf of a single client. The defense lawyer in a particular case may affect the outcome of the prosecution against her client, may embarrass witnesses, may be hero or villain on the evening talk shows, may make a prosecutor look foolish, and perhaps even redden the face of "the system" itself, but the prosecutor is a major player in the arena of criminal justice. It is the prosecutor who makes the vital choice: who gets charged with what. It is the prosecutor who then takes his case to court as champion of the people of the community, speaks in their name, and wraps himself in the mantle of righteousness.

"In just one year," D.A. Sam Shuster said, "I kick off my campaign for reelection." Shuster was in his first term as District Attorney of Commerce County, a large urban county in a populous state. His bureau chiefs, assembled for their monthly meeting, were not surprised by the announcement that the boss planned to run again. But they were pleased. They were proud of the team Shuster had assembled—proud, that is, of themselves. And they were just beginning to get the feel of the wheel, savor the gratifying rise of confidence. They were ready for more.

"Now I know each of you has done one hell of a job. And as we all know, the waters have not always been smooth and the breeze favorable." Pause for a grim smile all around. "But frankly, looking back over the last thirty-six months, I think my opponent—whoever that might be—will have one word to characterize our performance, and that word is 'lackluster.' And just among us here in this room I don't mind telling you there is some truth in that characterization."

The chiefs shifted uneasily. What was the boss getting at? "Now, I'm not criticizing anyone in particular," he went on. "I have complete confidence in this team. And in many ways, we've done fine. Our dispositions are up and holding steady; I think our pleas have been fair. We've had a couple of tough acquittals, but generally the trial staff has turned out a commendable conviction flow. We got rid of the political deadwood we inherited, and our younger recruits make a good impression for the office: integrity, energy, competence. Not bad for the salaries we pay!" He smiled, counting on the staff to relish the reminder of their favorite complaint. But they were still uneasy. Shuster resumed, "But you probably remember when I ran for this office, I promised action. And action is what I intend to see that the voters get during the next twelve months." He paused for effect, letting the word "action" ring in the air for a moment.

"So," he continued in a lower key, "what I want to do today is hear from each of you what you presently have under investigation, what you have under consideration, and where we can make ourselves felt in this community over the next few months. I know we will all treat this meeting as 'maximum sensitivity,' so let's be completely candid and bring our collective experience to bear. What I want to know is where and when are we going to produce some indictments in major cases." He looked around the room.

Then, with an emphatic gesture, he said, "Now, you all know I don't give a damn what they say about us in the media—we know it's all lies anyway. But they are still waiting for us to produce, and it seems to me they're starting to get a mite impatient. Whatever we think of this tribe of jackals, we have to remember, this is how the public learns about our work, so I have to consider how the case will play on the evening news. Do I make myself clear?" He did. He wanted some high-publicity blockbusters, and he wanted them fast.

"Let's start with you, Tom," Shuster said, looking at Tom Hartanian, the chief of the Commercial Crime Bureau. This unit investigated and prosecuted official corruption and white-collar crime. "Are we getting anywhere with that bid-rigging business on the school security contract?"

Tom shook his head, pursing his lips. "No, Sam. That's pretty much dead in the water at this stage."

"What's your best guess, Tom? Give it to me straight."

"If only we'd been able to keep our snitch productive! I was pretty optimistic. I was only that far from going for some taps," he said, holding up his thumb and forefinger. "But when she clammed, we were out in the cold."

"Why did she turn reticent on you, Tom?"

"Well, Sam, you can only expect so much from someone who comes to you to settle a score. Grievance mongers, I call them. They're just not reliable stools. They are likely to have a change of heart one day, or realize they are getting in pretty deep. So they pull out. I just wish we had something hanging over her head. For a while, I pursued the idea of bringing a charge against her just to keep her honest, but that got nowhere."

"And those Swiss bank accounts?"

"When we finally got ahold of our prime's bank records, we found a lot of suspicious stuff, but all untraceable as far as we could figure out. That left pretty much another big nothing."

"Is the case still alive, Tom?"

"It's still alive, Sam, but frankly, I've had to put my people on some other cases that need attention. I'm not saying we can't make this one, but it's going to take a major effort or some real lucky break. Maybe both."

Shuster swallowed it, nodding his head slightly, then turned to Robert Rosenthal, his chief of the Organized Crime Bureau. "How about it, Rob, any good news?"

"Well, Sam, the biggest pot on our stove is still that video outlet investigation. As you know, I've had the feeling for some time that the mob is trying to muscle into the video business, starting with the porn joints. I still don't have much hard evidence. I'm not even really clear on which gang it is, but I keep getting these hints from here and there all pointing the same way: the next big industry in this county that the mob is itching to get control of is video."

"So far no open moves?"

"Not that we know about, Sam. That doesn't mean that the stores haven't felt the squeeze. I just haven't any specific examples in hand."

"You don't have grand jury on this yet, do you, Rob?"

"Not yet. I don't even know whom to call. No witnesses, no cases. I can't just call every dealership in, get all the books and records. It would be a pig in a poke at this stage. What I really need is a sting, but I don't know whether you are ready to spring for that tab with only my hunch to go on."

"We'll talk about that again, Rob." Shuster now swiveled around and faced Elizabeth Varelli, chief of his Major Crimes Bureau. "Betsy, what can you tell us about that Syrian bomb plot? What's the latest?"

"It's pretty complicated, Sam. I don't know if you want me to go over the whole deal right now. It would take a while, and there are still more than a few black holes in the picture."

"You can spare us the nitty gritty, Bets. What I'd like to know is where we stand at the moment and, if possible, a projection."

"Well, Sam, just going back briefly for those in the room who may not know the background, you remember we got pretty lucky at the outset. We found these two Middle Eastern guys in the Department, one in Consumer Affairs and the other doing deep cover for Narcotics. We named them Mutt and Jeff. They seemed perfect. We briefed them and sent them in. They both managed to infiltrate this Islamic Friendship Federation, where the plot seemed to be hatching. They played the militant, anti-Semitic number beautifully, and before long they were both in touch with the radical cell in the organization. It helped a lot when Jeff told them that his brother-in-law is a mechanic in the Air National Guard and he could get them a pass to the hangars and a diagram of the ignition system of the Air Cobra. That really gave a shot in the arm to their sabotage planning."

"Right, I know all about that," Shuster said. "And what's happening now?"

"Frankly, Sam, right now I'm beginning to worry about Mutt. He's missed two meets with his control, and his info has gotten pretty thin. I'm afraid he may be going over. We got some hints on the last debriefing that he thinks this fringe imam has a point about the American persecution of his countrymen. Not that he's about to blow his cover or put Jeff at risk. That would be stupid—too dangerous. But I don't fully trust him at this point."

"And Jeff, how's he doing?"

"I have a different problem with Jeff just now. This radical cell has decided to go out and do some big-buck stick-ups to finance their operation. They are pressing Jeff to take an active part. It may not be designed as a test of his loyalty, but it sure would wash him out if he refused."

"I can see the problem," Shuster said, "and I'd like to go over it with you thoroughly as soon as we can."

"Let me interject at this point," Rosenthal said. "Have you coordinated this operation with the FBI?"

"Why, no." Varelli replied. "Do you think I should?"

"It certainly seems to me they may have some helpful stuff on this gang. And in any case, don't you think they should know we're into it?"

"I know where you're coming from, Rob," Shuster said. "You had a good relationship with them on that trucking union case. But this is different. We don't need their help at this point and if we brought them in, they'd want to take it over. I'm not sure we're ready to give it up."

Rob backed off. He understood. It's our show and if we can pull it off, we're the stars on the evening news. Sure, why not? That's part of the game too.

This glimpse of the work of Shuster's office reveals a host of discretionary decisions popping through the clutter on the prosecutor's desk. Some he'll worry about, a few may resonate with him in terms of the power of his office and the nature of his mission. Most will be made in the ordinary course— nothing remarkable, just doing the job.

Most obvious, perhaps, is the gravitational pull of the political imperatives on much of the prosecutor's agenda. Prosecutors, state and federal, are either elected directly or appointed by elected officers of the executive branch. A case can be made that the appointed prosecutors—notable among them being the United States Attorneys—are insulated from the tyranny of the electorate. And, although the record of the prosecutor may cast some light or shadow on the reputation of the appointing politician, the ambitions of the latter will rarely depend on the performance of the former.

Thus, there is some truth to the theory that the decisions of the appointed prosecutor may be made heedless of their political consequences—"on the merits." But to have the prosecutor beholden to the chief executive for his job may impair the freedom of the prosecutor to train his sights on the administration of his benefactor or those who support it. And it can also be argued that the prosecutor should be directly answerable to the people, that the delegated authority the prosecutor enjoys should carry political responsibility. Prosecutorial discretion being broad and powerful, our democratic plan demands control. And political control, for all its faults, may be the best device we have to direct the power of government.

So it should be no surprise when an elected local prosecutor like Sam Shuster takes account of the reaction of the news media, chooses targets to please the electorate, even times his prosecutions to coordinate with his campaign schedule. How can we hold our prosecutors politically accountable and then fault them for calculating the effects of their choices on their electability?

Yet I find the political factor in the calculation of discretion to be profoundly offensive, bordering on unethical. The standards governing the professional conduct of public prosecutors enjoin them to act "in the interests of justice"—and that does not mean the justice of their own reelection. Perhaps my revulsion stems from my own experience in the office of a District Attorney who was resolutely oblivious to the political consequences of his decisions. He had a high regard for his constituents, but he believed that they would approve of his own conscientious choices. And they did, reelecting him over and over, unopposed. He was, in effect, appointed by the people rather than elected. His successor has followed much the same course. These D.A.s may be aberrations, but at least they proved that political independence is not necessarily a political liability.

In the relations between prosecutors of overlapping authority, politics of a different sort may be seen. Remarkably, though state and federal jurisdictions cover much of the same criminal conduct, we don't really have a plan for coordination. Odd as it may seem, who gets a case is pretty much a matter of who gets there first. And there are undoubtedly rivalries. There's no pushing and shoving when it comes to trying the street-level drugs sales that violate both state and federal laws; that's a chore. But the high-visibility cases—official corruption, major underworld figures, shocking crimes, celebrity defendants of one sort and another—for these marquee cases, competing jurisdictions may sacrifice the benefits of coordinated effort to reap the rewards of public approbation on their own turf.

More interesting (to me, at least) than the humdrum of politics and publicity in the prosecutor's agenda is the discretionary deployment of the extraordinary techniques of investigation: surveillance and espionage. Here, the prosecutor decides—often on no stronger reed than a hunch—to intrude on the private affairs of a citizen, to watch, listen, and perhaps participate in the hopes of discovering evidence of crime. The ordinary tools of this extraordinary endeavor are deception, betrayal, and ambush.

It would be unfair to describe the mood of the courts with regard to this sort of activity as either enthusiastic or neglectful. But courts have been generally tolerant of such forays. And Sam Shuster would be a strange breed indeed if he felt the slightest moral compunction at the proposals and reports of his chiefs. Serious crimes—judges and prosecutors agree—often occur beneath the surface, producing no waves by which they may be detected. Either there are no immediate victims or those who are injured are, for one reason or another, unlikely to complain. If law enforcement confined itself to the investigation of complaints or manifest injuries (like homicides or arsons), corruption and racketeering would flourish with impunity. Covert operations, courts and prosecutors believe, are virtually the only way to penetrate the smooth surface of silence.

There's a lot of truth to that. But we are talking, too, about some important personal rights in jeopardy. The constitutional right to security in one's home and personal affairs, the inchoate right to have the government play an honorable part: the right to be free of arbitrary official intrusions and secure against government corruption of one's trusted associates. Without denying the general right (if not obligation) of the government to investigate subterranean crime, I have at least two major quarrels with the prevailing mode. They will emerge from a general review of the implications of Shuster's staff proposals on their several projects.

Let's start with Tom Hartanian's snitch. No one would suggest that the government should turn a deaf ear to any person who comes for whatever reason—noble or ignoble—to tell tales of crime. Skeptical, yes, but welcoming. And people do come, spontaneously, and provide valuable and verifiable information that would otherwise be forever buried. Vengeful associates, jealous lovers, spiteful employees, and even (on rare occasions) a conscience-stricken co-conspirator. More common than these—and perhaps, as Hartanian says, more easily controlled by the prosecutor—are the people, themselves under suspicion or indictment, who are seeking to work off some of the onus, to lighten the punishment they face by "cooperation." These "turned" defendants may assist the prosecution (usually for unstated but firmly expected consideration) by supplying information, by providing testimony, or in some instances by going back into the company of their unsuspecting associates and serving as a government spy.

As a spy, the former trusted friend is no different from the two agents, Mutt and Jeff, recruited by Elizabeth Varelli to infiltrate the suspected Syrian terrorists. Both are making fresh and deceptive penetration into the private councils of their targets. In each instance, the target is reposing trust in a visible person, thereby according the government access to events and disclosures that would have been denied had the truth been known. Has the government made an unlawful search and seizure by fraud and deception? Or has the target simply made an unwise choice?

The Supreme Court's most famous pronouncement on the subject came in 1966 while reviewing a criminal conviction of James Hoffa, the legendary gangster president of the Teamsters' Union. Jimmy Hoffa had been selected by the Justice Department as its prime target (the Attorney General, Robert Kennedy, showing a fresh and fervent interest in organized crime in general, and the criminal corruption of labor unions in particular). While prosecuting him on one criminal charge (known as the "Test Fleet" case), the Justice Department heard rumors that Hoffa had been making overtures to jurors with bribery in mind. So they wisely began making preparations for the next prosecution. ("Wisely" because the corrupted jury in the Test Fleet case could not reach a unanimous verdict, and Jimmy escaped conviction.) They located an old union cohort of Jimmy's named Edward Partin who was in jail somewhere awaiting trial on some pretty serious charges, including embezzlement, kidnapping, and homicide. They apparently offered to let him out, forgive him his trespasses, and put his wife on the government payroll if he would spy on his old buddy. The specific terms of the contract are not altogether clear because the government was loath to confess the details. But Partin did suddenly turn up at the Andrew Jackson Hotel in Nashville, Tennessee, where Hoffa and his defense team were quartered for the Test Fleet trial. Somehow he managed to insinuate himself into the entourage and was soon hanging around, making himself useful, and reporting regularly to the government what scraps of information he could glean. Partin's good work helped to convict Hoffa of jury tampering, and thereafter the charges against Partin all evaporated.

Briefing and arguing the case to the Court, the parties raised a great controversy over whether Ed Partin had been "placed" by the government in Hoffa's hotel suite or had merely placed himself there. This was not a trivial question. As I shall insist, there is a big difference for constitutional purposes between a rat and a mole. A government agent is a mole, placed by the government like an electronic bug (to pursue the zoological metaphor), while a rat is only a citizen who chooses to inform, a matter of no constitutional significance.

Unfortunately, the Court didn't see it this way. Justice Stewart, writing the majority decision, said the Court would take the case as though the government had purposely inserted Partin into the Hoffa camp but declined to accord the fact any significance. Yes, Stewart acknowledged, Hoffa had a constitutionally protected right of privacy in the hotel suite, but it was not the security of the *place* he was relying on when he spoke in Partin's presence. Rather, he put his trust in the fidelity of his companion. And the Constitution, Stewart wrote for the Court, does not protect "a wrongdoer's misplaced belief that a person to whom he voluntarily confides his wrongdoing will not reveal it."

In effect, the Court held that, although the person who gains the confidence of the "wrongdoer" does so by deception, there is no constitutional right to have reality match appearance.

Thus put—the Constitution does not underwrite misplaced confidence in apparent friendship and loyalty—the lesson of the Hoffa case is well taken. After all, the Constitution is not Mother, the benevolent presence that heals all wounds and shields the tremulous soul from the searing light of experience. It's just a document; a porous canopy of finite dimension.

Still, to say Jimmy Hoffa must assume the risk that his old buddy may turn against him is not to say that he must assume the risk that the government will induce the betrayal, that the government will use his trusted associate like a human transmitter. The Constitution does not require that we assume the risk that the telephone we speak on is tapped, that the private rooms we speak in are wired for sound. Even those individuals, like Hoffa, who had every reason to believe that Bobby Kennedy was surveilling his every move, are protected by the Fourth Amendment from the intruding ear of the government. Why should we have to assume the risk that our trusted associates have been converted into covert government agents?

Not that the government may not employ surreptitious electronic monitors. It may, but only according to law, in compliance with statute, within the limits of the Constitution, and by permission of a judge. Why not control the government's use of human transmitters in the same way? Taking seriously the issue argued by the parties, the Court might have held that, as a planted agent, Partin was a human bug, a mobile listening device indistinguishable for constitutional purposes from his electronic counterpart. As such, the government could employ him only in compliance with Fourth Amendment and statutory constraints—roughly the same sort of warrant procedures as apply to searches for physical evidence. Indeed, whether wired or not, the human spy performs the same function as the electronic monitor—with the same intrusiveness—and should be available only by judicial order.

A good idea whose time is not yet. Perhaps we are not ready to forbid espionage on hunch alone. Perhaps we count on the reports of our secret spies to provide the probable cause for further investigation and cannot hold off for lack of what only they can provide. And those (like me) who insist that ordinary necessity never was—and should never be—a good reason to penetrate protected security simply cannot be heard.

In any event, for the present, the uses of both rats and moles—Hartanian's snitch or Varelli's Mutt and Jeff—are beyond the notice of the Constitution. They are entrusted to the good judgment of the prosecutor or police commander who must develop his own official, fiscal, or personal guidelines for their employment. The factor of invaded privacy need not count heavily in these discretionary calculations, and rarely counts at all.

Rob Rosenthal wanted to mount an expensive sting to get some evidence of the mob muscling in on video outlets. One of Betsy Varelli's undercovers stimulated the appetite for sabotage in his target group by promising to help them get in and mess with the ignition of the Air Guard aircraft. To an alert defense lawyer, these operations raise the red flag, and on that flag, writ large, is the word: ENTRAPMENT! What is entrapment, and what is so bad about it?

To start, it's not an exclusionary rule, and it does not derive from the Constitution. It is a defense, a heavy duty defense. A defendant who was entrapped is not guilty. Because the defense of entrapment is a creature of local statute, the nature of the beast varies, but generally it exculpates a defendant for conduct that would otherwise be criminal if the behavior in question was induced by law enforcement efforts. It is not precisely like the defense of duress, but it is the same idea. The defendant does not have to be forced to engage in the criminal conduct to avail himself of the defense of entrapment, but the conduct must be the result of implanted criminal intention.

Actually, there are two dramatically different theories of the defense of entrapment. One, called the objective theory, is the universal favorite of scholars, law reformers, and almost everyone who thinks clearly about the issue. The other, the subjective theory, is the perennial winner among lawmakers and judges, including a stubborn majority of the Justices of the Supreme Court.

According to the subjective view, a person is not morally culpable if she did the criminal deed only because someone else talked her into it. To put it in terms of social efficiency, it is foolish for the law to punish behavior that was created entirely by law enforcement officers. In moral terms, a person should not be judged guilty for conduct that did not emanate from her own evil disposition. The question, in this version of the defense, is whether the defendant acted only because she was induced to do so by the undercover cops or whether they merely afforded her the opportunity to do what she was disposed to do anyway. This is a question of fact for a jury to decide. And, once the question is raised by the defense, it is generally the burden of the prosecution to prove beyond a reasonable doubt that the defendant was predisposed to criminal conduct and hence not entrapped.

It's easy to see how this rule developed out of two old cases in the Supreme Court. The facts in both drove the outcome. In the first, *Sorrells v. United States,* decided in 1932, an agent—a veteran from the same division as his target—repeatedly asked his old buddy for a drink as they reminisced about their wartime exploits. Again and again, the target sadly told his guest that he had no booze and that the town, locked in the grip of national Prohibition, was dry as a desert. Finally, in deference to his comrade's persistent thirst and his hostly duties, the target agreed to go out and look for some liquor. When he finally managed to produce a bottle, he was arrested for violating the Prohibition Act.

The other case, twenty-six years later, was even worse. In *Sherman v. United States,* a government informer met his mark in a doctor's office where both were receiving treatment for drug addiction. There, claiming that the therapy was not working for him, the informer importuned the mark to get him some drugs. After several solicitations, underscored by protestations of suffering, Sherman finally complied. The informer promptly turned Sherman in to law enforcement agents, boasting that "he had another seller for them." After observing three deliveries, federal agents arrested Sherman.

The Court did not choose the element of heightened susceptibility (which is what makes the two cases so compelling in my mind) nor the deplorable conduct of the government (which makes them so offensive) but focused instead on the innocent disposition of the targets before they were subjected to government persuasion. In a famous phrase, Chief Justice Earl Warren wrote: "To determine whether entrapment has been established, a line must be drawn between a trap for the unwary innocent and a trap for the unwary criminal." In other words, only the pure in heart are entitled to the defense of entrapment.

One of the major problems with this dominant theory of entrapment is that it puts purity of heart and innocence of disposition in issue before the jury. Some might say that we would be better off with a criminal justice system that convicted on character generally rather than conduct. And— except in those jurisdictions, like the federal, that are tightly bound to "guidelines"—when it comes to deciding on the appropriate sentence for a convicted offender, judges routinely do take character into serious consideration. But on matters of guilt and innocence, our system (for better or worse) is resolutely conduct driven. We take elaborate precautions that a jury will not decide that a defendant committed the criminal acts because "that's just the sort of thing a person like him would do." Yet when a defendant raises the defense of entrapment, the jury will be asked to decide whether the defendant was predisposed to commit the crime, an issue on which they will be allowed to consider all the defendant's prior bad acts and crimes, which would otherwise be screened from their sight. It's an anomaly.

On several occasions since 1958, the Court has been urged to abandon a position that carries the curious consequence of virtually precluding a defense, regardless of its merits, where the defendant suffers the onus of a criminal record. But the majority has, to date, refused to adopt the minority position expressed by Justice Roberts in 1932 and since endorsed by such diverse heavyweights as Justices Frankfurter, Harlan, Douglas, Stewart, Brennan, and Marshall, to say nothing of the legions of law professors.

The minority view, the objective theory, is modeled on the exclusionary rule. It would bar evidence procured by police who use such overwhelming or persistent persuasion that it would induce even a person not otherwise so inclined to commit the crime. Focus is on the nature of the police conduct, measured by the susceptibility of a hypothetical law-abiding person. The issue is usually for the judge rather than the jury, the burden of proof is on the defendant, and the particular character of the defendant on trial that might incline him toward criminal conduct is irrelevant.

The sting that Shuster's staff was thinking about, presumably, would entail setting up a phony video outlet—maybe X-rated—and waiting for the mob to show up and take an interest (pun intended). As long as the government passively played the sitting duck, no one could cry "Entrapment!" And that is what most stings do: they merely afford the opportunity for the criminally inclined to do their wont in the alert presence of the evidence gatherers. The trouble is that some of these stingers, bored with waiting around, may tender some encouragement, even persuasion. Thus some few years ago, a small group of swarthy, black-mustached FBI agents in appropriate headgear set up a phony outfit called Abdul Enterprises, Inc., and let it be known on Capitol Hill that a Middle Eastern oil sheikh was interested in buying some sympathetic congressmen. One senator and six congressmen and several other public officials swam to the Abscam bait and accepted gifts of cash—on camera. You can bet the cry of entrapment was heard in the halls of Congress, but to no avail.

More recently, the Supreme Court had a sting case that evidently shocked them deeply enough to find the defense of entrapment had been established as a matter of law. In 1992 the Court decided a case in which Keith Jacobson, a 56-year-old Nebraska farmer, was convicted of violating the child pornography act of 1984. Justice White, writing for the majority in a 5–4 split, recounted in painful detail the elaborate, devious, persistent campaign of the postal investigators to induce Jacobson to break the law. The official summary of the opinion tells the story:

> At a time when federal law permitted such conduct, petitioner Jacobson ordered and received from a bookstore two Bare Boys magazines containing photographs of nude preteen and teenage boys. Subsequently, the Child Protection Act of 1984 made illegal the receipt through the mails of sexually explicit depictions of children. After finding Jacobson's name on the bookstore mailing list, two Government agencies sent mail to him through five fictitious organizations and a bogus pen pal, to explore his willingness to break the law. Many of those organizations represented that they were founded to protect and promote sexual freedom and freedom of choice and that they promoted lobbying efforts through catalog sales. Some mailings raised the specter of censorship. Jacobson responded to some of the correspondence. After 2½ years on the Government mailing list, Jacobson was solicited to order child pornography. He answered a letter that described concern about child pornography as hysterical nonsense and decried international censorship, and then received a catalog and ordered a magazine depicting young boys engaged in sexual activities. He was arrested after a controlled delivery of a photocopy of the magazine, but a search of his house

revealed no materials other than those sent by the Government and the Bare Boys magazines. At his jury trial, he pleaded entrapment and testified that he had been curious to know the type of sexual actions to which the last letter referred and that he had been shocked by the Bare Boys magazines because he had not expected to receive photographs of minors. He was convicted, and the Court of Appeals affirmed.

While reaffirming their *Sorrells* view that entrapment occurs only when government action creates criminal conduct in an innocently disposed person, the majority held in *United States v. Jacobson* that a criminal disposition itself may be induced by overwhelming government pressure. And such creative activity is also entrapment. Excerpting from Justice White's opinion, the reasoning ran thus:

> [T]here can be no dispute that the Government may use undercover agents to enforce the law. "It is well settled that the fact that officers or employees of the Government merely afford opportunities or facilities for the commission of the offense does not defeat the prosecution. Artifice and stratagem may be employed to catch those engaged in criminal enterprises." [Citations omitted in these excerpts.]
>
> In their zeal to enforce the law, however, Government agents may not originate a criminal design, implant in an innocent person's mind the disposition to commit a criminal act, and then induce commission of the crime so that the Government may prosecute. Where the Government has induced an individual to break the law and the defense of entrapment is at issue, as it was in this case, the prosecution must prove beyond reasonable doubt that the defendant was disposed to commit the criminal act prior to first being approached by Government agents. . . .
>
> By the time petitioner finally placed his order, he had already been the target of 26 months of repeated mailings and communications from Government agents and fictitious organizations. Therefore, although he had become predisposed to break the law by May 1987, it is our view that the Government did not prove that this predisposition was independent and not the product of the attention that the Government had directed at petitioner since January 1985. . . .
>
> Law enforcement officials go too far when they "implant in the mind of an innocent person the disposition to commit the alleged offense and induce its commission in order that they may prosecute." Like the

Sorrells court, we are "unable to conclude that it was the intention of the Congress in enacting this statute that its processes of detection and enforcement should be abused by the instigation by government officials of an act on the part of persons otherwise innocent in order to lure them to its commission and to punish them." When the Government's quest for convictions leads to the apprehension of an otherwise law-abiding citizen who, if left to his own devices, likely would have never run afoul of the law, the courts should intervene.

Because we conclude that this is such a case and that the prosecution failed, as a matter of law, to adduce evidence to support the jury verdict that petitioner was predisposed, independent of the Government's acts and beyond a reasonable doubt, to violate the law by receiving child pornography through the mails, we reverse the Court of Appeals' judgment affirming the conviction of Keith Jacobson.

Back to our story. Tom Hartanian, investigating municipal bid rigging, managed to get the bank records of his suspect, albeit to no avail. But how did he get them? Aren't the transactions we have with our banks private? Can the government read our private financial records at will? Isn't that like tapping phones or opening mail?

One might well think so. But the Supreme Court has held otherwise. The depositor, the Court reasoned, having freely disclosed his financial affairs to the bank, has no claim of privacy in those records. "Wait!" the depositor protests. "I disclosed those records only to the bank and only for banking transactions. I did not intend to relinquish privacy to the government for purposes of investigating my business. Is privacy an all-or-nothing proposition in the eyes of the Constitution: either I have the full protection of the Fourth Amendment or none at all?" Right.

The Court recognizes no selective surrender of security. When you use the telephone and necessarily disclose the numbers dialed for billing purposes, you lose all claims of privacy in the call records. (The conversations, of course, are private and the government may listen only by court order for a wiretap, but the numbers called are fair game.) When you put the garbage out at the curb for collection, no rights of security are invaded if, instead of the garbage collector, law enforcement agents take the sack to look for traces of criminal activity.

This seems rather odd to me. It's not the best definition of the security offered by the Fourth Amendment, but the Supreme Court did choose to describe it as protection for "reasonable expectations of privacy." And it does not seem unreasonable to expect that the record of deposits and withdrawals that you make to your bank account will remain private to everyone except the bank. But the Court has taken a binary view of Fourth Amendment security: you have it or you don't. And matters disclosed to a designated recipient for a limited purpose are treated as though opened to the world at large for all purposes. True, your financial records can be obtained from you by subpoena, but this gives you notice and an opportunity to oppose and maybe even defeat the quest. Should you have any less protection because the records reflect transactions you had with your bank? But there it is: there are some holes in the security blanket our Constitution provides for us.

And—surprise—it makes little difference that the transactions were conducted with a Swiss bank. The banks of Switzerland are legendary for their impregnability. Until 1977, the famous "numbered accounts" promised anonymity to scoundrels, pirates, and tyrants of all nations. It was an article of faith that funds could effectively be hidden from curious government investigators, along with everyone else, behind the great facade of a Swiss bank. No longer. A treaty between the United States and Switzerland—along with some internal revisions of the Swiss banking laws—opened the granite vaults for official inquiry. Now, on little more than the demand of a subpoena— routed through diplomatic channels, of course—law enforcement agencies can get what they need: bank records. Of course, the end of legendary Swiss impenetrability simply moved the illicit depositors to other nations who still offer anonymity. (The Cayman Islands seems to be a current favorite.)

Betsy Varelli has sent a couple of agents, undercover, to infiltrate a foreign group thought to be plotting terrorism. To promote his own acceptance in the gang, one of the agents promised the conspirators an essential ingredient for the sabotage of an Air Guard plane. Had the sabotage gone to completion, this assistance would have raised the entrapment issue in a somewhat different form. Not persuasion of the reluctant, but provision of the ingredient without which the crime would have been impossible, even at the hands of the most eagerly disposed. So far, the Supreme Court has not found a case that they deem appropriate for this variant of the entrapment defense. In 1973, they had one—*United States v. Russell*—in which an agent supplied a hard-to-get reagent for the manufacture of an illegal drug known on the street as "speed." No, the Court said, although the agent made it easier to commit the crime, it would not have been impossible without his help. So the defense will not work. But the interesting thing was, they did not rule out this exotic sport.

This essential-ingredient theory is quite different from the prevailing formula of entrapment: overwhelming persuasion of the innocently disposed. A person of guilty disposition may be entrapped, the Court now blithely suggests, if law enforcement agents supply an ingredient without which the crime would have been impossible to pull off and which would have been otherwise unavailable to the defendant. This conclusion is simply incompatible with the subjective view of entrapment favored by the majority, the theory that the Court has insisted is the essence of the entrapment defense. Furnishing the means of commission of the crime to a criminally inclined person is altogether different from implanting a criminal disposition in an innocent mind. The words of the Court in *Russell* propose a radical alternative: a constitutional basis for an objective entrapment defense. Here's what Justice Rehnquist wrote (before he became Chief Justice): "While we may some day be presented with a situation in which the conduct of law enforcement agents is *so outrageous that due process principles would absolutely bar the government from invoking judicial processes to obtain a conviction,* the instant case is distinctly not of that breed" [emphasis mine].

It's more than twenty years, now, and they have not yet seen the case. When it comes, the Constitution will open its eyes and take its first notice of this sort of law enforcement activity. Plus, we may see the development of a theory closer to the objective version than the Court has yet come. For the concept of due process enjoins the government to avoid conduct that is offensive to objective standards of civilized government. That will be a most interesting development in the evolution of the doctrine of entrapment.

Meanwhile, the lower federal courts have had several cases in which they found that the participation of the government in the criminal enterprise was so excessive that due process required reversal of the resulting conviction. They are careful to assert that the ground for reversal is not "entrapment" as such, nor are they switching to an objective theory—but excessive government participation in the creation or execution of a crime looks a lot like entrapment to me.

Back to Betsy Varelli's moles, Mutt and Jeff. Both are presenting the prosecutor, their "control," with serious moral choices.

Mutt appears to be going over. The literature of espionage is full of tales of deep-cover spies who are gradually seduced by the life of the enemy. A cop inserted into the councils of the underworld no less than a Soviet officer in the diplomatic whirl of London may find himself attracted by the style of his own masquerade. And, deprived of contact with his own family and friends, removed from the reinforcement of his own corps, the agent may find himself making personal attachments in the enemy camp. After you go fishing with the mobster, one former spy reported, after you attend the baptism of his nephew and the wedding of his daughter, you begin to think of your target as family. The moral sensibilities scream as the officer comes to the point of betrayal. It's a hazard of the trade that may not be calculated among the several more obvious dangers when the plan is hatched.

But beyond the significant cost of putting young officers at such extraordinary risk, moral and physical, the phenomenon of going over tells another story. It is not so much the lure of the counter life, the slide toward marginality. To me it is the power of personal interaction, the strength of the human bond. People want to be loyal, to be true to the trust others repose in them. In close quarters, they come to see even their targets as fellows of the species, and they respond with warmth and attachment that may be stronger than any abstract identification—like who is on which "side." Though Betsy Varelli is not likely to see it so, I find that somehow heartening in this cynical world where antagonism often seems the ruling theme of interaction.

Betsy Varelli's other mole, Jeff, has a problem that is probably even more common and more troubling. Every time a prosecutor decides to put a spy in a criminal conspiracy, a decision must be made: how much criminal activity will the agent be allowed to do in order to prove his mettle to his new associates? If the gang to be infiltrated is active and suspicious (as will most likely be the case), no one can expect that they will tolerate a passive observer in their midst. Trust among criminals is usually won by demonstrated criminality. If it is a drug conspiracy, the crime the agent is called upon to do may be no more serious than handling contraband, but it may involve using it. Excuses may fail, suspicion may rise, and the agent finds he must sniff the coke to prove himself trustworthy. That raises serious problems, including the development of addiction and weakening of credibility if and when the agent emerges from cover as a witness at the trial.

Jeff presents another, more portentous dilemma. He is being called upon to participate in a serious crime with a substantial danger of injury or death to someone. The valuable information on an even more serious crime—deadly sabotage and terrorism—will be cut off before fruition if the agent suddenly ducks out. But he may be in personal peril if he stays.

Insofar as the law provides any help to Shuster and Varelli, it might provide a legal excuse for Jeff if he goes along on the stick-up: guilt depends not only on the conduct of the actor, but on the criminal intention with which it is performed. If his part in the robbery is governed by an overriding law enforcement purpose, maybe a court would find a criminal intention is incompatible. Maybe.

But the issue for the prosecutors does not really sound in legal terms. It is one of those perplexing moral questions for which the concept of executive discretion was designed. Most prosecutors probably apply some sort of sliding scale: petty crimes are a tolerable price for a major crime payoff, more serious crimes cannot be condoned for any purpose, however worthy. Still, we haven't really been tested. If the opportunity had arisen, should a good prosecutor instruct an agent to participate in a serious and dangerous crime like armed robbery if it might avert a catastrophe like the bombing of the World Trade Center in New York? Or the tragic destruction of the plane over Lockerbie, Scotland? And these decisions must be made before the outcome can be known. Obviously, the wise exercise of this discretionary authority calls not only for conscientious judgment of the highest sort, but for an uncanny gift of prescience. In the most carefully constructed system, many of the most important decisions must remain the province of individual judgment. And we can do nothing to enhance the process but hope for the best.

9 Plea Bargaining

Cheap Crimes, Costly Trials

To hear people talk about it, you would think the practice of plea bargaining had consumed the whole system of deliberative justice, substituting for it either the moral imperatives of a Moroccan bazaar or the social ethics of a Las Vegas casino. Due process, jury trial, presumptive innocence, equal justice, just deserts, and the rest of the treasures of the temple of adjudication are forgotten in the crass commerce of the marketplace, or (if you prefer the image) the bluff and risk of the gaming tables. Here the innocent are induced to sell themselves into prison while the deeply guilty walk away with a slap on the wrist. Issues of guilt and innocence are superseded by the bettor's odds (8 to 5 you'll do five-to-eight) and the implacable imperative of efficiency (get the most dispositions in the shortest time). In the usual description, the plea market is the antithesis of the courthouse, a place where the outcome of a case depends entirely on caseload, comparative anxiety, and the respective negotiating skill of counsel. And it is in this bizarre bazaar, not in the stately courthouse, that 90 percent and more of the business of justice is conducted.

It's not a pretty picture. Is it a fair representation?

I don't suppose people would object to a guilty person pleading guilty to the noncapital crime with which he is charged and throwing himself on the mercy of the court, as the expression goes. And I would guess that most people would not think justice had been compromised if the judge took the remorseful confession of the accused into account in imposing sentence. It might even be tolerable for scales to tip slightly toward leniency because the plea saved the state the expense of a trial and the victim the agony of reliving the crime. No explicit bargain has been struck, to be sure, but many of the same features are operating. The defendant has assessed the strength of his defense and the reputation of the judge and concluded that he would lose at trial and receive a heavier sentence than the sentence he could reasonably expect by making a contrite concession of guilt. The judge will respond to the relieved pressure on the docket and perhaps to the show of penitence. The judge will reward the defendant's choice and encourage others to do likewise. The prosecutor can get on to the next case. Everyone is happy.

The main difference is that, in a disposition by plea bargain, the guilty plea is offered *in exchange* for either a reduced charge or (more likely) a settled sentence lighter than the one the criminal would probably face on conviction by verdict. This is a settlement that requires some negotiation, inducement, and perhaps persuasion. It's odd how this added factor of "bargaining" transforms the process—in the public perception, at least—into a disreputable business. The blend of reality and misunderstanding that fuels popular opinion is a potent cocktail and all but impossible to examine analytically. Still, because plea bargaining in one form or another is the American way of processing criminal cases, I must give it a try.

At the start, it's not easy to construct a paradigm of the plea process (and hence I will offer no fictionalized scenario in this chapter). Practice varies widely. The low-volume jurisdiction looks nothing like the high-volume; policies vary from state to state, county to county—often from courtroom to courtroom. And federal plea practice is, in many ways, unique. For one thing, federal criminal laws are not drafted to lend themselves to reduction for plea purposes. For another, because federal prosecutors for the most part choose their cases (except for petty drug cases, which are thrust upon them), they control their caseload to keep the demand for expeditious disposition at a manageable level. Still, the feds have developed a form of plea bargaining, too. Obviously, I cannot hope to describe all the many shapes the monster takes as he ranges through state and federal courthouses, but I've consorted with him in at least one major habitat, so perhaps I can identify some of his more prominent features.

During the years when I did plea bargaining for the county prosecutor, there was a lot of pleading but not much bargaining. The standard drill in our office was for the defense lawyer to come by and ask, What's the offer? We would take out the file, scan the sketchy reports it contained, and usually offer to recommend the acceptance by the court of a guilty plea to a crime a notch or two below the most serious count charged by the grand jury. Because accusation—and, by extension, mitigation of a charge—is traditionally an executive function, the law requires the prosecutor's acquiescence in any reduction of the charged crime by judicial acceptance of a lesser plea. Factors we considered: the gravity of the injury, the prior criminal history of the defendant, the relationship between the victim and the defendant, provocation, and the projected strength of our case. Some cases—some homicides or other brutal crimes with more aggravating than mitigating circumstances— got no offer of reduction: plead to the indictment or try it. Others took a little further investigation. Talk to the cops, the witnesses, check out the forensics, then make an offer. In a few, very few, we were moved by the pleas of defense counsel for leniency on grounds of the defendant's exemplary character. In some cases, our prepleading investigation led to a motion to dismiss the charges.

Take the crime of robbery. The law in our hypothetical jurisdiction (whose sentencing laws are mercifully simple) says that stealing property by threatening the victim with a dangerous instrument is robbery in the first degree and is punishable by a term of imprisonment of not more than fifteen years. Along comes a case where a nineteen-year-old boy, on probation for car theft, flashes a knife blade in front of his victim's face, pulls the gold chain off of her neck, and runs. A serious, frightening crime. But the young assistant D.A. knows that no judge is going to sentence that robber to fifteen years, even after a protracted trial that includes the perjury of the defendant. No way. That crime is "worth," in the ordinary commerce of the courts of the jurisdiction, something like two or three years behind bars and another six to ten on parole. That's no mere "slap on the wrist" in a jurisdiction where the average time served by killers is five to seven years in prison. Of course, averages mean little where some murderers are still in after thirty years and others are out in thirty months. To God, perhaps, all human life is equally valued, but on the streets of today's big cities, there are murders and murders.

So the assistant D.A. tells the defense lawyer, OK, we'll go for a rob three (robbery in the third degree) here, with an understanding that he gets two-to-five (which means, in that jurisdiction, actual jail time of, say, eighteen to twenty-four months, the rest of the sentence to be served on parole). Defense counsel argues, He's really a good kid, supports his mother, bad crowd, etc. The D.A. stands pat. Counsel goes back to his client. We could win, he says, but it's a long shot. Can't say what the judge would do if you get convicted by a jury, but if you get a bad draw you could get three years easy. Maybe more. Take the D.A.'s offer and you'll be out before your twenty-first birthday. They agree: let's take it. The lawyer comes back to the D.A. A done deal, if the judge goes for it—and he usually will.

Now the question is, has something disgraceful happened here? Has the crime of robbery been devalued? Has the adversary design of adjudication been corrupted? Has an innocent person been seduced to sell his freedom? If so, I was a regular party to the crime. And I take subversion of justice as a serious offense.

What I thought I was doing, mainly, in the run-of-the-docket case, was discounting the "top count" crime—the heaviest charge, usually spelled out in the first count of the indictment. On my initiative, and with defense counsel's agreement, I was rewriting the law, modifying the judgment of the legislature to fit the circumstances of the crime, in accord with what I per-ceived to be the prevailing ethic in the courts of my time and place. That's all. Just remaking the law—by contract—to fit the crime. The plea bargainer's motto was: every individual case is different from the statutory model. And the corollary: justice lives in the subtle differentiations. The laudable job of the worthy plea bargainer is to refine with mercy and judgment the crude, harsh, remote, blind judgment of the legislature into a particular response to the unique aspects of a particular case. A somewhat arrogant job description perhaps, but were we defiling a beautiful design of justice? Would justice have been better served if we had required the young robber to take the extra year or two or three or four that a judge might give after trial?

In addition to reappraising the crime, I was frankly offering an inducement to dispose of the case by guilty plea. A case like that could take anywhere from three days to a week and a half to try to a jury. Courtroom trial time is an expensive commodity. In most places, a month's addition to the felony docket packs hundreds of hours more potential trial time than the trial courts have to give in four weeks. And in many—like New York City—the disparity can be measured in thousands of courtroom hours. In busy jurisdictions, the court system can barely keep up with the intake by trying less than 10 percent of the indictments. And "busy" does not necessarily mean "large"; it is a proportion of available trial time to felony case flow. So it is extremely important to the economy of the courtroom, in most urban state jurisdictions at least, to produce a substantial number of guilty pleas. Prosecutors generally feel they owe some deference to the interests of judicial economy. Still, they want to hold the offers high enough to keep the public faith.

What, precisely, is the inducement to plead guilty with a promised sentence that, though considerably below the "book value" of the top count, may not be significantly lower than a judge is likely to think the case merits after a verdict of conviction? Especially since to take the plea option is to forgo all chance of total acquittal? And in some places today, that's a very good chance indeed—as high as 40 percent, perhaps, including some cases that looked to the defense like dead losers.

There certainly never was, in my experience, any explicit threat that the defendant who declined the plea offer would receive a longer sentence if he was convicted after trial. No judge I ever worked with would say to a defendant or his lawyer, Get yourself convicted by a jury and you're looking at three years on top of the five you'll do on a guilty plea. There were, of course, reminders of the long sentence he *could* receive under the statute. And perhaps some veiled suggestion that the plea deal was at the low end of the likely. But judges are frank to say—and sometimes to the defendant as he is about to enter his plea—that they occasionally hear facts, or get impressions from trial evidence that moves them to impose a *lower* sentence on a defendant convicted after trial than they would have imposed had he pleaded guilty. Hearing that, why would any rational defendant plead guilty?

It's a very delicate matter. Factor in this: the Legal Aid Society or public defender's office represents a significant majority of the defendants. They know that if they refuse to plead all of their clients to the offered dispositions, they can drive down the market. A plea strike would hopelessly jam up the docket and force the dismissal of many, many cases for failure to provide the speedy trial guaranteed by statute and the Sixth Amendment to the United States Constitution. On the other hand, a plea strike might be broken by concerted action by the bench to impose the maximum on every defendant convicted by verdict. On ethical grounds, both moves are highly questionable. But the background prospect helps to keep offers at the low end, where the organized defense Bar considers them "fair," while holding them above the level of token punishment.

Two considerations probably induce the plea. One is the element of certainty. Even for a veteran offender, getting indicted for a felony opens a frightening array of unknowables. What kind of lawyer will you get? Who is in the wings ready to testify against you, and how vulnerable will these witnesses be? What other evidence does the prosecution have? Did the cops do a sloppy job or a thorough one in putting the case together? Can they be made to look bad? Can the prosecutor impeach you, if you testify, with your prior crimes or other misdeeds? What kind of jury will you get? Who will be the presiding judge, and how sympathetic will he be—especially if you testify and the judge thinks your story is blatant perjury? And what surprises—breaks or blows—will materialize from left field during the trial? In the contemplation of these uncertainties, the plea and sentence, settled in advance, have a certain appeal.

The other factor is the sense—right or wrong—that the offered disposition is a significantly better deal than can be expected from the judge's unfettered discretion. If conviction seems likely, the plea offer may be taken as a true bargain. And—importantly—defendants *believe* it is. I don't think any social scientist has tried to test the prevailing assumption that makes the ship sail: that, in most cases, a pleading defendant would be convicted by a jury and receive a substantially longer sentence. Perhaps it never will be verified in view of the difficulty of holding variables constant. But if it is true enough (as I suspect it is in many high volume jurisdictions), a major and disturbing question is raised: if the plea bargain is a reward for waiving the trial, then the system is imposing a penalty for the exercise of a basic right, the right to trial by jury.

The logic of this formulation seems irrefutable to me, but it's a bit tricky to raise in a case. A defendant, convicted after trial, might try to get her sentence reduced by claiming that it is longer than the sentence she was promised if she had waived trial and pleaded guilty. An appellate court would doubtless respond, Sorry, but sentence is a matter in the discretion of the trial judge and, unless the judge said on the record that the sole reason for the sentence imposed was to penalize you for electing a jury trial (not very likely), we will assume that the increment was due to unfavorable things the judge learned about you or your crime during the course of your trial. The issue might also be raised if a defendant, on second thought, tries to withdraw his guilty plea by claiming that it had been entered under duress—the duress being the threat of a longer sentence if he went to trial. But that threat, usually implicit at best, would be very hard to demonstrate.

Apart from the difficulty of raising the point, its chances of success in court are dim. Those few courts that have been moved to consider the claim that the plea bargaining system puts a tax on the right to trial have barely broken stride. Giving favorable consideration to a defendant for his choice to plead guilty, they say with a straight face, even apart from its (dubious) significance as an act of contrition, does not imply that the defendant who chooses to put the charge to a jury test is suffering a disadvantage on that account. Remember, they will explain patiently, the defendant could be acquitted if he goes to trial. The risk of a greater sentence is offset by the chance of acquittal. Because the defendant acts according to the dictates of his own self-interest (the chance is worth the risk), we cannot say he is being penalized for his choice. The greater sentence, after all, is what he deserves; the plea sentence is a break.

Justice Stewart, speaking loudly and clearly for the Supreme Court in in a 1978 case called *Bordenkircher v. Hayes,* endorsed the prevailing view. The issue was sharply presented because the threat was clearly articulated. Hayes was negotiating a plea on a forgery charge (two to ten years) when the prosecutor told him that if he rejected the offer and went to trial, the government would go back to the grand jury and get a habitual offender charge; if convicted after trial of the forgery as a habitual offender, Hayes faced a mandatory life sentence. Stewart noted at the start that the situation was the same as if "the grand jury had indicted Hayes as a recidivist from the outset, and the prosecutor had offered to drop that charge as part of the plea bargain."

Hayes rejected the deal, the prosecutor was as good as his word, and, after Hayes was convicted on both counts at trial, he was sentenced to life in prison. The Supreme Court held that offering a break for the plea was not penalizing Hayes for standing trial. Justice Stewart wrote for the Court:

> To punish a person because he has done what the law plainly allows him to do is a due process violation of the most basic sort and for an agent of the State to pursue a course of action whose objective is to penalize a person's reliance on his legal rights is patently unconstitutional. But in the "give-and-take" of plea bargaining, there is no such element of punishment or retaliation so long as the accused is free to accept or reject the prosecution's offer. . . . By hypothesis, the plea may have

been induced by promises of a recommendation of a lenient sentence or a reduction of charges, and thus by fear of the possibility of a greater penalty upon conviction after a trial.

While confronting a defendant with the risk of more severe punishment clearly may have a discouraging effect on the defendant's assertion of his trial rights, the imposition of these difficult choices is an inevitable—and permissible—attribute of any legitimate system which tolerates and encourages the negotiation of pleas. It follows that, by tolerating and encouraging the negotiation of pleas, this Court has necessarily accepted as constitutionally legitimate the simple reality that the prosecutor's interest at the bargaining table is to persuade the defendant to forgo his right to plead not guilty.

I am reluctant to use the word "sophistry" when describing the work of a Justice of the stature of Potter Stewart—but the word does come to mind. "Free to accept or reject the prosecution's offer"? Free to choose trial, a constitutional right, but only at the cost of risking a life sentence that he would not otherwise face? OK, let's not call it a "penalty" for the choice—after all, he was, in fact, a multiple offender. But it surely was a *cost,* Justice Stewart, was it not? He might have gotten off completely, that's true, too. But even risk is a cost. If a cop says to a suspect, Here's the deal: you can either confess to this homicide or I'll turn you loose, count to three, and start shooting at you as an escaped prisoner—would anyone contend that the resulting confession was the product of a free choice in the "give and take" of interrogation? After all, the cop might have missed, the prisoner might have gotten away.

Imagine a defendant facing a mandatory ten-year sentence on the top count. That is what the legislature had decreed his crime deserves, and he will surely get it if he is convicted of that count after trial. The prosecutor, eager to avoid a long and costly trial, offers a plea to a lesser charge and a sentence of seven and a half years. The defendant with his lawyer figures that the discount on the sentence is not worth it because the prosecutor has only a 40 percent record of convictions in cases of this sort. He refuses the offer. By this peculiar arithmetic, our apologists might call the ensuing trial cost-free to the defendant, because the 60 percent chance of acquittal outweighed the 33 percent sentence increment he risked.

Apart from the absurdity of calculating chances of acquittal numerically, I would respond that the cost to the defendant of the exercise of his trial option was the increment in sentence discounted by the risk of conviction: .40 x 30 months, or 1 year behind bars. By this arithmetic, any risk of conviction, however slight, applied to any surcharge on sentence, produces a cost. Even though the defendant might sensibly think the odds made a trial the best course, there is no denying that the system imposed a tax on the exercise of that choice. I also have an argument that does not require arithmetic. It is this: the chance of acquittal is implicit in the right to trial. The Constitution guarantees a chance of acquittal, and that promise cannot be diminished by using it to discount a sentence received after its exercise.

Notwithstanding its dubious constitutional posture, in the end I have to say that I am glad the Court accepted plea bargaining and recognized that fairly "persuading" the defendant to plead guilty may include the outright threat to exact the full punishment allowed by law as a surcharge for electing the right of jury trial. The consequence of a contrary holding would have been unimaginable—an endless, untriable docket of serious cases, provably dangerous people free on bail awaiting trials that never come. Or, if some alleviation of the crisis is attempted, we will have summary dispositions of thousands of major felonies without trial, convicting not on proof but on the allegations supporting the arrest. Either way, under the sheer weight of the criminal docket, we face total meltdown: virtually free crime or blatant tyranny.

Apart from (1) discounting the common crimes and moderating the legislature's constituent-driven, vindictive punishment levels (not a sin of the cardinal grade for an executive officer in my book), and (2) extracting implicit penalties for the exercise of the constitutional right to trial (a small matter that our High Court has counseled us to ignore), what other charges might be made against me—and the legions of my fellow bargainers—for degrading criminal justice?

We have, let us frankly confess, usurped the traditional judicial function to some extent. Fixing sentence is—or was, until Congress largely supplanted it in federal courts by the notorious sentencing guidelines—a uniquely judicial prerogative. Difficult as this part of the job may be, judges take their sentencing responsibilities seriously. And the federal bench is furious that the congressional response to sentence disparities was to drain judicial discretion. In my own defense, I should say that, in my day, we were wary of this accusation and bargained only for a reduced charge (the traditional prerogative of the executive branch), leaving the selection of sentence, within the scope allowed by the plea, entirely up to the court. But things have changed.

Today, criminal cases are often settled by an agreement to a specific sentence. In truth, that does offend somewhat my old-fashioned ideas of division of responsibility. To hear defense counsel get up in court and say, "The defendant is prepared to plead guilty to three-to-nine," seems inappropriate. Or for the prosecutor to say to a judge, "The prosecution offers a minimum of three years," sounds wrong. But it happens all the time today. Plea bargaining in many state courts has become sentence bargaining between the parties, the judge left with a veto power only. In federal courts, under the rigid guidelines, designated aggravating and mitigating factors can be fed into the "grid" in advance and the mechanism will grind out the sentence with great precision—a tab from which the judge may deviate only for exceptional, stated reasons.

The state judges' veto over the sentence agreed upon by the parties and the federal judges' sharply reduced discretion in sentencing are pretty weak residues of a once grand judicial power. We are not talking of civil cases, after all, where the outcome need satisfy only the parties to the dispute. In a criminal case, the community at large has an interest. And, though the prosecutor represents the public, the judge has the ultimate responsibility to see that the broad policies of the community standards are not compromised by the narrower interests of the adversaries. I'm with the judges on this one. I think the judge should take a more active part in arriving at a settled disposition, urging the zealous young prosecutor to be a bit more merciful in this case, counseling the stubborn defense lawyer to be a bit more realistic in that one, and ultimately deciding the actual terms of punishment.

Does the disposition mill put the poor and friendless criminal at a disadvantage? I've heard it said that the rich and organized criminals, who can afford high-priced counsel, get tried (and perhaps acquitted) while the plea market shunts the marginal predator straight to prison without even a decent point to argue on appeal.

I don't see the support for this claim. If anything, it seems to work the other way around. Defendants without funds to retain private counsel are represented by assigned lawyers, either from a publicly funded office or from a list of private practitioners who are compensated from the public treasury. The public defenders get paid by the month, the same salary whether they plead the client or take the case to trial. And many young lawyers working for the public defender are eager to strut their stuff before a jury—that's the main reason most of them joined the staff in the first place. There's no bonus for the number of dispositions they get. Assigned counsel are paid by the hour or the day, not the case, and can raise the paltry fee they get by adding days of trial time to their vouchers. And in most places these are volunteers looking for trial experience, not busy lawyers stealing time from their more remunerative business. So, for many, pleading their impecunious clients guilty is against the attorney's personal, financial, and professional interest.

It's the wealthier clients who pay a regular fee to private counsel who should worry about whether their chosen champion has a personal economic incentive to dispose of the case as quickly as possible and get on to the next case. High-priced criminal trial lawyers—and, to my knowledge, that phrase is redundant—generally take a hefty retainer up front and do not bill substantially for their time thereafter. (It's just the opposite for the high-priced commercial Bar, whose fees are computed largely on an hourly basis.) Lawyers in the private criminal Bar are heavily booked, and turning over cases with dispatch allows them to take that many more retainers. Of course, as we have noted, many of them allow themselves to become seriously overbooked, but then the pressure from the bench becomes very unpleasant.

The solution: plead out of some of these turkeys. Several of these lawyers have told me that getting tied up on a protracted trial can be financially disastrous—even with the added fees for trial days, one client cannot possibly compensate his counsel for the lost retainers of multiple clients during the same period. Unless you are one of the handful of lawyers on very high, continuous retainers from some very bad clients, I was told, "it's a volume business." And high turnover is the key to volume.

There are, of course, a few defendants with virtually limitless funds or an extremely prominent position in the world who can mount a defense, based on an extensive and expensive investigation, that outshines the case the prosecutor can afford from the public budget. They do have a distinct advantage over the rest of the common herd. But they do not always employ that advantage to claim the right to jury trial. A Vice President of the United States, a Chief Judge of the New York Court of Appeals, and the Croesus of the inside traders all bargained and pleaded guilty.

Perhaps what disturbs the watching public most about the plea bargaining system is the sense that crime is cheapened, that dangerous criminals get away with trivial punishment. Is there any truth to this perception? Indisputably, crimes are discounted for plea purposes, reduced well below the stretch the legislature sets as the maximum, and somewhat below what a judge might give in the free exercise of discretion following a verdict. But do these reductions undermine the authority of law?

Let's start by recognizing that leniency is a murky concept. I am frank to say that I have never been able to formulate a sound theory for deciding on an absolute basis whether a sentence is harsh, light, or just right. I have a pretty good idea of what the prevailing rates are, but no sense of whether they are high or low. Is three years—four seasons a year, twenty-four hours a day, in state prison with only other criminals for company—a long time? For some people, it would be an eternity. For others, maybe not.

Perhaps we might solve this riddle by asking, "long" for what purpose? I don't suppose there are many left who would offer rehabilitation as the purpose of imprisonment—though it was the favorite not so long ago. We are too realistic today to indulge the comforting myth that prisons reform character. The modern objectives most usually cited are isolation and punishment.

Isolation—putting the malefactor out of contact with the law-abiding world—is a good idea. A large chunk of the crimes are committed by a small slice of society, striking repeatedly. To be faithful to the goal of isolation, of course, would mean locking people away according to a prediction of recidivism rather than according to the gravity of the crime of conviction. We don't do that.

There are some obvious problems with a policy of locking away the potential repeaters. We have pretty good evidence that family killers are among the least likely to kill again (or commit any future crimes), while petty criminals like car thieves and bad check writers will almost certainly repeat. Yet no one argues that car thieves and forgers should be isolated longer than murderers. Isolation seems to be an incidental benefit rather than a controlling objective.

Punishment or retribution, once regarded universally as the unworthy purpose, is thought by some today to be the central objective. Retribution means that we law-abiding people can reaffirm the social values embedded in the criminal code while visiting upon the civic enemy his just deserts. It makes everyone feel better—maybe even the criminal. In service of this purpose, sentencing is keyed to the enormity of the criminal conduct, the injury inflicted, and the character of the offender. The punishment, carefully imposed by a court according to law, substitutes for the spontaneous, private impulse for revenge, crudely—perhaps brutally—pursued. When people complain about light sentences, they usually mean that their gut instinct for vengeance is unsatisfied. Some, of course, speak out of ignorance, expressing a more general frustration by repeating the common myth that criminals are "coddled" by the "system."

But how does one calibrate vengeance? How to put numbers on just deserts? Perhaps it's easiest at the high end. To many people, at least, it seems obvious that the sane and deliberate act that caused the horrible death of 167 innocent men, women, and small children in Oklahoma City can be atoned, if at all, only by death. But how does one calculate the myriad other factors of aggravation and mitigation that go into an ordinary crime and come up with the precise number of months behind bars that will satisfy a civilized craving for retribution? That is just what the federal sentencing guidelines purport to do. The notorious guidelines (and they provide more than mere guidance) construct a numerical grid that adds and subtracts standardized weights for the factors of gravity, impact, and character that judges normally consider in fixing a sentence. And everyone who has any business with the system agrees: it doesn't work.

Putting aside my problems with the concept of leniency, I will bravely attempt to answer the question: are negotiated sentences too lenient? To begin, I must divide all the jurisdictions of the nation into two groups, stressed and unstressed. Then (even before I define those terms) I must posit a natural plea level. The natural level is the rate at which accused defendants would plead guilty if no inducement were offered. For I believe that a certain number would throw in the towel just to gamble on the favorable consideration judges give defendants who own up to their culpability without excuse or expensive contest (actually, not an unwise gamble). Call it the "guilty-with-an-explanation" crowd. This natural plea level might be lower or even higher, but call it 30 percent for now.

Now the definitions. An unstressed jurisdiction is one where the ratio of available courtroom trial hours to intake rate of new felonies is such that a trial can be accorded to all who request it (70 percent in my hypothesis) within a short enough time after demand that statutory and constitutional standards for a speedy trial are easily met. A stressed jurisdiction—which can be graded in degrees—is everywhere else. One caveat is required. "Available courtroom hours" must take into account not only the number of courtrooms and sitting judges, but the number of prosecutors, public defenders, private counsel, jurors, level of trial time waste, and various wild cards that contribute to inefficiency—delays in transcribing grand jury minutes, police vacation schedules, transportation delays in bringing prisoners to court, etc., etc.

And let's not forget that plea level also reflects, to some extent, the prevailing strength of the prosecution cases. An indictment with strong evidence supporting it is more likely to fetch a guilty plea—and to a higher offer—than a case the defendant thinks he can beat before a jury. A good police corps produces more and higher pleas. So, too, if a prosecutor screens cases carefully at an early stage, reducing and dismissing the losers, the plea rate will be higher. Of course, in addition to the higher proportion of innocent defendants benefiting from a policy of careful evaluation, many guilty people will go free because the person they robbed was a drunk, or the person they shot was a rival drug dealer, or the rape victim keeps changing her story, or the only person who saw the defendant climbing out of the burglarized flat has a criminal record.

Some prosecutors think it's cowardly to try only the easy winners. They are willing to suffer the lower disposition rate to gain the boast that, if they think the defendant is guilty, they indict notwithstanding trial defects and allow the cases to go to the judgment of the jury. That's a policy call. Such a policy, however, is more likely to thrive in a less stressed jurisdiction because it is bound to result in more trials.

I must also insert this datum: drug cases throw off all calculations. Repetitive, tedious, frustrating user and small dealer busts clog calendars, defy judicial wisdom, and stymie prosecutors who must unexpectedly try cases long buried by the avalanche of others just like them and all but forgotten by the cops who made the collars and who must now testify confidently in the spotlight of adversary cross-examination. Everyone knows that law enforcement doesn't solve the drug crisis, but few want to live in a society of unrestricted drug consumption. And it's hard to imagine any drug enforcement policy without this nasty infestation of drug cases on the criminal dockets, state and federal.

But in those jurisdictions, state and federal, with a severe drug problem (and that probably describes most places today), the courtroom pollution mirrors the situation on the streets. Legislators strive dumbly to respond to constituent outcry with the usual punitive reflex. But they have learned that simply increasing sentences for drug crimes doesn't work, so they now try to limit plea bargaining, providing that an indictment for a certain grade of drug crime cannot be disposed of by a plea to a crime below a specified grade.

These politically motivated efforts to force more severe punishment in selected areas of the criminal process reflect an unrealistic view of petty crime and jam the general judicial economy.

The thesis, then, is simply put: excessive leniency is directly proportional to the grade of perceived stress in the jurisdiction.

Of course, the real world is hardly so neatly formulaic. In fact, the market can get sort of circular. I remember one year while I worked as a prosecutor, when we were running at somewhere near 95 percent guilty pleas, my boss replied to a critic with some heat: we were not coercing pleas or giving away the courthouse to get them. In fact, he said, we were so unstressed that we could guarantee a trial to any defendant who wanted one within six weeks of his demand (well within the speedy trial standard). Of course, he was right— as long as we continued at the 95 percent plea rate.

One final element is—and probably should continue to be—a big card in the deal: cooperation. The accused defendant who has important information to disclose in aid of law enforcement, who is willing to risk his life to spy or to testify for the prosecution against some colleagues, that person has a valuable consideration to give for which a prosecutor is usually ready to trade significant reductions in the pending charges. It is the coin of the realm. And it is a large part of the public prosecutor's job to determine whether the case against the ultimate defendant is worth the break to the instrumental defendant. If a soldier in the troops of the mob has a credible story against a boss, especially if the government has little else of probative value against the major figure, the soldier will be probably be compensated generously for cooperation.

The judgment is not always easy to make: who is the bigger fish, the corporate executive buying votes against a clean water bill or the congressman who sells his? And is the evidence (always impeachable) offered by the rat really an indispensable strand in the case against the ultimate defendant? But prosecutors make these judgments all the time and, as far as I can see, the handsome bargains they choose to award their helpers are not resented by the public. So in my ideal schema, I will allow the special case of the customized major discount, negotiated for a particular service in the interests of a greater law enforcement triumph.

Most disturbing of the claims made by critics of plea bargaining is the contention that the system tends to put the innocent in jail. Disturbing because—although one can never know—I have long suspected that there is more than a modicum of truth to the point. More innocent people are in prison on their own guilty pleas, I suspect, than by false verdicts of conviction.

To be brutally realistic—perhaps even somewhat cynical—plea bargaining is not about guilt and innocence. Some remorseful creatures probably do plead guilty because they are guilty (and for no other reason), and some righteous souls probably do go to trial (refusing all offers of leniency) because they are innocent. But only the most naive novice would say that those folk are typical.

Mainly, the pleading game is all about the credibility of the stories that will be told by prosecution and defense through their witnesses and exhibits. The innocent defendant with an incredible (though true) defense is in no better position than his guilty counterpart with an incredible and false defense. The stark, simple, and ugly fact is that true stories can be as incredible as false ones. Maybe more so since the false story is fabricated to seem true. And jurors cannot be trusted any more than any of the rest of us to sort the true from the false with a high degree of accuracy.

A good lawyer, sizing up a case for plea purposes, is less interested in claims of innocence (to be taken with a tablespoon of salt) than in how the story will play to the jury. Is this defendant a believable person? What's his record, his lifestyle, his warmth or personal appeal? How about his witnesses? And these cops, can they be attacked for carelessness, inconsistency, unfeeling character? How badly was the victim hurt? What sort of impression will the victim make on the stand—nervous, unsure, slippery, hostile, vindictive? Or clean, sober, human, and family-loving? On the weakness of the defense position—not its falsity—the lawyer can tell the client, Friend, guilty or innocent, you'd better take the best offer you get, because your story will not sell in the jury room. It's advice any defendant can understand, and the innocent along with the guilty—convinced by the lawyer's calculus—may go willingly to the plea.

If the prosecutor has good reason to believe her witnesses are lying, that the defendant is in fact innocent, then of course the prosecutor is under a strict ethical obligation to dismiss the case. And prosecutors take that obligation seriously. But the prosecutor is not the jury. The prosecutor is under no obligation, ethical or conscientious, to reach a conclusion on the issue of credibility. And if (as is sometimes the case) the prosecutor simply does not know whether the identification her witness swears to is accurate, whether the alibi the defendant offers is true, whether the strongest inference is that the gun was purposely aimed and fired or accidentally discharged, the prosecutor is entitled to bring the facts out fairly and fully and let the jury decide.

How about the court? Doesn't the trial judge have some obligation to see that only the truly guilty plead guilty? Well, yes and no.

The law requires that, before accepting a plea of guilty, the court satisfy itself that there is a "factual basis" for the plea. For most judges, most of the time, that requirement is fulfilled by the allocution, when the judge says to the defendant: "Your counsel has informed the court that you wish to withdraw the plea of not guilty heretofore entered, and that you now wish to plead guilty to the crime of robbery in the second degree. Is that your wish?" Prompted by his lawyer standing at his elbow, the defendant (who may not have fully understood the judge's inquiry) says, "Yes, Your Honor." I have heard it so many times I can recite it in my sleep. The judge says next, "Has anyone threatened you or promised you anything to induce you to take this plea?" "No, Your Honor." Standard, required response. Above all, the plea of guilty must be voluntary (as the Supreme Court has repeatedly warned). Of course, the truth is that the defendant was promised a reduced sentence to induce him to plead guilty. But that doesn't count.

Then the judge, according to his or her style, solicits the necessary factual basis. "Tell me in your own words what you did here," is a popular form of the question. But this is likely to elicit a long story, full of mitigation and self-justification. So some judges prefer to lead the culprit through the requisite catechism of self-inculpation. "By your plea, do you now admit that you did, by the use of a weapon, that is a seven-and-a-half-inch knife, take property, that is, a gold necklace, from the victim, Ms. Roberta Quinones?" "Yes, Your Honor." And so forth. Whether the allocution really elicits a reliable acknowledgment of culpable facts or whether the canny defendant, coached by counsel, simply goes along with an obligatory courtroom ritual is open to some debate.

Actually, the factual basis need not come from the pleader himself. Assurance from the prosecutor that witnesses have given evidence under oath to the grand jury that, if true, would establish the guilt of the defendant—the necessary foundation for a valid indictment—is probably sufficient factual basis for the reception of the proffered plea. So a judge may accept a guilty plea from a defendant who not only will not confess his guilt, but persists in denying it.

This is not quite so shocking as it may at first appear. A defendant, fully informed of the case against him, cognizant of the risks of trial, who freely chooses to forgo a trial in exchange for an acceptable consideration, has made a voluntary bargain, and there is little reason to deny him the benefit of his chosen disposition merely because he will not perform the ritual self-inculpation. The Supreme Court has so held.

Justice Byron White summarized the facts in *North Carolina v. Alford* as follows:

> On December 2, 1963, Alford was indicted for first-degree murder, a capital offense under North Carolina law. The court appointed an attorney to represent him, and this attorney questioned all but one of the various witnesses who appellee said would substantiate his claim of innocence. The witnesses, however, did not support Alford's story but gave statements that strongly indicated his guilt. Faced with strong evidence of guilt and no substantial evidentiary support for the claim of innocence, Alford's attorney recommended that he plead guilty, but left the ultimate decision to Alford himself. The prosecutor agreed to accept a plea of guilty to a charge of second-degree murder, and on December 10, 1963, Alford pleaded guilty to the reduced charge.
>
> Before the plea was finally accepted by the trial court, the court heard the sworn testimony of a police officer who summarized the State's case. Two other witnesses besides Alford were also heard. Although there was no eyewitness to the crime, the testimony indicated that shortly before the killing Alford took his gun from his house, stated his intention to kill the victim, and returned home with the declaration that he had carried out the killing. After the summary presentation of the State's case, Alford took the stand and testified that he had not committed the murder but that he was pleading guilty because he faced the threat of the death penalty if he did not do so. In response to the questions of his counsel, he acknowledged that his counsel had informed him of the difference between second- and first-degree murder and of his rights in case he chose to go to trial. The trial court then asked appellee if, in light of his denial of guilt, he still desired to plead guilty to second-degree murder and appellee answered, "Yes, sir. I plead guilty on—from the circumstances that he (Alford's attorney) told me." After eliciting information about Alford's prior criminal record, which was a long one [he

had been previously convicted for (among other things) murder and robbery (nine times)], the trial court sentenced him to 30 years' imprisonment, the maximum penalty for second-degree murder.

Alford summed it up when he told the court: "I'm not guilty but I plead guilty." After noting that jurisdictions were divided on the question, Justice White explained his reasons for approving Alford's plea as follows:

> [W]hile most pleas of guilty consist of both a waiver of trial and an express admission of guilt, the latter element is not a constitutional requisite to the imposition of criminal penalty. An individual accused of crime may voluntarily, knowingly, and understandingly consent to the imposition of a prison sentence even if he is unwilling or unable to admit his participation in the acts constituting the crime.
>
> Nor can we perceive any material difference between a plea that refuses to admit commission of the criminal act and a plea containing a protestation of innocence when, as in the instant case, a defendant intelligently concludes that his interests require entry of a guilty plea and the record before the judge contains strong evidence of actual guilt. Here the State had a strong case of first-degree murder against Alford. Whether he realized or disbelieved his guilt, he insisted on his plea because in his view he had absolutely nothing to gain by a trial and much to gain by pleading. . . . In view of the strong factual basis for the plea demonstrated by the State and Alford's clearly expressed desire to enter it despite his professed belief in his innocence, we hold that the trial judge did not commit constitutional error in accepting it.

For those in a position comparable to Alford's, many judges today will accept what is called an "Alford plea"—and on considerably less factual basis than was provided in Alford's case.

Does the availability of the Alford plea encourage the innocent to plead guilty? It seems unlikely that more innocent people are taking attractive plea offers because they are not required to admit guilt in the allocution. Long before *Alford* was written, innocent defendants were saying what was required to get the bargain plea they wanted.

But the decision does show that the Constitution, at least, approves the plea primarily as an aware, voluntary, counseled choice, a waiver of rights for an agreed upon consideration. More a contract than a confession. Understanding the consequences, freely electing the course, the defendant is not required also to acknowledge guilt. Though Justice White strongly suggests that the court should approve the defendant's view of his self-interest, that is hardly necessary. It is enough that the judge is convinced that the defendant is sufficiently informed and competent to assess his own self-interest and that there is adequate basis for the defendant's prediction of conviction.

Many judges, it should be said, find this construction of the guilty plea personally offensive. They will not take a guilty plea and impose sentence, they say, on a person who has not fully acknowledged his guilt in open court. However strong the factual basis, however intelligent the choice, to these judges the essence of the guilty plea is the mea culpa. The break incorporated in the bargain is justified in large measure, they believe, by the willingness of the defendant publicly to acknowledge his wrongdoing. To me, this view only demonstrates how easily judges—even wise and sophisticated judges—come to believe in the forms and trappings of their own rituals. A mumbled assent or halting narrative, spoken because a lawyer told him that unless he said those words, the judge would not allow him to take the advantageous plea, comes to signify to the judge a soul-purging confession.

Putting it all together, I come to the conclusion that there is considerable value in the plea bargaining process wholly apart from its docket-clearing utility. I can think of at least two good things to say about it. First, I believe that the prosecutor and defense counsel are in at least as good a position as the judge and the probation officer to evaluate the gravity of the crime and the character of the defendant. Not that they should take over the sentencing responsibility from the court; I lament the courtrooms where that has happened to the pleading practice. Sentencing is, ultimately, what judges are for. But the lawyers may have an important contribution to make to the exercise of judicial discretion. And they are certainly better situated for the job than the legislature. In fact, the lawyers are there, in large part, to relieve the rigidity that the legislature imposes upon the process.

Ideally, disposition of criminal charges by guilty plea should be a responsibility nicely shared among the branches. The legislature identifies the crimes, divides them into degrees of gravity, and sets rather broad limits of sentence for each grade. These are essentially choices to be made by the representative branch. The executive determines who should be charged and with what. Prosecutors, as executive branch officers, "enforce the laws" by performing this job. The judge, after managing the process and assuring a fair, orderly disposition according to law, selects the appropriate punishment for each individual offender.

It's a nice schema. But it is vulnerable to the political process. The anger of the electorate at the high crime rates is loudly communicated to their elected representatives, who readily (and foolishly) agree that the problem stems from the excessive leniency of the executive and judicial branches. The easiest way a legislator can demonstrate concern is to enact legislation that limits discretion and forces the soft branches to stiffen up. Harsher sentences, minimum sentences, mandatory jail time, standardized "grid" sentencing, and restrictions on reduction of charges by guilty plea are some of the common results of this legislative ardor. The irony is that at the same time in many places, the legislators, wary of the high cost of building new prisons, connive at "early release" programs that let out dangerous people long before they are eligible for parole on their imposed sentences. These invisible little back-door, budget-wise, across-the-board jail deliveries are another testament to legislative hypocrisy, a small scandal waiting to happen.

It then becomes incumbent on the executive and judicial players to circumvent and undermine these measures wherever they see a case they believe demands a more realistic disposition. I believe that, insofar as the plea bargaining system brings individualized judgment and warranted compassion back into the system, insofar as it serves to make finer cuts on culpability than the gross legislative scheme allows, it is a good and valuable part of the process. It helps to keep the human dimension in the dehumanizing business of processing criminal cases.

My second good thing to say is that I think the criminal defendant is entitled to know with the greatest possible certainty what he faces. Because I do not take the process primarily as a confessional experience that will uplift the soul of the malefactor, I (like the *Alford* Court) tend to emphasize its contractual features. A criminal defendant, innocent or guilty, is entitled to know what he is risking and what he is settling for before he makes the important choice. So if the lawyers, with the agreement of the judge, have reevaluated his crime, factoring in all the aggravating and mitigating circumstances of his personal situation, and decided that his crime (which by genre, the legislature pegged at up to fifteen) is worth about five years in prison, the defendant should know it. I prefer an intelligent choice to the blind leap onto the "mercy" of the court. Not as romantic, I grant, but cold calculation seems the appropriate mode when a person—even a criminal—makes a vital decision.

This leads me to venture a model of what I would consider a healthy pleading process. I must postulate, first, a jurisdiction of only moderate stress, though the beauty of my plan is that it can be modified according to the grade of local stress without losing the structure. It would run like this:

For every defendant who comes out of the machinery of accusation (the mechanisms are various, but let us say by indictment from a grand jury), a conference should be held among opposing counsel and the presiding judge during which the individual case is fully evaluated on its special merits and an appropriate sentence settled upon. Of course, it is understood that any new facts bearing on gravity that come out at a trial would necessitate a new evaluation. Then a standard reduction should be allowed for the guilty plea, let's say a 20 percent discount for saving the state the time and risk of a trial, 40 percent if the prosecutor labels the case a tough one to prove. So if the case is called a forty-eight-month rap when it first comes down the chute, that is the sentence the defendant can expect if convicted by verdict. If he promptly pleads guilty, his sentence will be discounted 20 percent to 38.4 months, and if the prosecutor calls his own case problematic, the defendant can get away with 28.8 months on a guilty plea. These numbers, of course, are adjustable according to the grade of stress in the jurisdiction. In a nice slow jurisdiction, with plenty of court time available for criminal trials, I can see discount rates of 10 and 25 percent; in a really stressed jurisdiction, perhaps 33 and 60 percent, maybe even higher. We might also have a category for especially heinous crimes which are evaluated at the top of the range set by the law. These cases the prosecutor could withdraw altogether from the standard allowance. These presumably would be tried because the defendant would incur little risk by trial, aside from the revelation of facts that make the judge lower an already low opinion of the brute. We also need a flexible discount factor for the "cooperating" defendant.

In all, the prevailing system of plea bargaining seems both better and worse than its popular image. It is better because by and large it neither cheapens crime by overgenerous allowances nor discriminates against the poor and friendless defendant. Whether it induces guilty pleas from the innocent is hard to say, but it is probably true that most of those who plead guilty would be convicted on trial. At the same time, the system is worse than its image because it unavoidably levies a tax on those who elect to exercise their constitutional right to trial by jury. Perhaps some consolation might be found in the realization that few options in the criminal justice system are cost-free. Some elections necessarily entail the surrender of some incompatible right. One can enjoy the constitutional right to the assistance of counsel only at the expense of relinquishing the right to represent oneself. The right to testify in one's own defense is purchased only by the surrender of the constitutional right to remain silent about the crime.

I find such consolation false. Some years back, the Supreme Court considered a California statute that allowed a judge to instruct a jury on the precise inference that could be reasonably drawn from a defendant's decision not to testify. It was, of course, an essentially unfavorable inference because an innocent person would be reasonably expected to take the stand and deny the charge under oath. In that case, *Griffin v. California,* the Court struck down the statute under the Fifth Amendment right of silence. It cut down on the privilege, the Court said, by making its assertion costly. So too, I fear, the plea bargaining system cuts down on the right to trial by making its assertion costly.

Acknowledging this serious infirmity, I am nonetheless content to live with a plea-dependent system of adjudication. Here, virtual justice works better than the authentic model. I only wish more jurisdictions were less stressed (especially by drug cases) and that some sensible procedure could be worked out to improve the information upon which a defendant makes his plea contract.

10 Picking the Jury

Stacking the Randomly Drawn Panel

All trial lawyers will agree: choosing the jurors to sit on your case is half the battle. And most will confide that they have an uncanny knack, nurtured into a crucial skill, of recognizing favorably disposed fellow citizens when they are called to the jury box, and of decoding the extrasensory signals of unconscious hostility. The novice or chastened trial lawyer (if any can be found) can readily acquire from seasoned colleagues field-tested guides and surefire charts of juror propensity essential to produce a sympathetic jury on the minimal cues afforded by the selection process. And the defendant who really wants to buy himself a gold-plated defense can easily hire an expert jury picker from a small industry of psychologists and psychics who advertise that they can tell at a glance how potential jurors will vote six weeks down the line, after all the evidence is in (whatever it may be) and they are sequestered in heated debate with one another.

The curious thing is that the American system of adjudication affords lawyers and their hired advisers ample opportunity to display these supposed talents.

Katherine O'Leary was still in her twenties when she met Manuel Gomez, a handsome man in his forties. It was an old-fashioned love story. Katherine was swept off her feet by Manuel's legendary Latin ardor—amplified by his evident wealth. Manny told Katie that he was Venezuelan and in the import business. He had an elegant shop, The Treasure Chest, where he sold handsome furniture and other expensive items imported, he said, from Argentina and other South American countries. What he did not tell her was that his principal line of imports was cocaine, which frequently arrived cleverly concealed in beautiful inlaid chests and leatherbound books.

Manny and Katie would surely have married had not Manny admitted that he already had a wife in Venezuela, whom he did not love and had not seen in many years but could not divorce because "divorce is impossible under the laws of my country." Katie and Manny did live together as husband and wife and, within a year, they had a baby girl whom they called Esmeralda in honor of Katie's heritage. When Katie became restless—she had always had a job until she met Manny—Manny set her up in a clothing boutique, which appeared to flourish notwithstanding the extravagant prices of the merchandise. She called it The Emerald for the baby, but the name also conveyed some idea of the quality of the trade she attracted. Manny, a generous man of seemingly limitless resources, invested heavily in Katie's stock. Although he showed a great deal of interest in The Emerald, Manny was reluctant to discuss his own affairs in any detail, and Katie learned to respect his preference, asking few questions.

All in all, the couple appeared to flourish until the government concluded its long investigation of a Latino drug smuggling ring and the indictments came down. Gomez was charged as one of the principal importers. O'Leary was indicted as a co-conspirator. The government believed that her close association with Manny during the three or four years they were together, her observed participation in meetings with other co-conspirators (whom Manny had always introduced as friends in the business), her overheard telephone conversations in which she took messages about business dealings for Manny (not realizing the messages were, as the government alleged, in code) confirmed her complicity. Most significant, the government thought The Emerald was another "money laundering scheme," a means—like The Treasure Chest—for Manny to convert a portion of his illegal income into profit from a legitimate business. O'Leary, the government believed, must have known of and willingly participated in the conspiracy that supported her handsome lifestyle. They underestimated her tact and naïveté.

When the indictment came down, Katie O'Leary was devastated. She was outraged at Manny's duplicity, humiliated by her own wilful ignorance, and desperately concerned for the future of her child. She was immediately released on bail (which she raised easily enough), but Manny was held on the government's contention that, if released, he would immediately flee the country for parts unknown. Which would have suited Katie just fine.

In the weeks following her indictment, Katie was very busy. She liquidated The Emerald, sold what she could of their household belongings, and took little Esme to her sister's house, where they planned to stay for the foreseeable future. She also asked around a lot and finally retained Marjorie Dressler, Esq., to represent her. Dressler was only two years out of the U.S. Attorney's office, but she had already made a good name for herself. She was highly regarded as a prosecutor, especially for her successful prosecution of a major drug case, and she switched sides without spilling a drop of the reputation she carried.

It was clear from the start that no plea could be negotiated, so Marjorie set about preparing for a long trial. It was particularly important, she felt, for Katie to have jurors who would understand and sympathize with her position. A great deal depended upon the jurors' willingness to think about her as a human being separate and apart from the other conspirators being tried with her. As the trial date approached, the composition of the jury consumed Marjorie's thoughts about the case. Like all of her breed, Marjorie relied on a stockpile of personal biases, untested generalizations, and irrational guesswork as she went about the delicate task of jury composition.

First, there was the ethnic card. Ordinarily, Dressler assumed that these days, minorities voted for their own: she would expect a certain Latino solidarity with Gomez, especially among males, and that would also put them on Katie's side against the feds. In this case, though, Dressler expected to cast Gomez as the heavy, a macho rich Hispanic drug dealer who kept his pretty little wife as an innocent plaything while exploiting her ignorance to launder his illicit profits. That strategy might antagonize Latino jurors—certainly the men. Better keep them off. Irish, on the other hand, whom she usually thought were on the government side, would probably be the best jurors for her: they might see Katie as one of their little sisters who was taken in by this smooth Latin lover. Jews were a tougher problem. Jews also were generally law enforcement types, not likely to be sympathetic to Latinos, especially where drugs were involved. On the other hand, Dressler had always found them—and especially the women—to be suckers for a romantic story. And Katie O'Leary was, in many ways, just the heroine they could identify with.

Women in general were also a problem group. Unlike many minority jurors, women did not always sympathize with women cast as victims. They were suspicious of male stereotypes that painted women as helpless and dumb. And the portrait of Katie might be offensive to some and make them wonder whether she didn't really know more of what was happening than she let on. Marjorie finally decided that it was largely an age issue; older women would be better for O'Leary than younger women. Maybe that was true of men also. Go for the gray heads. Here she would have to trust her instincts—see what sort of feel she could get by looking them in the eye.

What about the blacks in a case like this? she wondered. Ah, that was truly an interesting question. Many blacks tended to align with other minorities and were unfavorably disposed to law enforcement agencies. But Dressler had often sensed a subtle and unspoken hostility toward Latinos. So if she could cast Katie as a victim of both her Latin lover and the heavy-handed DEA, she might get a sympathetic reaction from black jurors. On the other hand, she knew that black women were sometimes hostile to white women, especially those who took men from across the racial divide. And she feared that at least some of the younger black men might identify subconsciously with a smart, high-living dude who made a fortune in the drug trade while keeping a cute white chick in the dark. Again, go for the grayer heads—the younger blacks might be risky.

But what's going on here? Can a lawyer pick jurors like horses at a horse race, by the judicious application of impulsive hunch? Like candidates for lesser political offices, by the shameless employment of blatant bigotry and crude stereotype? Shouldn't the community be represented on the jury by some chance configuration of its constituent groups? What is a jury, anyway, and how should it be composed to serve the interests of criminal justice?

The modern jury is a highly evolved device for answering important, and sometimes unanswerable questions, like Just what happened at this particular moment in the past, who was the principal actor, and what was on his mind at the time? Putting those questions to a carefully randomized, professedly fair-minded, but uninformed group of ordinary citizens is an idea that belongs peculiarly to peoples whose native language is English.

It was not ever thus.

Into the early thirteenth century (as everyone knows), one of the conventional means of "trying" a criminal charge was the ordeal. Under ecclesiastical aegis, the accused was required to hold a red-hot iron bar in his bare hands; if he showed no burns or blisters twenty-four hours later, he was declared innocent. Or the defendants were bound and plunged into a body of water; if they sank to the bottom, innocence was proved, if they floated to the top, they were obviously guilty. The trial by ordeal had many equally brutal variations—all to the same end. Brutal, yes, but not pointless. The accusation, returned by a large chunk of the community at a time when everyone knew everyone else's business, was very likely to be true. The "trial" was, in effect, an appeal for a divine signal—a minor miracle—in the event of mistake.

Then one fine day, for reasons I know not, Pope Innocent III, at the Second Lateren Council of 1215 (the same year, coincidentally, as Magna Carta), decreed that priests would no longer preside at the ordeals. Withdrawing the Lord's official ministers effectively deprived the ordeal of its purpose. On the continent of Europe, the medieval methods were largely replaced by the Inquisition, which aimed at receiving confirmation of the accusation by the confession of the accused. Torture was commonly employed to facilitate this quest for "proof."

In the British Isles, a different solution was developing. The accused, at his option, could be "put upon the country," meaning that his case would be submitted to a small group of fellow citizens, who would declare him guilty or innocent. The choice of going to trial before a jury was not entirely free. An accused could be pressed to accept the trial. Literally pressed: forced to lie under a board as rocks were piled on until the accused signaled his decision to accept a jury trial. Some allowed themselves to be crushed to death, the surest way to preserve their property for their families, who would forfeit their inheritance in the event of a conviction after trial by jury. You might have gotten a wry smile had you told the poor fellow under the board that he was helping establish the great right to trial by jury, the centerpiece in the Anglo-American system of justice.

The trial jury was called the *petit jury* to distinguish it from the *grand jury* that had framed the accusation. Trial by petit jury in its early form did not resemble the modern trial. For one thing, witnesses were not invented for several centuries. The jury, all from the "vicinage"—the neighborhood— were presumed to know the facts. They were, in effect, a jury of witnesses. Unlike the European courts, the English juries were not required to arrive at virtual certainty before finding guilt. A reasonably good likelihood was sufficient—even in that era of pervasive capital punishment. Still, juries would often acquit out of pure sympathy or distaste for the law even though, during the seventeenth century, jurors could be fined or imprisoned for returning a verdict of acquittal that the court thought was unwarranted. Ironically, the lower standard of proof required to convict in England compared to the Continent may be the reason that court-ordered torture was rarely employed by our legal ancestors: confessions were not necessary for conviction.

As life became more complex in England, mobility increased and the growth of cities promoted anonymity. Witnesses were gradually brought in to assist the jury, which could no longer rely on personal knowledge of the parties and the occurrences at issue. Gradually, by the nineteenth century, the system came around 180 degrees and jurors were required to be ignorant of the facts. At about the same time, the notion grew that the accused in a criminal case had a right to be tried on the evidence by a representative group of fellow citizens who harbored no secret antagonism. The process of jury selection had begun in earnest.

When talking about the composition of a jury, people often toss off the phrase "jury of peers." It's a pretty tag line—and today, pretty meaningless. When originally inscribed in Magna Carta, the principle granted nobles the right to be tried by juries composed exclusively of members of the nobility— hardly the usage the phrase has today, when it is thought to grant each individual the right to be tried by people like himself. Obviously, there is no such right. A teenaged defendant cannot claim the right to a jury of adolescents, a college graduate cannot demand trial by a comparably educated jury, a defendant with three burglary convictions has no right to be tried by a jury of felons.

Rather, we translate "peers" to mean something like a "representative cross section of the community." But again, the popular phrase should not be read literally. It certainly does not mean that the various elements of the community (however they may be recognized—race, sex, age, education, occupation, or political philosophy) must be reflected in every panel of twelve, each in its just proportion. What it does mean is that juries must be drawn from pools (called the *venire*) from which no discrete segment of the community has been unfairly and systematically excluded.

Even that idea is not quite as simple as it sounds, and its meaning is frequently the cause of bitter lawsuits. Is poverty a significantly defining characteristic of a component of the community, such that the venire may not be drawn from voting lists, tax rolls, and telephone books because they "systematically" exclude poor people who are sparsely represented on those lists? Then, too, not all discrete elements of the community are entitled to be included. It is not unreasonable to exclude those with felony convictions, or those with mental diseases or other disabling impairments; and because evidence often comes in documentary form, literacy might be required. But what is a "disabling impairment"? Recently, courts have begun to consider the tough question of just what basic faculties are essential to the performance of jury service. Jurors who are fluent and literate in a language other than English might have an interpreter. But that is a costly way to maximize diversity and, it might be argued, a juror cannot judge credibility when a witness's answers are translated by the interpreter, who cleanses them of hesitations and mistakes and supplies her own inflections and tone of voice. The deaf claim that their handicap enriches their sensitivity to other cues. The blind have argued that they have compensating sensitivities and that their systematic exclusion denies the accused a fully representative cross-section of the community.

Exemptions are another problem. Among those summoned, are there any who should be entitled to an automatic excuse? Within my memory, women could decline service at will, and lawyers were never summoned. That has changed. Physicians in most places can still excuse themselves, and others who are deemed to perform vital public service are exempt. Should exemptions be allowed automatically for mothers of small children? Those who care for the sick or elderly? Public school teachers? Ambulance drivers? Firefighters? Who else?

From all this contention, commissioners in the various jurisdictions have managed to compile comprehensive rolls of qualified citizens from which panels may be drawn. Most have defended their raw pools from time to time against challenges and have adjusted to any discerned exclusions that the courts have thought unwarranted. In my opinion, the jury lists remain a potpourri that doesn't bear close examination. All I know is that among my friends—all to be found in the standard directories and rosters from which jurors are drawn—some are called regularly every few years while others have never been called. One of the mysteries of life.

After the comprehensive rolls are compiled, providing a vast list of eligible citizens with no unfair exclusions, we rely mainly on the laws of chance to ensure a fair representation on any given venire. It is odd how we place our faith in random selection. It is almost as if we hear the faint echoes of the ancient faith in divine intervention. All law students in their first year are exposed to the old English case of *Regina v. Dudley & Stephens,* the famous lifeboat dilemma. A boatful of shipwrecked sailors were dying of exposure, thirst, and starvation when they decided their only hope was to resort to cannibalism. They chose the weakest of their group for sacrifice and killed and ate him. They were rescued sometime thereafter and eventually stood trial for murder. (They were convicted and their death sentences commuted to six months' imprisonment.)

When I put the issue to law students, I am always surprised to see how many believe the moral wrong was in the selection of the victim by a rational process rather than by drawing lots. When life and death decisions are to be made, evidently, we should trust not the human mind but the hand of God manifest in the outcome of a seeming chance draw. This odd faith in justice-by-chance finds its way into law in various and humbler choicepoints. I remember reading recently about a school that was required to reduce the size of its faculty and, between two equally qualified faculty members, chose to discharge the white woman and retain the black (though the faculty did not lack racial diversity). The discharged teacher sued on the theory that the school should have made the selection not by considered choice but by thoughtless chance.

So we believe the "cross section" we have striven for in the composition of the universe of eligible jurors will be preserved in the random sample we draw for our venire, then from the venire (by lot) to the box to be examined for service in a particular case. Here we are, then, with twelve in the box, maybe fourteen if we plan to have two alternates, as pure and perfect a representative jury as we are able to compose. Do we leave it as we drew it and proceed to trial? Not on your life.

First, we must tinker with the group fate has delivered into the jury box. Even trust in the god of chance goes only so far. There may be some among them who have concealed some important bias that would prejudice them one way or the other in the case to be tried to them. Is some prospective juror married to an agent of the Drug Enforcement Agency, which made the case against Gomez and O'Leary? Has someone a child with a drug problem and thus a tendency to vote to convict anyone connected in any way with the drug trade? Does one of the twelve have a friend who was falsely accused by a DEA agent? Obviously, we have to ask a few dozen questions to discover these possible grounds for challenge "for cause."

In federal courts and many state courts, the judges do most of this examination. This voir dire will smoke out a few who admit to prejudice and discover others whose background affords strong suspicion that they will not be able to keep an open mind and decide the case exclusively on the evidence presented at trial (as the standard for service requires). We spin the wheel again and replace the excused jurors with others from the venire and repeat the voir dire with them. Challenges for cause have now been exhausted; do we swear the randomly drawn group, as adjusted to eliminate special grounds of disqualification? Not on your life.

We come now to one of the monumental paradoxes in the American criminal justice process. The peremptory challenge. Having scrupulously composed a potential jury, representative of the community as a whole and free of any bias, we allow the lawyers to superimpose their personal set of prejudices to recompose the jury as the most *favorably* biased group that each side can come up with before exhausting its store of peremptory challenges. Sometimes (if the attorneys are sufficiently astute—and have enough challenges), the adversarial setoff in the use of peremptories produces not a jury of opposed predilections but a bland compromise of jurors whose biases are well concealed or who have no predispositions of any sort. Needless to say, these people either are not the most forthcoming citizens or are not the most alert and sensitive, those who have the broadest experience with life. Maybe not the best kind to sit on criminal juries. But most of those who display an "outlook" or who appear to have given some thought to issues of crime and culpability have probably fallen to the peremptory axe.

For the glory of the peremptory challenge is that it allows the lawyers for both sides to excuse any potential juror without stating any reason for the challenge. The number of peremptories allocated to each side varies from place to place, and usually with the severity of the crime, but it is large. In the State of New York, for example, each side gets twenty peremptories in a murder case, fifteen in an armed robbery; in a case like O'Leary's the federal courts would allow the government six peremptory challenges and the defense ten. Although that number is rarely doubled or tripled when two or three defendants are tried together, it may be increased by some number at the discretion of the trial judge.

The protracted voir dire examination by counsel (tolerated by many trial judges) can stretch jury selection in a serious case to many days of precious court time. If the case has had a lot of press, it can take weeks to pick a jury.

Counsel are searching, probing for some little clue to the disposition of the juror. Is this a broad-brush painter, the sort of person who is impatient with details, who believes that where there's smoke there's usually a fire? Is this a person who is mistrustful of young people? Foreigners? Hostile to authority figures? What is there in the life experience of this person that might make him sympathetic or hostile to my witnesses, or to the defendant herself? Is this the kind of person who would dislike me, react badly to the personality I project? Or is this the kind I can usually charm?

I've voir dired many a venire, but I don't think I was ever very good at it. For one thing, I have little confidence in my ability to read personality or to predict disposition. People always seem to me full of surprises. Too often, I find people acting inconsistently with their "type," and I never seemed able to find the telling question that would crack the mystery of a stranger's personality. Though my uncertainties lengthened my examination beyond what a judge should tolerate, I cannot say it produced a more favorably disposed group.

But even if the exercise of my peremptories at the end was a shot in the dark, by then I had usually advanced a hidden agenda. In the process of examining the potential jurors for subconscious prejudices, I would "brainwash" them on my case (to use the conventional, but hardly appropriate term). I pretend to no originality here; everyone did it.

If I were Marjorie Dressler, for example, picking a jury for Katie O'Leary, I might ask a juror: "You may hear evidence from the prosecution in this case that makes you think that Katie must have been really naive. You may say that, in that situation, you yourself would have found out what was really going on. Now, madam, can you honestly give me your assurance that if the judge instructs you that this case must be decided on what Katie actually knew, not on what she should have known, you will be able to follow that instruction?" If I were the prosecutor (and the judge let me), I might ask a juror, "Now, sir, you may hear evidence in this case that the defendant, Ms. O'Leary, has a child of tender years. I want you to look into your conscience and tell me honestly: if you thought that the evidence established the defendant's guilt beyond a reasonable doubt, would you be tempted to vote not guilty solely to allow this mother to go home to care for her young daughter?" Questions of this sort allow counsel not only to discover some hidden springs of adverse sentiment but to extract from the jurors assurances that they would not hold the weaknesses of the case against the vulnerable party. You never know; these pledges might help some jurors over the soft spots in your case.

Looming large among the wide assortment of trusty prejudices in the trial lawyer's repertoire is race. The factor can become quite complex as lawyers ring elaborate changes on the several racial and ethnic elements of a community as they might appear in the array of players—cop, victim, and defendant, cross-referenced against the type of crime, age, sex, class, and a host of other variables. How, the lawyer might speculate, would a young, black, female, upscale juror react to an economic crime by a middle-aged Hispanic male merchant against a Vietnamese family, hinging largely on the credibility of an Irish cop and his Jewish partner?

But often the race card is as simple as it is blatant. Black jurors sympathize with black defendants, especially against white witnesses and white cops. If pressed, prosecutors will modify this gross axiom, but it still comes out: *most* or *some* or *working class* black jurors *tend* to sympathize, etc. Coupled with the universal maxim "better safe than sorry," the frequent result in criminal cases was predominantly white juries trying black defendants, especially for crimes against white victims. After all, that's what the peremptory challenge system is designed for: go with the odds.

Liberals weren't alone in finding something distinctly distasteful about the common picture in the courtrooms across the land—white cops bringing black defendants before white judges to be prosecuted and defended by white lawyers before white jurors. Even as more and more black faces appeared in uniforms, robes, and pinstripes, the peremptory challenge system allowed the jury to be largely purged of African-Americans on a trial-by-trial basis. The stain of white oppression seemingly operating through law remained offensive to most Americans. Including the Justices of the Supreme Court.

More than thirty years ago, in a case called *Swain v. Alabama,* the Court held that the state denies a criminal defendant his right to equal protection of the law under the Fourteenth Amendment to the Constitution by the pervasive exercise of peremptories to exclude blacks from petit juries trying black defendants. The principle was established but, as a practical matter, few defendants could prove repeated and systematic misuses of the challenge in cases beyond their own. All court watchers knew the principle required a more realistic delivery. But it took a while.

Twenty-one years after *Swain,* in 1986, the Supreme Court took another look at the problem. A solid seven signatures supported the Court's opinion in *Batson v. Kentucky,* but the case produced five separate opinions in addition to Justice Powell's for the majority. When six of the nine Justices want to express their own opinions in a case, you know you are looking at a hot item. It is also interesting that the two dissenters (who also wrote separately, but signed each other's opinions) were the then and future Chiefs: Warren Burger and William Rehnquist. In *Batson,* Powell made an effort to assure that peremptory challenges were not used by the state in any particular case to strike blacks solely on account of race.

The "rule" resulting from *Batson* has a number of problems both of application and of implication for other cases where the exercise of peremptory challenges has a particularly repellent odor. Indeed, for many of us, the problems are so intransigent that the great old tradition of the peremptory challenge is itself called into question.

For one thing, the *Batson* procedure is a bit cumbersome and more than somewhat foolish. Initially, the African-American defendant bears the burden of showing that potential black jurors have been challenged by the prosecution with a "discriminatory purpose." The court must decide, on the defendant's claim, whether the pattern of prosecution strikes, the sort of questions asked on voir dire, or some other visible cue supports the inference of an intentional purge of blacks because they are black. When and how does the prosecutor's secret purpose become manifest? With the first prosecutorial challenge to a black venirist who seems otherwise perfectly well qualified? After three or four challenges of blacks—even though one black was seated without challenge? By comparing the prosecutor's choices of whites or other races with choices among blacks of the same general description?

No rules to guide us in this, but let's assume that at some point, defense counsel rises and says, "Your Honor, I can see what is happening here and I don't like it. The prosecutor has now challenged four of the last five African-Americans called and I make a *Batson* objection." And let's assume further that somehow the judge gets a whiff of the forbidden purpose. At this point, the judge calls the lawyers up to the bench and in a low voice says, "Yes, Mr. District Attorney, I can see what counsel means. I assume that you have some good reason for these challenges?" The burden now shifts to the prosecutor to come up with a race-neutral explanation of the strikes.

It's something even a raw recruit should have no trouble crafting. This one had a relative in jail, that one didn't make eye contact, a third one had a bad experience with a cop. It doesn't take much to justify a move that can be justified by irrationality.

Or so I thought. In the spring of 1995, in an unsigned opinion (which nevertheless drew two dissents), the Supreme Court decided a case elaborating on the race-neutral basis for the challenge of a black venireman. Only a quotation in full can do justice to the explanation that the prosecutor came up with in *Purkett v. Elem* for his peremptory strikes of two African-American men:

> I struck [juror] number twenty-two because of his long hair. He had long curly hair. He had the longest hair of anybody on the panel by far. He appeared to not be a good juror for that fact, the fact that he had long hair hanging down shoulder length, curly, unkempt hair. Also, he had a mustache and a goatee type beard. And juror number twenty-four also has a mustache and goatee type beard. Those are the only two people on the jury . . . with facial hair. . . . And I don't like the way they looked, with the way the hair is cut, both of them. And the mustaches and the beards look suspicious to me.

The prosecutor's explanation passed several layers of review until the federal Court of Appeals for the Eighth Circuit said, Hold it! This nonsense was obviously "pretextual." It's a good thing the Supreme Court opinion is unsigned; it is one of the silliest pieces of reasoning in a long time. But the bottom line was: It may have been utterly implausible, but the D.A.'s explanation was "race neutral," and that's all *Batson* requires.

An uncertain question is, What is the remedy? What should the judge do about it, if she finds the prosecutor's disingenuous explanation has not dispelled the suspicion of a racial motivation? I suppose she must discharge the seated jurors and start again with a new venire—this notwithstanding the fact that the defendant likes the first batch of jurors selected. Maybe she must call back and seat those improperly discharged. The problem rarely arises because a good judge takes the pragmatic approach: "All right, counsel," she'll say sternly, "but I'm watching you and I don't want any problem with this record, do we understand each other?" "Oh, yes, Judge. Trust me." And in the next batch, black jurors will not be challenged by the prosecutor unless they are beyond the pale. So it works out, after a fashion. But the fact that it works smoothly every day in courtrooms all over the nation should not conceal the essential fact that the rule, within its own compass, is incoherent.

A much harder question, the question not yet completely answered, is, Where do we go from here?

It seems pretty clear from *Batson*'s heritage, running back to an 1880 decision called *Strauder v. West Virginia,* that the line is dedicated to eradicating the badges of slavery. The special care called for in the matter of race responds to lingering prosecutorial discrimination based on assumptions of racial stereotyping. On this theory, the rule should apply only when black defendants protest state exercise of the peremptories to remove black jurors.

However, it did not take long to realize that it was not only the prosecution that used race as a basis for peremptory challenge. In some cases white defendants attempt to purge the jury of blacks; sometimes black defendants do not want blacks (as, for example, when a black man is accused of abusing a black woman). Should *Batson* apply to *defense* peremptories exercised against black jurors?

Why not? Well, for one thing, there is a serious doctrinal obstacle. It's not the state that is doing the discriminating, and the Fourteenth Amendment only forbids state denials of equal protection. That little problem did not unduly trouble the Court, however, and, when they got the right case, *Georgia v. McCollum* in 1992, Justice Blackmun led the Court through some fancy doctrinal footwork and announced the "reverse-*Batson* doctrine." It's the trial *court* that does the discriminating, it turns out, when it allows the defense peremptory challenges. So criminal defendants are now under the same injunction not to exercise their peremptories to challenge African-Americans on the basis of race.

From there, it was a short step to wonder whether an impermissible discrimination is made whenever the race of the defendant is different from the race of the jurors challenged. Suppose a black complainant against a white merchant. The prosecution might decide that white jurors would be less sympathetic than blacks; could they challenge white jurors on account of race? And, of course, if we decide that all of these racially based peremptories, in all their permutations, offend the spirit of *Batson*, the irresistible next question will be, why limit the rule to black-white discrimination? Blacks are not the only group who have suffered the biased exercise of peremptory challenge. Latinos and Asians have surely felt it, as have others groups not characterized as racial or ethnic: women, homosexuals, artists and intellectuals, recent immigrants, old people, handicapped people, animal lovers. If our goal is to pick juries free of conventional prejudice, should we not apply the *Batson* rule whenever either side exercises peremptories on the basis of racial, ethnic, gender, or other socially unacceptable prejudice?

One of the latest cases from the Supreme Court is called *J. E. B. v. Alabama ex rel T. B.* and was decided in April of 1994. It was a child support case (the Court had already decided that *Batson* applied to civil as well as criminal trials) in which T. B., the child's mother, used nine of her ten peremptory challenges to remove men from the jury. In *J. E. B.*, Justice Blackmun, once again writing the lead opinion, held that "gender, like race, is an unconstitutional proxy for juror competence and impartiality."

It was only a month after *J. E. B.* came down that the Court declined to hear a case involving religion as a basis for challenging prospective jurors. A case called *Davis v. Minnesota* raised the issue of whether a juror affiliated with the Jehovah's Witnesses could be excused on that basis because the prosecutor said she believed that "[i]n my experience Jehovah Witness [*sic*] are reluctant to exercise authority over their fellow human beings in this Court House." The Minnesota court, reading *Batson,* concluded that the equal protection analysis applied only to juror discrimination based on race. The Supreme Court's refusal to hear the case brought a sharp dissent from Justice Clarence Thomas (joined by his usual ally, Justice Scalia). Thomas had joined the dissenters in *J. E. B.*, but he now wrote:

> I find it difficult to understand how the Court concludes today that the judgment of the court below should not be vacated and the case remanded in light of our recent decision in *J. E. B. v. Alabama ex rel. T. B.* which shatters the Supreme Court of Minnesota's understanding that *Batson*'s equal protection analysis applies solely to racially based peremptory strikes. . . . In extending Equal Protection Clause analysis to prohibit strikes exercised on the basis of sex, *J. E. B.* explicitly disavowed that understanding of *Batson.*
>
> Indeed, given the Court's rationale in *J. E. B.*, no principled reason immediately appears for declining to apply *Batson* to any strike based on a classification that is accorded heightened scrutiny under the Equal Protection Clause. The Court's decision in *J. E. B.* was explicitly grounded on a conclusion that peremptory strikes based on sex cannot survive "height-

ened scrutiny" under the Clause because such strikes "are not substantially related to an important government objective." . . .

I can only conclude that the Court's decision to deny certiorari stems from an unwillingness to confront forthrightly the ramifications of the decision in *J. E. B.* It has long been recognized by some members of the Court that subjecting the peremptory strike to the rigors of equal protection analysis may ultimately spell the doom of the strike altogether, because the peremptory challenge is by nature "an arbitrary and capricious right." . . . Once the scope of the logic in *J. E. B.* is honestly acknowledged, it cannot be glibly asserted that the decision has no implications for peremptory strikes based on classifications other than sex, or that it does not imply further restrictions on the exercise of the peremptory strike outside the context of race and sex.

Justice Thomas's position is undisputable by my lights. Tempted by our cultural inclination toward egalitarian justice, we come up hard against the very concept of the peremptory challenge. Free-ranging, unapologetic, irrational indulgence in prediction by assumption of subset behavior. In a word: prejudice. "While we recognize, of course," Justice Powell wrote—with dubious sincerity—in *Batson,* "that the peremptory challenge occupies an important position in our trial procedures, we do not agree that our decision today will undermine the contribution the challenge generally makes to the administration of justice." Certainly, the Court had no intention of abolishing the pernicious peremptory challenge, that ancient mainstay of the jury system. But they had surely set in motion an idea, couched as it initially was in equal protection terms, that was bound to undermine the foundations of the peremptory challenge.

States are now developing their own variations on the rule, and the last word has not been heard from the marble temple where the Nine Oracles do business. But for my money, Justice Thurgood Marshall said it right in *Batson.* After praising the majority for recognizing the "pernicious" employment of the peremptory challenge, he continued: "The decision today will not end the racial discrimination that peremptories inject into the jury-selection process. That goal can be accomplished only by eliminating peremptory challenges entirely. . . . Much ink has been spilled regarding the historic importance of defendants' peremptory challenges. . . . But this Court has also repeatedly stated that the right of peremptory challenge is not of constitutional magnitude, and may be withheld altogether without impairing the constitutional guarantee of an impartial jury and a fair trial. . . . If the prosecutor's challenge could be eliminated only at the cost of eliminating the defendant's challenge as well, I do not think that would be too great a price to pay."

Justice Marshall ignored only one problem: the obviously unfit venireperson who answers all questions on the voir dire in a perfectly acceptable way and who, for some reason, either one side or the other will not consent to excuse. Rather than examine the juror for hours in the hope of uncovering grounds for a challenge for cause, a peremptory challenge should be available. One or two of these for each side should take care of these problems without endangering the carefully randomized jury delivery system.

To sum it up, *Batson* was a good impulse, wrongly realized. Detection of the evil was uncertain and the remedy was unclear. It works only by the goodwill of the parties and the moral posture of the judge—hardly the model of a legal solution. Worse, it cannot be contained by any principled means; its logic requires application not only to defense challenges but to challenges based upon diverse stereotyping. The concept of justifying challenges as free of bigotry is simply incompatible with the ancient prerogative of peremptory challenge. Indeed, the peremptory challenge is incompatible with the whole notion of a randomly drawn panel of citizens of all stripes. Though the trial Bar trembles at the prospect of an unbiased jury sworn as they come down the chute, though lawyers cannot conceive of playing the trial with a fully shuffled deck, the only solution to the pernicious exercise of peremptory challenges is their virtual abolition. The stoutest defenders of the prerogative can advance not a single benefit from the blind exercise of challenges. In fact, what little anecdotal evidence we have suggests that the most meticulously stacked jury will often produce surprises. Trial lawyers will learn to live without their self-touted hunch about jurors, their crude, unverifiable, and often mistaken predictions of juror sympathy and disposition. We will replace a virtually unbiased jury with a panel more nearly unbiased in fact. And (in addition to expedition) the trial process will regain a measure of much-needed dignity.

11   Character as a Guide to Conduct and Credibility

A Grotesque Structure Adorns the Legal Landscape

We courtroom lawyers are all in the proof business one way or another. Most of the time, we are busily engaged in trying to establish that some fact is true or false, that some event really happened or really did not. As we assemble our evidence, we usually adopt the footprint theory of how to show who passed by. This theory holds that the past is preserved in the present by altered surfaces of matter and mind. It's a good theory. Passing events generally do leave some durable marks on the physical world and imprints on the minds of witnesses. Detect, inspect, collect, resurrect these traces and the truth is proved. It works for archaeologists and paleontologists; it works for us.

But it is not the only method. Another way to decide whether or not someone did something—much favored outside the courtroom—is by a careful inspection of the character of the suspect. Is this the kind of person, we want to know, who would do a thing like this? Even without the help of the psychologists we would have known that behavior follows personality. It's not just the sickies, like child rapists, who act consistently with twisted traits of character; burglars and check forgers and car boosters are likely to repeat their criminal actions because that's the kind of people they have decided to be. Or, if you prefer a more deterministic formulation, let's just say that one way or another, they have developed an antisocial personality, which expresses itself in characteristic behavior. In other words, criminals, along with the rest of us, have character—which to lawyers means a propensity to act in a certain way in given circumstances.

Yet the law has a great deal of difficulty with proof of character as proof of propensity as proof of the conduct in issue. No one could improve on the justly famous language of Justice Robert Jackson, writing for the Supreme Court in 1948 in a case called *Michelson v. United States,* on the subject of the law of character evidence: "We concur in the general opinion of courts, textwriters, and the profession that much of this law is archaic, paradoxical, and full of compromises and compensations by which an irrational advantage to one side is offset by a poorly reasoned counterprivilege to the other. But somehow it has proved a workable even if clumsy system when moderated by discretionary controls in the hands of a wise and strong trial court. To pull one misshapen stone out of the grotesque structure is more likely simply to upset its present balance between adverse interests than to establish a rational edifice." Things have not changed much since then.

Start with the premise that the law abhors proof by propensity. The logic of this ancient aversion runs thus: although inclination is some indication of conduct, many people are inclined to do many terrible things they never do. Many jurors (not being quite as well lit as the rest of us) may not appreciate this simple truth; hearing of the defendant's illegal propensity, they may be all too quick to conclude that he did what he was disposed to do on the occasion in question.

Even acknowledging that propensity really drives conduct, proof of propensity can lead to serious injustice. There are lots of muggers out there, let us say, all disposed to snatch the purse of any victim they can find. But that disposition should not convict any one of them of the theft of any particular victim's bag. Otherwise, anyone generally disposed to a particular variety of crime could be convicted of any particular instance of it. And the law stoutly insists that people should be convicted only for particular behavior and not for a general criminal disposition.

The consequences are well known to virtually everyone who has served as a juror in a criminal case. If the defendant does not testify on her own behalf, the jury learns of her criminal history (if at all) in a corridor conversation with the lawyers after the verdict is in. Hey, they then think, it really would have helped us decide whether this mother smothered her baby if we had known that she had abused her older child. Meanwhile, the jury has heard of the criminal records of others who testified as witnesses—the prior convictions for forgery of the mother's companion who found the child, let us say. And many jurors will think (perhaps with some annoyance) that a vital fact had been perversely kept from them by the very system that charged them with the duty to return a "true verdict according to the evidence." After all, doesn't the judging public at large seize upon information that a suspected terrorist had been previously associated with a violent political faction to confirm their suspicions? Aha! we all say with satisfaction, he's just the sort of person who would do something like that! Is justice served when jurors are forced to operate in ignorance of data deemed significant in the ordinary judgment of reasonable people outside the courtroom? Yes, we lawyers say, data that many consider helpful in ordinary life is frequently considered prejudicial in the courtroom. The datum about the mother's prior abusive conduct would have made it too easy to decide the homicide charge.

The concept of prejudice in law is as subtle as it is vital. The line separating prejudicial from probative evidence is drawn along the fault line of human intelligence, the point where a rational inference becomes an irrational supposition. It is the difference between a logical connection between two propositions and a facile, hasty, superstitious, or gratuitous conclusion. And how do we recognize that line? By the use of our own reason, the textbook would say. By the application of community convention, the skeptic would reply. Why, after all, will we say that certain forms of schizophrenia deprive the mind of the capacity to distinguish right from wrong but reject the notion that possession by the devil can do the same? The law smiles on those jurors who conclude that desire for revenge drove the defendant to the deed, but we will not indulge those who might say that an astrological alignment was responsible. Experts on psychopathy are welcome, experts on necromancy are turned away; evidence of the events giving rise to the motive of revenge will be received as probative, while astrological charts will be banned as prejudicial.

Character evidence puts the concept of prejudice to its most severe test. It's not that evidence of the defendant's associations with an underworld mob has no logical bearing on the question of whether he obtained a contract by coercion and threat. Rather, it is the danger that that fact will have too much influence on the jury's decision.

But what is too much? A lawyer will sometimes stand up and object to the admission of the murder weapon bearing the defendant's fingerprints (or some such damning item) as "prejudicial." The objection is laughable. He means prejudicial in the sense that the jury, hearing this evidence, will swiftly decide the issue against the defendant. But that's not prejudicial evidence, that's dispositive evidence. The best kind: strong and clear. But isn't evidence that the defendant is a mobster the same sort—relevant, if not dispositive, on the issue of whether he committed this racketeering crime?

It is in the sense that it leads easily to the conclusion that the defendant is guilty. But it is different in that it leads to that conclusion along a line of inference that we deem false—false in the sense that the inferential link is too weak to support the inferred conclusion. The proven fact that the victim's blood was on the defendant's glove supports the inference to the conclusion that the defendant stabbed the victim. That line of reasoning conforms to our idea about how the human mind works—when it is working well. This, we say, is how the facts of the real world beyond personal experience are learned by human intelligence, this is the rational process we believe in.

But the conclusion that the defendant coerced the contract because he is a racketeer and that is the way the rackets operate, though easily drawn, reflects an error of reason. It has the beguiling form of a true syllogism: Racketeers coerce contracts, Delta is a racketeer, therefore Delta coerced the contract at issue. Q.E.D. But it isn't. Many racketeers do not coerce contracts and many contracts are coerced by racketeers other than Delta. Not that the status of Delta as a racketeer has no bearing on the issue. It is a relevant datum in that the fact that Delta is a racketeer makes it more likely that Delta coerced the contract in issue than if he had been an honest and law-abiding citizen. The prejudice factor is the possibility that the jury might mistake an item of some relevance for a syllogistic inevitability. The danger is that a jury may find the inference more compelling than it should be.

Should be? By whose lights? By the lawmakers' belief that, in our time and place, some chains of inference are better lines of logical reasoning than others. The line of inference is strong enough to support whatever weight the jury chooses to place upon it, we say, if its underlying assumptions are sound by commonly accepted conventions, if mainline science approves, if its links conform to shared processes of inferential reasoning, and if it is undisturbed by questionable premises and irrational intuitions. This process of right-think is not altogether a matter of legal dogma following popular opinion. Virtually everyone, including people with engineering degrees from accredited institutions, may consult a dowser before drilling a well, but the law will not recognize the evidence of a person who thinks that a willow twig will bend toward water hundreds of feet below solid rock.

All right, so the law (in its wisdom) deems some inferences better, more rational than others—where does the notion of prejudice come in? Here we may detect some residue of the patronizing attitude of the educated judiciary toward the lay jurors. The concept of prejudice reflects the law's concern that ignorant jurors might erroneously assign probative weight to some datum that we privileged few understand is inappropriate, that they may think they have reached a conclusion across a bridge of inference without recognizing that the shaky old structure will never support the crossing. The notion of prejudice incorporates the benevolent purpose to protect defendants from naive, inflamed, or foolish mistakes that might fortify weak inferences in the dim minds of jurors.

So there is the general, time-honored rule regarding character evidence: proof of character to prove the commission of crime by the inference of propensity is prejudicial as a matter of law and never permitted. But having made that resounding and unequivocal declaration, a conscientious guide would have to follow immediately with: except sometimes, indirectly. And here is where the despair of Justice Jackson infects us all.

Now, we must look gently at the permitted uses of evidence of character or evidence of prior conduct of the defendant in assisting the jury to decide the ultimate, substantive issues of the case: did the defendant do the criminal acts charged, and with the requisite guilty intent?

Equipped with carpet cleaning equipment, an appropriately groomed young man presented himself at Ann Blair's door offering a free demonstration of a new rug shampoo, together with an offer of a free estimate on "an introductory offer" of a carpet cleaning. Thinking of having her carpets done, Ann invited the young man into the house. The moment he was in the door, the man showed a curved carpet knife and, threatening to cut her "from ear to ear" if she screamed or fought him, he demanded that she disrobe. As Ann Blair later recounted the incident, he commanded her to parade naked back and forth in front of him and "look sexy." He then told her to kneel in front of him and perform fellatio on him, repeatedly instructing her to "moan" as she did so. He then got on top of her and raped her.

Immediately after the young man left, Blair telephoned the police and told her story. During the investigation that followed, police turned up another open case that seemed to have certain features in common in addition to a general physical description of the rapist. In that case, the victim, Bettina Cortez, described the circumstances thus: She was home alone one afternoon some weeks before the Blair rape when a young man rang her bell and stated that he was a door-to-door salesmen of cosmetics and toiletries, and if she would allow him in to show his wares, he would give her some attractive free gifts regardless of whether she made any purchases. He was carrying a rather large black case that she assumed contained the merchandise, so she let him in. As soon as he opened the case, the man took out a container of a colorless liquid, unscrewed the top, and told her it was acid and he would throw it in her face if she did not undress and do as he told her. In fear, the victim complied and the defendant had sexual contact with her. First, however, he forced her to dance naked, telling her to "look seductive, baby, like you mean it." He also insisted that she kneel in front of him for oral sex before accomplishing vaginal penetration.

Neither Blair nor Cortez could make a photo ID, though both were shown dozens of facial shots of convicted rapists of the general description they provided.

Albert Parker was arrested a few weeks later on a lucky break. He approached a woman in the park and asked whether she was a model. When she said she was not, he introduced himself as a fashion photographer and said she had the attributes of a high-priced model and should really think about giving it a try. She smiled and said she was not ready to make a career change. He offered to take a couple of test photos of her free of charge and added that he had a studio nearby. The woman had nothing better to do for the next hour, and she went along into a commercial building near the park. When they got out of the elevator together, Parker drew a knife and ordered the woman into the stairwell. There he told her to take off her clothes. At that point the woman, Detective Marjorie Petrus, drew her service pistol from her handbag and placed Parker under arrest. At the time of his arrest, Parker claimed his name was Tucker and produced a driver's license in that name to prove it.

Petrus mentioned the collar to another cop at lunch who turned out to be the officer on the Blair case. He immediately suspected a connection, and a lineup was arranged at which Blair and Cortez independently identified Parker as their attacker. Because Parker had never before been arrested on a sex charge, his photo had not been among those the women had pored over fruitlessly. He did have a prior conviction for burglary, however, and it was that conviction (discovered by his prints) that gave the police his true name and address. The indictment for the Blair rape was tried first.

Here, we will pursue a few different suppositions.
Supposition one:

In his opening to the jury, Parker's lawyer tells the jury that they must be very careful in listening to the evidence. They will see that the whole case against Parker rests on the word of Ann Blair that Parker was the rapist. He tells them that their own common sense and experience should warn them that people are often mistaken when they think they recognize someone. He hints that the defense might even call an expert. "There are experts out there," counsel says. "Scientists. They can tell you that study after study has shown that people are wrong more often than not when they think they recognize a stranger weeks later. And their ability is even weaker when they saw that person only briefly, in a stressful situation, and the person is of a different race. And confidence has nothing to do with it; people who are wrong are just as sure they are right as people who are actually right." An objection to this comment is sustained by the court, but everyone gets the idea what the defense would be. Counsel concludes with this: "Now folks, you may very well find that this young woman was raped. We don't know anything about that one way or the other. But if you are true to your oath, you will also find that there is major doubt here—much more than reasonable doubt—that my client was the man who raped her."

When Ann Blair, the first prosecution witness, testifies, the defense strategy becomes clearer still. On cross-examination, she is asked whether she has many close friends who are African-Americans. She is asked whether, like most people of all races, she thinks that many people of a different race look a lot alike. At great length, counsel asks her to try to remember any really unusual features or markings on the man who attacked her; Ann Blair comes up with the description she gave initially, a recital that obviously could describe a lot of men in addition to the defendant. On redirect examination, of course, Ms. Blair again insists that she clearly recalls the rapist and she is completely certain that Albert Parker was the man.

Although no evidence has yet been adduced by the defense, it's clear at this point in the trial that the defense has put the question of identity squarely at issue. The prosecutor will now propose to call as her next witness Bettina Cortez. Defense counsel will raise the most vehement objection.

How can the prosecution do this? he will rage. This is outrageous! It would violate the most basic premises of American criminal justice—a person cannot be tried for his unrelated and uncharged misdeeds, for his bad character! Surely, the court will not permit this blatant effort of the prosecutor to introduce evidence of propensity! Propensity. The forbidden subject. Counsel pronounces it as though the word alone concluded any further discussion of the matter.

Counsel is getting a bit carried away with his own rhetoric, the prosecutor will coolly reply. He surely knows that, by a well-established, universally recognized, and long-standing rule of evidence, proof of prior bad acts will be received to establish the identity of the defendant as the person who committed the crime. She is right. The reasoning goes like this: where the identity of the perpetrator is in issue, the prosecution may prove that the defendant has done other things (including the commission of crimes) in a manner so closely resembling the way the crime on trial was allegedly performed that a reasonable person might conclude that both acts were done by the same person. The crime had the defendant's signature on it. Proof of ID by similar MO, it's called.

On the face of it, the rule seems sound. If it were given that every time that Alpha burglarized a residence he left a note explaining that he hoped the owners would understand that he was engaged in a self-help campaign to redistribute wealth and to remedy, in small part, the gross inequalities of economic advantage in American society (MO[A] = B), and that the evidence indicated that the person who committed the burglary in issue had left just such a note (MO[X] = B), we might logically conclude that the person who committed the burglary was Alpha (X = A).

One problem with the ID/MO rule is that the syllogism has at least a couple of hidden premises that judges are not too scrupulous about when applying the rule in court. One concerns the uniqueness of the "signature." Perhaps we might accept the fact that a written sociopolitical apologia from a burglar is sufficiently rare that it is virtually impossible that anyone other than Alpha would leave a calling card like Alpha's. But judges do not require that the signature feature be truly unique. The fact that a burglar gained access by climbing through a transom, for instance, has been accepted as a signature MO for ID purposes.

Were the means by which the rapist gained access to Ann Blair and to Bettina Cortez sufficiently unusual that we could say with some degree of confidence that the man who used one approach was the man who used the other? I find this a very difficult question. Though unusual, I suppose, the method is hardly unique. And if different men might try the same sort of device in the same city within a relatively short time (a premise that might require some empirical study), admission of the facts of the uncharged rape to prove the identity of the person who committed the charged crime provides only some small probative evidence while raising a strong likelihood of severe prejudice (as jurors overestimate its probative value). Yet I am quite confident that most judges would find the technique sufficiently unusual that they would overrule the defense objection and let it come in.

How about the circumstances of Parker's arrest? Harder question. There are some features in common—the masquerade, the offer of a freebie. But a pickup in a park leading to a hallway rape is quite different from the door-to-door salesman approach. This raises a refinement of the signature question: the matter of similarity. An unknown signatory may be identified by comparing signatures with a known exemplar not only because a signature is thought to be a unique gesture but because the unknown writing closely corresponds to the known.

How similar do the two MOs have to be to make the prior conduct relevant on the issue of identity? I am tempted to say, as with ordinary signatures, very close. Are the rapist's approaches to Cortez and to Blair "the same MO"? Yes and no is the best answer I can give. Yet, again, I must report that courts are habitually loose about this—having some features in common is generally good enough for the "same MO" stamp. Despite some logical misgivings, I am reasonably confident that our case would pass the tests of both uniqueness and similarity in most courtrooms.

Another problem in applying the MO/ID rule to real cases is that, unlike my paradigm, in which it was "given" that a known person had left the signature on the uncharged act, facts are rarely *given;* they must be proved. So the question arises, by what standard, to what degree of certainty need we be convinced that Parker raped Cortez (in his supposedly characteristic manner) before we will admit evidence of that act on the issue of whether he raped Blair? What we actually have is evidence of about the same probity in both cases: the sworn word of the victim. Will that do?

Granted that at some point repetition itself becomes evidence that strengthens a defendant's connection with any individual occurrence. There was once a case in which a man called the police to report a dead body in his living room. He told them that he had been out drinking with the man the night before, had offered him a place to sleep it off, and discovered him dead the next morning. Two weeks later, the same host came up with another corpse and the same story. Police started to get suspicious. Two or three more similar incidents would convince most of us that the defendant had more than a happenstance involvement in the deaths.

But when we only have one or two prior occurrences, it seems to me we should require, in addition to an unusual and similar MO, a connection between the defendant and the prior event that is stronger than the connection established between him and the crime on trial. Otherwise, we have only an accumulation of equivocal connections with no incremental proof to justify the danger of prejudice. That someone resembling the defendant did a similar rape might prove that someone resembling the defendant did the rape in question. But we already know that from the present victim. It adds nothing to the proof that the person resembling the defendant was, in fact, the defendant. Again, I fear it is a point lost on trial courts who will take such evidence without troubling to weigh the relative connective fibers.

Finally, there is some doubt about when identity is in issue. In my example, I drew a case where there could be little doubt that the defense put the fact in issue. But suppose that a defendant in a murder case simply pleads not guilty, making no concessions and offering no theory of innocence. Is identity in issue? One could easily say, Yes, identity is always in issue in a criminal case. In fact, even if the defendant defended on a theory of self-defense, acknowledging that he had dealt the mortal blow, one might say identity is in issue. No critical facts may be conceded in a criminal case; they may be uncontested, but they are not conceded. The difference is the jury must always find every critical fact against the defendant beyond a reasonable doubt in order to convict. Every critical fact, even those that are uncontested.

Under this theory, every prior bad act bearing some similarity in an unusual particular to the act on trial (under the courts' customary relaxed notions of similarity and peculiarity) would be admissible in every criminal trial. Perhaps that is what it comes down to. If so, as you can see, the exception for proof of identity comes pretty close to consuming the ancient prohibition against evidence of character to prove propensity to prove conduct consistent with that characteristic predisposition.

Supposition two:

In his opening to the jury, Parker's lawyer tells the jury that they will learn from the evidence that the accusation of rape was a spiteful conclusion to a mutually pleasant interlude. He says that the jury will learn from the evidence that after Ann Blair invited Albert Parker into her apartment, she became friendly and offered him a cup of coffee. She asked Parker for cocaine, but he laughed and said he didn't have any. She said, "I bet you can get some for me." They talked in an increasingly intimate way, ending up in bed. After engaging in consensual intercourse, the lawyer continues, Blair again asked Parker for dope and Parker again refused to supply any. Blair became infuriated, forcing him to beat a hasty retreat, and shouted at the door, "Believe me, you'll be sorry!" Listen carefully, the lawyer told the jury, you will hear not one word about injuries, scratches, bruises, not one word about evidence of struggle. When Blair testifies, defense counsel's questions all suggest that she had consented to sex with Parker in the hope of getting some cocaine in exchange. She categorically denies all such suggestions.

This defense of consent puts at issue the defendant's criminal intent. As every first-year law student learns, what distinguishes many normal, innocent—even pleasurable—actions from serious crimes is the element of criminal intent. From taking possession of someone else's property to coitus, from entering someone else's home to putting a sharp knife in his gut, the criminal is distinguished from the trustee, the lover, the dinner guest, and the surgeon by the state of mind in which the identical conduct is performed. It is not easy to define this critical element—*mens rea,* we call it. It is rarely expressed and never writ large across the actor's brow. It is, judges invariably instruct juries, to be inferred from behavior, from circumstances, filtered through that indispensable faculty by which the law lives—our common sense and ordinary experience. We are expected to be able to recognize this vital element of criminality from our life experience with the difference between the way in which guilty-minded and well-intentioned people behave.

One of the circumstances that the law allows juries to use as a predicate for the inference of criminal intent is prior conduct. So the defendant accused of pirating and selling videos who defends by claiming that he had no intention of infringing copyrights or depriving anyone of royalties may be shown to have previously made and sold prints of copyrighted artworks. Criminal intent may be fairly inferred, the theory goes, from an individual's previous conduct that should have informed him of the wrongness of such actions so that if he thereafter does something else like it, he is more likely to have done so with the intention of doing wrong—the essence of *mens rea*. It may not be airtight logic, but it is good law.

What of our rape case? Can a prior rape be admitted to prove that the sexual penetration at issue was made with criminal intent—to counter, that is, a defense of consent? Courts are divided on the question. Evenly divided. The jurisdictions do not line up neatly because issues are sometimes smudged by variations in underlying facts, but it looks as though of the jurisdictions that considered the question, nine said no, nine said yes.

Of those that refuse to admit the prior rape, several cite an old federal case from 1948 bearing the lovely name of *Lovely v. United States,* which holds that the fact that one woman was raped is no evidence that another did not consent to sexual contact. There's obviously some heft to that thesis. New Hampshire and Alaska note that the prior unrelated incident shows nothing more than the violent propensity of the defendant in sexual encounters—just the sort of evidence the law universally disallows. Even a similar MO in the previous rape has no bearing on the issue of consent/intent except to show that the defendant is predisposed to use a particular coercive method to obtain gratification. Again, it's hard to argue with that conclusion. At least one jurisdiction (again, New Hampshire) confuses things further by holding that a consent defense does not raise the issue of intent and hence the prior rape is inadmissible on that issue (though it might be admitted on the issue of a mistaken belief that the complainant had consented).

The reasoning of those courts that find evidence of prior rape admissible on the issue of consent is often fuzzy. Many opinions, for example, emphasize the similarity between the prior rape and the one charged. Several point to the similarity and find that the prior rape tends to establish a plan to commit forcible rapes and defend them as consensual (*plan* being one of the conventional and statutory purposes for which evidence of unrelated misconduct may be admitted). The underlying theory supporting this strain—not always articulated plainly—must be that a man's having previously overcome with force a woman's objection or resistance to sex is evidence that, on the occasion in question, he is likely to have responded to rejection in the same manner—by the intentional use of force as alleged. That theory, however, throws no light whatever on the critical issue: did the woman in the present instance consent or resist? And insofar as it says, "This is a man who characteristically takes sex by force," the theory is sufficiently close to proof of simple propensity—he did it before so he is likely to do it again—that it courts the charge of sophistry.

One other point is worth making on the subject of prior sexual conduct and its relevance to the conduct at issue. What about the character of the victim? Not so long ago, well within the memory of many of today's trial lawyers, the defense of consent entitled defense counsel to cross-examine rape victims on their prior sexual histories. Notwithstanding the general prohibition on propensity inferences, it was believed that a sexually promiscuous (or precocious) woman would be more likely to consent to sexual contact on any given occasion than a woman of "virtuous character." Like the disempowering but universal rule that the accusation of a rape victim required corroboration, this humiliating inference imposed by post-Victorian, masculist assumptions of relevance was followed in all courts without an audible murmur of disapproval, much less outrage.

Then a remarkable thing happened. Sometime in the mid-seventies, everyone awoke at once. All it took was a nudge, an appeal to contemporary sensibility, and centuries of unbroken practice crumbled with scarcely a voice lifted to preserve it. Today, no jurisdiction will allow a rape defendant, claiming consent, to ask the victim any questions regarding her general sexual activity. It's just not relevant, not relevant as a matter of law. In 1978, Congress added a new provision to this effect to the Federal Rules of Evidence. This rule allows questions on past sexual behavior in only two circumstances: (1) to show that someone other than the accused was the source of semen or sexual bruises attributed to the defendant's sexual contact with the victim, or (2) to bring prior consensual sexual relations between the accused and the victim to bear on the issue of whether the victim consented to sex on the occasion in question. Most states have similar prohibitions and allowances.

This small and quiet revolution in the way the law thinks of women's sexual equality is the more remarkable because its effect is to limit the defendant's constitutional right of confrontation. A rape defendant, like all others, has a right vigorously to cross-examine any adverse witnesses, and that goes double for his accusers. This right may be the most precious of all the constitutional protections with which we drape a criminal defendant. It is, after all, the basic instrument of defense, the prime object of the rights of fair trial, public trial, assistance of counsel, notice of charges, unbiased jurors, and the rest. And courts are extremely sensitive to any efforts to limit the exercise of this right. To the extent that some might still argue that a woman's attitude toward casual sex has some bearing on whether she consented to, let us imagine, the postparty sexual activity she now characterizes as date rape, a rule of law that precludes defense examination of the complainant on the subject of her prior sexual history surely cuts back on the defendant's right of challenge.

The Supreme Court has not passed on the rape shield laws, as they are called, but the few federal courts of appeal that have looked at the federal rule of evidence do not seem much impressed with the constitutional argument. Only the military jurisdiction has accepted wholeheartedly the argument that to curtail relevant cross-examination on prior sexual history violates the defendant's constitutional right of confrontation. Most of the scattered state courts that have written on the subject have gone off on the peculiar facts before them or otherwise avoided the hard question.

In all, the issue seems ripe to be transferred from law school moot courts to the Supreme Court docket. It has all the ingredients of a meaty constitutional question: the clash of major policies with heavy social overtones in a commonplace trial situation. As lower courts have been careful to note, the defendant's constitutional right of cross-examination is already subject to several curtailments. Rules of evidence with high social valences, like the professional privileges, can block the defendant's access to impeachment. A defendant, for example, cannot probe for a witness's prior inconsistent statement by asking: "Is that what you told your lawyer when you conferred with him about your testimony?" So the Supremes may one day hold that the rape shield law does not offend the confrontation clause because it reflects a sound legislative assessment of low probative value and high embarrassment potential.

But I would not be surprised to learn that, where a trial court finds the complainant's prior sexual conduct truly relevant to the likelihood that she consented on the occasion in question, the defendant's right to ask her about that conduct cannot be denied because sexual privacy should, ordinarily, be respected. Other victims, witnesses—even police officers—have their privacy rent by cross-examination; their shameful misdeeds may be dredged up and exposed for whatever illumination they may shed on credibility. What is so special about the victims of alleged sex crimes?

In any event, we need to hear it from the Court. Otherwise, trial courts will continue to flounder in improvised, ad hoc solutions, learned in doubt and disbelief from the faltering appellate tier.

Let's now try a *third supposition:*

Parker is convicted after trial of the rape of Ann Blair, and shortly thereafter he is brought to trial for the rape of Bettina Cortez. In spite of the jury's refusal to believe him when he testified on the Blair trial, Parker is determined to take the stand and try again.

"I've learned from my mistakes," he tells his new lawyer at their first meeting. "I can be pretty convincing, believe me. You leave that to me. Your job is to see that this jury hears nothing about the Blair case."

"Well," says the lawyer, "that may be easier said than done. Do you have a defense this time that puts in issue neither your identity nor consent?"

"You know it! Here's my story: it never happened. No sex, no penetration. Nothing. Just conversation plus the fevered imagination of a sex-shocked female."

"Is that the fact?"

"If I tell you that's the fact, counselor, that's the fact."

"How about medical evidence? Won't there be evidence of intercourse?"

"What do you think I'm stupid? My story can't be disproved that easily. This Cortez woman didn't complain for a week. I'll bet they didn't even bother to take a smear."

"Well," the attorney says tentatively, "that may keep out evidence of prior conduct on the prosecution's case-in-chief. Mind you, I say *may*. I can't guarantee it. But I may be able to get a ruling on the question before the trial begins."

"I'd like to know where I stand on that one."

"But if you testify, Mr. Parker, the D.A. may bring out your record to impeach your credibility."

"What? If it's in, it's in; if it's out, it's out. How can it be out and in at the same time?"

"Well, it may be in for a different purpose. Not to show you were the one who did it, not to show you intended to rape the woman, but to show you are lying when you said it never happened."

"Surely you must be kidding, counselor. Can the law be such an ass it thinks the jury will understand that distinction?"

Parker may be a rapist, but he's not stupid.

First, we will cast a sidelong glance at the nasty little ethical question poking through this conversation. It does look as though the defendant is concocting a false defense with the connivance—if not the active assistance—of his lawyer. Surely, the lawyer should do more to discourage perjury than the rather mild objection he raises here. And if Parker insists on going forward with his story tailored to circumvent the rules of evidence, shouldn't the lawyer withdraw?

Well, not exactly. As a matter of conscience, a lawyer might choose to challenge vigorously a highly suspect story told by his client. Some few lawyers might even go out and check it, try to disprove the story and thereby persuade the client to abandon it. But I must sadly report that there is no professional obligation binding a defense lawyer to such a course.

The prosecutor is a different creature. He has no client and he has a clear obligation to use every effort to see that justice is done. The prosecutor is bound to investigate fully, following all leads until a fairly clear picture of the truth emerges. Then the prosecutor is obliged to refuse to call witnesses believed to be false and to dismiss charges against a defendant believed to be innocent.

Defense counsel is not charged with any public responsibility to the truth. Defense counsel is bound to the energetic and faithful pursuit of the client's cause. Most lawyers do not consider discrediting the client to be part of that mission. Indeed, to bend too heavy an oar to the task might be interpreted by the client as disloyalty, might impair the confidence that the client must have in counsel to make the relationship work as it is supposed to. Although many lawyers claim that truth from the client helps them in conducting the defense, I fail to see how it helps if the truth is "I'm guilty and everything the witnesses say against me is true." Many more realistic lawyers look instead for a "story" that will wash without running. So Parker's snap retort was not too far off the mark.

Now what of this "credibility" dodge?

Basically, there are two ways we would be tempted to look to character to help a jury find the truth. If a defendant had, several years before, embezzled dues while serving as treasurer of a community action coalition, that fact might be adduced to establish that he had, as the present indictment alleges, defrauded investors in a later real estate deal. This line of proof goes like this: because his prior conduct reveals a sneaky, lying, cheating, larcenous trait in his character, it is more likely that he would swindle investors, as charged, than if he had never entertained a thought of thievery in his life. As we have seen, this is proof of propensity pure and simple, and it is firmly, clearly, and everywhere rejected. Alternatively, evidence of his prior dishonesty might be offered to prove that he lied when he testified in his own defense that he had not cheated anyone in connection with the charged investment fraud.

Maybe only a lawyer could appreciate the distinction. To use character as evidence that the accused had, as charged, defrauded investors may not seem so very different from using the same evidence to prove that he lied when he denied it. Proof of prior dishonesty is proof of a trait of character, and use of it to show that the witness lied on the stand is, after all, nothing but proof by propensity. Because of his sneaky, lying, cheating, larcenous soul he is more likely to have lied on the stand than more honestly disposed citizens. But at law, there is all the difference in the world.

In one of those maddening inconsistencies for which this doctrinal corner is notorious, when it comes to *testimonial* conduct, the law is fully ready to accept the evidence of mendacity on the issue of credibility. So if a witness—any witness, including the defendant testifying on his own behalf—has done anything from which one might suspect that he is not an altogether honest and scrupulously truthful person, the jury may hear of it as a basis for concluding that the testimony of that witness was false. That means, among other things, that a jury may disbelieve a chance eyewitness solely because the witness was convicted of misreporting his income eight years before.

It doesn't make a lot of sense. Why the character trait of mendacity gives rise to the only propensity recognized by law and why that propensity will be considered only on the issue of testimonial veracity—these stubborn incongruities remain, despite my best efforts, inexplicable mysteries of the law of evidence. And we lawyers have labored under this erroneous scheme everywhere and since the dawn of modern jurisprudence.

Actually, intuition might support a rule directly opposite. Knowing that a person had stolen automobile batteries before actually helps decide the issue of whether he stole the battery in question because we all know that a person who has the character of a thief is more likely to steal than a person who has never demonstrated that disposition. Of course, a criminal inclination does not *prove* the conduct in question in the sense that a theorem in geometry is proved. But it is proof in law insofar as it is relevant evidence. And we use the term *relevant* to refer to information that makes the existence of a fact more or less likely than it would have been without the datum. In this sense, then, evidence of a larcenous trait of character does tend to prove criminal conduct associated with that trait. On the other hand, forging someone else's name to use a stolen credit card says little about a person's disposition to lie under oath on the stand about an assault he witnessed while waiting for a bus a short distance away. Unless you indulge the behavioral assumption favored by law—but contrary to all good sense—that a person who is dishonest about anything is likely to lie about everything.

But (of course) nothing is simple. Acceptance of character evidence on the issue of testimonial credibility does not mean that *all* evidence of prior dishonest behavior comes in, or that *only* evidence of prior dishonest behavior is admissible on the issue of credibility.

Parker's lawyer will submit a motion to the judge asking for a ruling in advance that the judge will not allow any of the defendant's past conduct or criminal record to be introduced for impeachment purposes. He will cite various reasons: this one is in the wrong form, that one does not reveal the relevant trait, another is too prejudicial. The defendant's decision whether or not to testify may well hinge on the outcome of this motion. This common-place pretrial application has always struck me as a prime example of vital rights hanging on little more than judicial whim. Arguably even more important than the right of confrontation (and also granted by the Sixth Amendment) is the defendant's constitutional right to adduce evidence in his favor from any witness—including himself, if he wishes. Yet that option may be seriously impaired by the criminal record the defendant carries. Notwithstanding the exceptions, in most cases, all or most of the defendant's prior history will be shielded by the propensity rule as long as he remains mute. In these cases, the exercise of the defendant's right to testify may hang on the trial judge's decision on how much of that history the jury should hear as impeachment—a ruling made on standards that are elusive at best.

I hasten to say that judges I have talked to about this do not seem to feel the exasperating difficulty of the task imposed upon them. This has always been a wonder to me since I have yet to discover a rational basis for deciding which events, which prior convictions, which facts underlying those convictions have a real bearing on credibility, a probative value on that issue strong enough to overcome the presumptive—but also unmeasurable—prejudice that a defendant would suffer if the jury learned of his criminal past.

On the motion in Parker's case, the judge would have to consider several items of possible impeachment value.

The false ID on the driver's license. Here is solid evidence that Parker is a liar, and the law is happy to receive it to prove Parker's propensity to lie on the witness stand. Courts are happiest, however, when evidence of character comes from a "character witness," someone who will testify that the person in question has a reputation in the community as an honest or dishonest character. That's the way evidence of character has been traditionally proved. Only reluctantly have some jurisdictions expanded their tolerance to include evidence from the character witness of a personal opinion regarding character. In most places, courts continue to reject evidence of mendacity when it comes from a source other than the impeached witness himself in the form of evidence of a particular instance of dishonest behavior from which a dishonest character may be inferred. The Federal Rules of Evidence are explicit: "Specific instances of the conduct of a witness, for the purpose of attacking or supporting the witness's credibility . . . may not be proved by extrinsic evidence."

So what this means is that, if Parker testifies, a judge will permit the prosecutor to question him about his false identification papers. "Now isn't it a fact, Mr. Parker," the D.A. will ask on cross examination, "that you have lied about your own identity?"

"No, that's not the fact," Parker might reply.

"Well, at the time of your arrest," the D.A. will persist, "didn't you give your name as Tucker?"

"That's not true." Let's suppose Parker is stubborn (and knows the law on this point).

"Do you now deny, Mr. Parker, that you had in your possession a driver's license in the name of Leroy Tucker, address 757 South Main?"

If Parker admits it, the prosecution has proved the specific incident of dishonesty, and jurors may consider it for whatever bearing they think it has on his testimonial veracity. But (in one of those marvelous quirks you have to go to law school to discover) if Parker stubbornly insists that he never misrepresented his identity, even after the prosecutor takes out the license and waves it around in front of the jury, the prosecution is "bound by the answer." Meaning that, in federal courts and most state jurisdictions, the falsification may not be proved by the testimony of the cop who took the license from him and by the license itself (both "extrinsic" sources). This so-called extrinsic evidence rule was not invented by the modern evidence codes. It's an old, nasty little efficiency device to keep the jury's attention focused on the substantive issues. On matters going only to the credibility of the witness (collateral matters, we call them), the standard rules of evidence do not allow the cross-examiner to introduce proof other than the testimony of the testifying witness himself. Even when the extrinsic evidence would prove the witness to be a liar on a vital matter in contention, the trial will get out of hand, the jury will be hopelessly confused, and the real issues buried (so the law believes) if we allow counsel full rein.

The prior burglary conviction. In the old days, the very old days, any prior felony conviction would incapacitate a witness; convicted felons were conclusively presumed to be forever untrustworthy and therefore disqualified to give evidence. (In those days, too, Parker, like all defendants, would be deemed so biased in his own favor that a court would not allow him to give evidence in his own behalf.) Today, of course, no witness is tainted to the extent of disqualification (and the criminal defendant has the right to testify), but all jurisdictions allow the jury to hear of a witness's prior conviction for whatever tinge they may think it imparts to credibility.

At least, they may hear about *some* of the witness's criminal history. Especially if the witness is the defendant himself—who stands to lose the most by the effects of prejudice—most courts will filter the record to some extent. First, the judge will try to determine whether the crime for which the defendant was convicted involved "dishonesty" as well as simple lawlessness. Thus, a conviction for fraud or forgery will come in, but a conviction for robbery or assault probably will not. On this level, Parker's burglary conviction will probably be excluded. Except that some courts will take into consideration not only the elements of the crime but also the circumstances of its commission. If the burglary in question was committed when Parker gained access to a house by posing as a plumber and then stealing valuable items as he pretended to fix the pipes, some judges will find that the burglary "involved dishonesty" and allow it. The standard is so woefully imprecise, it is hardly surprising that judges are sharply divided on how to apply it.

If the judge finds that the prior crime did not involve dishonesty, he may still admit it for impeachment if he finds that its probative value on the issue of credibility outweighs its prejudicial potential. When, one might well ask, will a prior conviction for an "honest crime" have such a strong bearing on credibility? Most judges will look to the gravity of the prior crime. Judges think it's just silly to allow impeachment by a prior conviction for writing a single bad check but to keep from the jury a defendant's conviction for a series of brutal murders. So now judges must wrestle with questions like whether a conviction for a vehicular homicide while driving intoxicated has a greater probative valence than prejudicial potential if admitted against a defendant to impeach his veracity. And on this decision the defendant's exercise of his right to testify might well depend. You think it's easy to be a judge?

On this basis, a simple burglary probably will probably not qualify. But if it was especially aggravated, involving, say, a major theft or wanton and gross destruction of property, some judges might let it in. Who knows? It's a wild card—which is the reason defense lawyers seek a ruling in advance of trial.

The events leading to Parker's arrest. Parker was not convicted for the minor crimes against Detective Petrus—menacing, possession of a weapon. He wasn't even charged with attempted rape; the approach probably did not go far enough to amount to an "attempt." So no impeachment by prior conviction is contemplated here. But dishonest character need not be read from conviction only; any behavior that reveals the trait will do. And here, the photography gambit was patently false. So if the court thinks the incident is probative of Parker's dishonest character (as I would think it is), the judge might allow questions about it on cross-examination, with the same proviso as in the matter of the phony driver's license—that the prosecutor is "bound by the answers." Because of the sexual nature of the conduct, however, a judge might feel that the prejudicial potential—the temptation to use the evidence as indicative of the forbidden propensity—outweighs its probative quality on the issue of credibility.

Conviction for the rape of Ann Blair. Here we have a real test for the Solomonic wisdom of the judge who must decide Parker's motion. A prior conviction for a crime that (at least by one interpretation) "involved" dishonesty is prime evidence of a mendacious character and should be available to impeach any witness, including the defendant if he chooses to testify. In addition, even if it does not involve dishonesty, the crime of rape is sufficiently heinous that, according to prevailing, sweetly naive fiction, it manifests the sort of generally immoral character that would not scruple to lie under oath.

At the same time, the rape of Ann Blair is a crime so like the Cortez rape on trial that it would be exceptionally difficult for the jury to follow the court's instruction and consider the conviction only on the issue of Parker's credibility as a witness and not on the propensity of the defendant to rape

Bettina Cortez as he had raped Ann Blair. My best guess: Parker will win on this one. And if the jurors find out about it after their verdict is in, they will wonder why the law kept them in the dark on such an important datum.

The facts underlying the conviction for the Blair rape. Excluding evidence that Parker was *convicted* for the rape does not necessarily preclude evidence that he *acted* in a way revealing a dishonest character. Apart from his conviction, his conduct leading up to the Blair rape certainly revealed a duplicitous character that might betoken a perjurer. If the court decides that rape is not a crime involving dishonesty, nor grievous enough to come in otherwise, can Parker nonetheless be cross-examined about this conduct as he could be about the overtures he made to the detective that resulted in his arrest?

I cannot honestly think of a reason why not—unless, of course, the prejudice factor keeps it out. Yet, to my consternation, most authority on the point seems to hold that if the dishonest conduct eventuated in a conviction and the conviction is kept out, the underlying conduct is insulated as well. Even more surprising, most respectable pundits say that, even if the fact of conviction is allowed, the underlying conduct—evidence that might inform the jury of just how much weight to accord the witness's criminal record—should not be disclosed.

But this is just another example of the confusion generated by the erroneous premise of the law regarding character and credibility. The law's theory of human behavior, remember, is that a person who has previously acted dishonestly is more likely to lie under oath at a trial about anything than a person without such a visible blemish. In my view, provable incidents of prior behavior—even general repute composed of who knows what rumors and half-truths about who knows what sort of behavior in who knows what circumstances—do not figure very prominently in the decision to lie under oath at a trial. In a word, it is not character that determines testimonial veracity, it is circumstance.

As I see it (to state it bluntly), nearly all people decide whether to lie on the witness stand according to two determinants: the importance to them of having a falsehood believed and their confidence that their false testimony will achieve that end with minimal risk. Within this latter factor we may include the witness's security in his skill as a dissimulator, along with his perceived impeachability by inconsistent evidence.

Innocent defendants in criminal cases will, of course, tell the truth insofar as it promotes acquittal. But even they will lie or omit facts when the full truth would heighten suspicion: Did she have a fight with the deceased a week before the murder? Was he in the store shortly before the robbery?

All guilty defendants who choose to testify will lie on the stand about critical facts and anything else that might improve their chances and about which they imagine they can be persuasive. For virtually all—novice and experienced criminal—acquittal is the overriding, intensely desired goal, and the risks of perjury are minimal.

Victims of crimes and other witnesses in civil and criminal cases may also have diverse, if less pressing, interests in promoting some falsehood. The desire for revenge might induce a victim to add some aggravating details, or the urge to make someone pay might fortify the victim's otherwise uncertain recollection. An ordinary witness may have some open or secret affiliation with a party or sympathy with the party's position. It's natural to wish to portray oneself as more perceptive, heroic, or less forgetful and (notably in the case of police witnesses) to describe greater diligence or more faithful adherence to law or rules. These and a host of other interests may incline a witness, otherwise honest and law-abiding, to shade the truth.

There are undoubtedly some folk, perhaps even a sizable number, who will scruple to lie under oath for moral or religious reasons, though as defendants they might go to trial to make the state prove its case. As guilty defendants, these people will choose not to testify. Ordinary witnesses, subject to subpoena, have no such option. They will try to tell the truth, the whole truth, and nothing but the truth when their interest in promoting a falsehood is no stronger than their scruple. But raise the stakes (say a beloved child needs an alibi) and increase the certainty of impunity (it's only her word against mine), and even people who pride themselves in their honesty will either take their chances with perdition or convince themselves that their lies are true.

Compared with the strength of these determinants for all categories of witness, prior criminal conviction or a history of honest or dishonest behavior in a variety of unrelated circumstances is of marginal significance at best.

We have barely scratched the surface, but the wisdom of Justice Jackson's observation is becoming ever more apparent. The law seems truly confused— if not actually grotesque—when it comes to the important question: what to do with unrelated incidents of behavior as clues to the conduct in issue.

There are very few patches of legal doctrine that make me want to throw up my hands and shout: "Make sense, dammit, make some sense!" If law does not make sense, I fret, nothing will. The law relating to evidence of character—the wellspring of all conduct—is utterly baffling. The underlying behavioral assumptions can only be described as bizarre, and the rules that have sprouted from them are arcane and arbitrary, undermining all the claims of jurisprudence to rationality and predictability. Are we, in litigation, seriously concerned with human behavior, I ask myself—with discovering the most likely reconstruction of real events involving human actors? Or are we, like modern medieval monks, trying to reconcile artificial doctrine with imaginary behavior?

The human mind instinctively seeks personality predicates for the inference of behavior. The effort of the law to preclude such reasoning by jurors is foolish. The law's acceptance of evidence of "untruthful character" as an index of testimonial veracity is willfully naive about why people lie. And the slippery exceptions and vaporous conditions for their application only underscore the artificiality of the rules themselves. Above all, I find unwarranted the law's mistrust of the ability of jurors to recognize the limits of relevance of character evidence.

The obvious solution to the painful problem of character evidence, it seems to me, is to allow evidence of character for whatever purpose it is offered unless its probative weight is clearly outweighed by its potential for prejudice. This standard is applied all the time by trial judges to problematic evidence of all sorts. I see no reason why they should not be equipped to deal with proffered evidence of character in the same way.

Am I just casting a bushel of imponderables onto the trial judge's bench, hoping they will be buried beyond disturbance by the exercise of discretion? Am I resorting to "sound discretion," that old dodge of ad hoc justice, where I can find no principle that could be expressed as law? Perhaps I am. But I see no shame in it. That's why we have—and revere—judges. They are to do justice in the particular case according to their best lights. Law—judgment detached from the particulars—is not the higher truth by which the judge must always be guided. General principles of relevance (with limits) are traditionally the judge's domain. Character is nothing more than a subset of relevance, as far as I can see, and it is presumptuous of rulemakers to usurp the traditional precincts of good sense in this area. And the proof of that proposition is the mess they have made of it.

12 Of Witnesses and Jurors

A Tale of Confidence and Error

What's the story here? What happened? How did it happen? Who did it? In what state of mind did he do it? These are usually the questions in a criminal trial, and at least some of them are likely to be stone-hard nuts to crack. In most cases, however, these questions will be answered by a verdict agreed to by the jurors who have been selected partly because they don't have the slightest idea what the answers are. The jurors will form their conclusions (if they do the job right) from the evidence in the case, meaning primarily from the testimony of witnesses who say they know and remember exactly what happened—or at least some events that may illuminate the rest of the story. The accounts supplied by these witnesses will be elicited by lawyers, the jurors sitting in enforced passivity. The witnesses will first be gently led through their stories by their coaches; then they will face a hostile challenge from their adversaries, who are primarily interested in discrediting their harmful testimony.

So the jury will listen, more or less patiently, more or less attentively, striving, against all human inclination, to keep an open mind (as they were instructed) until they have heard all they are going to hear about it. Then they will retire, these twelve strangers from across a wide band of the social spectrum, and think about it, argue about it, pray, sulk, cajole, rethink, and tell each other personal secrets they thought they would never share, much less with strangers. And from the peculiar intimacy-of-necessity, they will come to a unanimous verdict on the extremely consequential question: is the accused guilty or not guilty, and of what?

It is really one of the minor miracles of our time that this system works at all, much less that it works every day in a way that most people (including judges), most of the time, seem to find completely satisfactory.

The trial of any case in the adversary mode, but especially a criminal case, relies heavily on the skill of a jury to recognize mistake and dishonesty in the renditions of witnesses. Most facts are proved by testimony. Even in those cases where documentary or physical evidence or the defendant's confession is available to assist the fact finder, the human recital—*viva voce*—is often crucial to the establishment of its authenticity or significance. Accordingly, we have developed elaborate forms and devices to assist our lay jurors in what is, under the most favorable circumstances, a highly problematic undertaking. Indeed, the adversary trial might be fairly described as a structured process for the determination of the credibility of strangers, many of whom will, for one reason or another, try to deceive those who rely upon their word. Our faith in the adversary system depends in large measure on our confidence that, assisted by courtroom procedure and the law of evidence, our jurors will usually return a verdict in accord with the historical fact. Of course, in some relatively few cases, the law of evidence—and the Constitution itself—works against this result. But, privileged exclusions aside, we must assume that verdicts are mostly true.

Understandably, few have tried to verify this critical assumption. As a practical matter, we have no better way to discover the historical truth underlying a case than the trial process itself. The only post facto checks we have on jury verdicts are dubious anecdotal complaints from disappointed parties or their lawyers, the rare postverdict appearance of some overlooked evidence, and occasional expressions of agreement or disagreement from presiding judges. Some commentators have placed great faith in the high correlation between judicial and jury conclusions. But I find the evidence of accord insignificant and the evidence of dissent insolubly ambiguous because, in most cases, the judge's opinion is based on little more than the jury had to go on. For all we know, the judge presiding at a trial is prone to the same errors of fact finding as the jury; experience on the bench may teach judicial temperament—even a little law—but I have yet to be persuaded that it sharpens the skills of detecting honest error and conscious falsehood in the renditions of strangers.

To illustrate the sorts of credibility issues sent to the jury room, as well as the kind of information jurors have on which to resolve those issues, I must sketch two separate cases on trial. Here's the first:

Ying Wo, a truck driver, had testified on direct examination to the events of the night of March 14, when his truck with its cargo of electronic equipment had been hijacked. He was climbing into his cab after a brief stop for a meal, he said, when a "dark-skinned Hispanic" fellow had suddenly stepped out of the shadows, put the muzzle of a pistol under his chin and demanded the keys. Ying surrendered them, and the man ordered him to return to the diner. He did as he was bidden and saw his accoster mount the vehicle and roar away, headed south. In the few minutes of their confrontation, Ying insisted, he saw the robber's features clearly in the light of the parking lot lamps and remembered him well. When he saw Hector Ramirez the next day in a lineup, he immediately recognized him and he is certain that the defendant in the courtroom, Ramirez, is the man who took his truck.

The government's case will continue with evidence of Ramirez's capture. Some four hours after the robbery, about 250 miles to the south, a cruising northbound state patrol car spotted the truck headed south on a remote stretch of four-lane state highway. Some while before, the trooper had heard a broadcast alarm and a good description of the vehicle, and, having calculated the time it would take the stolen truck to reach him, he was keeping an eye out when he spotted it heading toward him. He proceeded a short distance farther north until he came to a place in the divider where he could turn southbound. Swinging around, he switched on his crownlights and speeded toward the truck. As he rounded a curve, the trooper saw the truck pulled up to the side of the road. He approached and saw a man climb over the rail and begin to run toward the woods that bordered the highway. Using the bullhorn on the car, the trooper commanded the man to halt and when he did, the trooper walked over and placed him under arrest. The man, who turned out to be Hector Ramirez, told the trooper that he was a hitchhiker and that the driver had escaped. The trooper will testify that, when he first saw the truck as it roared past him on the highway, he had not noticed whether there was a person in the passenger seat. He will also testify that a handgun had been found on the floor of the cab, under the driver's seat. The government will prove that the gun had Ramirez's fingerprints all over it.

After the prosecution completes its case, the jury will hear the testimony of the defendant, Hector Ramirez. Ramirez will swear that he was looking for a ride at a truck stop about 100 miles north of where he was arrested. There he met a driver who "looked enough like me to be my brother." He was headed south and offered Ramirez a ride. As they were driving along, the driver, whom Ramirez knew only as "Spike," took a revolver out from under his seat, unloaded it, and asked Hector whether he would like to buy a gun, cheap. He handed the weapon to Hector, who looked it over carefully, "to be polite," then handed it back, saying he was not really interested. About an hour and a half later, they passed a state police car headed in the opposite direction. Spike slowed down, looking in his rearview mirror. Suddenly he said, "Holy shit! He's coming after us." He pulled the truck over, stopped, and jumped out, shouting, "Run for it, man!" Spike vaulted the low guardrail, sprinted for the woods, and disappeared. Ramirez got out, stood perplexed for a moment, then decided he, too, had better get out of there. He was making a half-hearted attempt to flee when he was halted by the trooper and placed under arrest.

With this preview of the case to come, we return to the testimony of Ying Wo. The government has concluded its direct examination of the witness. Defense counsel rises to cross-examine. This is a moment of small drama relished by court buffs and trial lawyers. A moment of silent anticipation, you can feel it in the air. Will the lawyer now rising slowly and moving into position be able to shake the witness? Find some soft spot in the story where the witness may be vulnerable, a witness who now seems so confident as he watches his adversary move into the spotlight? Can counsel aim a shaft so cleverly that it will penetrate and collapse what now seems a whole, intact, and plausible account?

Cross-examination is the part of a trial that most severely tests the skills of a small but highly visible subset of the Bar: the trial dogs. Books have been written about the technique, but it can't be taught. And of the many trial practitioners, most of whom believe themselves masters of the craft, most are inept to the point of embarrassment. The few good ones are worth watching; they are really good.

Now as counsel prepares to cross Ying Wo, she will probably adopt the common opening ploy: a friendly, nonthreatening, casual, almost bumbling style, to disarm her prey. It might go something like this:

Q: Uh, Mr. Wo—by the way, do you prefer to be called Mr. Ying or Mr. Wo?

A: It doesn't matter. Either way is OK.

Q: All right. Mr. Wo, my name is Mary McAllister and I represent Mr. Ramirez here. Now let's see (fumbling with papers). I just have a few questions I'd like to ask you about this business, OK?

A: Go ahead, ma'am.

Q: You are an experienced driver, sir. I believe you told us on direct examination that you have been driving trucks for eight years. For the same trucking company?

A: That's right.

Q: And I'm sure you are a very responsible person. You haven't had any trouble with your employer in all that time, have you?

A: That is correct.

Q: So I'm sure this was a very upsetting experience for you, Mr. Wo. I don't suppose anything like this had ever happened to you before, am I correct?

A: You mean getting my rig stolen out from under me?

Q: Well, yes. Everything you told us. Getting your rig stolen, getting a gun shoved in your face. The whole thing.

A: That's right, nothing like that had ever happened to me.

Q: So I take it you were pretty upset at the time?

A: I was mad, I was really mad. I thought, this can't be happening to me.

Q: Mad and scared, right?

A: Scared?

Q: I mean with the gun shoved in your face and all.

A: Sure, I was scared, wouldn't you be?

Q: I ask the questions, Mr. Wo, you answer them, OK?

A: Yes, I was scared.

Q: Now, you actually saw the gun in Mr. Ramirez hand, is that right?

A: That's right, I saw the gun.

Q: And there is no doubt in your mind that it was a gun? It couldn't have been a wrench or some other metal object, could it?

A: I told you already. I saw it. I saw it was a pistol.

Q: And there's no chance you could be mistaken about this, is there?

A: None.

Q: This was a very important part of the whole experience, wasn't it, Mr. Wo, not the sort of fact a person would forget, right?

A: I certainly will never forget it, I can tell you that.

Q: There came a time, Mr. Wo, when you were interviewed by the Federal Bureau of Investigation, is that right?

A: That's right. The next morning, two FBI guys came to my motel room and asked me a lot of questions. I don't know why—I'd told the whole story to the state trooper the night before, just after it happened.

Q: Well, for whatever reason, you did talk to the FBI, right?

A: Right.

Q: And at some point, did they ask you to sit down and write out what happened?

A: Yes, I gave them a written report, that's correct.

Q: Did you say anything about a gun in that report, Mr. Wo?

A: Well, yes, I think so. I mean I must have.

Q: I show you this document, Mr. Wo, and call your attention to the signature at the end. Is that your signature?

A: Sure looks like it.

Q: And is that document in your hand, sir?

A: It is.

Q: That's the statement you wrote for the FBI on the day after the theft, is it not?

A: Well, yes, it looks like the statement I wrote, yes.

Q: Now, Mr. Wo, I want you to read that statement all through and tell this jury whether you can find one word in it about a gun.

A [after a pause of several minutes]: No.

Q: So when you wrote that statement, you just forgot the part about the gun, is that it?

A: No, I didn't forget it.

Q: You just didn't think it was a fact important enough to include?

A: I told the trooper about it, I just didn't put it in the statement.

Q: I didn't ask you about what you told anyone, Mr. Wo. I'm just trying to understand how come you left it out of the written statement.

[At this point there might be a government objection and an instruction from the court to "move on to something else, counsel."]

Q: All right, Your Honor. Mr. Wo, let's talk about your friends and associates for a moment. Can you tell me how many close personal friends you have who are dark-skinned Latinos?

A: Close friends? What do you mean?

Q: Well let's say people who have been over to your house more than once.

A: More than once . . . I can't think of any just at the moment.

Q: Now when you are working, driving the truck, you normally drive alone, is that correct?

A: That is correct. I don't work with a partner. That's done only for the really long cross-country hauls, or when you are on rush and have to drive twenty hours or more at a stretch.

Q: I see. So it would be fair to say that in the last ten years or so you have never worked closely with a person of Latino origin?

A: Yes, that would be right.

Q: And on the night of March 14th, how long would you estimate that you had in view the face of the man you have told us is my client, Mr. Ramirez?

A: Oh, I don't know. A few minutes.

Q: Minutes, Mr. Wo? How many minutes, three? Seven? Sixteen?

A: Maybe two or three.

Q: That's a pretty long time, Mr. Wo. I'll bet you could run a half mile in that amount of time.

[Again, an objection would be sustained to this.]

Q: Well, I'll tell you what let's do. You just close your eyes, and when I say "begin," you just imagine everything that happened from the time this man stepped out of the shadows until he got into your truck and you lost sight of him, then you tell me "stop" and we'll see how long it takes. OK? Can you do that? In real time?

A: I think so.

[An objection to this would probably be overruled.]

Q: All right, begin.

A [after a pause]: Stop.

Ms. McAllister: May the record reflect that approximately thirty-five seconds have elapsed?

The Court: Hearing no objection, the record will so read. Please continue.

Q: Now, Mr. Wo, I have just one other thing I wanted to go over with you, please. Does your company have rules about leaving a load unattended in a truck?

A: There are rules, yes.

Q: And what are those rules, do you recall?

A: Whenever a driver leaves a load for a meal or other personal reasons, the cab must be locked and secure. And of course, the trailer is locked at all times.

Q: So, I suppose that if you had followed these rules, and the truck was stolen from you at gunpoint after you had unlocked the cab, you wouldn't be in any trouble with your employer, is that right?

A: How could you be in any trouble for getting robbed?

Q: All right. But if a driver had left the truck open, and someone got in and drove off with it while the driver was having a cup of coffee, that driver could be in serious trouble, right?

A: Wait a second, hold it—that's not what happened here.

Q: But if that had happened, Mr. Wo, if you had forgotten to lock the cab this one time, left the keys in the ignition, and you lost the truck, someone might think it was your fault, right?

A: But I told you, that's not what happened.

Q: And it is extremely important to you, Mr. Wo, is it not, to convince everyone here—these jurors especially—that that's not what happened, isn't it?

[An objection would be overruled and the judge would turn to the witness and say, "Is that important to you, sir?" The witness, his equanimity recovered, would reply, "It is important that people know the truth, Your Honor." Whereupon Ms. McAllister would smile and say, "No further questions, Your Honor," and resume her seat. On redirect examination, the government would try to adduce the fact that Ying Wo had explicitly told the state trooper that the truck was taken at gunpoint. If the judge knows the law (and trial judges are notoriously sloppy on points like this one), he should sustain an objection because the rules of evidence do not allow proof of a witness's prior statements consistent with his trial testimony under these circumstances. Ying is permitted to say, however, that he was in a hurry when he wrote the statement, that he wanted to get the interview over with and go home, and that he didn't think the written report was particularly important because he had already given a "full and complete" account orally.]

We have seen in this abbreviated transcript two of the tried and true methods of impeachment, and we are ripe for a third, more innovative technique. The first is impeachment by prior inconsistency. McAllister was trying to persuade the jury that they should not believe anything that Ying said under oath because he was the sort of person who says different things at different times. Writing out the story for the FBI without mentioning such an important detail as a gun pointed at your Adam's apple counts as an inconsistency and, no matter how many times Ying included that feature in other accounts, he may be impeached by the inconsistent prior statement. For purposes of impeachment, McAllister doesn't have to show that the prior written rendition was more likely to be true; the impeachment is accomplished by the inconsistency alone. Whichever version is true, the prior inconsistent statement tends to show that the reporter is generally unreliable.

What the jury makes of this sort of evidence is another question. Will they think that the omission was understandable? Or that in the circumstances, it was a minor lapse, detracting not a whit from the credibility of the witness as he testified? True, they did not receive directly the evidence of his other consistent accounts, but they got the hint. Jurors are not as dim-witted as the law likes to pretend. They heard the question from friendly counsel. Maybe it was phrased, "Now Mr. Wo, in your conversations with the troopers, did you tell them that your assailant had a gun?" The jurors heard the objection from defense counsel; she obviously didn't want the jury to hear the answer. Does anyone doubt that the jury figured out that if the witness had been permitted to answer, he would have said, "Yes"? All trial lawyers resort to this ploy on occasion, asking the objectionable question just to bootleg the probable answer into the jurors' understanding.

The jury will receive little if any help from the judge on how to evaluate the evidence of inconsistency. The judge is likely to instruct them only that they "should give it such weight as they think it deserves." If asked, the judge might also tell the jury that an unanswered question is not evidence and that the jury should not guess at what the answer might have been. But everyone knows the instruction is just a matter of form.

Evidence of prior inconsistency—when it can be found—is among the most persuasive counsel can muster on the issue of witness credibility. And for good reason. People who give different versions of the same event, particularly in circumstances of moment like sworn testimony or written statements to the FBI, are suspect. But at the same time, we all have it in our experience that reports, even meticulously honest reports, frequently vary in some particulars. Important facts may be omitted or stated differently from one situation to another. One excellent trial lawyer I knew used to tell the jury on summation after he had been unable by vigorous cross-examination to shake a witness whose story never varied in any detail: "As my mother used to say, 'Too good is no good.'"

The other tried-and-true means of impeachment employed by McAllister is called *bias*. Not as the term is commonly used to denote some inappropriate basis for judgment, but in the old-fashioned sense of *slant*. The law supposes that even those of us who are otherwise scrupulously honest may tend, consciously or otherwise, to slant our stories to favor our own interests or those of our friends and relations. Thus witnesses who have some stake in the outcome of a case, financial or affectional, are subject to the influence of interest—and the jury should know of this possible spin on their renditions.

Of course, most witnesses are biased to some degree. Critical witnesses are often connected in some manner to the party for whom they testify. The alibi witness who says the defendant was with her at the time of the crime is likely to be a friend or relation of the defendant—only slightly less biased than the defendant himself. The character witness who swears to the defendant's exemplary reputation is likely to be a longtime friend or associate. And prosecution witnesses? Police officers may have commendations or promotions riding on the quality of their work in the case. The clerk or salesperson of the robbed jewelry store probably has the company interest in mind—and the company may have an insurance claim that will be affected by the outcome. So with bias of some sort on every hand, what is the jury to do in deciding which story is likely to be pulled the furthest out of shape by its influence?

McAllister was obviously trying to show the jury that Ying was not a disinterested witness but had a heavy stake in the robbery version of the episode. She got her point across. But again, the true effect of bias on testimony is unknowable, and the jury will be left to its own resources to quantify this element of credence. And the central—and most disturbing— aspect of these devices for assessing veracity and accuracy is that jurors have no special gifts. They are no more qualified than the rest of humankind to hear the false ring of deception or detect the innocent error of the well-meaning reporter.

Though rarely so termed, both impeachment by bias and by prior inconsistency are, in essence, impeachment by another equally venerable means, one that we just discussed in Chapter 11: impeachment by bad character. These methods ask the jury to believe that, because the witness made the inconsistent statement, he is the sort of person who does not take the obligation of the oath seriously—that is to say he has the trait of character of treating facts casually. Or that because of his connection to a party or his stake in the outcome, he is likely to color the truth. Again, a character trait of placing less value on truth telling than on self-interest.

I come now to the new method of discrediting Ying's testimony, a method accepted by some courts and rejected by others. It's a beauty, Mary McAllister thinks, maybe an ace. Waiting in the wings, the defense has a witness who could easily cancel the government's strongest evidence: the unshaken testimony of the victim that when he saw the defendant on the day after the crime, he was absolutely certain he was the hijacker. The light was good at the scene, the view was clear, the felon's face was etched in the victim's memory, and the certainty quotient is 100 percent. That is the sort of evidence that sends many defendants to pump iron at state expense for long stretches.

The witness McAllister has up her sleeve is an expert: a psychologist thoroughly schooled in the empirical literature pertaining to the human faculties of recognition and recollection of the human visage. There's plenty of experimental data on this subject, it is professionally sound and substantial, it is virtually uniform, and it is dynamite in the courtroom.

If allowed to testify, this witness—aided by charts and statistical tables— will explain that repeated experiments have demonstrated that people are extremely weak in their ability to identify strangers—especially strangers of a different race perceived briefly under conditions of stress. Perhaps the expert will be permitted to tell of a famous experiment on television in 1974, when viewers were exposed to a twelve-second filmed incident in which a man stole a woman's purse, knocked her down, and ran toward the camera. Viewers then saw an array of photos of six faces and were invited to phone in if they recognized the "thief" or thought that he was not in the array. Nearly two thousand self-selected witnesses telephoned with their choices. Correct identifications were 14.1 percent, almost precisely the score we would expect from two thousand people who had not seen the filmed incident at all.

McAllister's witness will not say—will not be allowed to say—what the odds are that Ying made an accurate identification of Ramirez as the hijacker. But the witness's testimony will be carefully structured to focus on "people" in circumstances as close as possible to the eyewitness in the case on trial. So it will not take much imagination for the jury to supply the connection and apply the expert's testimony to the facts of the case before them. And that evidence will be devastating. It's impossible to discredit (all the experts will agree that respectable experiments yield those results), and it's hard to ignore. It is difficult to see how any jury, with such evidence in mind, could convict in a case that depends entirely on eyewitness identification evidence.

The expert's testimony creates reasonable doubt per se. And in a case like ours, where the D.A. is counting on Ying Wo's positive identification to overwhelm Ramirez's odd story, a good perception psychologist can sink the prosecution without a bubble.

Without the expert, jurors tend to generalize from their own experience. For those (like me) who think the cognitive faculty of remembering faces is little short of miraculous, the data come as no great surprise. But for others (like my wife) who can meet someone months after a brief chat at a party and recognize him and name the occasion on which they last met, the expert may have some important news to convey. Perhaps for all of us, the most profound shock the expert will deliver is that certainty has zero correlation with accuracy. Everyone—including cops and judges—takes the witness's expressed confidence—"I'm 99 percent sure that's the guy"—as some measure of the strength of the ID. The experts show us no mercy; we're just plain wrong, no two ways about it. People are just as certain of their errors as their correct hits, just as likely to be dubious about correct recognitions as false ones.

So we'll call this possible avenue of impeachment, with its golden payoff, impeachment by incompetence—a word in the lexicon of evidence that means that a witness doesn't really know what the witness professes to know. It's not surprising that courts divide on the admissibility of this sort of evidence. We have a long-standing tradition that the jurors are the best judges—and the exclusive judges—of the credibility of witnesses. Experts should not be allowed to instruct them, in effect, on whether or not to believe the testimony of an eyewitness—or anybody else. Plus, it is argued by some that experimental data, however well the tests are conducted, cannot inform a jury on whether a particular witness accurately identified the person he said he recognized. After all, however well or poorly some bunch of experimental subjects performed in other circumstances says little about the recognition skills of this particular witness in these circumstances. He could have my disability or my wife's facility in remembering faces. The courts' conflicting treatment of such evidence is another manifestation of a long-running dispute on the relevance of statistical probability.

At the same time, most jurisdictions are becoming considerably more relaxed on the admissibility of expert testimony. Even on subjects that used to be considered common knowledge, courts will usually allow an expert to contribute wherever the expert's opinion might be "helpful." Knowledge of human faculties, systematically collected and analyzed, will surely assist the jury lost in the mire of *maybe* and *sometimes*. In fact, the danger is that McAllister's expert will assist the jury too much, allowing them to abandon the tough job of sorting out and weighing the evidence in favor of the neat statistics expertly recited from the detached perspective of scientific study.

Let's pose another case, providing a somewhat different opportunity for counsel to try to discredit a witness by conventional techniques, with a less conventional means in reserve:

Jody Hacket was charged with murder. She had taken a hunting rifle belonging to her husband, Tom, and shot him once through the head as he lay sleeping. When the police arrived shortly afterward at the modest mobile home where the Hackets lived in a somewhat rundown trailer park, they found Jody sitting on the steps outside, weeping. The first thing she said to the officers was, "What have I done? He could be so good to me. What will I do now without him?" Inside, they found the rifle on the bed next to the body. When they took Jody down to headquarters, they thought they noticed bruises on her face, a swollen eye, but it was hard to tell because she was still crying.

Tom had worked as an automobile salesman at a dealership in town, where he was regarded as a personable, ambitious young man. Perhaps a bit too handsome for his own good, a fellow salesman confided. His male colleagues thought of Tom as a good companion with whom they often bowled after work. He liked to hang out with bachelors, one buddy said. You sometimes forgot he was married. If he had one fault, another recalled, it was his taste for old Jack Daniel's, and it was true he had a tendency to get mean when he was tanked. But, hey, a woman who worked in the office allowed, you forgave him every-thing when he flashed that cute smile of his.

This picture of the deceased emerged from the testimony of the prosecu-tion's witnesses, spiced by prosecution evidence that for several months Tom had been carrying on a clandestine affair with the office bookkeeper. To prove the liaison and establish a motive, the prosecution called the bookkeeper, An-nalee White. The witness, a frail, pale, hesitant young woman of some twenty-four years, was extremely reluctant to testify. She answered the prosecutor's questions in a barely audible tone, her eyes cast down as though she were reading the answers from the tops of her party pumps. Several times, the judge gently instructed Ms. White to speak louder; more than once he had to prompt her to answer the question as she sat there in silence, looking at no one.

Yes, she knew the deceased, Tom Hacket. Had she found him attractive? Well, he was nice. Yes, he had given her small gifts—a bunch of flowers he had picked from the side of the road on the way to work, candy from the supermarket, stuff like that. Yes, he had asked her to go out with him. No, she didn't have any other boyfriends. Did she go out with Tom? Mostly no, she said, because he was married and it would be wrong. Well, yes, she did go out with him a few times. To the movies once, usually they just drove around. Sometimes they would get a pizza at a late-night pizza joint. She didn't want to go anywhere they might be seen together. Were they ever seen together? I hope not. I don't think so, not by anyone we knew. No (with a flicker of heat), she never spent the night with Tom. She lived with her mother, she and Tom never had any place to go together. Sex? Did they ever have sex? Well (please, Ms. White, try to keep your voice up), sometimes they kissed and fooled around a little in the car. Intercourse? (Do I have to answer that question, Your Honor?) No, never. Well, maybe once or twice. Yes, she cared for Tom. He told her he loved her. He said he was very unhappy in his marriage and he planned to get a divorce as soon as he had saved some money so he could provide something for his wife when they broke up. Yes, she believed him. No, of course, she never told anyone about the affair. Except she did once talk about it to Sue, her best friend, when she was really confused about how she felt.

The state's theory of how Tom Hacket met his death was offered to the jury at the very outset of the case. Tom was a good-looking, fun-loving young man who never gave up his bachelor pleasures when he married Jody. Jody felt abandoned, angry, and—when she heard Tom was carrying on with another woman—inflamed with jealousy. They often fought, sometimes came to blows, but Jody was determined to hold onto her philandering husband. On the night of the shooting, Tom had come home late; the autopsy showed he had been drinking quite heavily during the evening. They probably had words, as they usually did in one of these frequent scenes. Perhaps Jody accused him of infidelity and maybe this time he didn't bother to deny it. Anyway, when Tom, exhausted, lay down and fell asleep, Jody, in a jealous rage, took his rifle from the back of his closet, deliberately loaded it from a box of ammunition he kept in a drawer, and with murderous intent took careful aim from close range and fired a bullet neatly between his closed eyes. Deliberate and premeditated murder, the most serious crime on the books.

Jody Hacket had a very different version of the facts. She did not deny shooting and killing her husband as he lay sleeping in their bed. But she claimed she had fired in self-defense. On direct examination, she told a harrowing tale of two years of brutality. About once a month, Tom would come home drunk, begin accusing her of keeping the house "like a pigsty," demand a hot meal, accuse her of squandering money and an assortment of other marital misde- meanors. Often his voice would be raised so loud that neighbors would begin shouting at them to knock it off and let them get some sleep. Several times police were called but she always told them it was OK, she didn't want to press charges. Tom had struck her many times, she said. Usually he would slap her with an open hand across the face. But he would hit her as hard as he could, often knocking her to the floor. Several times he had hit her with a stick. Her injuries included a broken nose and two broken ribs when he struck her with a baseball bat. Once, she sustained internal hemorrhages when he hit her in the midsection. And her only pregnancy was aborted after her husband kicked her in the belly. On those occasions, she had received medical atten- tion at the emergency room of the local hospital, but she had lied to the doc- tors about how she had sustained the injuries.

Cross-examination of Jody by the assistant district attorney went like this:

Q: So you just waited until he went to sleep, went and got his gun, and shot him dead, right?

A: I was desperate.

Q: Desperate, Mrs. Hacket? Why didn't you just leave?

A: I couldn't.

Q: Was someone blocking the door, Mrs. Hacket?

A: No, not physically.

Q: Not physically? Is there some other way to block a door?

A: Psychologically.

Q: Let me see if I understand you, Mrs. Hacket. You say that even though your husband was in bed, in a deep sleep, his ghost, or spirit, or some emana- tion of some kind was standing between you and escape, is that it?

A: No, not exactly.

Q: And this was not the first time you had had a fight with Tom, isn't that right?

A: That's right.

Q: And there were times, many times, when Tom was out—at work or what- ever—when you were completely alone?

A: Almost every day, yes.

Q: And you never took advantage of any of those many opportunities to get away from this monster you've been telling us about, did you?

A: No.

Q: Was anyone preventing you from leaving on those many occasions?

A: No, not physically.

Q: Oh yes, I forgot. You were barricaded in that place by invisible forces, tied down by psychological bonds you just couldn't break.

[On an objection, the judge will say, "Yes, Mr. District Attorney. No comments, please." "I'm sorry, Your Honor," the prosecutor will respond, "I just forgot myself for a moment." "Proceed," the court will say sternly.]

Q: Tell me, Mrs. Hacket, how long was Tom asleep before you went to get his rifle?

A: I don't know. Not long. Less than an hour, I would say.

Q: But it was more than a few minutes, wasn't it?

A: Oh, yes. Maybe an hour or so.

Q: You wanted to make sure he was really asleep, didn't you?

A: No, I just didn't know what to do. I just felt so bad. I was thinking, How had I provoked it? I should probably have had some supper waiting for him, like he said.

Q: You were thinking what to do?

A: I guess so, yes.

Q: Well, don't you remember what you were thinking?

A: No, not really. Well, yes, I guess I was thinking what I should do. I thought about leaving, but Tom needed me, I knew that, in spite of everything.

Q: So, thinking about how your husband needed you, you decided to kill him, right?

A: I don't know what I thought. I was very upset.

Q: Well, you weren't so upset that you couldn't find the gun, right? [No answer.]

Q: You weren't so upset that you forgot where Tom kept his ammunition, were you?

A: I knew he kept it with his socks.

Q: So when you took the gun and loaded it, you were planning to kill him, weren't you?

A: Maybe, I don't know.

Q: Well, you weren't planning to go out squirrel hunting in the middle of the night, were you?

[On an objection, the judge turns to the witness and says, "Mrs. Hacket, he wants to know did you plan to use the rifle to hunt squirrels, yes or no?" to which the witness replies, "No."]

Q: Now, when you took that loaded gun into the bedroom, Tom was obviously still asleep, right?

A: He was snoring, I remember very well.

Q: Snoring, all right. So you lifted the gun and aimed it. Now at that moment, Mrs. Hacket, please tell this jury: did you feel yourself in any physical danger from your husband?

A: Yes, I did.

Q: You did? You thought this man, deep asleep and snoring, would suddenly leap up and strike you?

A: Well, no, not exactly.

Q: Not exactly? Well, just how were you in mortal danger at that moment?

A: I can't explain. I always felt in danger. [Witness cries.] I'm telling you as best I can. For over two years, I never felt safe. I thought he would kill me. [Witness cries again.]

The Court: All right, we will have a brief recess, ladies and gentlemen. Ten minutes.

We can imagine that after the witness regains her composure and the trial resumes, the cross-examination might continue for hours along the same vein. It is perfectly obvious what the prosecutor is trying to do here. It's basic cross-examination. He is trying to discredit Jody Hacket (as the defense had earlier attempted to cast doubt on Annalee's story of the affair) by demeanor evidence and by incoherence.

It is very important in the American system of adjudication that witnesses come before the jury, live and in person, and tell their stories under oath, from present recollection, and subject to vigorous cross-examination in the presence of the fact finder. The principle is expressed in the prohibition against hearsay (a prohibition shot through with exceptions but nevertheless regarded as fundamental). In a criminal trial, the same idea is reinforced by a constitutional right belonging to the defendant, known as the right of confrontation.

Why is live testimony so important? After all, documents—records, reports, sworn statements—are often as reliable and probative. The reason is that a false document does not sweat, shift around in its seat, and look frequently at the ceiling. It is the faith of our adversary system (touching, really, in its superb naïveté) that any twelve ordinary citizens can detect an untruthful live witness by the visible clues of lying. This theory supposes that, for virtually all humanity, falsehood is so uncomfortable that, magnified by hostile interrogation, the liar's discomfort cannot be concealed. The lie (we customarily forget here the honest mistake) will betray itself in tone of voice (too loud, too soft, too aggressive, too submissive), manner of articulation (too many pauses, hesitations, equivocations), body language (crossed arms or legs, eyes aloft, rigid posture, shifting position, fingers nervously touching face and head), and other cues too subtle to describe but readily recognizable from across the courtroom well. These are the products of live testimony known as demeanor evidence, and the jury is explicitly told they may consider them in resolving the credibility issue.

So defense counsel presses Annalee White on cross-examination and the prosecutor returns the favor when Jody Hacket testifies. Each is trying to make the witness squirm, literally—to stammer, perhaps to lose her composure and show, even for a moment, the passions seething beneath the controlled courtroom delivery. By these inadvertent gestures, counsel hope the jury will perceive the indicia of mendacity. And no one in the courtroom has the slightest problem with this. Not just lawyers and judges, but apparently almost everyone else shares the belief that liars generally give themselves away to the close observer by the rebellion of the autonomic nervous system, the locus of the conscience that cannot abide falsehood.

That's the premise on which the polygraph—the "lie detector"—works. The black box makes finer measurements, of course, detecting activity of the sweat glands invisible to the naked eye, changes in blood pressure and respiration that might escape notice of the ordinary observer. And a skilled polygraph operator might be able (as they claim) to screen out the seasoned or "pathological" liar—something the jury observing the effects of the most skillful cross-examination might be unable to do. But otherwise, the premise is the same: human physiology does not easily countenance lying.

But for all the accord, there is very little evidence to support the notion that a lie waves a behavioral flag. People simply cannot—as they think they can—read falsehood in the vocal and bodily accompaniments to recital. Leaving the claims of the polygraph guild aside, the data are pretty clear that none of the supposed clues to falsehood is trustworthy. Regarding the data, however, I must insert this caveat. Sadly (*maddeningly* would be more honest), I found not one of the several experimental models to be a well-designed test of what really happens when a jury watches a witness testify in court. But there are many studies, some better than others, and they all agree—and the unanimous verdict can hardly be ignored. Professor Olin Wellborn, writing in the Cornell Law Review in 1991, reviewed the copious empirical data and reported:

> Taken as a whole, the experimental evidence indicates that ordinary observers do not benefit from the opportunity to observe nonverbal behavior in judging whether someone is lying. There is no evidence that facial behavior is of any benefit; some evidence suggests that observation of facial behavior diminishes the accuracy of lie detection. Nor do paralinguistic cues [that is, voice quality and inflection] appear to be of value; subjects who receive transcript[s] consistently perform as well as or better than subjects who receive recordings of the respondent's voice. With respect to body cues, there is no persuasive evidence to support the hypothesis that lying is accompanied by distinctive body behavior that others can discern.

So much for demeanor evidence. Some commentators (me among them) believe that coherence is the prime guide to credence. The plausibility factor: jurors asking themselves, Does this story make sense? This, I believe, is the final hurdle in selling a story to the jury, the last question they ask themselves before casting their final votes. And it is the prime task of the trial lawyer to take the bits and pieces recited by the witnesses, put them together with the physical evidence, expert opinions, and whatever else there may be that fits, and advance to the jurors a coherent series of events—a compelling story—in which a jury can concur, agreeing, yes, it makes sense that it happened just that way.

But what makes a story make sense? Most likely, plausibility testing involves some sort of cerebral matching. A set of actions and events as recounted by the evidence is held up against the juror's experience, imagination, and derived intelligence concerning the behavior and reactions of real and fictitious others: "Is this the sort of thing I might do in those circumstances?" "Would anyone I know have reacted that way?" "From what I've seen of cops on TV, would they have done it this way?"

The trouble, of course, is that frequently the cultural context and customs of the actors in the events narrated by the witnesses are alien to the jurors seeking a plausibility match. Probably none of the jurors nor anyone they are likely to know has had any experiences comparable to those described by Jody Hacket or Annalee White. And with no referent in experience, with no capacity to understand behavior and events by projection, and (let us hope) with appropriate mistrust of fiction, the jury's quest for coherence degenerates into a worthless assessment of possibilities. "It could have happened that way" gets the jury nowhere, because it could have happened any number of ways. It is far from a judgment on the most likely way it actually happened.

Thus, the well-worn tools of "common sense and ordinary experience," which jurors are directed to use in gauging credibility, may be useless as jurors listen to witnesses and contemplate circumstances far from the paths of their own lives. Even when some correspondence may be found between the jurors' lives and the events they are called upon to imagine, plausibility is a highly uncertain standard. "Sure, that makes sense" or "Oh yes, I knew someone just like her who might have done just that sort of thing" are hardly reactions by which a complex patchwork of past events may be stitched together with confidence. While some of us characteristically rely on the "ring of truth" for all sorts of important decisions, others of us (lacking perfect pitch) mistrust that ring and are constantly reminded that unlikely things occur in life all the time.

True, judgment by appeal to the sense of plausibility is at the heart of a criminal trial or any conceivable system for the reconstruction of past events. From historians to insurance claims adjusters, people rely on that critical element of judgment. But historians know that plausibility is culture driven, that what seems a plausible explanation to contemporary sensibility may have been unthinkable at the time, or in the culture under study. Jurors are not normally taught to discount their invisible, culture-bound mind-sets. In certain cases, I might like to request an instruction from the judge something like this: "Members of the jury, because the players in this case live in a different social milieu from most of you, please do not attempt to assess their conduct by the standards of behavior derived from your own experience. Instead, you should try to project yourselves, by the use of your imagination, into the world from which the participants come and judge the plausibility of their accounts from that standpoint." I'd like to ask for it, but I don't think I could persuade a judge to make such a radical departure from the boilerplate about "common sense and ordinary experience." Nor could I argue convincingly that anyone can perform that feat of imagination with any degree of reliability.

The uncertainty of the plausibility standard may be further aggravated by our adversary mode of trying cases. In the familiar American model, the jury—charged with the measurement of plausibility—has limited access to contextual detail and irrelevant bits of information that flavor the account laid before them. They don't hear the stories told in a natural and spontaneous way that might betray implausibility. They don't even get to ask the questions—and follow-up questions—that might, in other circumstances, lead them to a judgment on plausibility. The jury must take their raw material as it is dished up for them by the lawyers in the artificial and polarized forum of the courtroom.

Jody Hacket, our defendant, actually has a big problem in the coherence department. It comes from the law of self-defense. Like many other women in the same position, Jody has only the defense of self-defense. It's her only hope. And on some level it might be said that it is a fair and true construction of the situation. But the law is clear. For a defendant to escape criminal responsibility for an act that would otherwise be a homicide, the killer must believe, and with good reason, that a serious crime (robbery, rape, murder) is about to be committed against her or some other person, a crime that cannot be otherwise averted or escaped. It is a defense only for those in imminent danger, whose backs are truly up against the wall.

Applying the ordinary tests of credibility, comparing Jody Hacket's story with their own experience, jurors are very likely to find Jody's claim of imminent, inescapable mortal danger implausible. But again, the defense has a helpful expert waiting in the wings. In recent years, urged by the women's movement, psychologists have studied cases of women who eventually strike back after being viciously abused by their partners over an extended period. From these clinical studies, they have crafted what is now called the "battered-spouse syndrome."

Across the nation in recent years, courts have been remarkably receptive to evidence from these experts. Of the thirty states that have considered it, twenty-nine allow experts to describe the characteristic behavior patterns of the syndrome and to answer hypothetical questions drawn from the evidence on trial. The hold-out, Nevada, still has the question under consideration. In addition, two states, Maryland and Missouri, have granted executive clemency on the strength of the battered-spouse theory.

But in one of those quirks of the legal mind (with which we are becoming familiar), most courts will not allow the psychologist to testify that she examined the defendant in the case and found her to be suffering from the syndrome, nor to give the opinion that the conduct of the defendant in the case on trial was "consistent with" or "a product of" the battered-spouse syndrome. It's much the same as with the experts in recognition skills.

Although not clearly spelled out, judicial thinking on this is probably based on the "province of the jury" theory. Any psychologist who comes right out and says, "In my expert opinion, this defendant is suffering from a condition that made her believe that she was really acting in self-defense when she struck the lethal blow" is too blatantly usurping the jury's authority—the determination of guilt. Whereas the expert who testifies only that a hypothetical person in a hypothetical situation (having the characteristics of this defendant in this situation) "might be suffering from a clinical condition that has the following symptoms" leaves it to the jury's judgment whether this defendant in fact believed she was acting in self-defense. Another distinction without a difference? Such are the placebos of the legal mind.

This means that, most likely, Jody Hacket will be allowed to call her expert in the field of psychology. After stating her professional qualifications, the witness will be asked whether she is familiar with a psychological condition known as the battered-spouse syndrome. She will be asked whether that condition has received recognition in the field of psychology and she will reply that it has received wide recognition as a result of extensive clinical observation. Maybe counsel will expand on this a bit by eliciting the titles of respectable journal articles and such. The witness will then be asked to describe the condition. The witness will probably say something like this: "The battered-spouse syndrome is a characteristic condition of mind produced by an extended period of brutal abuse at the hands of a spouse or the functional equivalent thereof. The spouse, usually the female spouse, characteristically experiences feelings of guilt, mistakenly taking the blame for the abusive behavior of her husband. She comes to feel that somehow she must have deserved it. The abusive spouse, usually the male, characteristically expresses exaggerated remorse and concern following episodes of brutality, professes love and dependency, and resolves to reform. The abused spouse characteristically responds by forgiveness. Through many repetitions of this pattern, the abused spouse falls into a relationship of dependence from which she finds it virtually impossible to extricate herself. At the same time, she lives in fear of repetitions of the physical abuse. Commonly, she will make no complaint, usually disguising her injuries, out of fear that her spouse will retaliate for any betrayal with more severe punishment. In many instances, this syndrome will aggravate over time until the battered spouse comes to fear for her life. In some instances, she will be driven to the point where she kills her spouse to protect herself from what she believes is a certain fatal attack on herself and from which she feels there is no other escape."

The expert witness will then be asked a hypothetical question along these lines: "Now doctor, please assume the following facts are true. A woman, let's call her 'J,' has been married to a man, call him 'T,' for something over two years. J is a woman of limited education, having left school after the eighth grade to take a job, who had suffered abuse at the hands of her father when a youngster. T is a handsome and sociable young man who enjoys going out with his male friends. On occasion, he drinks too much and frequently arrives home drunk."

The questioning will continue thus, reciting carefully in hypothetical form, the particular details of the case as given by the witnesses in evidence. The form is utterly transparent, of course, as the jury recognizes every fact as corresponding to the evidence in the case before them. At the conclusion of the hypothetical recital, the psychologist will be asked whether she has an opinion concerning the condition of "J." Not surprisingly, the witness will reply that J was suffering from the classic symptoms of the battered-spouse syndrome. She will not be asked whether, in her view, J was acting in self-defense when she shot T; that is the ultimate issue for the jury alone to decide.

The odd thing about a court's accepting the testimony of these experts is that in effect it contradicts the standard instructions to the jury. Disregard the credibility assessments you might be led to make by the application of your own common sense and life experience, the experts might as well say. Things are not as they seem. We can tell you from our superior learning that human beings behave in ways you would not expect. And therefore, when a witness tells you a certain kind of story that you would not otherwise believe, you might nevertheless find it to be true.

The high court in the State of Connecticut, considering the admissibility of expert testimony on the battered-spouse syndrome, confronted the anomaly head-on. The case, decided in 1993, was called *State of Connecticut v. Bor-*

relli. It had unusual facts. The victim had made a sworn complaint of abuse, which she later recanted and denied. The state, prosecuting her husband on the basis of her initial statement, sought to have the jury discredit her subsequent disavowal by attributing it to the battered-spouse syndrome. The Supreme Court of Connecticut wrote:

> The defendant's final claim is that the expert testimony in this case was actually opinion testimony as to the credibility of a witness, and therefore should have been excluded because it improperly invaded the province of the jury. . . .
>
> Certainly, the jury had the right to consider [the expert] Stark's testimony in determining whether to believe the victim's prior statement or her testimony at trial. Stark did not testify, however, that the victim was in fact battered and therefore did not comment, directly or indirectly, on her credibility. . . . [T]he purpose of Stark's testimony was to present to the jury possible explanations for why a victim of abuse would completely recant her accusations, explanations that in all likelihood were beyond the jury's experience and knowledge. Stark neither presented opinion testimony as to the credibility of any witness nor indicated whether the out-of-court statement was credible. . . . Stark's testimony was relevant to describe the behavior patterns typically ascribed to battered women's syndrome. The trial court also cautioned the jury that expert testimony "is [not] binding upon you and you may disregard such testimony either entirely or in part. It is for you the triers of the facts to consider the testimony and with the other circumstances in this case, use your best judgment to determine whether or not you give any weight to the testimony and, if so, what weight you will give to it."
>
> Under the circumstances of this case, Stark's expert testimony was properly admitted "to assist the jury in understanding, not whether [the victim] was a credible witness on the witness stand, but whether her conduct . . . was consistent with the pattern and profile of a battered woman." We conclude that the expert testimony did not invade the province of the jury in determining the credibility of witnesses.

That's where it stands. The jury hears testimony, at least some of which is probably mistaken, consciously or unconsciously distorted, or an outright lie. They watch the witness and listen to her testimony as it is adduced by the lawyers in the highly artificial setting of a courtroom, where the fact finders are deprived of the usual subtle cues of spontaneous recitals—where, when, to whom, and in what order, and with what gaps the teller chooses to reveal the message. The jurors are not permitted to prompt, challenge, or even react with a raised eyebrow as they might in ordinary circumstances if trying to decide whether to credit a story they were being told. They are given the benefits of the traditional techniques of impeachment—evidence of bad character with regard to truth telling, prior self-contradiction, bias—and they are invited to consider the demeanor evidence of the testifying witness and to consider the plausibility and coherence of the story told.

With all this in mind, the jurors retire to hammer it out. And we are all generally satisfied that the verdict that comes out stands on a pretty accurate judgment concerning the credibility of the witnesses. In many instances, I would readily concede that our faith is justified. The facts seem plain to all the experienced players: cops, both lawyers, and the judge. And although no one can know for sure, and there are plenty of documented instances in which this collective certainty proved to be mistaken, still I suppose I would join with those who say that that small possibility of error must be ignored. What I am concerned about are the many, many cases where the attribution of credence is problematic, the cases where the lawyers would disagree or be forced to concede that they are unsure. "That's what we have juries for," they will add. But I say, what makes you think jurors are any better fixed to make that judgment? And if they are not (as I fear they are not), is our faith in the product of the adversary system justified?

There is another way to go about this fact-finding business. But its exploration will have to await the final chapter. In the meantime, it is enough to note our uncertainty over whether a jury can truly resolve either the case of the alleged hijacking of Ying Wo's truck or the responsibility of Jody Hacket for killing her husband. And in this connection, we should note (by way of segue into the next chapter) that sometimes the defense of those who murder brutally abusive spouses or parents is cynically referred to as the "the-bastard-had-it-coming" defense. The law recognizes the justification of self-defense but not fair retribution. But juries have it in their power to "recognize" by acquittal defenses unknown to law. We call it the power of nullification.

13 Jury Nullification

The Insanity Defense and Other Avoidances

It is probably inevitable, even in the most liberal, participatory democracy, that occasionally laws will seem unduly harsh or the application of a good law to a particular case will seem unjust. One of the virtues of the jury system— rarely celebrated—is that the jury has the power to take the law into its own hands and do justice despite the law.

Not since the earliest years of the republic has this power of the lay jury been officially recognized—and then only for the briefest period. In 1798, Congress passed a law, which remained on the books for only three years, called the Alien and Sedition Acts. It expressly conferred on the jury the power to decide the law as well as the fact in prosecutions for seditious libel. Under this law, the jury could, as judges of the law, lawfully decline to convict a defendant by deciding that his published attack on the government— however scurrilous—was not "seditious" as a matter of law. Even then, the law was an aberration.

Throughout most of our history as colony and nation, the jury has been the judge of the facts only, and today jurors are firmly instructed that they are bound by their oath to take "the law" from the judge (who, in turn, is bound to take it from higher courts and from the legislature). What nobody tells the jury (except for the occasional defense lawyer who braves an inevitable admonition from the judge) is that if the jury, for whatever reason, chooses to disobey instructions, to disregard clearly understood provisions of law, to acquit a defendant who is indisputably guilty under the law, there is nothing, but *nothing,* anyone can do about it. Jurors are no longer punished (as they were long ago) for erroneous verdicts. And in the English-American system, the government has no appeal from a verdict of acquittal. The principle of double jeopardy precludes a second trial even if the first verdict was indisputably wrong. If, after returning a verdict, a juror has a pang of conscience and submits an affidavit to the court saying, in effect, "We, the jury, decided in this case to disregard the law and acquit this defendant just because we felt like it," the court will turn a deaf ear.

So there is no dispute that, de facto, the American jury has an awesome power of nullification. The only dispute—and an engaging controversy it is—concerns whether the jurors should be told of the power that is theirs. Odd though it feels, I find myself among those who believe that they should not be told. I think it is right that they be instructed (as they are) just the contrary: that, like it or not, they must take the law from the court and they must return a verdict according to law. I think they should exercise their extraordinary power only in cases that are truly extraordinary, cases in which they feel so strongly about the interests of justice that they are willing to disobey their sworn duty in order to accomplish a just end.

Nullification pure and simple occurs when a jury hears evidence that a doctor placed a mask over the face of a living person, knowing full well that through that device a lethal dose of carbon monoxide would be delivered when the person pulled a string; when the jury is fully charged that the law provides that any person, even a doctor, is guilty of the crime of assisting suicide if he or she does anything to help another person in any way to commit suicide, regardless of whether that person is in full possession of his or her senses and freely chooses to end his or her life; and when the jury, understanding all this, nonetheless returns a verdict of not guilty. That decision is nothing more or less than canceling the will of the legislature regarding such situations, effectively rewriting the law to fit the jury's notions of justice in the particular case.

Quasi-nullification—virtual nullification—presents itself to the jury openly as a legal means to avoid the harsh consequences of the law just as surely as if they were nullifying it. Unlike performing "true nullification," this jury will be obeying the court's instructions. Nullification in this form is a subtler creature, taking several forms, most of which are too familiar to attract much notice, but none announces itself for what it is: nullification.

Deliberately killing another human being, a crime that would otherwise be murder, is reduced in grade to manslaughter if it was done "in the heat of passion" or "under extreme emotional disturbance." Thus, a jury may partially excuse the person who grabs a knife and plunges it into the heart of a man whom he has just discovered in the act of raping the killer's ten-year-old daughter. By finding he acted in the heat of passion—a partial excuse—the jury can nullify the murder count under which the intentional homicide would otherwise belong.

Entrapment is another example. Bribing a police officer is justified if the jury finds that the defendant, who had not the slightest intention of offering money to the cop, was induced to do so by the cop, who persuaded him that the case was hopeless, the penalty severe, and the only hope of a fair disposition lay in a crossing the officer's palm with silver. So a jury, finding that the criminal idea was implanted by an overzealous officer, might excuse the person who tenders the payment that would otherwise be criminal.

Insanity is, of course, a perfectly "legal" defense, but it, too, provides jurors with a means of nullifying a law because it seems wrong to them to apply it in a particular case. Pretty much everywhere, the law provides (with some variations in language) that when an act that would otherwise be criminal is committed by a person who, by reason of mental disease or defect, does not fully understand the nature and quality of the act or appreciate that it is wrong, the person shall be found not guilty.

The defense was developed in England midway through the nineteenth century, well before Freud invented psychoanalysis. It does not mean (despite one ill-fated effort to translate it thus) that a person diagnosed as psychotic is not responsible for crimes associated with that disease. Nor does it mean that a person can escape conviction if his crime is sufficiently bizarre and repugnant. Just because "normal" people do not commit multiple murders, eat the flesh of their victims, and keep their severed heads in the refrigerator does not mean that the person who does is, for legal purposes, insane.

The insanity defense reflects the basic idea that it is unjust to hold responsible a person whose mind is so weak or disoriented that he or she lacks even the basic understanding that a weapon is lethal, or that death might result from striking another person repeatedly on the head, or that it is evil to kill an innocent person. Though most frequently asserted in homicide cases, the defense is equally available when mental disease robs a man of his understanding that it is wrong to have coitus with a child, or that setting fire to a home has consequences beyond a lovely bright blaze to watch.

The immediate predecessor of our old and current definition of insanity held that a person could not be deemed guilty if he had no more understanding of his conduct than a wild beast would have. It's still the same idea. And it still makes good sense. There is something peculiarly human about the concept of guilt, and it should be applied only to those who have the basic trait of an adult human animal: moral understanding.

Today we have swarms of experts on moral understanding. They are not (as some might suppose) theologians or moral philosophers. They are psychologists (alienists, we lawyers used to call them in a wonderfully descriptive term). Because "mental disease or defect" is generally part of the definition of legal insanity, psychiatrists, psychoanalysts, and clinical psychologists are regularly called upon to give their opinions on the mental condition of the defendant who asserts this defense.

The lawyers' resort to the psychiatric guild for their guidance presents an amusing clash of intellectual cultures. It was precisely this juxtaposition that first attracted me to law in general and criminal law in particular. I saw it— and still see it—not only as a reflection of an age-old conflict, but as a central paradox of any legal system. Shrinks, like most "modern" theorists, are basically determinists. They believe in something they call the personality (orthodox Freudians have a somewhat more complex lexicon), which is composed (in a disputable mix) of nature and nurture, of genetic traits and the myriad impressions of experience. Behavior is the product of personality. If a person kills another human being and no one made him do it, he did it because he was required to do it by his own personality. External circumstances, the events of the moment, do not cause behavior, though they may stimulate forces within the stored potentials of personality. All the things we are, civilized and primitive, are the determinants of all the things we do.

Law—especially criminal law—posits a very different motive agent in behavior, a concept without which there would be no crimes. Free will. According to this quaint idea, people are endowed with the capacity for free and intelligent choice. Adults, therefore, are responsible for their choices. Guilt, under this rubric, is the social response to a faulty choice—not a feeling, as the shrinks would have it, but a moral status. If we act only as we must, according to the wiring of our personality, we cannot be held responsible—morally or criminally—for any action. To be responsible—guilty—implies that an alternative course could have been chosen.

How, then, can we punish as criminals people who did what they did because, given who they are, they could have done nothing else? This is the disturbing paradox throbbing in the courtroom every time a shrink takes the stand to testify on the issue of insanity. As she holds up her hand to take the oath, the psychiatrist will be thinking, "Everyone behaves as his psyche demands; abnormal personalities will engage in abnormal conduct, including murder. I can tell them whether this person was suffering from an abnormal personality. I can tell them whether this behavior was symptomatic of a mental disease. On everything else, I'll have to wing it."

The lawyer will then ask questions designed to elicit an opinion on moral judgment. "Tell me, doctor," he will say with a dramatic pause, "in your opinion, did this defendant, by reason of his mental condition, know or appreciate that what he did was wrong?" Or in some jurisdictions, the question might be, "Could the defendant freely choose to act lawfully?" They're asking me, the doctor realizes with dismay, questions about moral capacity and free will. Funny, I can't recall anyone ever mentioning these things at the psychoanalytic institute.

In this fix, a candid alienist once confided, I have a simple escape. These lawyers seem to be talking about a condition they call insanity. "Insane" is a diagnosis unknown to the medical profession. So I don't know what I am doing here, under oath, in the first place. But they seem to think that there is some correspondence between insanity (whatever that is) and recognized mental diseases. So I will play it their way and silently translate into a more familiar language. Thus the lawyer's standard question, "In your opinion, Doctor, did this man know or appreciate the nature and quality of his actions" becomes, "Was he psychotic?" The free will/moral capacity junk then becomes surprisingly easy. If he was psychotic, a prisoner of his disease, the cognitive processes cannot be said to function freely and the moral judgment must reflect the delusion. The resulting evidence the doctor gives is probably heard by the jury as: "Because of his mental disease, this person should not (or should) bear moral responsibility for what he did." So the lawyers and the doctors talk their different languages at each other, and the jury usually gets enough information to do the right thing.

This dissonance, I hasten to say, is the sort of thing that may be readily dismissed as an academic conundrum. In the workaday world of the courts, happily, no one seems to notice the silent clash of medieval notions of personal responsibility and modern deterministic ideas. And it's a rare court worker who wonders whether the aperture of insanity should be wide, narrow, or abolished altogether as a means of virtual nullification. Only the academic crank worries about whether we can claim to take the defense seriously and still go on convicting the serial killers and child rapists as though psychopathy were a case of poison ivy.

On the other hand, if we were serious about the requisite control and moral appreciation components of "guilt," criminal justice would be reserved for the few (are there any?) whose crimes can honestly be said to be detached from their social and psychological determinants. And the more heinous, sadistic, and brutal the crime, the more readily it would be excused. Because we are not headed in that direction, the Doctor's Solution to the linguistic bind goes unheeded. We do not conclude from a diagnosis of psychosis—nor do we expect juries to so conclude—that the moral capacity is gone. Free will, and the responsibility it implies, survive even the most catastrophic collapse of the cognitive faculties. So the question arises, what is left of the defense of insanity?

In many places, following David Hinckley's attempt on President Reagan's life (and his acquittal on grounds of insanity), an ingenious new category was invented. In a brilliant stroke, incompatibles were fused; a new verdict (or guilty plea) was born: *guilty but insane.* Jurors are relieved of the choice that so bedeviled the Hinckley jurors—how can we bring ourselves to convict this nutcake? You can now do both, you can vote him in need of psychiatric help and vote him culpable at the same time. Let the prison officials sort it out. It's only a question of housing, after all—the conventional slammer or its medical equivalent? This development goes a fair distance toward the abolition of the insanity defense.

Still, we probably need legal pegs for juries to hang an excuse on, means to exercise the vital power of virtual nullification. And there are surely cases of high stress that would not meet the usual insanity definition but in which a jury may be moved to find extenuation sufficient to ameliorate or excuse otherwise culpable conduct. Let's draw a case:

Bruce A. Talbot Jr. grew up in a small town in Iowa. His father was a farmer, a religious man, and a strict disciplinarian of the old school. Bruce's earliest memory was the time his father had discovered a doll that Bruce had found in the attic and liked secretly to dress up and play with in his room. His father had pulled his "baby" out of his arms and murdered it, viciously slamming its sweet, bewigged head against the wall until it broke. He had then whipped the sobbing boy to teach him never again to play with sissy toys. Early in adolescence, Bruce had the uncomfortable feeling that he was somehow "different" from the other farm boys he played with in school. Though he was strong and well built, he was never really interested in joining in their sports. His father insisted that he go out for the football team, but he missed many practices, preferring to read or draw in the school art room.

During this period, his early teens, Bruce, like everyone else in the small farm community, greatly admired his father, emulated his strong and purposeful demeanor, and adopted his views. Together they would often express admiration for the masculine heroes of history, of war, and of sports. Bruce can still remember, however, how these treasured moments of shared masculine companionship with his father would induce a feeling of intense discomfort and anxiety in him. He stayed awake nights wondering what was wrong with him, repeatedly resolving to put more effort into becoming the sort of man his father admired.

It was in such a desperate mood that Bruce, soon after turning eighteen, enlisted in the Marines. His father made no effort to conceal his approval. "It'll make a man of you, son," he said, patting him on the back just like in the posters. He basked in his father's pride when he came home on leave in his uniform and bristling haircut and recounted the arduous training he endured.

For the first year or so of Bruce's service, he was the model marine, all spit and polish and rigorous self-discipline. He began to think he was getting his anxieties under control. True, he avoided trips to town, where his buddies would visit the local bars and try to introduce him to the painted and provocative young women who hung out there. But he told himself that his reluctance to go along on these adventures was simply the result of his strict religious upbringing. "I'm saving myself for my wife," he would tell his scoffing friends. And he half believed it.

He was planning to invent a fiancée during his second year when he met another young marine, and his life changed forever. There was something in Tod's eyes, a certain sadness. And wisdom beyond his years, as though he understood more about what was in Bruce's heart than Bruce knew himself. Before long, the two young soldiers became friends and would find opportunities for long talks. Bruce found himself telling his new companion things he had only dimly perceived in the shadows of his soul. Very carefully, secretly, as their love for each other deepened, Bruce allowed himself to acknowledge what he had always known.

By his third year of service, Bruce was as open about his sexual orientation as his military career and his strained relations with his parents allowed. He went home infrequently now and felt a new and painful distance from his dad. During this time, Bruce and Tod decided to take a leave and join (out of uniform, of course) a protest rally at the Pentagon. It was early in Bill Clinton's tenure, and it looked as though he was going back on his commitment to open the military services to gay men and women. People were coming from all over the country to express their dismay at this apparent breach of a campaign promise. Bruce was still proud of being a marine, of his rank, and of the many citations and commendations he had won for exemplary performance. But it galled him that if the Corps knew the truth about his private life, they would unceremoniously—and dishonorably—discharge him.

Outside the great citadel of the Pentagon, Bruce and Tod found themselves at the edge of vast sea of people—mostly young, mostly male. Singing, chanting slogans, waving hand-painted signs, the throng seemed—at first—good-humored, almost festive. Bruce felt an unexpected surge of good feeling. So many guys, so many men like himself. He felt buoyed by the sheer numbers of this clan. All he wanted was to lose his individual identity, his history, his uncertain future, and become one of this great and convivial throng.

It was hard to say just when it turned ugly. But there was a subtle mood change in the crowd. The songs and laughter were replaced by angry shouts and some surging and shoving. It might have been provoked by the counter-protesters gathered in knots around the edges, not far from where Tod and Bruce stood. An ill-sorted lot, they were a mix of young toughs in their motorcycle jackets, beer cans in their fists, and older, local redneck types. From behind the wooden police barricades, they laughed, sniggered, let fly an occasional epithet ("Hey, faggot" or something equally imaginative), and for the amusement of one another burlesqued the gait and gestures they associated with homosexual men.

Now angry words were being exchanged between the men in the protest and their hecklers outside. Bruce remembers feeling the anger well up in him. Why were these drunken thugs and bigots starting trouble? Who the hell did they think they were, the epitome of virtue and civility? The tougher sorts from Bruce's group were pushing toward the edge, exchanging insults and threats with the hoods. Members of each group felt secure among their cohorts, and both sides felt challenged to turn back all the hostility they received, raising the level with each volley. Bruce felt himself swept up with his fellows. If they were going to make trouble, let them come, he would stand with his kind and defend the group.

Police in riot gear were moving toward the trouble spot. Bruce saw them out of the corner of his eye as he moved toward the frail barricades, partly impelled by those crowding behind him, partly drawing the others in the wake of his mounting anger. Still, Bruce thought he had himself in control. He was just moving forward in case things got physical and his skills in martial arts were needed.

At that point an older man who, Bruce recalled, looked something like his father, focused a glare of hatred on Bruce, spat, and said, "Whatsamatter, sonny, didn't your daddy ever teach you which hole to stick it in?" He did not remember what happened next, but witnesses—corroborated by a memorable bit of news videotape—said Bruce came crashing through the barrier, grabbed a gray-haired man by the shirt, and hit him hard across the face several times. He then flung him to the ground, and when the man rose and turned to flee, Bruce suddenly aimed a kick at his head, catching him just behind the right ear with the reinforced toe of his boot. The man fell in a heap, and the police grabbed Bruce. The kick had fractured the man's skull, causing serious cerebral hemorrhaging. Though the victim survived, he was seriously and permanently incapacitated from Bruce's sudden attack.

Bruce Talbot was tried for attempted murder, assault, and various other crimes. From the videotapes and the many prosecution and defense witnesses, the jury got the whole story in detail. As its final witness, the defense called Professor Horace C. Robinson, Ph.D., chair of the Department of Sociology at the state university. After introducing himself by reciting his position and degrees, Professor Robinson told the jury that his field of specialty was social pathology, a field in which he had taught, studied, and published for some thirty years. Among his published papers was a monograph entitled *Mob Mentality: Three Studies in Stressful Collective Action*. Another bore the title *The Subjective Impact of Concerted Behavior: Muffling the Superego*. Among his several books, Professor Robinson mentioned in particular *Mob Mania: The Effects of Group Action on Personal Control Mechanisms*. He was obviously superbly qualified for the task he was about to perform.

Prompted by counsel, and over the objection of the prosecution, the professor was allowed to explain what, in his opinion, can happen to the mind of a person swept up in a large and unstable demonstration. An otherwise fully controlled, law-abiding person, Professor Robinson explained, surrounded by others in a state of high excitement, sharing a sense of social purpose, and agitated by opposition, may lose the faculty of detached judgment. He becomes infected, the Professor testified, by "mob mania." Mob mania, he explained, is a condition of mind wherein the normal mechanisms of behavioral control and social interaction are temporarily suspended to be replaced by a pathological, sociopathic disorientation.

"Could you put that in plain English for us, Professor?" Robinson was asked.

"It means," he said, "that, under those conditions, a person may lose his judgment of what is good and bad conduct and do bad things he would not otherwise think of doing. Typically," he added, "it lasts only a short time."

"In your opinion, Professor, is 'mob mania' a mental disease or defect?"

"It is a pathological condition of mind, yes."

"And does that mean, Professor, that during the time a person is suffering from 'mob mania,' he does not have the capacity to understand the nature of his conduct or that it is wrong?"

"That is correct," the professor replied.

In response to a further question, the professor told the jury that the mob mania syndrome could be triggered by some remark or incident that "reverberated in the unconscious with some deep anxiety or repressed trauma." Following this explanation, Talbot's lawyer asked the witness a long hypothetical question, asking him to assume as true virtually all the facts the witnesses had told the jury about Bruce's life and the incident that brought him to trial. On the basis of those assumed facts, the professor stated his opinion that such a person would be "a classic case" of the condition he had described as mob mania. Professor Robinson was cross-examined at length, of course, but the prosecutor could not make a dent in his testimony. Two experts were called in rebuttal, a psychiatrist and a professor of clinical psychology. Neither could claim any particular qualifications in the field of "social pathology." Both said they did not recognize a condition of "mob mania" as an established mental disease or defect, but both admitted on cross-examination that they were familiar with the work of Professor Robinson and thought it "professionally respectable."

After all the evidence was in, defense counsel requested the court to charge the jury that if they found that at the time Talbot went berserk he was suffering from mob mania, they should return a verdict of not guilty owing to temporary insanity. If they believed the expert, he argued, they would have to find that mob mania was a mental disease or defect and that it resulted in the loss, albeit temporary, of the ability to understand the nature and consequences of conduct or to appreciate its wrongfulness. Therefore the appropriate verdict would be not guilty.

Is this *law?* It sounds more like what's going on here is an appeal to some inarticulable human sympathy for Bruce. Hey, he's no criminal. He's just a guy trying to get along in this world with a load of heavy emotional baggage. He a good, patriotic, law-abiding citizen who snapped and went haywire under severe provocation. How can you call him guilty and send him off to prison? Maybe a little psychotherapy will help him get comfortable with his situation, but jails weren't built for people like this. It's not a *legal* argument. But, in their persistent efforts to align law with justice, courts are surprisingly tolerant of this sort of thing.

It's good to know there is a place reserved in the severe precincts of law for purely human reactions. But there must be some limits to this sort of defense. Just because conduct can be explained does not mean it should be excused. The man kicked by Bruce will spend the next twenty years in hell, partially paralyzed, disoriented, severely impaired, virtually helpless. *Justice* to him and to his family is not satisfied by *justification.* Tell the legalist that Bruce went haywire under stress, that he aimed a lethal boot at an unarmed heckler because he had problems due to his sexual identity and unresolved ambivalence toward his father. The legalist will reply, all crimes—especially serious crimes—can be explained. Some explanations may mitigate culpability, some may cancel it, but only as the democratically elected branch of government decides they should. Some explanations affect the severity of punishment appropriate to the case, but guilt and punishment are two different things. Justice, the legalist will insist, is uncomfortable with ad hoc defenses predicated on some improvised theory of moral justification, impelled by sympathy, and built on some pseudoscientific theory of mental impairment. To allow virtual nullification, the argument runs, is to replace law with impulse—not a good thing.

Still, there is something compelling about Bruce Talbot's defense. He did produce a highly qualified expert who gave it as his professional judgment that, temporarily at least, Bruce fit the classic legal definition of insanity— and the defense of insanity is hardly the invention of some trendy liberal fashion in multicultural jurisprudence (like "black rage" or "premenstrual syndrome").

Maybe momentary insanity is no defense in Virginia, where Talbott's crime occurred. They have not yet thought about the precise question, but if it came up, Virginia might well refuse to recognize as exculpatory such a fleeting condition. Many jurisdictions do not. Maybe we require for a mental "disease or defect" a named condition indexed in the shrinks' handbook of official diseases of the mind—which mob mania is surely not. But if we were writing our own code for a just state, and if we accepted the universal excuse of insanity, why should we hesitate to grant the defense motion, instruct the jury accordingly, and allow them—if they credit Dr. Robinson—to return a verdict of not guilty? And if courts today are generally disposed favorably to the battered-spouse-syndrome version of self-defense, should they be reluctant to allow mob mania as a subset of insanity?

These are not easy questions. In our uncertainty, we lawyers turn to the experts. The issue of whether a legal excuse or justification can be predicated on a novel theory of inducement, duress, or mental irresponsibility frequently comes down to the question of whether a respectable expert can be found who will describe the condition in terms familiar to traditional concepts of culpability. That means that if you really could find a well-qualified expert like Professor Robinson who would really testify as Robinson did, you might stand a chance of getting your mob mania defense to the jury.

But there is something strange and disturbing about abdicating to the experts. There are no experts in culpability—except the jurors themselves. Some jurisprudents might claim to have discovered the essence of criminality, to know the fundamental elements of justification or excuse. For the rest of us, crimes are those defined behavioral incidents that the body politic formally declares are punishable. There are old crimes and new, serious and minor. There are even crimes that scholars call *malum in se*—inherently evil—and offenses that are *malum prohibitum*—wrong only because it is against the law. There are acts that are universally called crimes and those that are culturally specific. And the same might be said of defenses. But in our tradition of legality, we do not allow either punishment or excuse because some wise and erudite person, thinking carefully and dispassionately after the fact, concludes that under the circumstances the conduct was wrong and inexcusable or that it was justified. Even if a lay jury agrees.

Nullification by the jury is tolerable—just barely—under the principle of legality. It is tolerable to me because it is an extraordinary device, an escape hatch for those extreme cases in which jurors are so deeply motivated that they are willing to kick over the traces. Virtual nullification, manufactured by an expert who can convince a jury that a defendant does not deserve punishment, I find abhorrent. These experts do not pretend to be specially anointed in moral judgment; they would deny that they presume to redefine criminality to fit a particular case. But it seems to me that is precisely what they are doing. To give it as an expert opinion that a mass murderer should be excused as insane because he was suffering from black rage or she was in the throes of premenstrual syndrome, to say that a killer was unbalanced when he shot the mayor of San Francisco and Harvey Milk because he had been eating Twinkies all afternoon, to argue that Bruce Talbot was not criminally responsible because he had succumbed to mob mania—or, yes, even to suggest that a battered woman who slays her partner as he sleeps was justified because she was acting in self-defense—comes very close to asking a jury to acquit a guilty person because he or she does not morally deserve conviction. To me, these improvised defenses do not seem so very different from asking them to convict a person who has violated no criminal law because he morally deserves conviction.

14 The Judge

Promoting the Quest for Truth in the Adversary Mode

Seated at the center of the American criminal process is the trial judge. Robed on a raised bench, attentive but detached, severe but compassionate, involved but disinterested, the judge is the central figure of authority—and mystery—in the mysterious and authoritarian morality play we call criminal justice.

It is important to believe in our scientists, teachers, our journalists, and (God help us) even our elected politicians. But if we do not believe in the integrity, the wisdom, the good judgment, and the fairness of our judges, we will be utterly lost. Few of us will ever stand before a judge but somehow the way a court handles its criminal docket is of deep concern to us all. Perhaps we carry vivid pictures of the atrocities of tyrants that seem somehow associated with criminal laws. Perhaps it is an atavistic memory of childhood and the craving for the just and good parent. Perhaps it is simply the association of crime with the disintegration of civility and security, a demand for the judicial vindication of imperiled social values. Whatever the reason, the figure of the judge is crucial to urgent community concerns.

In fact, the judge is an extremely complex figure, playing a role compounded of the most diverse elements—and, for the most part, playing it extremely well, given that our system affords virtually zero training. Judges are aware of many of the contradictory, superhuman demands of the role. They know that when they put on the robe, they must put off the personal piques and prejudices of private life; that when they speak from the bench, they speak in the voice of the community; that in their public persona they are charged to "uphold the law" regardless of private ideology, to "protect the rights" of even the most villainous, and to "dispense justice evenly, without fear or favor" even in the glare of public hostility. And with a remarkable degree of success, I believe most trial judges do just that—to the best of their ability.

They also know that they have responsibility for the courtroom and everything that happens in it. And that is a bushel full of nitty-gritty. A good judge runs the courtroom—potentially a forum of chaos and endless contention—with dignity. Efficiency is a term hardly appropriate to the work of adjudication, but a judge must have an eye to the productivity of the process. Each case must be treated as though it were the only concern of the court while the docket builds behind it with relentless pressure for prompt disposition.

It's a demanding job. I ought to know. I'm married to a judge sitting in a state court of general felony jurisdiction. But I hasten to say she is not my only source. I have worked in those precincts, and over the years, friends and former colleagues have contributed anecdotes from behind the bench. So I should know enough to recognize the foolishness of composing a "typical judge," a "typical court," or a "typical day on the bench." There is little that typifies judges. Intelligence, experience, attitude, appetite, and energy run the gamut, and all inform the way a judge does the job. Courts in cities and towns across the country share few features in common, and even in the same building, the regime varies greatly from courtroom to courtroom. Nonetheless, this is what I propose to do. With full and vigorous caveats, I shall attempt to illustrate the stresses, demands, triumphs, and frustrations of the role by imagining a day in the life of a typical judge (not my wife) in a typical court that tries the heavy criminal cases:

Karen Meadows was somewhere in the middle of her class at a first-rank law school. She was never really sure why she went to law school in the first place. While she enjoyed some of the puzzles her professors were so fond of inflicting on the students, and she developed a taste for crime and the Constitution, the commercial courses that permeated the curriculum bored Karen to tears. So it wasn't surprising that when graduation cast her upon an unsuspecting profession, she took the vow of poverty, deviated from the customary path, and chose a job with the public defender. (Youthful idealism inclined her to serve those she thought of as "victims of the system.") She did her time with the endless, repetitive, and meaningless buy-and-bust drug cases until one day she woke up to discover that she could not remember a case she had tried the previous week. Her supervisor took pity, and her caseload was salted with a variety of real cases. She was now taking felony pleas and even trying an occasional rape or robbery.

Karen was truly excited by courtroom work. She felt good addressing a judge, the law of evidence actually made sense to her (well, most of it anyway), and she found that she had a way with jurors—they listened attentively when she spoke to them, smiled with her when she smiled, frowned when she frowned, and even occasionally voted to acquit her client. So, for a few years, her success carried her along. She looked forward to the challenge of each new trial and relished the small ways in which her talent was evident.

But slowly Karen began to notice that something was happening to her attitude. And she didn't like it. It started when she noticed a new, urgent tone in her voice as she told her friends, wryly, as she had so many times before, "I just wish I could have a client I *like* once in a while." It was not that she had never had a client who just might be truly innocent. Even some of the guilty ones had stories that could break your heart. But for the most part, her clients were indifferent, suspicious, unrepentant, and ungrateful. And, let's face it, they were in the main the predators of her community. Every now and then as Karen stood to challenge, discredit, even humiliate a victim of her client's callous aggression, she asked herself, Why am I doing this? There must be a better way to have fun while earning a living.

Karen began quietly considering the alternatives. She still couldn't face the idea of disappearing into some commercial law firm, even with the promise of a post in their "litigation department." She understood that "litigation," with a bank or a big corporation as your client, bore no resemblance to the trial work she knew and loved. She listened with new interest to the career stories of her friends. She put out some feelers to the prosecutor's office. She wasn't really enthusiastic about crossing the street, but it might be interesting to be on the side of the victim for a change, and to carry the burden of proof. Nothing came of it. Hiring was tight in public offices, and the truth was she hadn't made a lot of friends in the higher echelons of the adversary camp. The job that finally took her out of the courtroom was a faculty position as clinical professor of law at a local law school.

She became totally immersed, her customary approach. She really loved her students: bright, eager, excited by war stories that had come to seem stale to her. She saw herself in their avid commitment to "justice" and "the rights of the defendants." She did her best to recreate for them the situations she knew so well of actual criminal practice for the defense. With great trepidation, she undertook to supervise a modest program in which students actually went to court and represented defendants. The cases were as small as could be found—peddlers, prostitutes, and panhandlers, that sort of thing—but the students treated them like murder one. It was very gratifying in a way. But Karen could not conceal from herself a longing to return to the courtroom. "I can't seem to get it out of my blood," she conceded to a friend after a few years at the school. "It's stupid, I know, but sometimes I actually feel like I'm mourning a lost life, that I'm faking, I'm not really living my own life—you know what I mean?"

She was in this state of mind when the opportunity of a lifetime burst upon Karen. She remembers well the moment the idea detonated. She was sitting at her desk one night, preparing for a simulation the following day, when an old boyfriend from her student days phoned. He always had been something of a pol and he told Karen he was very active in judicial selection. Had she ever thought about going on the bench, he asked her. Not until that moment, she replied. Judges were old, she said, and she was barely past forty. You're way out of date, her friend assured her. Your résumé is perfect. Perfect. This is your year, grab the moment. Carpe diem, baby.

He had been right. Karen had no problem—breezed right through the screening committees, got the nod, attended a few political functions and, without even mounting a campaign, found herself a few months later being fitted for a black robe.

In the six years since that day, Judge Meadows discovered that judging was what she had been designed for from the beginning. In her robe, she found expression for all the diverse elements of her personality. She was tough, controlling, insistent on decorum and professional performance. She was compassionate, sensitive to the trauma of witnesses and the ordeal of defendants. She was engaged by the human drama, the stories behind the cases. Never a scholar, she found herself absorbed by the legal issues that thrust through her daily docket. "Hey," she told her law clerk one day, "I just discovered something I never understood at law school: law is interesting!" At the same time, she was habitually focused narrowly on the peculiar facts of the case before her. She was diligent to the point of exhaustion, but she was expedient and productive. She could not be pigeonholed; whatever the charge, both sides were glad if the case landed on Meadows's docket.

She was not typical of her breed, but she was not the only one of her ilk. The role has a way of bringing out the best in many lawyers of unsuspected talents.

On the morning on which we will follow Judge Karen Meadows, she awakes thinking about the case on trial before her. It's really quite a story. Life, she was forced to conclude, imitates pulp fiction. The defendant, Herb Adler, a young man with a good job in an investment brokerage firm, has been separated from his wife, Sybil, for more than a year. In the last month, he had become distracted at work and frequently absent. Herb's erratic behavior was so uncharacteristic that his colleagues began to worry about him. His boss, familiar with occupational stress, made some discreet inquiries about Herb's personal life ("Is everything OK, buddy?" he inquired one day with his usual masculine finesse. "Any personal problems I should know about?") and suggested to Herb that he might wish to have a few visits with the office counselor ("My treat, fella"). Herb assured him that everything was fine ("Some digestive distress is all, Chief; I hear that sort of thing happens to all recycled bachelors.")

Sybil, meanwhile, had started receiving disturbing phone calls. At first, the phone would ring at odd hours; when she answered, all she heard was the caller hanging up. She stopped answering her phone. Then with increasing frequency, she would hear an obviously disguised voice say to her answering machine something cryptic like, "Your problem, Miss, is you wouldn't know a good thing if you fell over it." Or, "The Sex Monitor is watching, so be careful, don't enjoy yourself too much." She suspected Herb, of course, and made a report to the police. They told her she had no proof that the calls came from Herb and, anyway, no threats had been made as yet. At their suggestion, she had a device installed that records the number of the incoming calls, but she recognized none of the numbers; when she checked, she learned that the caller had used several public phones.

Of late, she has come to believe that she is being stalked. On several nights, she noticed the same car parked across the street. She couldn't read the plate and she couldn't be sure, but she thought she could see a figure sitting behind the wheel. Twice, during her lunch hour, when she walked up the block with friends to a neighborhood deli, she had the uneasy feeling that she was being followed, though she was embarrassed to turn and confront the man. She could have been mistaken. She felt she was becoming a bit paranoid. When she got a good look at the man who had followed her into the movies one night, he looked nothing like Herb, unless Herb had invested in outlandish disguises.

Things came to a head one cold, windy night in March. Sybil had just put a couple of bags of groceries into the trunk of her BMW in the parking lot of her local supermarket. As she opened the driver's door, a man suddenly stepped from the shadows and was standing very close to her. She was startled but saw at once that it was Herb in a wig. "Get in," he said. "I have a gun in my pocket and I'll use it if you make a fuss." There was something in his voice, something in his eyes. Sybil was frightened. "I thought he had actually gone crazy," she later explained. "I didn't know him any more. I didn't know what he would do next. It was really scary."

She got behind the wheel. Herb ran around the car and got in beside her. "Drive," he commanded, "and don't pull anything funny." She tried to reason with him. "Herb," she said, "why are you doing this? What's the matter with you?" But he said only, "Drive. And shut up."

"Where to?" she asked.

"Your place," he said. "Our place," he corrected himself. Sybil suddenly remembered her anger when she had discovered that Herb had bought himself a second Rolex but refused to share the expense of recovering the sofa.

When they arrived, Sybil said, "I can't let you in, Herb. Not in the state you're in."

"You'll let me in or I'll kill you right here on the doorstep," Herb said. And he sounded like he meant it. Herb withdrew his hand from his pocket and Sybil could see the dark metal of the gun in his fist. She felt a sudden cold chill. She fumbled for the key and let both of them into the pleasant apartment they had once shared. Herb immediately went around the place unplugging all the phones. Then, with one of the phone cords, he securely bound Sybil's wrists behind her back. Forcing her to sit on a straight chair in the dining room, he used another cord to tie one ankle to the leg of the chair. Then, pacing back and forth, the gun still in his hand, obviously agitated, Herb began what Sybil later described as "a long, rambling, incoherent diatribe." He accused her of having an affair with a man from her office with whom she'd had lunch a few times. He slapped her across the face, hard. He accused her of having seduced the handsome young handyman who had come to her apartment to install new blinds on the windows. He grabbed one of her breasts and squeezed it viciously, saying he should cut it off "and see how your new lover likes it." He claimed she had secretly called his boss and told damaging lies about him. He charged that she had poisoned their mutual friends against him, mocking him, telling them he picked up whores and used drugs. At first she denied all the accusations, but, seeing that her protests only fed his anger, Sybil fell silent and waited it out.

Finally, at about two in the morning, Herb gave out. Exhausted, he started crying and told Sybil he still loved her, needed her, wanted her. He said he wanted to sleep with her, "just this one last night." Then he would let her go and get out of her life forever. Sybil didn't know what to do. She certainly was in no mood to crown the torture by lying in the arms of her tormentor, but she saw it as her best chance of escape. "OK," she said, "if that's a promise. One last time." Herb untied her, they both got undressed and fell into bed. To her surprise, Sybil, exhausted by her ordeal, fell asleep at once; her last waking memory was of Herb awkwardly climbing on top of her.

Several hours later, Sybil awoke, the events of the previous night coming back to her like a bad dream. But it was no dream; Herb was still asleep next to her. She got quietly out of bed and was slipping on some clothes to make her escape when Herb awoke. "Where in hell do you think you're going?" he demanded, groping under the bed for the pistol.

"You promised," she said.

"That was yesterday," he said. "Today I have a better idea."

"Please, Herb," she begged, "be fair."

"We're going away together," Herb said. "I have a small cabin in the woods. It's perfect. I'll leave you there to think things over for a while. I'll take the car."

Sybil interrupted his fantasy. "Herb," she said. "You can't do that. I have a very important appointment with a client this morning. We're closing a really big deal. You know what that means. I can't default on this one."

Herb hesitated. "What time is your appointment?"

"Ten. It's taken weeks to set this up."

"OK," Herb said. "I'll drive you down to the office and wait outside. You come down when the meeting's over."

"Sure, Herb," she said, "anything you say."

Sybil dressed for the office and Herb drove her downtown. Sybil, briefcase in hand, disappeared into her office. As soon as she got to her desk, she telephoned the police. They arrived ten minutes later and found Herb sitting behind the wheel of the car Sybil had described. He was placed under arrest and a pistol was taken from the glove compartment of the car.

At least that was Sybil's story as she told it from the witness stand. Judge Meadows, like the jury, sat entranced as the tale unfolded. Sybil was a compelling narrator. Attractive, articulate, she testified in a straightforward manner, reciting the events with little explanation or embellishment. She needed little prompting from the prosecutor and only once or twice showed the emotions she appeared to be holding in check. The story was odd, but the telling of it was wholly convincing. Why would a woman like this lie about such a thing?

She couldn't say how the jury reacted to Sybil's story, but Judge Meadows and the jury did not get much help from Herb Adler's lawyer. Marvin Sussman was an old lefty lawyer who had picked up some publicity recently representing high-profile clients. As far as Judge Meadows could see, his trial skills had two main features. First, his flamboyant style called attention to himself, often substituting his own personality for his client's as the center of jury interest. His second talent was what Judge Meadows thought of as "the sneer and snarl" technique, a method of interrogation designed less to elicit information for the fact finder to chew on than to convey the scorn the witness's story provoked in the interrogator. Marvin Sussman's trial preparation, Judge Meadows imagined, must consist of standing in front of a mirror practicing hand gestures and lip curls to convey outrage, disbelief, sincerity, and entreaty: his idea of the elements of advocacy. But she had to admit, Marvin Sussman also had a way of coming up with some outlandish defenses that somehow clicked with the jury. So he had a few celebrated acquittals in hopeless cases. It helped not to be a stickler for the law.

In his cross-examination of Sybil Adler, Sussman concentrated on the wealth and privilege of the Adlers. Questions abounded on the subject of their income, their rent, where they took vacations, even the make and model of the car. What all this had to do with the events at issue, Judge Meadows could not guess. But the judge could see where counsel was headed. He was setting up the jury for a who-cares defense. He wanted to get up on summation and, with some dismissive gesture, tell the jury: these spoiled, rich yuppies deserve each other. Why should we honest, hardworking folk care about the escapades of the rich and decadent? A jet-set marital dispute, that's all, not a real crime.

The young assistant D.A., Robin Mancuso, out of policy or timidity, did not object. Some assistant D.A.s, Judge Meadows had noted, rarely objected to questions for fear that the jury would think they were trying to conceal some relevant fact. Maybe it was office policy, she thought, or perhaps in their office training sessions, the unfledged assistants were taught the tactical ploy as a way of currying juror confidence.

In any case, the D.A.'s passivity put Karen Meadows in a classic dilemma, which we have visited before. She could allow flagrant irrelevancy on the theory that the rules of evidence merely provide a tactical option for counsel, waivable at will, or she could insist that they are established by law to protect the jury from distraction, boredom, and prejudice and that the judge is bound to enforce them regardless of counsel's preference. Judges were forever divided on this one, and many had no principled and consistent policy. Karen generally let counsel have their heads, amending the rules of evidence (in effect) as they wished. But there were limits. And when Sussman asked (in his cute manner), "By the way, Ms. Adler, I hope I'm not being too nosy, but that bag you're carrying looks to me to be a Gucci. Would I be right about that, by any chance?" Judge Meadows looked sharply at Mancuso, who maintained her immobility of form and feature. "Objection sustained!" Judge Meadows said. "Please move on to something else, counsel."

Sussman was all injury and incredulity. "But Your Honor," he emitted painfully, in the classic reaction of defense counsel, "this is cross-examination."

"I am aware of that, counsel," Meadows said. "Enough on this subject. Anything further?"

"Is Your Honor cutting off my cross-examination?" A challenge. You know and I know, Judge, that a criminal defendant has a constitutional right to cross-examine the witnesses against him. You cut off my cross and I go hollering foul to an appellate court—they reverse you in a trice.

"I am not cutting you off, Mr. Sussman. You go ahead and ask your next question. But please, counsel, confine yourself to relevant matters." Point to the court. A hint to the jury (the merest hint—not enough to subject the court to a charge of partiality) that the lawyer is wasting their time.

"But Your Honor, they taught me at law school that everything is relevant to credibility." Pushing a bit harder in the baiting game. Maybe he could draw a flash of anger, something to give the jury the sense that he must fight an unfair judge.

"You were misinformed, counsel," Judge Meadows says coolly, claiming her right to the last word. "But I'll have no more colloquy. Put your next question or sit down."

Sussman was saving his best stuff for his cross of the arresting officers. This was Sussman's strongest suit and his greatest pleasure. He prided himself in his intimate knowledge of police procedure and the regulations. He liked nothing better than to show up a young cop (or a veteran) for his sketchy knowledge of the manual of his own department. He had perfected the tone of voice that could most often get the goat of a cop—the hint of disrespect, the faint innuendo of incompetence that might provoke a bit of defensive strutting, perhaps a break in professional cool—the sort of thing that put off jurors.

But in the Adler case, Sussman did not seem to have much to go on. The story of the arresting officer was short and sweet, her role had been brief and inconsequential. Responding to a radio call, Officer Janette Beranski had driven with her partner to the described location. There they had at once spotted the vehicle indicated, which bore a plate number matching the alarm. A man was inside the car. Because he was said to be armed, she approached the driver's side with her own gun in hand and told him to exit the vehicle, keeping his hands in sight. The man had complied at once, but once on the street, he had looked around and started to bolt around the vehicle. Her partner took one step to the right and the subject ran right into his arms. She then put handcuffs on the subject. She saw her partner retrieve a pistol from the vehicle. And that was about it. Mancuso had the officer on the stand for all of about ten minutes.

Sussman went on a fishing expedition. He asked Beranski about details of the booking procedure, he tested her knowledge of police rules regarding identification, interrogation, meals, commendations, anything he could think of. With little effect other than a growing sense of impatience among the jury. Then he asked by way of a parting shot, "By the way, officer, is there pending, or have you in the past been the subject of any disciplinary proceeding in the department?"

"Yes," Beranski replied quietly, "I have."

This disclosure rocked the courtroom and threatened to capsize the trial. "Why," Sussman demanded with high indignation when the jury had been excused, "why, I repeat, why was I not served with this information?" Here we go.

"When did your office learn of this, Ms. Mancuso?" Judge Meadows inquired.

"Not until this moment, Your Honor. It's news to me."

"But Your Honor, if I may." It had been a dry season and Sussman could hardly contain himself. "She should have known. That's the point. I certainly do not suggest that this young woman purposely hid from me this devastating bit of news. She just didn't do her job and failed to discover what she should have known all along."

"I have your point, sir."

"Your Honor has no choice but to dismiss this case with prejudice, I submit."

"Please lower your voice, Mr. Sussman. I will not have you shouting at the court. Now, Ms. Mancuso, you do put the court in an awkward position. When can you have those records?"

All and all, it had been a difficult moment, Judge Meadows recalled. Defendants are entitled to see all material the prosecutor has, knows about, or should know about that might tend to exculpate the defendant, as well as statements or other material that might be used in discrediting a prosecution witness. And that usually means they must be allowed to inspect the material long enough in advance to make effective use of it. Here, fortunately, the disclosure came on a Thursday. By excusing the jury on Friday and working through the weekend, Judge Meadows managed to get the trial back in motion by Monday afternoon. The incident was trivial—Beranski's name had been mentioned by an informer in connection with a payoff ring at the precinct, but investigation proved the accusation vindictive and groundless and no action was taken. Because the files contained information that might disclose the identity of the informant, however, the department was extremely reluctant to provide the records—even to a court. It took strenuous effort by the judge to get hold of the files, sift through them, and decide what should be shown to counsel for the defense. Then she had to control how far the officer could be impeached by this incident.

All this had precious little to do with what went on in Sybil Adler's apartment but, Judge Meadows recognized, it did go to the credibility of a witness who had provided some evidence of importance on the merits—evidence of an attempt by the defendant to flee. Sussman had a field day. First, it took several lengthy and heated declarations to ventilate his fury at not being served all of the documents bearing on the matter and at not being accorded a full week to study them and plan his line of attack. Then, when he regained sufficient equanimity to proceed with what he had, Sussman spent half a day suggesting that Beranski was a corrupt and dishonest cop who had managed to hoodwink the authorities and escape without the censure she so richly deserved. There were times—whole stretches of time—when a visitor to the courtroom might be excused for believing he was attending the prosecution of a police officer on a charge of official corruption. Throughout this display, Mancuso, true to form, never lifted an eyebrow, much less rose from the seat to which she was apparently glued, to cut short this peripheral excursion or to protect her witness from the insistent and baseless calumny.

When it was finally over, the defense called Herbert Adler to the stand and the jury heard an entirely different version of the critical facts. First, he firmly denied that he had ever stalked Sybil. As he described it, they had split by mutual agreement and both had led their separate lives with little contact since. They would, however, bump into one another from time to time and, Herb insisted, their relations were cordial. He had other romantic relationships, he said, and did not wish to resume with Sybil. Asked whether he could account for Sybil's testimony, Herb replied, "She always was a bit paranoid or, shall we say, had a lively imagination." Asked whether he had been morose and inattentive at work preceding the evening in question, Herb said, yes, he could see how others might view it thus. Asked to account for it, he said that there were two things weighing on his mind at that time. He felt that an important relationship he was then in was "coming apart" and would soon end, and, coincidentally, he was becoming disaffected from the investment banking business.

"I had just turned forty," Herb testified. "You might say I was having my midlife crisis early. I was asking myself, do I want to buy and sell money for the rest of my life? Serve the greed of strangers? There must be something else for me to do with my talents. That sort of thing."

On the evening in question, he had gone down to the hardware store on the mall for a plumbing fixture (which he couldn't find). Returning to his Ferrari, he saw Sybil pushing a cart full of groceries. They greeted each other in their customary friendly manner, and he walked with her to her car, helping her to stow the groceries in her trunk. She asked him what was new and he told her that he felt he was at a "critical juncture" in his life, that he was contemplating a major career change but he didn't know what he wanted to do. She had had some of the same feelings and invited him to come back to her apartment for a cup of coffee to talk about it. He left his car in the lot and rode with her to her apartment. There they had talked and had a little wine until they had both gotten really sleepy.

It was really late by then and Sybil, Herb testified, had invited him to sleep over. Herb didn't think it was such a good idea, but he figured by the time they recovered his car and he got home, half the night would be gone. So he agreed. It had felt strange he said, but they had both gotten into the same bed and found that they were both aroused. So they had had sex and slept soundly. The next morning, Sybil had an early appointment at the office but was then free for a few hours, so she offered to drive him back to his car if he came with her and waited for thirty or forty minutes. He was waiting for her when the police arrested him. He had never tried to escape, he said, though he had not the slightest notion of why they were taking him into custody. He figured it must be "a case of mistaken identity" that would be quickly cleared up at the police station. He had walked around the car to get his jacket which was hanging in the back of the car, when he was roughly seized by the other officer. As to the gun, taken from the car, Herb said he had never seen it before.

Like Sybil, Herb was a good witness. He was intelligent, certain, and understated. He answered questions simply and directly. His story made perfectly good sense. And Ms. Mancuso did very little to undermine its plausibility. Maybe she lacked the confidence acquired by experience, maybe she just did not have the personality of an effective advocate—the relentless skepticism, the instinct for the weakness in a narrative—but her performance was tepid. One sensed that she was herself half convinced by Herb's story. She never hammered at the edges of Herb's story where it might be weakest: just what plumbing fixture was he looking for? Had he no business at his office on the morning after his night with his ex? Didn't he even phone in to explain his absence? Instead, Robin Mancuso concentrated on the center of the story, where Herb was unmovable. Why had he chosen to confide his problems in Sybil in the middle of a parking lot? She had always been interested and helpful and he trusted her advice. But didn't that seem like a strange place to have a heart-to-heart? Maybe. But she had asked how things were going and this career problem was uppermost in his mind, so he just answered truthfully. Et cetera.

It was obvious to Judge Meadows that the D.A. was taken completely by surprise when she heard Herb's story from the stand. Under our adversary system, both sides may hold their cards close to the vest. Even on his opening statement to the jury, a defendant need not announce what his defense will be. So Robin, listening to her witnesses in her office, was completely convinced and imagined the trial would be a cinch. She did not push her witnesses as hard as she might, she did not direct a follow-up investigation. She did not have the gun examined for fingerprints—why should she bother if she had no doubts of Sybil's story? She did not go out to locate the hardware store clerk to see whether he remembered Herb from the night in question, whether the store carried the part Herb said he couldn't find, even whether the store was open as late as Herb claimed. And because the adversary model puts the whole responsibility for such investigation on the parties—if the D.A. (or the police) don't do it, no one will. And if the defense has investigated and found that the facts do not support its theory, it is under no obligation to provide the court or the prosecution with the results. Of course, some say even defense lawyers have an ethical obligation not to stand silently by while one of their witnesses lies under oath, but if so, Karen had the sense that the word had not yet gotten out to the practicing Bar.

Now, as Karen Meadows heads down to the courthouse, she wonders once again whether there is any hope that the truth will emerge from this process. Once again, she wishes that she could ask the questions, that she could direct the investigation. And that she could mix the two, asking questions, checking the stories, and returning with more questions. Driving downtown, she imagines how she would have done it in the Adler case. For one thing, she would have concentrated on the divorce. Neither counsel had asked a single question on the subject. But what were the facts? Were they planning on a divorce? Was the issue in contention, bitter contention perhaps? Maybe a third story would emerge; maybe Sybil had set the whole thing up, seduced Herb up to her apartment and into her bed just to spring a story that would benefit her position in the divorce. Then, too, she'd want to know a lot more about that gun. Was it sold legally? Where, when and to whom? And what about Herb's supposed career crisis—did he ever confide in anyone else? Was there in fact another relationship that might account for his distress? Maybe she couldn't get the truth by her own investigation/interrogation plan, either, Karen thinks, but she sure had a much better shot at it.

The fact-finding method that Karen Meadows was dreaming of resembles the criminal process of western Europe. Although some features of the American trial are being adopted in European courts, the continental descendants of the Roman Empire have generally retained a system of criminal adjudication quite different from the adversary model developed in the British Isles and inherited by the United States. In a French, Dutch, or Italian trial, witnesses are not chosen, coached, and examined by the lawyers, alternately gently and aggressively, with the lay fact finder manipulated by their tactical choices and forensic skills. The European judge, far from the passive referee that most American judges appear to be during the course of the trial combat, directs the investigation, calls the ungroomed witnesses, and conducts the major part of the interrogation. And the judge (sometimes assisted by lay "advisers") finds the facts. In an unfortunate word with overtones of ancient abuses, we call this model *inquisitorial.*

I'm sure many American trial judges are perfectly content to sit back and leave the laboring oar to counsel, ruling when called upon to do so, otherwise maintaining a benign, detached demeanor, reassuring to jurors and conducive to orderly proceedings. These judges bristle at the idea that they would serve as inquisitors. But many other judges and commentators, exasperated by the failures of the adversary mode, are looking with increasing interest at the inquisitorial alternative. Like them, I am increasingly troubled by a system that leaves so much to the fortunes of battle, the distributions of skills and resources, the luck of the moment. To me, serious fact finding takes place in a disinterested investigation, not in a clash of opposed interests. Facts are better found by an earnest investigator than by a randomly assembled group of spectators.

An investigation-driven adjudication system would, I think, most hurt the guilty defendants who today put their hopes on the vagaries of an adversary contest. A detached investigation, focused on facts and undistracted by courtroom theatrics, is likely to point the finger unwaveringly at the guilty person; there are no windfalls in an well-conducted investigation—there may be a few inconclusives, but fewer outright errors. And that is not a system favored by the guilty. It is not a group I bleed for. Would the innocent defendant also fare worse? It is difficult to know with certainty. Those who use a modified inquisitorial method say that the innocent are rarely prosecuted at the conclusion of a fair and thorough investigation, and of those who are, no more are convicted than under an adversary system. This testimony is not to be lightly dismissed. We adversarians must concede that some—an unknowable number—of innocent defendants get convicted under our system. True, we have a high burden of proof on our prosecutors and all sorts of escape hatches for our defendants, but a solid—if mistaken—witness, together with highly suspicious circumstances, can put away an innocent defendant as easily under the adversary system as the inquisitorial. Maybe more easily, because the inquisitorial investigation is neutral (in theory, at least), and defense leads are as diligently pursued as any.

The toughest test of the inquisitorial system is the case with political overtones, in which the interest of the government is hardly neutral, the police investigation is likely to be driven by a political goal, and the defendant—an accused neo-Nazi terrorist in Germany, let us say—will have little opportunity to contradict the evidence assembled against him. Still, I'm sure there are those who would argue that the Irish terrorist tried in England is not in a much better spot. I myself believe that some adversary elements—such as vigorous confrontation and diligent adverse counsel—were they incorporated into the continental model, might counteract the government's special interest in the prosecution of the troublesome political case.

Whatever the comparative virtues of the inquisitorial model, stout resistance to any shift of style from adversary to inquisitorial would come from our guild of courtroom lawyers. Granted that in a Swiss courtroom, for example, lawyers who try cases are a tame and colorless breed compared to our own heroes. Little more than ministers of justice or counselors to the accused, continental lawyers view with amusement the Great American Courtroom Romance. With the judge firmly in charge, European lawyers are not the producers, stage managers, and featured actors that they are in our beloved trial drama.

Even allowing the importance of theatre as public participation in the legal system, it is hard for the rest of us to mourn the loss of a stage for forensic thespians. I have been gratified when, during one of our periodic courtroom spectaculars, I find the media blitz provoking general debate on issues usually explored only in law school classrooms (the plain-view exception to the warrant rule under the Fourth Amendment, for example). It's great to get major constitutional questions out into a lively public forum. The Constitution should not be an esoteric document for scholarly dissection; it belongs to everybody, everybody should care what it says and means. But I find it hard to believe that the adversary extravaganza that is today's supertrial is the only means of getting the public involved. A crime does not become newsworthy by the means of its eventual trial. Surely, great and dramatic cases remain in the public eye while tried in a European courtroom. And lawyers do not lose their role as advocates by moderation of the all-out adversary performance. Continental lawyers remain active advisers to the court, contributing in important ways to the direction and substance of the court-led fact-finding mission.

The American problem that Karen Meadows finds hard to accept is our circumscribed definition of the judge at a criminal trial. The role of umpire works, she finds, when you are lucky enough to have two first-rate lawyers, each working hard to present the most convincing version, neither hiding anything, exaggerating anything unduly, or "orchestrating nonsense" (as Karen liked to call such meaningless excursions as Sussman's attack on the character of the arresting officer). But even then, it is hard to know that the pretrial investigation—often out of counsel's hands—was really adequate and that the jury is not reacting to some inconsequential fact of personality or deportment. And, Karen thinks wryly, how often do I get two really good lawyers in the same case?

Sussman's excursion was a voyage of discovery. As lawyers use the term, *discovery* means what a lawyer may learn directly from an adversary before the trial begins. Designed to moderate the venerable adversary tactic of ambush, pretrial discovery has come to dominate civil litigation but is still a relatively scarce resource in criminal cases. In most jurisdictions, prosecutors are entitled only to very few tips on a defense, matters that they may want to go out and investigate for themselves in preparing for trial: whether insanity will be the defense, whether the defendant will assert an alibi (the claim that he was elsewhere at the time of the crime). But, as a matter of due process (under the Fifth and Fourteenth Amendments to the Constitution), a criminal must receive from the prosecutor's files all potentially helpful evidence.

This sort of material is catalogued under the names of the two decisions in the Supreme Court that announced the entitlement. *Jencks*—both the case and the federal statute that codified its holding—pertains only to statements previously made by government witnesses that differ from their trial testimony. *Brady* material is a broader category. It refers to anything that might tend to exculpate the defendant or might enable him more effectively to meet the prosecution case against him. It includes all sorts of evidence and leads to evidence on the merits, as well as material that might be used to impeach the credibility of government witnesses, such as deals they made with the prosecutor in exchange for cooperation. However, as the Court has pointed out more than once, a conviction will be reversed for failure to divulge Brady material only when there is a reasonably good chance that the missing evidence might have had an effect on the outcome.

State as well as federal criminal trials are bedeviled by this small but deadly serpent of the adversary process. Long after the verdict is in, a convicted defendant will discover that, unknown to the prosecutor, some insignificant notation was made or omitted by some witness (probably a police officer) in some record buried in the bureaucratic avalanche of paper. The prosecutor never saw it but *should have* known of it on the theory that what is known to one agency of government is presumed known to all. The defense, had it had the information, might have discredited the witness and introduced the reasonable doubt that would have changed the result. The case must be reopened, the judge must hear evidence, endure much bitter wrangling, and reach an almost impossible decision based on could have, should have, and might have.

Karen Meadows could see it coming. *The one thing we don't need in this crazy case is a bitter postconviction battle. Not that the defendant is entitled to have all the data on every prosecution witness that might possibly detract from credence. But what if the cop had been disciplined for fabricating evidence? Surely that sort of impeachment has a close enough bearing on culpability to amount to Brady material.*

Painfully aware of the Brady factor (as they are), should prosecutors routinely ask their cops whether there's anything in their personnel files that could hurt the case? Probably they should. But if the answer is only that a complaint was dropped, the prosecution probably doesn't have to disclose anything. Of course, once the defense finds out about such a complaint, cross-examination can be brutal. That's what the adversary system is all about: blast away at your adversary's denial; she may be lying. A complaint filed gives a good-faith basis. Maybe the cop is really dishonest and the official vindication is false. So open fire.

The Adler trial was not the only matter on Judge Meadows's calendar that day. The first thing she faced when she took the bench was a tough *Massiah* motion. She'd read the papers. It was not an unusual case. Regine Leveq was charged with running a discreet "escort service" with a small and crafty corps of male and female prostitutes, runaways in early adolescence whom Leveq sheltered and fed like a large family. Her client list included some men prominent in politics and business. Blackmail was an associated venture. The case broke when greed pushed Regine's extortion demands beyond a stubborn client's tolerance. He went to the police, Leveq was arrested, indicted, and held on high bail in view of her reputed hideaways in foreign parts.

The prosecution had been unable to push the investigation further than the single extortion charge, together with some counts of promoting prostitution and contributing to delinquency. The prosecutors were convinced that other extortions had occurred and that, somewhere, big-name victim/clients were, at that very moment, cringing in fear of discovery. But Leveq kept no little black book that they could find, and the young prostitutes had been well trained to furnish no help whatever.

At this point, word reached the prosecutor's office that an inmate named Phyllis O'Connor, being held on a serious drug charge in the same lockup as Leveq, had information regarding the Leveq racket that she was willing to trade for leniency in her own case. An interview was arranged. O'Connor told the ADA that Regine was boasting about her rich and powerful friends who would soon post the bail for her. "They owe me," Regine had supposedly said. She had mentioned a name or two that had meant nothing to O'Connor, so she could not recall them. But she said she was sure she could easily reopen the conversation and get some names. Maybe more.

Even though the story of a fellow inmate, traded for a promise of leniency, is not the most credible piece of evidence, it would be a start. So the prosecutor made the deal. O'Connor's cooperation would be taken into consideration in the disposition of her case if she would encourage Regine to boast, keep her ears open, and remember and report whatever she learned. From O'Connor's efforts, the authorities obtained the leads that allowed them to broaden the investigation and add several megaton counts to the indictment against Leveq.

Now in the critical pretrial phase, Leveq's counsel has moved to dismiss these latter counts as the product of an unconstitutional investigation. O'Connor's betrayal violated the *Massiah* doctrine, they claimed. Karen Meadows knew she was going to have to spend some time with the books on this one; the arguments she heard from the lawyers only reminded her that this was one of those delicate issues on which the appellate courts had painted the doctrine into a tight corner. It was her job to escape from the doctrinal trap and try to do justice in the particular case before her without doing violence to the constitutional principles involved.

Massiah v. United States, a 1964 decision of the Supreme Court, collapsed the boundary between the investigative and adversary components of the American criminal justice system. To those (like me) who like their doctrine as unclouded as possible, the U.S. Constitution is rather neatly divided into provisions limiting the criminal investigative powers of the government (the

Fourth Amendment and parts of the Fifth) and provisions governing the adversary process (the Sixth Amendment). The Sixth Amendment, by its terms, accords rights only to those who have already been accused of committing a crime. The language of the Amendment itself speaks of the rights of "an accused" and, as read by the courts, the status is acquired when a person is accused of a crime by some formal document like an indictment or information, an instrument upon which he may be tried and convicted. Some seven rights are specifically enumerated in the Sixth Amendment—including rights to speedy and public trial, a stated charge, an impartial jury, subpoena power to compel testimony from witnesses, and the right to "confront" (that is, cross-examine) adverse witnesses—all obviously trial-related. Last of the enumerated rights is the right "to have the assistance of counsel for his defense."

Winston Massiah had been a sailor aboard the SS *Santa Maria*. The ship was found to be carrying three and a half pounds of cocaine, which was linked with Massiah and another member of the crew, one Colson by name. Both were indicted and Colson decided to become a government spy in its continuing investigation of the smuggling operation. One night, while awaiting trial, the two bailed shipmates sat in Colson's secretly wired car and talked at length about the case. The conversation was broadcast to Agent Murphy, who later testified to Massiah's inculpatory statements. The Supreme Court reversed Massiah's conviction, holding that his right to counsel had been violated by a secret interrogation by a covert government agent, after accusation, an interrogation that "deliberately elicited" incriminating statements without according him the assistance of counsel. The evidence— the overheard conversation with Colson—was therefore obtained in violation of Massiah's Sixth Amendment right to counsel, the Court held, and must be excluded.

This was no coerced confession—not even an interrogation of a suspect in custody without appropriate warnings. It offended none of the restraints on investigation of the Fourth or Fifth Amendments. Rather, the Court had taken the right to counsel of the Sixth Amendment out of the courtroom context in which it was provided and used it to limit investigatory access to the thoughts of the defendant.

Clearly, Justice Stewart and his majority did not mean literally that the government should have put Massiah's lawyer into that vehicular broadcast studio to explain to him the risks of speaking freely to a supposed confederate. Saying a person has a right to counsel during questioning is just another way of saying he should not be questioned. Because a lawyer will simply tell him not to converse with police or their agents. The Supreme Court itself once acknowledged as much when it wrote that "any lawyer worth his salt" will say only one thing to the client: keep your mouth firmly shut. So, on a practical level, what the Court was saying in 1964—and has clearly reaffirmed several times since—is that after formal accusation, no deliberate elicitations, period.

Symbolically, by borrowing the counsel provision from the Sixth, the Court was also saying the adversary process begins before the case even gets to court—at least for those who have been formally accused. The "assistance" that a charged defendant has a right to expect from counsel, they decided, goes beyond help in navigating the treacherous waters of motions, pleas, trials, appeals, and writs. The sort of thing many thought was the peculiar province of people with J.D. degrees. No, it includes help in limiting the government's access to damaging evidence, assistance in blocking the investigation.

This revelation comes as a shock to people like me who never believed that the right to a defense entitled a person to block lawful evidence gathering. That takes the adversary model to a new level of reverence. Let me not overstate it. *Massiah* does not hold that the defendant, once he ascends to the status of "an accused," has the right to have his lawyer present to block any investigation the prosecutor may still be engaged in—forensic comparison of blood samples, for example. It holds only that there is one source of evidence—hitherto accessible—that is out of bounds now that the indictment has come down: the mind of the accused himself. Even though the solicitation is perfectly lawful in all other respects. And the reason (though never stated as such by the Court) is not hard to find. The Court, wedded to the adversary ideal, wants that inquisitorial window to be to be as narrow as they can make it.

The idea that inquisition is evil, that the American system—proudly premised on the superiority of adversary confrontation—can tolerate only the narrowest modicum of free government access to the mind of the suspect, is surely a boon to the guilty (and possibly remorseful) criminal. Those who praise this aspect of American criminal justice also claim that it represents an apotheosis of enlightened respect for the sovereign worth of the individual. Perhaps so. Others (including me) tend to focus on the violated sovereignty of the victims and of the rest of society that lives, constricted, in the shadow of crime.

The hard point in all of this is to determine whether adversary blockage of investigation at this stage actually does enhance the dignity of the individual, our treasured legacy of the Enlightenment. It may, as claimed, cool somewhat the government's ardor to hear the inculpatory word from the defendant that would confirm their informant's story or fortify their interpretation of suspicious circumstances. But these covert, postindictment forays hardly pose a threat of outright persecution in contemporary American criminal justice. The *Massiah* rule also might, to some small degree, encourage law enforcement people to look for evidence elsewhere, thereby insulating somewhat the sanctum of the mind. But let's remember that virtually all of the inquisitorial probing of the suspect's mind—and certainly that form of questioning that is most likely to be called "oppressive"—takes place before accusation, a stage at which we have chosen not to insert the adversary inhibition.

These thoughts, troublesome as they may be to jurisprudes, probably do not enter Judge Meadow's calculus as she moves to a decision of the motion to dismiss the extortion counts against Leveq. What she wrestles with are the several decisions applying the *Massiah* rule to cases of perfidious jailmates. She is grateful, at least, that she needn't worry about *Miranda* in this situation. Until the Supremes stepped in, a pretty good argument could be made that because the suspect behind bars was obviously in custody, and because the faithless buddy was acting as a government agent, the suspect should be given the *Miranda* liturgy before any conversation that could lead to self-incrimination. To this absurd scenario the Supremes, in a radiant moment of realism, said, "Absurd!"

So Judge Meadows must decide only whether O'Connor "deliberately elicited" Leveq's comments. It will all come down to minuscule questions like: Who brought up the subject first? Did O'Connor say, "Tell me more about your racket," or did she say, "OK, I'm listening" when Leveq said, "Let me tell you more about my racket?" Or: Did O'Connor say only "uh-huh" when Leveq was talking about her escapades, or did she by chance say, "Oh, and then what happened?" On the answers to these questions will depend the gravity of the crime charged to the defendant and very possibly her convictability on the charges.

Judge Meadows has her hearing. The questions are asked and the witnesses differ in their responses. Apart from the impossibility of saying with assurance just how those jailhouse conversations actually went (spies are often wired to alleviate this problem), the judge feels some frustration that the important substantive issues in the case have been transformed (by the adversary process, saith I) into these marginal and fundamentally inconsequential questions.

The final matter on Karen Meadows's calendar this morning is a case on for sentence, a difficult matter that she must attend to before calling in the jury and resuming the Adler trial. What makes the case hard is not that a weak defense counsel had failed to provide for the jury evidence or argument that might have given rise to doubts that changed the outcome. It wasn't that the legislature had tied the hands of the judge, compelling a more onerous sentence than the judge in the exercise of unfettered discretion might have thought appropriate. It wasn't even that the D.A., in an excess of zeal, had overindicted the defendant, resisted all efforts at mitigation by lesser plea, and won a jury conviction that forced the judge to impose prison time for a charge far more serious than she thought the facts warranted. Lord knows, Karen Meadows (like all of her colleagues) had had more than enough of those cases of irremediable, forced injustice.

No, what had bothered her for weeks, as she collected her thoughts on the sentence of Kareem Jackson, was different. Jackson was a young black man from an intact family (as the probation officer likes to put it). His parents were both employed in white-collar positions; his mother was a bank teller, his father was an insurance adjuster. Kareem fulfilled their fondest hopes. A good student and at six feet, five inches a star basketball player, he had completed his first year at Princeton and was the pride of his family and neighborhood. His future was bright and cloudless.

Then one night during midwinter vacation, two young police officers stumbled on what looked like a drug transaction or possibly the robbery of a drug dealer in an empty lot in a rundown section of town. As soon as the officers announced their presence, the knot of young men split and ran off in different directions. A rookie named Theresa McDonald chased one through the dark lot as her partner, Tommy Garcia, went after the other. Suddenly a shot was heard and Theresa went down. Tommy gave up his pursuit and ran to his fallen partner. She died in his arms. He put the alarm over the radio and a few minutes later another team spotted Kareem Jackson running down a deserted street.

They stopped him and took him in for questioning. He had no weapon on him and explained that he was in the neighborhood, alone, doing research for a paper for school, when he heard a shot followed by police sirens converging from all directions and became frightened. He did not want his parents to learn that he had been in that part of town so late at night—so he ran. Under his parka, Kareem was wearing a grey sweatshirt with a large orange *P* on the chest.

There is nothing like the murder of a cop to energize the force. The police combed the neighborhood. In a trash can between the scene and the place where Kareem was arrested, they found the murder weapon, but it was clean of prints. The stoolie network turned up a drug dealer with a long record who told a story about two young men who had said they were looking to score crack. One had pulled a gun and demanded the dealer's money when the crime was interrupted by Garcia and McDonald. The robbers were new to the neighborhood and he did not recognize them. But he did remember that one of them, a tall, well-spoken young man, wore a sweatshirt with a orange *P* on it. He was the one who held the gun, the dealer said. Though Kareem generally resembled the robber with the gun, the dealer said, it was too dark in that lot for him to get a good look at his assailant's face, so he couldn't say for sure whether it was Jackson. Another witness was turned up who had been looking out her second-floor window some while before the crime and recalled that she saw two or three young men "just hanging out together" on the corner. She had seen Kareem's photo in the newspaper after his arrest and said she recognized him as one of the men she had seen. She also picked him out of a lineup.

The case received a lot of publicity and both sides were well represented. Moreover, it was one of those cases in which the jury hears everything anyone knows about the case. The prosecution, admittedly, was relying on "circumstantial evidence" and a fairly weak eyewitness I.D. But circumstances can be pretty compelling. As the witnesses testified and the prosecutor drew the plausible inferences, the case sounded pretty strong and the defense looked concocted. The defense, aside from all the evidence of good character, was largely consistent with the story Jackson first told: he was planning to do a paper over the Christmas break about drug crimes. So he had gone once or twice to heavy drug areas to observe whatever he could on the streets. After he became more familiar with and to the dealers, he planned to try to do some interviews. He never saw the murder weapon and knew nothing further of the crime.

Karen Meadows, as she heard the evidence and the arguments, could understand how the jury had voted guilty after a long and agonizing deliberation. But she was still troubled. What bothered her, when she looked squarely at it, was that both sides had seemed to her too good to be entirely true. The witnesses were all too certain and unshakable, all the details had been recalled and explained. Both versions were clear and perfect. She was ready to bet that a lot of rehearsal—and possibly some scriptwriting—had gone into the perfection of these competing stories. Not that the lawyers were instructing the witnesses what to say. But they had gone over things so many times, tried so hard to iron out the little inconsistencies and fill in the little gaps, that it was hard now to recall what the spontaneous version really was. And then the story was rebuilt again in the lawyers' narratives that fitted together all the strands of favorable evidence into a coherent picture, made it sound like actual reality.

What she and the jury had received, Karen Meadows began to suspect, was "virtual reality," a version of the historical facts that seemed real, that had been constructed—in good faith, perhaps—to accord with shards of reality. Two versions of the historical truth, each of which sounded absolutely true, but that could not both be true. How should she respond? If the prosecutor's version was the actual truth, the crime was very serious indeed and the punishment should reflect that, regardless of the defendant's academic accomplishments and promise. But if the defense was right, any sentence would be an abomination. The verdict should be set aside. Can these two extremes be justly compromised into a moderate sentence? The hard part was, of course, that the judge had no better basis than had the jury to choose between the competing stories. After all, the judge consoled herself, that's what we have juries for.

To me, sentencing defies rational analysis. Yet it is probably the heart and essence of the judge's job. It's not that I can't understand how one person can condemn another to prison. There are many people who stand before a court for judgment of whom it is all to easy to say, "Lock him up!" My problem, rather, is how do you decide what length of time is the right one for the particular case? In most cases, it seems to me, any stretch is both too long and too short. Fortunately, I'm not a judge and I don't have to come to terms with this dilemma. And just as fortunately, the judges I know do not seem to have inordinate difficulty with the task. Not to say there are no frustrations. Inadequate scope (usually due to conscious legislative purpose to limit judi-

cial discretion), insufficient background information on the convict, ambiguous indicators of remorse and future disposition, all sorts of things require
any judge to struggle occasionally to find the just punishment. But in most
cases, judges seem to have—and to trust—a feel for what sentence a case
"deserves."

Every now and then—possibly in as many as 10 percent of the cases—a
judge comes up against a dilemma of a different order of magnitude. That's
the demon that Karen Meadows is wrestling with now as she swivels around
in her chair and paces her chambers. The jury has handed her a verdict
convicting a man who may be innocent. There is no basis for her to set aside
the verdict; there's plenty to support it. Yet the judge cannot help but feeling,
That's OK for the jury, they did their job in good faith. But I have my own
responsibility to my conscience. Can I impose a sentence—and a good long
one, at that—on a person before I am *myself* persuaded of his guilt beyond a
reasonable doubt?

If I were an orthodox theorist, truly wedded to doctrine, I would say to
Judge Meadows, "Relax, Karen, your job description does not require you to
decide whether Herb kidnapped, assaulted, and raped Sybil. Your task does
not include evidence gathering. It does not require you to know to a moral
certainty whether Kareem Jackson shot a cop. Relish your passivity. All you
have to do is take the decision of the jury. And it will be a lot easier if you do
not try to second-guess them. There's comfort in the division of labor—if
only you can accept your own limited role."

The problem is, I am not an orthodox theorist. I would feel just as Karen
does. A judge is not merely a civil servant and should not have recourse to
that timeless, dehumanizing dodge of the civil service: "Sorry, it's not my
job." All of it is the judge's job. And for my money, the broader the job
description, the better for justice. Let the judge supervise the investigation,
let him direct the presentation of the case and carry the prime responsibility
for eliciting the evidence. And let the judge participate in the fact finding so
that when the ultimate onus of pronouncing sentence arrives, he will not feel
that he is doing second-hand justice, taking a verdict he had no part in finding
as the predicate for his exercise of serious state power.

So in the end, what can we say? The law provides no release for Judge
Meadows in her agony. It's the agony of decision making for which she was
elected, which she does about as well as anyone could. She will be influenced
by all the things that would affect any of us in every decision she makes. The

facts—the peculiar, unique circumstances of each case—above all. And the American system of criminal justice expects it will be so—and wants it thus. But Judge Meadows cannot help but think from time to time that the inherent strain of her job is exacerbated by the adversary system, that she could more responsibly perform her duties, could concentrate her energies more efficiently, if she were not compelled to be a spectator at a contest of gladiators in a colosseum of ego where participants are goaded by the public and the media to present the important business of justice as theatre. The judge cannot help but feel that the American process of investigation and adjudication sometimes distracts her—and its other players—from the ends of literal justice and subtly substitutes the gratification of virtual justice.

Conclusion

Having come with me so far along this bumpy road, you are entitled to a conclusion. Still, I approach the task of concluding with great trepidation. I hate conclusions—I love introductions, but I hate conclusions. Partly, it is because nothing ever really concludes. Not only does this story—like all stories—continue, but my thinking about the things I have already described goes on changing. I am always uneasy when asked—by students, for example—"So? Where does that leave us? What do you recommend?" And when I read the conclusions of others, I am usually disappointed. Following a thoughtful exegesis of some perplexing puzzle, the author reaches a solemn conclusion. It usually cheapens all that has gone before. Conclusions, I find, generally come in one of two forms: the *think seriously* type and the *pat proposal* type. I know them well; I've used them both several times.

In the first form, I lower my voice a tone or two, furrow my brow, and inform the reader that these matters deserve careful consideration. My object, I avow, has been to sharpen our focus, to illuminate some dark corners, and to stimulate further thought on matters of some importance. But it is obvious I am myself clueless where such cogitation will lead. Although conclusions in this form are supposed to lend an air of serious purpose to the undertaking, I fear that my readers will perceive that their guide has led them into a cul de sac he is unable to lead them out of.

In its customary other form, the author cobbles a neat solution: I have gone so far as to draft a law or rule to solve the problem I have expatiated.

Not that I expected anyone to enact my tidy formulation (nor, so far as I know, has anyone done so). I did it merely to demonstrate that I could think *constructively* about the problem. Sometimes conclusions in this genre take on a radical flavor that bespeaks nothing so clearly as the disgusted frustration of the commentator. Here, the writer shakes his analytic head, throws up his intellectual hands, and angrily concludes: let's just get rid of the whole miserable business and start again. I ran across one of the more imaginative proposals in this genre in *The New Yorker* magazine, where Dr. Park Elliott Dietz, a redoubtable expert witness in insanity cases, played with the idea of abolishing altogether the insanity defense in all its guises. We should, he mused, simply acknowledge that people do all sorts of horrible deeds for all sorts of reasons beyond their rational control. They should be routinely locked up in moderately comfortable quarters ("a kind of Holiday Inn setting" is the way Dietz put it) and fed and clothed adequately for the rest of their dangerous lives. Then we institute a *sanity* defense by which the defendant could prove that he committed the act in the exercise of free choice and evil purpose, in which case he could escape the usual incarceration and be flogged instead. Well, at least it's a conclusion.

So I know I could select the *think seriously* conclusion and say something like this: Too much of what passes for criminal justice in this country is only a close approximation. It seems as though justice is done—most of the time anyway—but seeming is not being. Our faith in virtual justice has suffered some notable dents and tears of late. And it's time we recognized that the problem is not the occasional aberration but the systemic flaws that are bound to produce the distortion. Faith is not boundless. Virtual justice—like virtual reality—may not be good enough. So we should take these problems with our system seriously and try to work out some improvements.

It's an honest statement. It's an earnest hope. And I suppose I do believe that thinking seriously about a problem is not an altogether useless occupation. But when it comes to the deep-down fundamental weaknesses of the American system of justice, our cultural commitment to the forms that conceal malfunction, my hope for the remedial powers of deep thought flags.

Or I might make some *pat proposal* like: We should import this feature or that of the inquisitorial model, according our judges greater control over the fact-finding process and reducing the distortions attributable to the adversarial method. I am not the first to suggest that a system that focused more intensely on full and fair investigation and less on the contentious adjudication of the product of that investigation might improve the quality of justice in the criminal justice system. I believe it. But I know that the excellent arguments of like-minded scholars have produced no discernible tremors in the Great American Model. No movement has been reported among the legislatures to devise basic modifications in their criminal procedure. And I am frankly a bit dubious about whether selective incorporation of features of an integrated, alien system, driven by a theory altogether foreign to ours, can be successfully accomplished.

Thus, I find the only honorable conclusion of this tour to be one less than satisfactory for those who like their conclusions neat. I can only restate at the end what has been apparent all along.

In many ways—some ingenious—the necessities of law enforcement have inspired improvisation to repair or disguise failures of law. In several other places, a little common sense or administrative initiative could put things right. Like all great and complex mechanisms of the social order, criminal justice must compensate for points of foolish design by bursts of sensible administration. Some of these improvised accommodations are far from trivial—major elements of justice have been and can be rescued by informal devices. I applaud those we have and urge those we might make. But I am not content that spot improvisation, even legislative reform, can rescue our system from its fundamental contradictions.

For in the end, I think the American system of criminal justice fails to deliver true justice. I conclude that the law, in some places, fails to provide a realistic framework for effective investigation and adjudication within appropriate constraints. I appreciate the value of criminal trials as a Theatre of Moral Values, and I endorse the thesis that the acceptability of verdicts is an important civic value. But I believe that the accuracy of verdicts is ultimately the most important ingredient of their acceptability.

I do not think the fault is in the constitutional structure. Though the Constitution was certainly drafted with the common-law model in mind, the fundamental catalogue of rights and obligations that found their way into the text do not require the full adversary mode that we have engrafted onto it. The citizen can be secure against unreasonable searches and seizures with far greater scope for court-sanctioned investigations. Our ingrained notions of the limits of interrogation and the consequences of silence are not dictated by the words of the Fifth Amendment that none shall be compelled to be a witness against himself. And certainly the right to the assistance of counsel in one's defense does not necessitate the adversary circus or the lawyerly shield against the fair acquisition of evidence against the accused defendant.

The excesses of constraint on investigation and the pervasive bane of a combat mentality are principal among the deep faults in the system. But I think the major discontinuity between virtual and true justice lies at the sacred center of the process: the jury. The democratic drapery that surrounds it—the voice of the people on the ultimate issue of liberty and justice— insulates the jury from cold critical appraisal. The difficulty of assessing the accuracy of verdicts (because the truth is not knowable by any better process) and the general concurrence of judges in the product (because they usually have no better basis for judgment) put the institution further beyond re- proach. And our legally enforced determination not to examine the way juries actually perform their crucial task reflects our resolute refusal to doubt. Like the priestesses of old, the jury enjoys an immunity from question born of irrational—but indispensable—faith. Even those relatively few high-visibility cases (and we seem to have had a rash of them lately) in which the jury verdict (usually acquittals, interestingly enough) disappoints the public— seems, indeed, an outrage of justice—fail to cast the system of jury decision itself into disrepute.

Yet I am coming closer and closer to the conclusion—and with increasing sadness—that jurors simply cannot be expected to do what they are required to do. There are certainly cases, maybe most cases, in which the evidence submitted to the jury shouts "guilty" or "not guilty" loudly and clearly. Any jury, even half asleep and suffering severe reality deprivation, could not fail to see the actual truth nestled in there among the evidentiary facts. For such cases, any sort of fact finder will do. But in a significant number of cases, vital credibility calls must be made between witnesses, neither of whom is off the wall. A trial does not have to drag on for months and months, testimony and documents do not have to fill shelves of transcript for a factual pattern to be complex. Pieces have to be fitted together, discarded, and amplified by imag- ination to recreate a true picture of a multifaceted event.

Jurors are no better equipped for that task than anyone else. In fact, many have never before grappled with a tough fact pattern, tried to make sense out of disparate reports, evaluated scientific expert opinion along with the frag- mentary and bumbling accounts of chance witnesses. The courtroom setting is to jurors, as it is to participants, an artificial place in which to absorb information. The enforced, sometimes restless passivity of the jury, the masked performance of the witnesses, and the ferocious partisanship of the lawyers hardly allow the jurors room for the development of opinion and the play of personal judgment that nourish most decisions in ordinary circumstances. And the rules of evidence, beloved of trial advocates, rarely improve the flow of intelligible information to the jury box. Sending such issues into jury rooms on clouds of faith is often nothing more than inviting jurors to trust their hunches, do what they feel in their bones is right, and give us any result we can live with. This is not fact finding. This is settling for virtual justice.

Whether we should settle for virtual justice is a harder question, a question that will sadly demonstrate my difficulty in reaching conclusions. The American trial jury, for all its failures, is deeply embedded in the legal and cultural fabric of our nationhood. To try to devise any other mechanism for delivering verdicts in criminal cases in the United States is pretty much an empty academic exercise. We have allowed a couple of minor changes in the definition of a jury and of a verdict when we overcame our mystical attachment to the number twelve and decided to tolerate less-than-unanimous conclusions in criminal cases. But that's about it. It's virtually impossible to imagine an American criminal trial without a defendant's option to have the issue of guilt judged by a more or less random collection of ordinary folk with neither special knowledge nor experience relating to the case, who will receive their facts largely from coached live witnesses in a fully adversary battle. You'd have to burn the Sixth Amendment to change these components of the right to "trial by an impartial jury." We're not about to do that. And nibbling around the edges—such as the abolition of peremptory challenges or the proposal that trial judges more commonly exercise their authority to call experts rather than sit by passively as these technical issues are plunged into the adversary fracas—will not do much to address the central problems of the contentious jury system.

So perhaps the course of wisdom would be to counsel contentment. Let's conclude with the homily that we be grateful for what we have, that we celebrate a system that most people, most of the time are reasonably comfortable with. I once surveyed experienced federal trial judges and found that almost 95 percent of them thought juries came out right more than 75 percent of the time. (Only a little more than half would venture 90 percent or better.) That's not a bad endorsement—not great, but not bad. I'd bet that the public comes out about the same way, maybe a bit more content. So the important thing may be, after all, acceptability: if we *believe* that we are well served by the system in place, we *are* well served. Don't make trouble.

Still, as a conclusion, this sort of bland shrug rankles. Although (as I have taken no pains to conceal) I am a realist to the extent that I readily accept the facts of life in a system based on the mysterious firing of cerebral cells, I hate to think that we have built a structure that doesn't really work. A reluctant realist, you might say. Criminal justice is too important to the communal endeavor to be smiled at with "Oh, well. Not the worst. Good enough." We constructed our justice system—it wasn't given to us like the neurons of our brains. We can rebuild it to work better, I want to shout.

I wish I had the illusions of the true reformer, the zeal of the revolutionary. It would lend some fire to this conclusion. But alas, I must express my discontent within the strictures of the possible. I must conclude, with regret, that we probably must learn to live with our own brand of virtual justice, to find satisfaction, if not with the special talents and exceptional insights of juries, then in a society that empowers its ordinary members, in disparate array, to sit as judges, qualified only by their unbiased sense of plausibility. We must take some comfort in the common perception that the criminal justice system, with all its improvisation, its excesses and failures, adjudicates criminal charges in a manner that—by and large—seems to win public approval. And, little by little, here and there, we will all work to narrow the gap between virtual and actual justice.

Index

Abandoned property as admissible evidence, 36

Abstract questions on appeal, 12

Acevedo v. California, 74

Accused persons entitled to counsel, 123, 132

Adams v. Williams, 92

Adjudication, 5

Administrative alternatives to the exclusionary rule, 68

Administrative search: criminal consequences of, 25; defined, 105

Adversary system of adjudication, 122, 241; faith in, 242, 265; weakness of, 261; alternatives to, 293

Advice, cops' unwillingness to solicit, 42

Alford, North Carolina v., 194

Appeal, 8

Arraignment, 3

Arrest: what constitutes, 45, 47; as "accusation" for Sixth Amendment purposes, 48; consequences of unlawful, 49

Arrest warrant, 78

Assistance of counsel: the right to competence, fidelity, zeal, 136

Attorney-client privilege: theory and fact, 114; coverage, 115; documents in lawyers'

hands, 116; waiver by disclosure, 128; between joint clients, 149

Automobiles: expectations of privacy within, 72; as inherently dangerous instrumentalities, 105

Automobile stops, on suspicion, 106

Autonomy, client, in relationship with attorney, 150

Bail, 3

Bank records, obtained by subpoena, 173

Batson v. Kentucky, 211

"Battered spouse syndrome," 261

Bias, as a means of impeachment, 249

Blackmun, Justice Harry, 214

Bordenkircher v. Hayes, 183

Borrelli, Connecticut v., 263

Bostick, Florida v., 45

Brady bill, 89

Brady material, 295

Brennan, Justice William: 52, 59

Burden of persuasion, 14

Burger, Chief Justice Warren, 211

Burger v. New York, 105

Camara v. Municipal Court, 25, 105

Canine sniff "searches," 97